Dante's
INFERNO

Indiana
Masterpiece
Editions

MARK MUSA EDITOR

Dante's
INFERNO

The Indiana Critical Edition

Translated and edited by
Mark Musa

Indiana University Press

BLOOMINGTON AND INDIANAPOLIS

This book is a publication of

Indiana University Press
601 North Morton Street
Bloomington, Indiana 47404-3797 USA

http://iupress.indiana.edu

Telephone orders 800-842-6796
Fax orders 812-855-7931
Orders by e-mail iuporder@indiana.edu

Manufactured in the United States of America

Library of Congress Cataloging-in-Publication Data

Dante Alighieri, 1265–1321.
[Inferno. English]
Dante's Inferno : the Indiana critical edition / translated and
edited by Mark Musa.
p.   cm. — (Indiana masterpiece editions)
Includes bibliographical references and index.
ISBN 0-253-33943-X (cloth). — ISBN 0-253-20930-7 (pbk.)
1. Hell—Poetry. 2. Dante Alighieri, 1265—1321. Inferno.
3. Hell in literature. I. Musa, Mark. II. Title. III. Series.
PQ4315.2.M775   1995
851'.1—dc20   94-20237

5 6 7 8 08 07 06 05

For Alec Marc Musa
on his entrance to the world

CONTENTS

▼

PREFACE

Accompanying my verse translation of Dante's *Inferno* are ten essays which offer diverse approaches to a number of different aspects of the first canticle of the *Divine Comedy*.

In the opening essay Lawrence Baldassaro regards the "starting point that necessitates the pilgrim's difficult journey through Hell" to be the allegorical landscape of Canto I of *Inferno*, "a physical manifestation of the pilgrim's contaminated soul." Because of his fallen condition, the way up and out of the "selva oscura" is closed. Climbing the hill is impossible because of the pilgrim's pride, which will be erased in Purgatory in a similarly allegorical setting. Baldassaro asks, if Inferno is a representation of universal sinfulness and Purgatory a point-by-point erasure of sin, how does Inferno exhibit these sins? The allegory of Canto I gives way to dramatic manifestations, he says, in which the pilgrim interacts and gradually arrives at a "subjective awareness of his own capacity for wrongdoing," recognizing step by step the degree of his own contamination. Dante uses himself as an example; he depicts his sinners "not as awkward allegorical representations of specific sins, but as compelling human beings." The pilgrim's "mimetic response to the sinners he encounters" brings him and them to life dramatically, not didactically.

The allegorical first scene is "negative potentiality" and the rounds of Hell fulfillment of it. This is not a fact-finding journey the pilgrim is taking. His behavior that "calls attention to itself" reflects the "ironic stance that distinguishes the voice of the poet from that of the pilgrim." Each of the sinners the pilgrim meets is a "potential other self." The pilgrim is a "reader" who tests "'texts'" in the Inferno, one who cannot see the whole and whose limitations are indicated by his imitative responses. In turn, the reader is a pilgrim to whom Dante speaks directly in his addresses to the reader. But Baldassaro disagrees with Auerbach that Dante misleads us by misleading his protagonist; rather he gives us credit for being able to sort out the "ironic duality of the distinct voices of the poet and pilgrim." The compelling reality of the action does not distract from the "professed redemptive function of the poem," as Auerbach concluded, but is "part of the poet's strategy, part of the challenge he poses both to his protagonist and to his reader." The goal is to gain perspective by completing the journey. In XX, 19–26, for example, what seems a request for pity is instead a subtle acting out of the sin depicted, the pilgrim weeping for suffering which is God's just punishment. The pilgrim "fails to read the text properly," allowing himself to be seduced and beguiled by sin. Why does Dante place "stumbling blocks" in the way of our understanding? To force us to work to understand him. Dante's characters in the *Inferno*, in fact, are sometimes so real "they may seem to be living human beings temporarily misplaced in the eternal environment of Hell." However, they are not "lead players" but signs, leading the way to redemption; each one points out a necessary first step.

Guy P. Raffa stresses in his essay Virgil's importance for Dante as articulator of a shared political philosophy, as explorer of the fictional Underworld, and as prophet, but even more to the point, as a faulted man: "a tragic figure whose intellectual, emotional and psychological complexity accounts for much of the dramatic energy" of the *Divine Comedy*, especially in the *Inferno*. Dante mined Virgil for mythological, historical, and political material and for the mechanism, or structure, for translating his poetic vision into verse form. He created his own terza rima with Virgil's model in mind, borrowing from him extensively while transforming the material into something entirely new.

Raffa ranks Virgil's importance for Dante according to three measures: his poetic excellence first, then his wisdom regarding poetic truth, and lastly his susceptibility to falsehood. In the beginning, Dante refers and defers to Virgil as a respected "author" and "authority," whose pagan religious views he will christianize in the *Divine Comedy* on the strength of the *Fourth Eclogue* (where the appearance of the virgin and new-born son will bring about a golden age). Dante's debt to him is so great that he attributes his own reputation to him and places him first among his teachers. His "'deep love'" for him is translated into situations in the *Comedy* that make for a believable and intimate reciprocity between the *Comedy* and the *Aeneid*. Dante's comparisons between his own enterprise and Virgil's epic are "daring—yet prescient." (Virgil comes away, in a sense, "second best.") The *Aeneid* provides a primary source for Dante's imagery, for instance, the metamorphosis in *Inferno* XIII, which both poets used to dramatize history. The image is given a new form in the *Inferno* that both reaffirms Virgil and implies a critique of him that Raffa refers to as a "staged competition."

Dante's christianizing of Virgil derives from the reputation of his *Fourth Eclogue* as prophecy, but Raffa finds a "flip side" to it in Virgil's popular reputation as a sorcerer. He hears an echo of Virgil's "incantations" at several points in the poem, even in Dante's verses describing his own celestial vision in *Paradise* XXXIII. Although Dante allows Virgil to restore his good name by defending himself, he does so ambiguously, showing him to be racking up new faults to correct the old. In Virgil's interactions with the pilgrim and the sinners they meet, the poet, prophet, historian and guide is sometimes revealed as the windy logician and alterer of facts, the superstitious naif and faulty reasoner who speaks and acts unpredictably in the windings of Hell. Deep in the recesses of fraud, Virgil is shown to be not only a flawed figure but a comic one whose dignity is gravely compromised in subtle and not so subtle ways. "In this sense," Raffa concludes, "the pilgrim learns at Virgil's expense" in the *Inferno*. And the reader gains as the Latin poet emerges in his complexity, brought down to our level as fully human.

What is Hell good for? Denise Heilbronn-Gaines in her critical essay on the opening canto of the *Divine Comedy* offers an answer to this question with an in-depth study of the canto's language, symbols and extended meanings for the *Inferno*. She concludes by taking a fresh look at the first words actually spoken in the poem by the pilgrim, "miserere di me," which break the silence that has weakened the pilgrim's sight. Canto I finds the pilgrim in a "negative moral landscape" which Dante evokes to terrify both reader and pilgrim, not only because of its bleak aspect and threatening beasts but because of its familiarity as nightmarish dream: there is no way out of it without help. What the pilgrim sees is a dark wood, low valley, and distant inaccessible hilltop lit by the sun, all symbolically suggestive, all seeming "to mean something more than themselves while lacking a clearly objective reality of their own." In addition to being visually shrouded in this darkness, to which the pilgrim's eyes gradually adjust, the landscape is also deprived of sound; in fact, its striking feature, Heilbronn-Gaines points out, is its silence. Even the darkness is expressed as silence, the sun is mute, the cacophony of Hell is absent. She recalls Psalm 50 (as interpreted by St. Augustine), in which it is said that God is silent for those who do not hear, but that he speaks through the faithful whenever they utter the truth. This truth Heilbronn-Gaines finds at the turning point of the canto, when the whole mechanism of the *Divine Comedy* begins to move as the pilgrim utters his first words. Verses 61–66 represent the turn from a "subjective mode whose literal meaning remains singularly elusive" to "the objective narrative of a journey through the other world, whose primary sense is literal." In these verses the pilgrim first sees Virgil, divinely "offered" to the lost traveler as he is about to hit bottom, emerging out of the "unreal, visionary" ambiance of the first part of the canto to assume the shape of one "who because of long silence appeared faint." Heilbronn-Gaines interprets this *lungo silenzio* not as Virgil's but as the pilgrim's and closely argues her reasons why: it is Dante who had been silent too long. Going back to Psalm 50 and the repentance the Biblical David expressed in the words "miserere mei"—which Dante echoes in verse 65 with his *miserere di me* ("have pity on me")—she suggests that Dante saw a way of binding "his own spoken Tuscan to the scriptural language of the psalmist . . . making it capable of expressing the highest form of praise." Not only was David's language and metaphoric richness a source for Dante's poetry, but his example, that of the great sinner who repented and spoke out and was saved, gave him a hope which he wanted to communicate through his *Comedy* to mankind. Thus Hell is good for enabling Dante not only to break out of the "disconnected space" in which he found himself in Canto I but to break a silence which put him there in the first place. He frees himself to sing of God's grace and goodness, symbolized in all three canticles of the *Comedy* by the sun and stars, a hope made literal and concrete.

Amilcare A. Iannucci begins his essay by dividing the *Comedy*'s cantos into two types: one, the "local," whose action ends with that canto; and two, the "structurally determining" canto, whose influence extends throughout the poem. One of the latter, he will demonstrate, is Canto IV of the *Inferno*. It is on the threshold of Limbo outside Hell proper that Dante introduces his tragic theme, one which he will pursue in many other contexts on into Paradise. This theme is like a "Greek tragedy of necessity rather than a Christian tragedy of possibility" and it is revolutionary in its concept. The traditional theological and poetical conception of a two-phased Limbo (*limbus patrum* and *limbus puerorum*) is jettisoned and replaced with one, in which those "irrevocably stained by the sin of the first Adam" languish unbaptized, without hope of rescue, although still desiring to find peace in God. In this canto, Dante also revises the medieval idea of the Harrowing of Hell to exclude the virtuous pagans, Christ having redeemed only the righteous Hebrews when he descended into the underworld. Thus Virgil and his cohabitants of Limbo are tragically left behind, contained within their seven sets of walls, on the other side of the river of baptism, confined to a castle, symbols serving to segregate this category of the damned from the others in Hell but also to "contain" them from any hope of grace. Even the glow surrounding the noble castle acts as a negative factor, a half-light which Iannucci compares with the shadow that fell over "disenfranchised man" when he sinned originally. This "Eden of unredeemed time" has the function not of a kind of consolation prize for the pagan philosophers and poets, but of a prison in which they are shackled "to the timebound pattern of their own thought." "The terrestrial 'comedy' of the virtuous pagans becomes an eschatalogical 'tragedy,'" that of predestination. "Pursued by an unsympathetic fate" determined by "the God of Christianity Himself," their tragedy is meant to evoke pity and compassion in the reader, but without hope of a dramatic catharsis, or of a Christian happy ending.

In my essay "A Lesson in Lust," I make the connection between the self-pity that the protagonist of the *Vita nuova* experiences and that pity for another which the Pilgrim feels when he meets Francesca in Canto V of the *Inferno*. In both cases, experience teaches the wrong lesson, and Dante fails for the moment to learn the nature of his mistake, a victim of his own tendency toward sentimentalization. And this abject failure, the subjection of reason to sentiment, is symbolized by the Pilgrim's figure, prostrate and unconscious, on the floor of Hell. Pity for the delicate and aristocratic Francesca da Rimini, so seductive in her speech, has robbed him of even his traitorous senses. Francesca's basic weakness is her self-centeredness, evident in every word and gesture; a craving to be noticed, to be heard and to be pitied that is best delineated by her domination of the scene as she subjects all about her to her words. Not only does she seem to demand all the attention (the weeping Paolo remains silent), but she embellishes her speech with grandiose images, revealing a histrionic self-consciousness in her introduction to her tale that suggests a figure plunged into grief by the Pilgrim's question, but heroically forcing herself to comply with his desire, attempting to adopt a philosophical attitude— only to remind us at the end of the tears she is restraining. Grandiloquence, pomposity, pedantry, but also self-delusion are evident in Francesca's presentation, in which she elegantly draws the Pilgrim in to her own personal tragedy as a victim of an irresistible force. Love cannot be denied, and in this sense she would excuse herself from responsibility for her sin. She exploits the words of the poets (the *dolce stilnovisti*) in the interests of self-justification, bending their concept of virtuous love to her purposes in her well-bred but superficial manner ("whereby gentility leads insensibly to hypocrisy"). Even more tellingly, she misreads the tale of Lancelot and Guinevere, transferring to Lancelot the act of initiating the adulterous kiss. I conclude from these and other signs that Francesca, not so much deliberately as disingenuously, confuses and alters facts in order to put herself in a better light, to obliterate, momentarily, the ugly fact of her punishment. Francesca, who is the first sinner to speak in the *Comedy*, stands for Eve, the first human being to sin in Christian history. Insofar as the Pilgrim is seduced by her words, he participates in her sin—not only the essence of lust but also the essence of sin itself.

According to Christopher Kleinhenz's essay, the events in Cantos XXI–XXIII are determined by two contradictory thematic currents: devilish playfulness and diabolical cunning, grotesque humor and profound seriousness. While the devilish antics provide a superficial unity for the action, the machinations contrived by both devils (Malacoda's lie, which aims to entrap Dante and Virgil) and sinners (Ciampolo's ruse, calculated to free himself from the Malebranche) underlie and consistently undermine this "good-humored" surface narrative.

Several factors contribute to the successful representation of this duality: the ironic dichotomy between appearance and reality and the use of certain parodic elements, such as the "trumpet" blast, on whose note Canto XXI ends ("and he blew back with his bugle of an ass-hole," 139) and the marvelous mock-heroic introduction to Canto XXII (1–12), where Dante effectively lowers the tone to its proper level and underscores its base nature. Irony is also present in the parodic use of religious art. In Canto XXI the Santo Volto ("Holy Face") of Lucca provides an appropriate referent for the irreverent remarks of the devils, who refer to the upturned rump of the unidentified Lucchese barrator (grafter) blackened with pitch in this manner. The devils' humorously grotesque and sacrilegious identification of the sinner's blackened rump with the "Holy Face" is especially pertinent to the events at hand because of its dark wood and particular veneration in Lucca. Works of art have already been used in similar ways in the *Inferno*; in Canto XIX, e.g., the upended position of the Simonists in the "baptismal fonts" recalls the usual representation of Simon Magus in medieval art. Just as medieval art establishes a frame of reference for the interpretation of Canto XIX, so does Dante, through the allusion to one work of art (the Santo Volto), give us an indication here in Canto XXI of how we should read and interpret the entire episode. The arrival of the devil with the anonymous Lucchese barrator on his shoulders was likened by Benvenuto da Imola to that of a butcher carrying the carcass of an animal. However, the figure of the devil who carries the sinner would appear to be a direct imitation and parody of the artistic representation of Christ the Good Shepherd, who bears the lost sheep on his shoulders. Several passages in the Bible provide the literary basis for this manner of depiction, e.g., the parable of the lost sheep in Luke (15:4–6) and the more explicit passage in John (10:11, 14, 27–28).

Besides specific references to this tradition in patristic literature, the Good Shepherd was a very popular figure and theme in early Christian art. Early on, as demonstrated by his appearance on numerous sarcophagi, the *Pastor Bonus* was associated typologically with the concepts of baptism and resurrection. In addition to these associations, the notion of Christ as Good Shepherd is complemented and enriched by the description of him in the apocalypse (7:15–17) as the *Agnus* who functions in the role of psychopomp, the conductor of souls to the afterlife. These two related aspects of Christ—*Pastor Bonus* and *Agnus Psychopompos*—were conflated early in the Christian era. A consideration of the artistic and literary background of the Good Shepherd enables the scene in Canto XXI to assume greater significance: the devil who hauls the sinner so crudely on his shoulders would be the antithesis of Christ, who gently bears the lost sheep (= repentant soul) back to the fold.

Parodic inversion is a staple of Dante's art in the *Inferno*, which is replete with ironic emblems: three-headed Lucifer represents the infernal perversion of the Trinity; the figure of Farinata, emerging waist up from the sepulcher, parodies the image both of the resurrected Christ and of Christ the Man of Sorrows; and so on. Infernal perversions, however, often have their divine counterparts elsewhere in the poem. Thus, just as the devil parodies the action of the Good Shepherd in Canto XXI, so Virgil in the same context "imitates" that action in Canto XXIII by carrying Dante down into the next *bolgia* in order to rescue him from the enraged Malebranche. Significantly, Virgil carries his protégé on only two other occasions in the *Inferno*—in Cantos XIX and XXXIV. Moreover, Virgil is described as a shepherd in *Inferno* XXIV and *Purgatory* XXVII. By carrying Dante or by standing watch over him, Virgil would be imitating the *Pastor Bonus*, and the several instances of this activity are intended first of all to counterbalance the parodic scene of the devil carrying the sinner. More generally, in Dante's political ideology or "theology," the emperor is necessarily a *typus Christi*, one who assumes the identity of both Good Shepherd and sacrificial *Agnus Dei*. Thus, in these pertinent instances from the *Comedy*—and especially in *Inferno* XXI–XXIV—Virgil, the poet of Empire, would embody the notion of the temporal shepherd, the one charged with leading humankind (and in the context of the poem, Dante the Pilgrim) to earthly felicity.

Robert Hollander's article sets up an intriguing opposition of text, character, poet, and commentary in a reading of *Inferno* XXI and XXIII that goes a long way toward explaining Dante's complex and "deft manipulations" of character in their passages. With his own elucidations of their sustained action, in which the fallout from Virgil's and the pilgrim's meeting with the *malebranche* in the *bolgia* of the barrators (grafters) is described and reconsidered, Hollander invites a response from the reader which may imitate Dante's response to his situation, enabling us to make our own intuitive bridge for his allusions. The fable about the mouse, the frog and the kite is recognized to be as much about cognition, in fact, as it is about text.

Hollander arrives at the conclusion that the frog in the picture ultimately was intended to be Virgil. "No matter how good his intentions" were in interpreting signs as he did, Virgil led the pilgrim into danger. "Dante understands that for the demons he himself is the mouse" tied to the "unwitting frog" Virgil, about to be seized by the ten *malebranche* (kites) once they have redeployed from their rout over the boiling pitch. Commentators from earliest times have read the fable (partly in response to Dante's instructions) as a parallel only for the scene the two travelers have just witnessed. But Dante was also inviting the reader to match his main characters with the fable's mouse and frog, not just the various demons acting out their comedy. This becomes clear from Hollander's discussion of how the use of the terms *mo* and *issa* in *Inferno* XXIII, 5, both words meaning "now," is more than a casual choice of terms: "It is as though, while rehearsing the fable and the *rissa*" (rout) Dante "unconsciously insisted on the relevance of both matters to what is to happen in the immediate future." The mouse Dante escapes, but not before we are made to see how, "having tied himself to his guide, he has put himself absolutely at risk beneath the vicious birds of prey. Dante would not be 'crossing' (or actually *not* crossing) in this manner had it not been for Virgil's bad advice." In revealing the "symmetries and judgments" of this "elaborately developed chain of events," Hollander provides a crucial link to the role that the "praised and damned" Virgil actually played in the development of Dante thought.

Ricardo Quinones tells us that we are gradually learning to focus our critical attention not only on the story of the *Divine Comedy*—that single line of spiritual development—but also, which is now more valuable, on the stories within the *Commedia*. One of the more remarkable unfolding stories occurs exclusively within the *Inferno*. This drama is made up of a series of encounters between the two travelers, Dante and Virgil, and a number of demonic challengers: Charon, Minòs, Cerberus, Plutus, Phlegyas, the demons at the Gate of Dis, the Furies who emerge on the ramparts, the Minotaurs, and later the Malebranche. These encounters are extraordinarily distinctive because through them are revealed the great patterns of Christian eschatology in which individual souls knowingly or unknowingly participate: the contest in heaven, the fall of the rebellious angels (with their resultant roles as devils in Hell), the death of Christ, and the Harrowing of Hell. It is significant that these encounters exist outside and apart from the exchanges between Dante and the sinners. They thus form a separate line of development, one in which the larger patterns of Dante's journey is established. Only here is his journey taken outside of history and placed in universal myth. (That other line of development, the municipal one of Dante's exile, is confined to exchanges with sinners, and thus participates in history.)

Yet the mythical pattern is not a full one. It stops short at the Harrowing of Hell without going on to later triumphs. Christocentric, to be sure, it gives us only a limited version of the Christian story. This is crucial because it indicates that the mythical pattern is mainly concerned with the issues of its major topos, the visit to the Underworld, and this means the issues of sponsorship and justification. Who grants the right of entrance? But more importantly, it asks, Who guarantees the ticket of return? To go to Hell might be considered easy; far more difficult is to return from that experience. Hence the concern with the Harrowing of Hell. The more dramatic energy of mythic patterning is provided by Book VI of the *Aeneid*, which Dante comprehends in its innermost nature. Like Virgil, he fully appreciates the singularity, the rarity, the difficulty of the journey. Yet, despite this genuine indebtedness, the journey to Hell in Dante's poem, in the unfolding of one of its discrete story lines, quickly becomes a debate over Virgil. It is only here that Virgil himself becomes the contested personage in the unfolding plot-line that is so revealing, dramatic, and poignant.

"Hell as the Mirror Image of Paradise" by Joan M. Ferrante explores the political and church history of the period in which Dante wrote to add compelling detail to our knowledge of the *Comedy*. "The political message is integral to the poem," Ferrante writes; "all the sins and virtues have social or political implications." By placing the roles and claims of Church, city-state and emperor beside Dante's powerful criticisms, she shows how Hell resembles the city-state Florence, ruled and inhabited by the selfish who act against the common good; how Purgatory provides a transitional healing process for the repentant within the community of the spiritual church, and how Paradise—an "empire" justly formed and administered according to divine plan—answers to the major sins of Hell with an ideal society based on law and an enlightened monarchy motivated by love. The world, by analogy, only awaits the arrival of a just emperor to fulfill Dante's vision of Paradise here on earth.

Ferrante makes a strong argument for an interpretation of the sins of Hell within a socio-political moral context rather than a purely religious one. Even suicide, squandering, and usury are sins more against society than against the person, as demonstrated by the individuals Dante chooses to people his regions of Hell. The damned souls "frequently seem to implicate their city in their sins" so that Florence (representing the most flagrantly lawless and offensive of the city-states) takes on the coloration of a Babylon challenging a pagan Rome for hegemony. But the greater enemy in the *Comedy* is the papacy, in particular its representative, Pope Boniface VIII, a power figure Dante attacks as far along in his poem as *Paradise* XXX. Boniface as a focus of attention in the *Comedy* is most succinctly drawn in the analogy between Satan, with his upturned legs in Hell's last region, and the Simonists in Canto XIX whom Boniface will join when he dies. To counter his evils, Dante "intended the empire to set the world straight and the church to have a spiritual role, as guide to salvation, without any temporal power or wealth. . . ." Ferrante stresses the importance of commerce in the language and situations of Hell, illicit profit of various sorts deserving the most painful punishments: "Dante is reminding us at the end of Hell that we create Hell, that we are living in it and, by obstinately committing such sins, we damn ourselves here and there." Hell's images are meant to be negatives of the solutions offered in Purgatory and mirror images of the eternal empire of the sky, where differences find their place in the harmony of a shared purpose. For this reason Ferrante concludes that one cannot understand Dante's Hell without knowing his Paradise.

The concluding essay, by John P. Welle, talks about Dante in the movies. In addition to his considerable presence in high culture—his influence, for example, on modern world literature, Dante has also been adapted in popular culture. He has been the source of numerous films from the early years of the silent cinema until the present decade dominated by video and television. While all Dante movies shed light on the *Divine Comedy's* seemingly infinite adaptability, the history of Dante's reception in the Italian cinema, Welle argues, points to the centrality of film and literary interaction in the development of modern Italian culture. Because he is considered to be the "father" of the Italian language and has been constructed since the late eighteenth century as the Italian national poet, Dante movies have a particular significance within Italian culture.

Welle's essay demonstrates that evolution of Dante movies over the course of the twentieth century parallels and sheds light on the trajectory of other social, linguistic, and cultural phenomena. These phenomena include 1) the link between the nineteenth-century cult of Dante and Dante's strong presence in the early Italian cinema, and 2) the development of a truly national Italian language, "national memory," and national consciousness. Thus, by tracing the history of films stemming from the *Divine Comedy*, Welle examines an important and overlooked feature of Dante's reception in modern culture and emphasizes Dante's particular contribution to the creation of Italian national identity from political unification in 1870 until the present.

Dante's
INFERNO

SYNOPSIS

CANTO I 19

HALFWAY through his life, DANTE THE PILGRIM wakes to find himself lost in a dark wood. Terrified at being alone in so dismal a valley, he wanders until he comes to a hill bathed in sunlight, and his fear begins to leave him. But when he starts to climb the hill his path is blocked by three fierce beasts: first a LEOPARD, then a LION, and finally a SHE-WOLF that fills him with fear and drives him back down to the sunless wood. At that moment the figure of a man appears before him; it is the shade of VIRGIL, and the Pilgrim begs for help. Virgil tells him that he cannot overcome the beasts which obstruct his path, but that some day a "GREYHOUND" will come to drive the wolf back to Hell. Rather by another path will the Pilgrim reach the sunlight, and Virgil promises to guide him on that path through Hell and Purgatory, at which time another spirit, more fit than Virgil, will lead him to Paradise. The Pilgrim begs Virgil to lead on, and the Guide starts ahead. The Pilgrim follows.

CANTO II 27

BUT THE PILGRIM begins to waver; he expresses to Virgil his misgivings about his ability to undertake the journey proposed by Virgil. His predecessors have been Aeneas and St. Paul, and he feels unworthy to take his place in their company. But Virgil rebukes his cowardice, and relates the chain of events which led him to come to the aid of the Pilgrim. The VIRGIN MARY took pity on the Pilgrim in his despair and instructed ST. LUCIA to aid him. The Saint turned to BEATRICE because of Dante's great love for her, and Beatrice in turn went down to Hell, into Limbo, and asked Virgil to guide her friend until that time when she herself would become his guide. The Pilgrim takes heart at Virgil's explanation and agrees to follow him.

As the two poets enter the vestibule that leads to Hell itself, Dante sees the inscription above the gate, and he hears the screams of anguish from the damned souls. Rejected by God and not accepted by the powers of Hell the first group of souls are "nowhere," because of their cowardly refusal to make a choice in life. Their punishment is to chase after a banner forever, and to be tormented by flies and hornets. The Pilgrim recognizes several of these shades but mentions none by name. Next they come to the River Acheron where they are greeted by the infernal boatman CHARON. Among those doomed souls who are to be ferried across the river, Charon sees the living man and challenges him, but Virgil lets it be known that his companion must pass. Then across the landscape rushes a howling wind which blasts the Pilgrim out of his senses, and he falls to the ground.

Waking from his swoon, the Pilgrim is led by Virgil to the First Circle of Hell, known as Limbo, where the sad shades of the virtuous non-Christians dwell. The souls here, including Virgil, suffer no physical torment, but they must live, in desire, without hope of seeing God. Virgil tells about Christ's descent into Hell and His salvation of several Old Testament figures. The poets see a light glowing in the darkness, and as they proceed toward it, they are met by the four greatest (other than Virgil) pagan poets: HOMER, HORACE, OVID, and LUCAN, who take the Pilgrim into their group. As they come closer to the light, the Pilgrim perceives a splendid castle where the greatest non-Christian thinkers dwell together with other famous historical figures. Once within the castle, the Pilgrim sees, among others, ELECTRA, AENEAS, CAESAR, SALADIN, ARISTOTLE, PLATO, ORPHEUS, CICERO, AVICENNA, and AVERROËS. But soon they must leave; and the poets move from the radiance of the castle toward the fearful encompassing darkness.

From Limbo Virgil leads his ward down to the threshold of the Second Circle of Hell where, for the first time, he will see the damned in Hell being punished for their sins. There, barring their way, is the hideous figure of Minòs, the bestial judge of Dante's underworld; but after strong words from Virgil, the poets are allowed to pass into the dark space of this circle, where can be heard the wailing voices of the LUSTFUL, whose punishment consists of being forever whirled about in a dark, stormy wind. After seeing a thousand or more famous lovers—including SEMIRAMIS,

DIDO, HELEN, ACHILLES, and PARIS—the Pilgrim asks to speak to two figures he sees together. They are FRANCESCA DA RIMINI and her lover PAOLO, and the scene in which they appear is probably the most famous episode of the *Inferno*. At the end of the scene, the Pilgrim, who has been overcome by pity for the lovers, faints to the ground.

CANTO VI   56

ON RECOVERING consciousness the Pilgrim finds himself with Virgil in the Third Circle where the GLUTTONS are punished. These shades are mired in filthy muck and are eternally battered by cold and dirty hail, rain, and snow. Soon the travellers come upon CERBERUS, the three-headed, doglike beast who guards the Gluttons, but Virgil pacifies him with fistfuls of slime and the two poets pass on. One of the shades recognizes Dante the Pilgrim and hails him. It is CIACCO, a Florentine who, before they leave, makes a prophecy concerning the political future of Florence. As the poets move away, the Pilgrim questions Virgil about the Last Judgment and other matters until the two arrive at the next circle.

CANTO VII   62

AT THE BOUNDARY of the Fourth Circle the two travellers confront clucking PLUTUS, the god of wealth, who collapses into emptiness at a word from Virgil. Descending farther, the Pilgrim sees two groups of angry, shouting souls who clash huge rolling weights against each other with their chests. They are the PRODIGAL and the MISERLY. Their earthly concern with material goods prompts the Pilgrim to question Virgil about Fortune and her distribution of the worldly goods of men. After Virgil's explanation, they descend to the banks of the swamp-like river Styx, which serves as the Fifth Circle. Mired in the bog are the WRATHFUL, who constantly tear and mangle each other. Beneath the slime of the Styx, Virgil explains, are the SLOTHFUL; the bubbles on the muddy surface indicate their presence beneath. The poets walk around the swampy area and soon come to the foot of a high tower.

CANTO VIII   69

BUT BEFORE THEY had reached the foot of the tower, the Pilgrim had noticed two signal flames at the tower's top, and another flame answering from a distance; soon he realizes that the flames are signals to and from PHLEGYAS, the boatman of the Styx, who suddenly appears in a small boat speeding across the river. Wrathful and irritated though he is, the steersman must grant the poets passage, but during the crossing an angry shade rises from the slime to question the Pilgrim. After a brief exchange of words, scornful on the part of the Pilgrim, who has recognized this sinner, the spirit grabs hold of the boat. Virgil pushes him away, praising his ward for his just scorn, while a group of the wrathful attack the wretched soul whose name is FILIPPO ARGENTI. At the far shore the poets debark and find themselves before the gates of the infernal CITY OF DIS where howling figures threaten them from the walls. Virgil speaks with them privately, but they slam the gate shut in his face. His ward is terrified, and Virgil too is shaken, but he insists that help from Heaven is already on the way.

CANTO IX

THE HELP FROM Heaven has not yet arrived; the Pilgrim is afraid and Virgil is obviously worried. He reassures his ward by telling him that, soon after his own death, he was forced by the sorceress Erichtho to resume mortal shape and go to the very bottom of Hell in order to bring up the soul of a traitor; thus Virgil knows the way well. But no sooner is the Pilgrim comforted than the THREE FURIES appear before him, on top of the tower, shrieking and tearing their breasts with their nails. They call for MEDUSA whose horrible face has the power of turning anyone who looks on her to stone. Virgil turns his ward around and covers his eyes. After an "address to the reader" calling attention to the coming allegory, a strident blast splits the air, and the poets perceive an ANGEL coming through the murky darkness to open the gates of the City for them. Then the angel returns on the path whence he had come, and the two travellers enter the gate. Within are great open burning sarcophagi from which groans of torment issue. Virgil explains that these are ARCH-HERETICS and their lesser counterparts.

CANTO X

THEY COME TO the tombs containing the Epicurean heretics, and as they are walking by them, a shade suddenly rises to full height in one tomb, having recognized the Pilgrim's Tuscan dialect. It is the proud FARINATA who, in life, opposed Dante's party; while he and the Pilgrim are conversing, another figure suddenly rises out of the same tomb. It is the shade of CAVALCANTE DE' CAVALCANTI who interrupts the conversation with questions about his son Guido. Misinterpreting the Pilgrim's confused silence as evidence of his son's death, Cavalcante falls back into his sepulchre, and Farinata resumes the conversation exactly where it had been broken off. He defends his political actions in regard to Florence and prophesies that Dante, like himself, will soon know the pain of exile. But the Pilgrim is also interested to know how it is that the damned can see the future but not the present. When his curiosity is satisfied, he asks Farinata to tell

Cavalcante that his son is still alive, and that his silence was caused only by his confusion about the shade's inability to know the present.

CANTO XI 89

CONTINUING THEIR WAY within the Sixth Circle where the heretics are punished, the poets are assailed by a stench rising from the abyss ahead of them which is so strong that they must stop in order to accustom themselves to the odor. They pause beside a tomb whose inscription declares that within is POPE ANASTASIUS. When the Pilgrim expresses his desire to pass the time of waiting profitably, Virgil proceeds to instruct him about the plan of punishments in Hell. Then, seeing that dawn is only two hours away, he urges the Pilgrim on.

CANTO XII 95

THEY DESCEND the steep slope into the Seventh Circle by means of a great landslide which was caused when Christ descended into Hell. At the edge of the abyss is the MINOTAUR, who presides over the circle of the VIOLENT and whose own bestial rage sends him into such a paroxysm of violence that the two travellers are able to run past him without his interference. At the base of the precipice, they see a river of boiling blood which contains those who have inflicted violence upon others. But before they can reach the river they are intercepted by three fierce CENTAURS whose task it is to keep those who are in the river at their proper depth by shooting arrows at them if they attempt to rise. Virgil explains to one of the centaurs (CHIRON) that this journey of the Pilgrim and himself is ordained by God; and he requests him to assign someone to guide the two of them to the ford in the river and carry the Pilgrim across it to the other bank. Chiron gives the task to NESSUS, one of the centaurs, who, as he leads them to the river's ford, points out many of the sinners there in the boiling blood.

CANTO XIII 102

NO SOONER ARE the poets across the Phlegethon than they encounter a dense forest, from which come wails and moans, and which is presided over by the hideous harpies—half-woman, half-beast, birdlike creatures. Virgil tells his ward to break off a branch of one of the trees; when he does, the tree weeps blood and speaks. In life he was PIER DELLE VIGNE, chief counsellor of Frederick II of Sicily; but he fell out of favor, was accused unjustly of treachery and was imprisoned, whereupon he killed himself. The Pilgrim is overwhelmed by pity. The sinner also explains how the souls of the suicides come to this punishment and what will happen to them after the Last Judgment. Suddenly they are interrupted by the wild sounds of the hunt, and two naked figures, LANO DA SIENA and GIACOMO DA SANT' ANDREA, dash across the landscape shouting at each other until one of them hides himself in a thorny bush; immediately a pack of fierce, black dogs rush in, pounce on the hidden sinner, and rip his body, carrying away mouthfuls of flesh. The bush, which has been torn in the process, begins to lament. The two learn that the cries are those of a Florentine who had hanged himself in his own home.

CANTO XIV

THEY COME TO the edge of the Wood of the Suicides where they see before them a stretch of burning sand upon which flames rain eternally and through which a stream of boiling blood is carried in a raised channel formed of rock. There, many groups of tortured souls are on the burning sand; Virgil explains that those lying supine on the ground are the BLAS-PHEMERS, those crouching are the USURERS, and those wandering aimlessly, never stopping, are the SODOMITES. Representative of the blasphemers is CAPANEUS who died cursing his god. The Pilgrim questions his guide about the source of the river of boiling blood; Virgil's reply contains the most elaborate symbol in the *Inferno*, that of the OLD MAN OF CRETE, whose tears are the source of all the rivers in Hell.

CANTO XV

THEY MOVE OUT across the plain of burning sand, walking along the ditch-like edge of the conduit through which the Phlegethon flows, and after they have come some distance from the wood they see a group of souls running toward them. One, BRUNETTO LATINI, a famous Florentine intellectual and Dante's former teacher, recognizes the Pilgrim and leaves his band to walk and talk with him. Brunetto learns the reason for the Pilgrim's journey and offers him a prophesy of the troubles lying in wait for him—an echo of Ciacco's words in Canto VI. Brunetto names some of the others being punished with him (PRISCIAN, FRANCESCO D'ACCORSO, ANDREA DE' MOZZI); but soon, in the distance, he sees a cloud of smoke approaching which presages a new group, and because he must not associate with them, like a foot-racer Brunetto speeds away to catch up with his own band.

CANTO XVI

CONTINUING THROUGH the third round of the Circle of Violence, the Pilgrim hears the distant roar of a waterfall which grows louder as he and his guide proceed. Suddenly three shades, having recognized him as a Florentine, break from their company and converse with him, all the while circling like a turning wheel. Their spokesman, JACOPO RUSTICUCCI, identifies himself and his companions (GUIDO GUERRA and TEGGHIAIO AL-DOBRANDINI) as well-known and honored citizens of Florence, and begs for news of their native city. The three ask to be remembered in the world and then rush off. By this time the sound of the waterfall is so deafening that it almost drowns out speech, and when the poets reach the edge of the precipice, Virgil takes a cord which had been bound around his pupil's waist and tosses it into the abyss. It is a signal, and in response a monstrous form looms up from below, swimming through the air. On this note of suspense, the canto ends.

CANTO XVII   128

THE BEAST WHICH had been seen approaching at the end of the last canto is the horrible monster GERYON; his face is appealing like that of an honest man, but his body ends in a scorpion-like stinger. He perches on the edge of the abyss and Virgil advises his ward, who has noticed new groups of sinners squatting on the fiery sand, to learn who they are, while he makes arrangements with Geryon for the descent. The sinners are the USURERS, unrecognizable except by the crests on the moneybags hanging about their necks which identify them as members of the GIANFIGLIAZZI, UBRIACHI, and SCROVEGNI families. The Pilgrim listens to one of them briefly but soon returns to find his master sitting on Geryon's back. After he conquers his fear and mounts, too, the monster begins the slow, spiraling descent into the Eighth Circle.

CANTO XVIII   134

THE PILGRIM DESCRIBES the view he had of the Eighth Circle of Hell while descending through the air on Geryon's back. It consists of ten stone ravines called *Malebolge* (Evil Pockets), and across each *bolgia* is an arching bridge. When the poets find themselves on the edge of the first ravine they see two lines of naked sinners, walking in opposite directions. In one are the PIMPS or PANDERERS and among them the Pilgrim recognizes VENEDICO CACCIANEMICO; in the other are the SEDUCERS, among whom Virgil points out JASON. As the two move towards the next *bolgia*, they are assailed by a terrible stench, for here the FLATTERERS are immersed in excrement. Among them are ALESSIO INTERMINEI and THAïS, the whore.

CANTO XIX   140

FROM THE BRIDGE above the Third *Bolgia* can be seen a rocky landscape below filled with holes, from each of which protrude a sinner's legs and feet; flames dance across their soles. When the Pilgrim expresses curiosity about a particular pair of twitching legs, Virgil carries him down into the *bolgia* so that the Pilgrim himself may question the sinner. The legs belong to Pope Nicholas III, who astounds the Pilgrim by mistaking him for Boniface VIII, the next Pope who, as soon as he dies, will fall to the same hole, thereby pushing Nicholas farther down. He predicts that soon after Boniface, Pope Clement V will come, stuffing both himself and Boniface still deeper. To Nicholas' rather rhetoric-filled speech the Pilgrim responds with equally high language, inveighing against the Simonists, the evil churchmen who are punished here. Virgil is much pleased with his pupil and, lifting him in an affectionate embrace, he carries him to the top of the arch above the next *bolgia*.

CANTO XX

In the Fourth *Bolgia* they see a group of shades weeping as they walk slowly along the valley; they are the Soothsayers and their heads are twisted completely around so that their hair flows down their fronts and their tears flow down to their buttocks. Virgil points out many of them including Amphiaraus, Tiresias, Aruns, and Manto. It was Manto who first inhabited the site of Virgil's home-city of Mantua, and the poet gives a long description of the city's founding, after which he names more of the condemned soothsayers: Eurypylus, Michael Scot, Guido Bonatti, and Asdente.

CANTO XXI

When the two reach the summit of the arch over the Fifth *Bolgia*, they see in the ditch below the bubbling of boiling pitch. Virgil's sudden warning of danger frightens the Pilgrim even before he sees a black devil rushing toward them, with a sinner slung over his shoulder. From the bridge the devil flings the sinner into the pitch where he is poked at and tormented by the family of Malebranche devils. Virgil, advising his ward to hide behind a rock, crosses the bridge to face the devils alone. They threaten him with their pitchforks, but when he announces to their leader, Malacoda, that Heaven has willed that he lead another through Hell, the devil's arrogance collapses. Virgil calls the Pilgrim back to him. Scarmiglione, who tries to take a poke at him is rebuked by his leader, who tells the travellers that the Sixth Arch is broken here but farther on they will find another bridge to cross. He chooses a squad of his devils to escort them there: Alichino, Calcabrina, Cagnazzo, Barbariccia, Libicocco, Draghignazzo, Ciriatto, Graffiacane, Farfarello and Rubicante. The Pilgrim's suspicion about their unsavory escorts is brushed aside by his guide, and the squad starts off giving an obscene salute to their captain who returns their salute with a fart.

THE NOTE OF grotesque comedy in the *bolgia* of the *Malebranche* continues, with a comparison between Malacoda's salute to his soldiers and different kinds of military signals the Pilgrim has witnessed in his lifetime. He sees many GRAFTERS squatting in the pitch, but as soon as the *Malebranche* draw near, they dive below the surface. One unidentified NAVARRESE, however, fails to escape and is hoisted up on Graffiacane's hooks; Rubicante and the other *Malebranche* start to tear into him, but Virgil, at his ward's request, manages to question him between torments. The sinner briefly tells his story, and then relates that he has left below in the pitch an Italian, FRA GOMITA, a particularly adept grafter, who spends his time talking to MICHEL ZANCHE. The Navarrese sinner promises to lure some of his colleagues to the surface for the devils' amusement, if the tormentors will hide themselves for a moment. Cagnazzo is skeptical but Alichino agrees, and no sooner do the *Malebranche* turn away than the crafty grafter dives below the pitch. Alichino flies after him, but too late; now Calcabrina rushes after Alichino and both struggle above the boiling pitch, and then fall in. Barbariccia directs the rescue operation as the two poets steal away.

THE ANTICS OF CIAMPOLO, the Navarrese, and the *Malebranche* bring to the Pilgrim's mind the fable of the frog, the mouse, and the hawk—and that in turn reminds him of the immediate danger he and Virgil are in from the angry *Malebranche*. Virgil senses the danger too, and grabbing his ward as a mother would her child, he dashes to the edge of the bank and slides down the rocky slope into the Sixth *Bolgia*—not a moment too soon, for at the top of the slope they see the angry *Malebranche*. When the Pilgrim looks around him he sees weeping shades slowly marching in single file, each one covered from head to foot with a golden cloak, lined with lead that weights them down. These are the HYPOCRITES. Two in this group identify themselves as CATALANO DE' MALAVOLTI and LODERINGO DEGLI ANDALÒ, two Jovial Friars. The Pilgrim is about to address them when he sees the shade of CAIAPHAS (the evil counselor who advised Pontius Pilate to crucify Christ) crucified and transfixed by three stakes to the ground. Virgil discovers from the two friars that in order to leave this *bolgia* they must climb up a rockslide; he also learns that this is the only *bolgia* over which the bridge is broken. Virgil is angry with himself for having believed Malacoda's lie about the bridge over the Sixth *Bolgia* (Canto XXI, 111).

AFTER AN ELABORATE simile describing Virgil's anger and the return of his composure, the two begin the difficult, steep ascent up the rocks of the fallen bridge. The Pilgrim can barely make it to the top even with Virgil's help, and after the climb he sits down to catch his breath; but his guide urges him on, and they make their way back to the bridge over the Seventh *Bolgia*. From the bridge confused sounds can be heard rising from the darkness below. The scene reveals a terrible confusion of serpents, and THIEVES madly running. Suddenly a snake darts out and strikes a sinner's neck, whereupon he flares up, turning into a heap of crumbling ashes; then the ashes gather together into the shape of a man. The metamorphosed sinner reveals himself to be VANNI FUCCI, a Pistoiese condemned for stealing the treasure of the sacristy of the church of San Zeno at Pistoia. He makes a prophecy about the coming strife in Florence.

CANTO XXV 182

THE WRATHFUL VANNI FUCCI directs an obscene gesture to God, whereupon he is attacked by several snakes, which coil about him, tying him so tight that he can not move a muscle. As soon as he flees, the centaur CACUS gallops by with a fire-breathing dragon on his back, and following close behind are three shades, concerned because they cannot find CIANFA— who soon appears as a snake which attacks AGNÈL; the two merge into one hideous monster which then steals off. Next, GUERCIO, in the form of a snake, strikes BUOSO, and the two exchange shapes. Only PUCCIO SCIAN-CATO is left unchanged.

CANTO XXVI 189

FROM THE RIDGE high above the Eighth *Bolgia* can be perceived a myriad of flames flickering far below, and Virgil explains that within each flame is the suffering soul of a DECEIVER. One flame, divided at the top, catches the Pilgrim's eye and he is told that within it are jointly punished ULYSSES AND DIOMED. Virgil questions the pair for the benefit of the Pilgrim. Ulysses responds with the famous narrative of his last voyage, during which he passed the Pillars of Hercules and sailed the forbidden sea until he saw a mountain shape, from which came suddenly a whirlwind that spun his ship around three times and sank it.

CANTO XXVII 196

AS SOON AS ULYSSES has finished his narrative, another flame—its soul within having recognized Virgil's Lombard accent—comes forward asking the travellers to pause and answer questions about the state of affairs in the region of Italy from which he came. The Pilgrim responds by outlining the strife in Romagna and ends by asking the flame who he is. The flame, although he insists he does not want his story to be known among the living, answers because he is supposedly convinced that the Pilgrim will never return to earth. He is another famous deceiver, GUIDO DA MONTEFELTRO, a soldier who became a friar in his old age; but he was untrue to his vows because, at the urging of Pope Boniface VIII, he counseled the use of fraud in the Pope's campaign against the Colonna family. He was damned to Hell because he failed to repent his sins, trusting instead in the Pope's fraudulent absolution.

CANTO XXVIII 203

IN THE NINTH *Bolgia* the Pilgrim is overwhelmed by the sight of mutilated, bloody shades, many of whom are ripped open with the entrails spilling out. They are the SOWERS OF SCANDAL AND SCHISM, and among them are MAHOMET, ALI, PIER DA MEDICINA, GAIUS SCRIBONIUS CURIO, MOSCA DE' LAMBERTI, and BERTRAN DE BORN. All bemoan their painful lot, and Mahomet and Pier da Medicina relay warnings through the Pilgrim to certain living Italians who are soon to meet terrible ends. Bertran de Born, who comes carrying his head in his hand like a lantern, is a particularly arresting example of a Dantean *contrapasso*.

CANTO XXIX 210

WHEN THE PILGRIM is rebuked by his mentor for his inappropriate interest in these wretched shades, he replies that he was looking for someone. Virgil, who can read the Pilgrim's mind, knows that this was GERI DEL BELLO. They discuss Geri until they reach the edge of the next *bolgia* where all types of FALSIFIERS are punished. There miserable, shrieking shades are afflicted with diseases of various kinds and are arranged in various positions. Sitting back to back, madly scratching their leprous sores, are the shades of GRIFFOLINO DA AREZZO and one CAPOCCHIO, who talk to the Pilgrim, the latter shade making wisecracks about the Sienese.

CANTO XXX 216

CAPOCCHIO'S REMARKS are interrupted by two mad, naked shades who dash up, and one of them sinks his teeth into Capocchio's neck and drags him off; he is GIANNI SCHICCHI and the other is MYRRHA of Cyprus. When they have gone, the Pilgrim sees the ill-proportioned and immobile shade of MASTER ADAMO, a counterfeiter, who explains how members of the Guidi family had persuaded him to practice his evil art in Romena. He points out the fever-stricken shades of two infamous liars, POTIPHAR'S WIFE and

SINON, the Greek, whereupon the latter engages Master Adamo in a verbal battle. Virgil rebukes the Pilgrim for his absorption in such futile wrangling, but his immediate shame wins Virgil's immediate forgiveness.

CANTO XXXI 223

THROUGH THE MURKY AIR they move, up across the bank which separates the *Malebolge* from the pit of Hell, the Ninth (and last) Circle of the *Inferno*. From a distance is heard the blast of a mighty horn which turns out to have been that of the giant NIMROD. He and other giants, including EPHIALTES, are fixed eternally in the pit of Hell; all are chained except AN-TAEUS, who at Virgil's request, lifts the two poets in his monstrous hand and deposits them below him, on the lake of ice known as COCYTUS.

CANTO XXXII 230

THEY DESCEND FARTHER down into the darkness of the immense plain of ice in which shades of TRAITORS are frozen. In the outer region of the ice-lake, CAINA, are those who betrayed their kin in murder; among them, locked in a frozen embrace, are NAPOLEONE and ALESSANDRO of MANGONA, and others are MORDRED, FOCACCIA, SASSOL MASCHERONI and CAMICION DE' PAZZI. Then the two travellers enter the area of ice called ANTENORA, and suddenly the Pilgrim kicks one of the faces sticking out of the ice. He tries to force the sinner to reveal his name by pulling out his hair, and when another shade identifies him as BOCCA DEGLI ABATI, the Pilgrim's fury mounts still higher. Bocca, himself furious, names several other sinners in Antenora, including BUOSO DA DUERA, TESAURO DEI BECCHERIA, GIANNI DE' SOLDANIER, GANELON, and TIBBALD. Going farther on, the Pilgrim sees two heads frozen in one hole, the mouth of one gnawing at the brain of the other.

CANTO XXXIII 236

COUNT UGOLINO IS THE SHADE gnawing at the brain of his onetime associate ARCHBISHOP RUGGIERI, and Ugolino interrupts his gruesome meal long enough to tell the story of his imprisonment and cruel death, which his innocent offspring shared with him. Moving farther into the area of Cocytus known as PTOLOMEA, where those who betrayed their guests and associates are condemned, the Pilgrim sees sinners with their faces raised high above the ice, whose tears freeze to lock their eyes. One of the shades agrees to identify himself on condition that the ice be removed from his eyes. The Pilgrim agrees, and learns that this sinner is FRIAR AL-BERIGO and that his soul is dead and damned even though his body is still alive on earth, inhabited by a devil. Alberigo also names a fellow sinner with him in the ice, BRANCA D'ORIA, whose body is still functioning up on earth. But the Pilgrim does not honor his promise to break the ice from Alberigo's eyes.

CANTO XXXIV 243

FAR ACROSS the frozen ice can be seen the gigantic figure of LUCIFER, who appears from this distance like a windmill seen through fog; and as the two travellers walk on toward that terrifying sight, they see the shades of sinners totally buried in the frozen water. At the center of the earth is Lucifer in all his ugliness: he has three heads and is made more fearful by the fact that in each of his three mouths he chews on one of the three worst sinners of all mankind, the worst of those who betrayed their benefactors—JUDAS ISCARIOT, BRUTUS, and CASSIUS. Virgil with the Pilgrim on his back begins the descent down the shaggy body of Lucifer. They climb down through a crack in the ice, and when they reach the Evil One's thighs, Virgil turns and begins to struggle upward (because they have passed the center of the earth) still holding onto the hairy body of Lucifer until they reach a cavern where they stop for a short rest. Then a winding path brings them eventually to the earth's surface, where they see the stars.

Dante's
INFERNO

CANTO I

Midway along the journey of our life
   I woke to find myself in some dark woods,
   for I had wandered off from the straight path.   *3*

How hard it is to tell what it was like,
   this wood of wilderness, savage and stubborn
   (the thought of it brings back all my old fears),   *6*

a bitter place! Death could scarce be bitterer.
   But if I would show the good that came of it
   I must talk about things other than the good.   *9*

How I entered there I cannot truly say,
   I had become so sleepy at the moment
   when I first strayed, leaving the path of truth;   *12*

but when I found myself at the foot of a hill,
   at the edge of the wood's beginning, down in the valley,
   where I first felt my heart plunged deep in fear,   *15*

I raised my head and saw the hilltop shawled
   in morning rays of light sent from the planet
   that leads men straight ahead on every road.   *18*

And then only did terror start subsiding
   in my heart's lake, which rose to heights of fear
   that night I spent in deepest desperation.   *21*

Just as a swimmer, still with panting breath,
   now safe upon the shore, out of the deep,
   might turn for one last look at the dangerous waters,   *24*

so I, although my mind was turned to flee,
   turned round to gaze once more upon the pass
   that never let a living soul escape.   *27*

I rested my tired body there awhile
    and then began to climb the barren slope
    (I dragged my stronger foot and limped along).   *30*

Beyond the point the slope begins to rise
    sprang up a leopard, trim and very swift!
    It was covered by a pelt of many spots.   *33*

And, everywhere I looked, the beast was there
    blocking my way, so time and time again
    I was about to turn and go back down.   *36*

The hour was early in the morning then,
    the sun was climbing up with those same stars
    that had accompanied it on the world's first day,   *39*

the day Divine Love set their beauty turning;
    so the hour and sweet season of creation
    encouraged me to think I could get past   *42*

that gaudy beast, wild in its spotted pelt,
    but then good hope gave way and fear returned
    when the figure of a lion loomed up before me,   *45*

and he was coming straight toward me, it seemed,
    with head raised high, and furious with hunger—
    the air around him seemed to fear his presence.   *48*

And now a she-wolf came, that in her leanness
    seemed racked with every kind of greediness
    (how many people she has brought to grief!).   *51*

This last beast brought my spirit down so low
    with fear that seized me at the sight of her,
    I lost all hope of going up the hill.   *54*

As a man who, rejoicing in his gains,
    suddenly seeing his gain turn into loss,
    will grieve as he compares his then and now,   *57*

so she made me do, that relentless beast;
    coming towards me, slowly, step by step,
    she forced me back to where the sun is mute.   *60*

While I was rushing down to that low place,
    my eyes made out a figure coming toward me
    of one grown weak, perhaps from too much silence.   *63*

And when I saw him standing in this wasteland,
　　"Have pity on my soul," I cried to him,
　　"whichever you are, shade or living man!"　66

"No longer living man, though once I was,"
　　he said, "and my parents were from Lombardy,
　　both of them were Mantuans by birth.　69

I was born, though somewhat late, *sub Julio*,
　　and lived in Rome when good Augustus reigned,
　　when still the false and lying gods were worshipped.　72

I was a poet and sang of that just man,
　　son of Anchises, who sailed off from Troy
　　after the burning of proud Ilium.　75

But why retreat to so much misery?
　　Why aren't you climbing up this joyous mountain,
　　the beginning and the source of all man's bliss?"　78

"Are you then Virgil, are you then that fount
　　from which pours forth so rich a stream of words?"
　　I said to him bowing my head modestly.　81

"O light and honor of the other poets,
　　may my long years of study, and that deep love
　　that made me search your verses, help me now!　84

You are my teacher, the first of all my authors,
　　and you alone the one from whom I took
　　the beautiful style that was to bring me honor.　87

You see the beast that forced me to retreat;
　　save me from her, I beg you, famous sage,
　　she makes me tremble, the blood throbs in my veins."　90

"But your journey must be down another road,"
　　he answered, when he saw me lost in tears,
　　"if ever you hope to leave this wilderness;　93

this beast, the one you cry about in fear,
　　allows no soul to succeed along her path,
　　she blocks his way and puts an end to him.　96

She is by nature so perverse and vicious,
　　her craving belly is never satisfied,
　　still hungering for food the more she eats.　99

She mates with many creatures, and will go on
    mating with more until the greyhound comes
    and tracks her down to make her die in anguish.   *102*

He will not feed on either land or money:
    his wisdom, love, and virtue shall sustain him;
    he will be born between Feltro and Feltro.   *105*

He comes to save that fallen Italy
    for which the maid Camilla gave her life
    and Turnus, Nisus, Euryalus died of wounds.   *108*

And he will hunt for her through every city
    until he drives her back to Hell once more,
    whence Envy first unleashed her on mankind.   *111*

And so, I think it best you follow me
    for your own good, and I shall be your guide
    and lead you out through an eternal place   *114*

where you will hear desperate cries, and see
    tormented shades, some old as Hell itself,
    and know what second death is, from their screams.   *117*

And later you will see those who rejoice
    while they are burning, for they have hope of coming,
    whenever it may be, to join the blessèd—   *120*

to whom, if you too wish to make the climb,
    a spirit, worthier than I, must take you;
    I shall go back, leaving you in her care,   *123*

because that Emperor dwelling on high
    will not let me lead any to his city,
    since I in life rebelled against his law.   *126*

Everywhere he reigns, and there he rules;
    there is his city, there is his high throne.
    Oh happy the one he makes his citizen!"   *129*

And I to him: "Poet, I beg of you,
    in the name of God, that God you never knew,
    save me from this evil place and worse,   *132*

lead me there to the place you spoke about
    that I may see the gate Saint Peter guards
    and those whose anguish you have told me of."   *135*

Then he moved on, and I moved close behind him.

1–10

The reader must be careful from the beginning to distinguish between the two uses of the first person singular in the *Divine Comedy:* one designating Dante the Pilgrim, the other Dante the Poet. The first is a character in a story invented by the second. The events are represented as having taken place in the past; the writing of the poem and the memories of these events are represented as taking place in the poet's present. We find references to both past and present, and to both pilgrim and poet in line 10: "How *I entered* there *I cannot* truly say."

1. *Midway along the journey of our life:* In the Middle Ages life was often thought of as a journey, a pilgrimage, the goal of which was God and Heaven; and in the first line of the *Divine Comedy* Dante establishes the central motif of his poem—it is the story of man's pilgrimage to God. That we are meant to think in terms not just of the Pilgrim but of Everyman is indicated by the phrase "the journey of *our* life" (*our* journey through sin to repentance and redemption).

The imaginary date of the poem's beginning is the night before Good Friday in 1300, the year of the papal jubilee proclaimed by Boniface VIII. Born in 1265, Dante was thirty-five years old, which is one half of man's Biblical life span of seventy years.

8–9. *But if I would show the good:* Even though the memory of this "wood" brings back his "old fears" (6), Dante must talk about "things other than the good" which led to the final "Good" (his salvation) by contributing to the learning process of the Pilgrim.

13–15. *but when I found myself at the foot of a hill:* Once we leave Canto I, which is the introduction to the whole of the *Divine Comedy,* the topography of the various regions of Hell will be described with elaborate carefulness. But in this canto all is vague and unprepared for; the scene is set in a "nowhere land"—the region of undifferentiated sin. Suddenly the Pilgrim awakes in a forest (which is not described except in terms that could apply to Sin itself: "wilderness, savage and stubborn"); suddenly, as he is wandering through it, there is a hill—whereupon the forest becomes a valley. Other suggestions of this dreamlike atmosphere (which, under the circumstances, must be that of a nightmare) will be found throughout this canto.

17–18. *morning rays of light:* The time is the morning of Good Friday.

30. *I dragged my stronger foot and limped along:* A literal translation of this line which has puzzled all Dante critics would be "So that the firm foot (*piè fermo*) was always the lower." Let the two feet represent man's loves: when Gregory the Great comments on Jacob's wrestling with the angel, he identifies one foot as love of God and the other foot as love of the world (*Homiliarium in Ezechielem,* lib. II, hom. 2,13; *PL* 76, 955–56). The "stronger foot" then, symbolizes the love of this world, for at this point in the Pilgrim's journey, this love is obviously "stronger" than the other; if he were not more strongly attracted to the things of this world than to God there would be little reason for him to make the journey. In order to ascend (to God) the Pilgrim must exert great force to drag upward his "stronger foot" (which is always the lower because its natural tendency is always downwards) and prevent himself from slipping back into the "dark woods."

32–60

The early critics thought of the three beasts which block the Pilgrim's path as symbolizing three specific sins: lust, pride and avarice, but I prefer to see in them the three major divisions of Hell. The spotted Leopard (32) represents Fraud (cf. XVI, 106–108) and reigns over the Eighth and Ninth Circles where the Fraudulent are punished (XVIII–XXXIV). The Lion (45) symbolizes all forms of Violence which are punished in the Seventh Circle (XII–XVII). The She-Wolf (49) represents the different types of Concupiscence or Incontinence which are punished in Circles Two to Five (V–VIII). In any case the beasts must represent the three major categories of human sin, and they threaten Dante the Pilgrim, the poet's symbol of mankind.

32–36. *sprang up a leopard:* Note the sudden appearance of the colorful Leopard as if from nowhere. Then the trim, swift, spotted beast disappears as such to become a symbol: a force that is everywhere, blocking upward movement.

40. *the day Divine Love set their beauty turning:* It was thought that the constellation of Aries, which is in conjunction with the sun in the spring equinox, was also in conjunction with the sun when God ("Divine Love") created the universe.

46–50. Note the triple use of the verb *seem* (which is a faithful reproduction of the original), intended to blur the figures of the Lion and the She-Wolf—in harmony with the "nowhereness" of the moral landscape.

55–60. *As a man who . . . the sun is mute:* It must be admitted that this simile is not one of Dante's most felicitous. The pilgrim, having gained some terrain toward his goal is forced back by the She-Wolf, thus losing all he has gained. But in the parallel imagined by the poet, we have not only the phase of gaining followed by the phase of losing, we are also told of the victim's emotional reaction to his experience—of which there is no trace in the factual narrative.

60. *she forced me back to where the sun is mute:* In other words, back to the "dark woods" of line 2.

62. *my eyes made out a figure coming toward me:* The shade of Virgil miraculously appears before Dante. The Roman poet, who was born (70 B.C.) in the time of Julius Caesar (*sub Julio*), represents Reason, Natural Philosophy. The Pilgrim cannot proceed to the light of Divine Love (the mountain top) until he has overcome the three beasts of his sin; and because it is impossible for man to cope with the beasts unaided, Virgil, as Reason, has been summoned through the chain of divine command to guide the Pilgrim and help him overcome his sins by understanding and, later, repudiating them.

63. *weak, perhaps from too much silence:* The voice of Reason has been silent in the Pilgrim's ear for a long time. Others have interpreted this line as referring to that period in the Middle Ages when Virgil's art was not understood.

73–75. *I was a poet and sang of that just man:* In the *Aeneid* Virgil relates the *post bellum* travels and deeds of Aeneas (son of Anchises) who, destined by the gods, founded on Italian soil the nation which, in the course of time, would become the Roman Empire.

87. *the beautiful style that was to bring me honor:* In the years before the composition of the *Divine Comedy* Dante employed in his sonnets and *canzoni* what he calls the tragic style, reserved for illustrious subject matter: martial exploits, love, and moral virtues (*De Vulgari eloquentia* II, ii, iv). His respect for the Roman poet is boundless. The reasons for the poet's selection of Virgil as the Pilgrim's guide (instead of, shall we say, Aristotle, *the* philosopher of the time) are several: Virgil was a poet and an Italian; in the *Aeneid* is recounted the hero's descent into Hell. But the main reason surely lies in the fact that, in the Middle Ages, Virgil was considered a prophet, a judgment stemming from the interpretation of some obscure lines in the *Fourth Eclogue* as foretelling the coming of Christ. In this regard Dante saw Virgil as a sort of mediator between Imperial and Apostolic Rome. Moreover, Dante's treatise *De monarchia* reflects the principal concepts of the Roman Empire found in the pages of his guide.

91. *But your journey must be down another road:* Dante must choose another road because, in order to arrive at the Divine Light, it is necessary first to recog-

nize the true nature of sin, renounce it, and pay penance for it. Reason (or Natural Philosophy), symbolized by the figure of Virgil, is of course the means through which man may come to an understanding of the nature of sin. With Virgil-Reason as his guide, Dante the Pilgrim will come to an understanding of sin on his journey through Hell and will see the penance imposed on repentant sinners on the Mount of Purgatory.

101–111

This obscure forecast of future salvation has never been explained satisfactorily: the figure of the Greyhound has been identified with Henry VII, Charles Martel, and even Dante himself. It seems more plausible that the Greyhound represents Can Grande della Scala, the ruler of Verona from 1308–1329, whose birthplace (Verona) is between Feltro and Montefeltro, and whose "wisdom, love, and virtue" (104) were certainly well known to Dante. Whoever the Greyhound may be, the prophecy would seem to indicate in a larger sense the establishment of a spiritual kingdom on earth, a terrestrial paradise in which "wisdom, love, and virtue" (these three qualities are mentioned again in Canto III, 4–6, as attributes of the Trinity) will replace the bestial sins of this world.

107. *the maid Camilla:* She was the valiant daughter of King Metabus, who was slain while fighting against the Trojans (*Aeneid* XI).

108. *and Turnus, Nisus, Euryalus died of wounds:* Turnus was the King of the Rutulians who waged war against the Trojans and was killed by Aeneas in single combat. Nisus and Euryalus were young Trojan warriors slain during a nocturnal raid on the camp of the Rutulians. In subsequent literature their mutual loyalty became a standard measure of sincere friendship.

117. *and know what second death is:* The second death is the death of the soul, which occurs when the soul is damned.

122. *a spirit, worthier than I:* Just as Virgil, the pagan Roman poet, cannot enter the Christian Paradise because he lived before the birth of Christ and lacks knowledge of Christian salvation, so Reason can only guide the Pilgrim to a certain point: in order to enter Paradise, the Pilgrim's guide must be Christian Grace or Revelation (Theology) in the figure of Beatrice.

124. *that Emperor dwelling on high:* Note the pagan terminology of Virgil's reference to God; it expresses, as best it can, his unenlightened conception of the Supreme Authority, that to his mind was, and could only be, an emperor.

133–135. *lead me there to the place you spoke about:* These lines are baffling. Many commentators interpret "the gate Saint Peter guards" as referring not to the gate of Heaven (in the *Paradise* no gate is mentioned) but to the gate of Purgatory, for in Canto IX of the *Purgatory* we are told that its gate is guarded by an angel whose keys have been given him by Peter. Thus the Pilgrim would be saying: "lead me to the two places you have just mentioned so that I may see those in Purgatory and those in Hell."

But it is difficult to believe that "the gate Saint Peter guards" refers to the entrance to Purgatory: neither the Pilgrim nor his guide could have known in Canto I anything about the entrance to Purgatory, nor could they have known about the absence of a gate in Paradise. Surely the Pilgrim's allusion must reflect the popular belief that the gate to Heaven is guarded by Saint Peter. But if line 134 refers to Paradise then it is difficult to make sense of the Pilgrim's words. The reference to Heaven in line 134 could follow quite easily from 133 if we interpret the two lines as meaning: "lead me to the two places you have just mentioned, Hell and Purgatory, so that ultimately I will be able to go to Heaven." But then how is the reference in line 135 to be understood? "Take me to Hell and Purgatory so that I may see (not only Heaven but) Hell" makes no sense!

But perhaps line 133 does not mean "lead me to both the places you have just mentioned" but rather "lead me to the place you mentioned last," i.e. Purgatory (the literal translation of the Italian is: "lead me there where you said"). In that case the Pilgrim would be saying "take me to Purgatory so that I may see Heaven—and (since this is unfortunately necessary) Hell too." This would betray some confusion or agitation, but what would be more natural at this stage when the Pilgrim is just about to begin his journey?

*   *   *

It is impossible to understand all of the allegory in the first canto without having read the entire *Comedy* because Canto I is, in a sense, a miniature of the whole, and the themes which Dante introduces here will be the major themes of the entire work. Thus, this canto is perhaps the most important of all.

The moral landscape of Canto I is tripartite, reflecting the structure of the *Divine Comedy* itself. The "dark woods" suggests the state of sin in which Dante the Pilgrim finds himself, and therefore is analogous to Hell (the subject matter of the first canticle) through which Dante will soon be travelling. The "barren slope" (29) suggests the middle ground between evil and good which men must pass through before they reach the "sunlight" of love and blessedness at the mountain's peak. It is analogous therefore to Purgatory, the subject of the second part of the *Comedy*. The "joyous mountain" (77) bathed in the rays of the sun is the state of blessedness toward which man constantly strives, described in the third canticle, the *Paradise*.

CANTO II

The day was fading and the darkening air
    was releasing all the creatures on our earth
    from their daily tasks, and I, one man alone,   *3*

was making ready to endure the battle
    of the journey, and of the pity it involved,
    which my memory, unerring, shall now retrace.   *6*

O Muses! O high genius! Help me now!
    O memory that wrote down what I saw,
    here your true excellence shall be revealed!   *9*

Then I began: "O poet come to guide me,
    tell me if you think my worth sufficient
    before you trust me to this arduous road.   *12*

You wrote about young Sylvius' father
    who went beyond, with flesh corruptible,
    with all his senses, to the immortal realm;   *15*

but if the Adversary of all evil
    was kind to him, considering who he was,
    and the consequence that was to come from him,   *18*

this cannot seem, to thoughtful men, unfitting,
    for in the highest heaven he was chosen
    father of glorious Rome and of her empire,   *21*

and both the city and her lands, in truth,
    were established as the place of holiness
    where the successors of great Peter sit.   *24*

And from this journey you celebrate in verse,
    Aeneas learned those things that were to bring
    victory for him, and for Rome, the Papal seat;   *27*

then later the Chosen Vessel, Paul, ascended
　　to bring back confirmation of that faith
　　which is the first step on salvation's road.   30

But why am I to go? Who allows me to?
　　I am not Aeneas, *I* am not Paul,
　　neither I nor any man would think me worthy;   33

and so, if I should undertake the journey,
　　I fear it might turn out an act of folly—
　　you are wise, you see more than my words express."   36

As one who unwills what he willed, will change
　　his purposes with some new second thought,
　　completely quitting what he first had started,   39

so I did, standing there on that dark slope,
　　thinking, ending the beginning of that venture
　　I was so quick to take up at the start.   42

"If I have truly understood your words,"
　　that shade of magnanimity replied,
　　"your soul is burdened with that cowardice   45

which often weighs so heavily on man
　　it turns him from a noble enterprise
　　like a frightened beast that shies at its own shadow.   48

To free you from this fear, let me explain
　　the reason I came here, the words I heard
　　that first time I felt pity for your soul: 51

I was among those dead who are suspended,
　　when a lady summoned me. She was so blessed
　　and beautiful, I implored her to command me.   54

With eyes of light more bright than any star,
　　in low, soft tones she started to address me
　　in her own language, with an angel's voice: 57

'O noble soul, courteous Mantuan,
　　whose fame the world continues to preserve
　　and will preserve as long as world there is,   60

my friend, who is no friend of Fortune's, strays
　　on a desert slope; so many obstacles
　　have crossed his path, his fright has turned him back.   63

I fear he may have gone so far astray,
   from what report has come to me in Heaven,
   that I may have started to his aid too late.   66

Now go, and with your elegance of speech,
   with whatever may be needed for his freedom,
   give him your help, and thereby bring me solace.   69

I am Beatrice, who urges you to go;
   I come from the place I am longing to return to;
   love moved me, as it moves me now to speak.   72

When I return to stand before my Lord,
   often I shall sing your praises to Him.'
   And then she spoke no more. And I began,   75

O Lady of Grace, through whom alone mankind
   may go beyond all worldly things contained
   within the sphere that makes the smallest circle,   78

your plea fills me with happy eagerness—
   to have obeyed already would still seem late!
   You needed only to express your wish.   81

But tell me how you dared to make this journey
   all the way down to this point of spacelessness
   away from your spacious home that calls you back.'   84

'Because your question scarches for deep meaning,
   I shall explain in simple words,' she said,
   'just why I have no fear of coming here.   87

A man must stand in fear of just those things
   that truly have the power to do us harm,
   of nothing else, for nothing else is fearsome.   90

God gave me such a nature through His Grace,
   the torments you must bear cannot affect me,
   nor are the fires of Hell a threat to me.   93

A gracious lady sits in Heaven grieving
   for what happened to the one I send you to,
   and her compassion breaks Heaven's stern decree.   96

She called Lucia and making her request
   she said, "Your faithful one is now in need
   of you, and to you I now commend his soul."   99

Lucia, the enemy of cruelty,
    hastened to make her way to where I was,
    sitting by the side of ancient Rachel,   *102*

and said to me: "Beatrice, God's true praise,
    will you not help the one whose love was such
    it made him leave the vulgar crowd for you?   *105*

Do you not hear the pity of his weeping,
    do you not see what death it is that threatens him
    along that river the sea shall never conquer?"   *108*

There never was a worldly person living
    more anxious to promote his selfish gains
    than I was at the sound of words like these—   *111*

to leave my holy seat and come down here
    and place my trust in you, in your noble speech
    that honors you and all those hearing it.'   *114*

When she had finished reasoning, she turned
    her shining eyes away, and there were tears.
    How eager then I was to come to you!   *117*

And I have come to you just as she wished,
    and I have freed you from the beast that stood
    blocking the quick way up the mount of bliss.   *120*

So what is wrong? Why, why do you delay?
    why are you such a coward in your heart,
    why aren't you bold and free of all your fear,   *123*

when three such gracious ladies who are blessed
    watch out for you up there in Heaven's court,
    and my words, too, bring promise of such good?"   *126*

As little flowers from the evening chill
    are closed and limp, and when the sun shines down
    on them, they rise to open on their stem,   *129*

my wilted strength began to bloom within me,
    and such good zeal went flowing to my heart
    I began to speak as one free in the sun.   *132*

"O she, compassionate, who moved to help me!
    And you, all kindness, in obeying quick
    those words of truth she brought with her for you—   *135*

you and the words you spoke have moved my heart
　　with such desire to continue onward
　　that now I have returned to my first purpose.　　　　　*138*

Let us start, for both our wills, joined now, are one.
　　You are my guide, you are my lord and teacher."
　　These were my words to him and, when he moved,　　　　*141*

I entered on that deep and rugged road.

NOTES

5. *of the journey, and of the pity:* The theme of the Pilgrim's pity is a major motif of the *Inferno* and one which is particularly important for the education of the Pilgrim; this is the first mention of pity in the *Divine Comedy.*

7–9. *O Muses! O high genius! Help me now!:* Dante links his own poem to the classical epic tradition by invoking the Muses. As Canto I is an introduction to the entire *Comedy,* it is appropriate that Dante give his invocation in Canto II, the beginning of the *Inferno* itself. This passage is balanced at the beginning of the *Purgatory* and the *Paradise* by similar invocations to the Muses.

The phrase "O high genius" may refer to Dante's own poetic skill or to that of Virgil (or both).

10–48

In the first major movement of Canto II, Dante the Pilgrim expresses fear of a journey such as Virgil proposes, for he finds himself wholly unworthy beside the two who have been allowed to visit "eternal regions" before—Aeneas and St. Paul. The comparison between Dante the Pilgrim and Aeneas and Paul is significant. For Virgil, Aeneas' journey had but one consequence: empire; for Dante, however, it signified both empire and the establishment of the Holy Roman Church, the "City of God" where all popes reside and reign. The fundamental concepts of Church and State, their government, their conflicts and internal problems were very important to Dante, and form one of the central themes of the *Comedy.* It is also true that the Pilgrim and Aeneas are searching for perfection according to the standard of their respective ages: moral virtue obtainable in a pagan culture, spiritual comprehension in a Christian one. The comparison between Dante the Pilgrim and the Apostle Paul is also significant: by extending the simile (as was done in the case of Aeneas), the reader may consider the Pilgrim, like St. Paul, a "Chosen Vessel," one who, granted sufficient grace for his journey, will strengthen the faith of mankind through it (by writing the *Divine Comedy*).

13–21. *young Sylvius' father:* Sylvius was the son of Aeneas by Lavinia, his second wife and daughter to Latinus.

In the *Aeneid* Virgil recounts the history of the founding of Rome. After the fall of Troy, Aeneas, the legendary hero of the epic, embarked on his divinely inspired journey that eventually led him to the shores of Italy, where he was to establish his city and nation. Before arriving at the Lavinian shores, however, he was obliged to descend to the Underworld where his father, Anchises, revealed the glories of the Rome that was to be.

28–30. *the Chosen Vessel, Paul:* In his *Second Epistle to the Corinthians* (12:2–4) the Apostle Paul alludes to his mystical elevation to the third heaven and to the arcane messages pronounced there. The medieval *Visio Sancti Pauli* relates his journey through the realms of the dead. Paul's vision served to strengthen the Christian faith, that same faith which is basic to the Pilgrim's (and by extension, Everyman's) salvation ("the first step on salvation's road"—which the Pilgrim took when he turned away from the "dark woods" in Canto I).

37–42. *As one who unwills what he willed, will change:* One of Dante's favorite poetic devices is to imitate the "action" stylistically. Here the Pilgrim's confused state of mind (his fear and lack of conviction) is reflected by the involved structure of the lines.

49–142

The second major movement in Canto II includes Virgil's explanation of his coming to the Pilgrim, and the subsequent restoration of the latter's courage. According to Virgil, the Virgin Mary, who traditionally signifies mercy and compassion in Christian thought, took pity on the Pilgrim in his predicament and set in motion the operation of Divine Grace. Lucia, whose name means "light," suggests the Illuminating Grace sent for by the Blessed Virgin; without Divine Grace the Pilgrim would be lost. Beatrice, whose name signifies blessedness or salvation, appears to Virgil in order to reveal to him the will of God who is the ultimate bestower of Divine Grace. The three heavenly ladies balance the three beasts of Canto I; they represent man's salvation from sin through Grace, as the beasts represent man's sins. The Pilgrim's journey, then, actually starts in Paradise when the Blessed Virgin Mary takes pity on him; thus the action of the *Divine Comedy* is in one sense a circle which begins in Heaven, as related here, and will ultimately end in Heaven with the Pilgrim's vision of God (*Paradise* XXXIII).

52. *I was among those dead who are suspended:* In the *Inferno* Virgil is assigned to Limbo, the dwelling place of those virtuous shades not eligible for heaven because they either lived before Christ's birth or remained heathen after the advent of Christianity (see Canto IV, n. 34).

61. *my friend, who is no friend of Fortune, strays:* See n. 76–78.

74. *often I shall sing your praises to Him:* Exactly what good it would do for Beatrice to sing Virgil's praises to God is not too clear, since those shades assigned to Limbo have no longer a chance to escape (see Canto IV, 41–42).

76–78. *O Lady of Grace, through whom alone mankind:* Virgil recognizes Beatrice as one who has meaning for *all* mankind. To his pagan soul, she represents the kind of contemplation that for Aristotle was perfect happiness, and by which alone man can transcend his human state. Her realm is above the lunar sphere ("the sphere that makes the smallest circle"), and to that realm of permanence and happiness we may ascend through contemplation. "Within the sphere" of the moon (i.e. on earth) is Fortune's realm, the region of change and corruption. Virgil, then, recognizes Beatrice in his own perspective, according to pagan thought; and she respects his point of view when, speaking to him (61) she refers to the Pilgrim as "my friend, who is no friend of Fortune's."

94. *A gracious lady sits in Heaven grieving:* The Virgin Mary.

102. *sitting by the side of ancient Rachel:* In the Dantean Paradise Rachel is seated by Beatrice: she represents the contemplative life.

108. *along that river the sea shall never conquer:* The river has the same kind of reality as the wood and the road of Canto I—all three belong to a stage of *our* life and have their existence in time rather than space (hence, the river will never be conquered by the sea). This river flows through the heart of Everyman (cf. Canto I, 20) and may be thought of as the *concupiscentiae fluctus* of St. Augustine: the

waters of cupidity for this world that flow in the heart of man.

119–126. *and I have freed you from the beast that stood:* The Pilgrim's initial fail-
ure to climb the mountain (due to the presence of the She-Wolf, I, 49–60) and his
subsequent state of desperation are recalled in these lines. Freed now, however,
from this peril by Virgil, and assured of success by the "three gracious ladies," he
should no longer be hindered from his journey by fear or any hesitation. Virgil
must make the Pilgrim move; and he accomplishes this through the purely ra-
tional arguments established by the events of the first two cantos and recapitu-
lated in this passage.

CANTO III

THROUGH ME THE WAY INTO THE DOLEFUL CITY,
  THROUGH ME THE WAY INTO ETERNAL GRIEF,
  THROUGH ME THE WAY AMONG A RACE FORSAKEN.   *3*

JUSTICE MOVED MY HEAVENLY CONSTRUCTOR;
  DIVINE OMNIPOTENCE CREATED ME,
  AND HIGHEST WISDOM JOINED WITH PRIMAL LOVE.   *6*

BEFORE ME NOTHING BUT ETERNAL THINGS
  WERE MADE, AND I SHALL LAST ETERNALLY.
  ABANDON HOPE, FOREVER, YOU WHO ENTER.   *9*

I saw these words spelled out in somber colors
  inscribed along the ledge above a gate;
  "Master," I said, "these words I see are cruel."   *12*

He answered me, speaking with experience:
  "Now here you must leave all distrust behind;
  let all your cowardice die on this spot.   *15*

We are at the place where earlier I said
  you could expect to see the suffering race
  of souls who lost the good of intellect."   *18*

Placing his hand on mine, smiling at me
  in such a way that I was reassured,
  he led me in, into those mysteries.   *21*

Here sighs and cries and shrieks of lamentation
  echoed throughout the starless air of Hell;
  at first these sounds resounding made me weep: *24*

tongues confused, a language strained in anguish
  with cadences of anger, shrill outcries
  and raucous groans in time to slapping hands,   *27*

34

raising a whirling storm that turns itself
    forever through that air of endless black,
    like grains of sand swirling when a whirlwind blows.   *30*

And I, in the midst of all this circling horror,
    began, "Teacher, what are these sounds I hear?
    What souls are these so overwhelmed by grief?"   *33*

And he to me: "This wretched state of being
    is the fate of those sad souls who lived a life
    but lived it with no blame and with no praise.   *36*

They are mixed with that repulsive choir of angels
    neither faithful nor unfaithful to their God,
    but undecided in neutrality.   *39*

Heaven, to keep its beauty, cast them out,
    but even Hell itself would not receive them
    for fear the damned might glory over them."   *42*

And I: "Master, what torments do they suffer
    that make such bitterness ring through their screams?"
    He answered: "I will tell you in few words: *45*

these wretches have no hope of truly dying,
    and this blind life they lead is so abject
    it makes them envy every other fate.   *48*

The world will not record their having been there;
    Heaven's mercy and its justice turn from them.
    Let's not discuss them; look and pass them by."   *51*

And so I looked and saw a kind of banner
    rushing ahead, whirling with aimless speed
    as though it would not ever take a stand;   *54*

behind it an interminable train
    of souls pressed on, so many that I wondered
    how death could have undone so great a number.   *57*

When I had recognized a few of them,
    I saw the shade of the one who must have been
    the coward who had made the great refusal.   *60*

At once I understood, and I was sure
    this was that sect of evil souls who were
    hateful to God and to His enemies.   *63*

These wretches, who had never truly lived,
    went naked, and were stung and stung again
    by the hornets and the wasps that circled them   66

and made their faces run with blood in streaks;
    their blood, mixed with their tears, dripped to their feet,
    and disgusting maggots collected in the pus.   69

And when I looked beyond this crowd I saw
    a throng upon the shore of a wide river,
    which made me ask, "Master, I would like to know: 72

who are these people, and what law is this
    that makes those souls so eager for the crossing—
    as I can see, even in this dim light?"   75

And he: "All this will be made plain to you
    as soon as we shall come to stop awhile
    upon the sorrowful shore of Acheron."   78

And I, with eyes cast down in shame, for fear
    that I perhaps had spoken out of turn,
    said no more until we reached the river.   81

And suddenly, coming towards us in a boat,
    a man of years whose ancient hair was white
    screamed at us, "Woe to you, perverted souls!   84

Give up all hope of ever seeing heaven:
    I come to lead you to the other shore,
    into eternal darkness, ice and fire.   87

And you, the living soul, you over there
    get away from all these people who are dead."
    But when he saw I did not move aside,   90

he said, "Another way, by other ports,
    not here, shall you pass to reach the other shore;
    a lighter skiff than this must carry you."   93

And my guide, "Charon, this is no time for anger!
    It is so willed, there where the power is
    for what is willed; that's all you need to know.   96

These words brought silence to the woolly cheeks
    of the ancient steersman of the livid marsh,
    whose eyes were set in glowing wheels of fire.   99

But all those souls there, naked, in despair,
    changed color and their teeth began to chatter
    at the sound of his announcement of their doom.   102

They were cursing God, cursing their mother and father,
    the human race, and the time, the place, the seed
    of their beginning, and their day of birth.   105

Then all together, weeping bitterly,
    they packed themselves along the wicked shore
    that waits for everyman who fears not God.   108

The devil, Charon, with eyes of glowing coals,
    summons them all together with a signal,
    and with an oar he strikes the laggard sinner.   111

As in autumn when the leaves begin to fall,
    one after the other (until the branch
    is witness to the spoils spread on the ground),   114

so did the evil seed of Adam's Fall
    drop from that shore to the boat, one at a time,
    at the signal, like the falcon to its lure.   117

Away they go across the darkened waters,
    and before they reach the other side to land,
    a new throng starts collecting on this side.   120

"My son," the gentle master said to me,
    "all those who perish in the wrath of God
    assemble here from all parts of the earth;   123

they want to cross the river, they are eager;
    it is Divine Justice that spurs them on,
    turning the fear they have into desire.   126

A good soul never comes to make this crossing,
    so, if Charon grumbles at the sight of you,
    you see now what his words are really saying."   129

He finished speaking, and the grim terrain
    shook violently; and the fright it gave me
    even now in recollection makes me sweat.   132

Out of the tear-drenched land a wind arose
    which blasted forth into a reddish light,
    knocking my senses out of me completely,   135

and I fell as one falls tired into sleep.

5–6. DIVINE OMNIPOTENCE . . . HIGHEST WISDOM . . . PRIMAL LOVE: These three attributes represent, respectively, the triune God: the Father, the Son, the Holy Ghost. Thus, the gate of Hell was created by the Trinity moved by Justice.

18. *of souls who lost the good of intellect:* That is, those souls who have lost sight of the *Summum Bonum*, the "Supreme Good," or God.

22–30. *Here sighs and cries and shrieks of lamentation:* Entering the Vestibule of Hell, the Pilgrim is immediately stunned by the screams of the shades in the Vestibule, borne to him in the form of an awesome tempest. In this first encounter with eternal punishment, he receives, as it were, an acoustical impression of Hell in its entirety. Bearing this in mind, the reader should note, as he follows the Pilgrim's passage through Hell, the recurrence of the descriptive elements contained here.

35–42. *who lived a life . . . with no blame and with no praise:* The first tormented souls whom the Pilgrim meets are not in Hell itself but in the Vestibule leading to it. In a sense they are the most loathsome sinners of all because in life they performed neither meritorious nor reprehensible acts. Among them are the angels who refused to take sides when Lucifer revolted. Appropriately, these souls are all nameless, for their lack of any kind of action has left them unworthy of mention. Heaven has damned them but Hell will not accept them.

52–69. *I looked and saw a kind of banner:* In the *Inferno* divine retribution assumes the form of the *contrapasso*, i.e., the just punishment of sin, effected by a process either resembling or contrasting to the sin itself. In this canto the *contrapasso* opposes the sin of neutrality, or inactivity: the souls who in their early lives had no banner, no leader to follow, now run forever after one.

Moreover, these shades that were on earth untouched and unmoved by any care are here "stung and stung again by the hornets and the wasps."

60. *the coward who had made the great refusal:* The difficulty of identifying this figure has plagued critics and commentators for over seven hundred years. Among the candidates suggested are the Emperor Diocletian who in his old age abdicated the throne, Esau who relinquished his rights of primogeniture to Jacob, Vieri dei Cerchi (incompetent head of the Florentine Whites), Giano della Bella, Frederick II of Sicily, etc. But most critics say that it is Celestine V who renounced the Papacy in 1294 five months after having been elected. However, Celestine, considering himself inadequate to the task, resigned his office out of humility, not out of cowardice. And the fact that the ex-Pope was canonized in 1313 indicates that his refusal might well have been interpreted as a pious act.

Perhaps it is most likely that this shade is Pontius Pilate who refused to pass sentence on Christ. His role, then, would be paralleled to that of the "neutral angels": as they stood by while Lucifer rebelled against God, so Pilate's neutral attitude at the trial of Christ resulted in the crucifixion of Christ. Again, it is significant that Pilate (if the identification proposed be correct) would be the first individual pointed out to us after the Pilgrim enters the Gate of Hell. The *Inferno* concludes with the climactic figure of the rebellious Lucifer; thus, a parallel would be suggested between the archtraitor to God in Heaven and the cowardly Pilate whose irresolution amounted to a betrayal of Christ on earth.

78. *upon the sorrowful shore of Acheron:* Acheron is one of the rivers of Hell whose origin is explained in Canto XIV, 112–120; it serves as the outer boundary of Hell proper.

83. *a man of years:* This is Charon, the boatman of classical mythology who transports the souls of the dead across the Acheron into Hades.

91–93. *Another way, by other ports:* Charon, whose boat bears only the souls of the damned, recognizes the Pilgrim as a living man and refuses him passage. This tercet contains a prophecy of Dante's salvation: "by other ports" he will pass to "reach the other shore (of the Tiber)," and go to Purgatory and eventually to Paradise.

100. *But all the souls there, naked, in despair:* Though we must assume that all the damned in the *Inferno* are naked (except the Hypocrites: Canto XXIII), only occasionally is this fact pointed out.

112–117. *As in autumn when the leaves begin to fall:* Dante's great debt to Virgil's *Aeneid* includes figures of speech such as this simile (cf. *Aeneid* VI, 309–310). Dante, of course, always adapts the imagery to his own use and frequently makes it more vivid.

124–126. *they want to cross the river, they are eager:* It is perhaps a part of the punishment that the souls of all the damned are eager for their punishment to begin; those who were so willing to sin on earth, are in Hell damned with a willingness to go to their just retribution.

132. *even now in recollection makes me sweat:* The reality of the Pilgrim's journey is enhanced through the immediacy of the remembrance and the effect it produces on Dante the Poet. There will be many such auctorial comments in the course of the *Divine Comedy*.

136. *and I fell as one falls tired into sleep:* The swoon (or sleep) as a transitional device, is used again at the end of Canto V. Note also the opening lines of Canto I where the Pilgrim's awaking from sleep serves an introductory purpose.

CANTO IV

A heavy clap of thunder! I awoke
　　from the deep sleep that drugged my mind—startled,
　　the way one is when shaken out of sleep.　　　　　　　　　*3*

I turned my rested eyes from side to side,
　　already on my feet and, staring hard,
　　I tried my best to find out where I was,　　　　　　　　　*6*

and this is what I saw: I found myself
　　right on the brink of grief's abysmal valley
　　that collects the thunderings of endless cries.　　　　　　*9*

So dark and deep and nebulous it was,
　　try as I might to force my sight below
　　I could not see the shape of anything.　　　　　　　　　*12*

"Let us descend into the sightless world,"
　　began the poet (his face was deathly pale):
　　"I will go first, and you will follow me."　　　　　　　　*15*

And I, aware of his changed color, said:
　　"But how can I go on if you are frightened?
　　You are my constant strength when I lose heart."　　　　*18*

And he to me: "The anguish of the souls
　　that are down here paints my face with pity—
　　which you have wrongly taken to be fear.　　　　　　　　*21*

Let us go on, the long road urges us."
　　He entered then, leading the way for me
　　down to the first circle of the abyss.　　　　　　　　　*24*

Down there, to judge only by what I heard,
　　there were no wails but just the sounds of sighs
　　rising and trembling through the timeless air,　　　　　*27*

40

The sounds of sighs of untormented grief
    burdening these groups that were diverse and teeming,
    made up of men and women and of infants.   30

Then the good master said, "You do not ask
    what sort of souls are these you see around you.
    Now you should know before we go on farther,   33

they have not sinned. But their great worth alone
    was not enough, for they did not know Baptism
    which is the gateway to the faith you follow,   36

and if they came before the birth of Christ
    they did not worship God the way one should;
    I myself am a member of this group.   39

For this defect, and for no other guilt,
    we here are lost. In this alone we suffer:
    cut off from hope, we live on in desire."   42

The words I heard weighed heavy on my heart;
    to think that souls as virtuous as these
    were suspended in that limbo, and forever!   45

"Tell me, my teacher, tell me, O my master,"
    I began (wishing to have confirmed by him
    the teachings of unerring Christian doctrine),   48

"did any ever leave here, through his merit
    or with another's help, and go to bliss?"
    And he who understood my hidden question,   51

answered: "I was a novice in this place
    when I saw a mighty lord descend to us
    who wore the sign of victory as his crown.   54

He took from us the shade of our first parent,
    of Abel, his good son, of Noah, too,
    and of obedient Moses, who made the laws;   57

Abram, the Patriarch, David the King,
    Israel with his father and his children,
    with Rachel whom he worked so hard to win;   60

and many more he chose for blessedness;
    and you should know, before these souls were taken,
    no human soul had ever reached salvation."   63

We did not stop our journey while he spoke,
   but continued on our way along the woods—
   I say the woods, for souls were thick as trees.   66

We had not gone too far from where I woke
   when I made out a fire up ahead,
   a hemisphere of light that lit the dark.   69

Though we were still some distance from that place,
   we were close enough for me to vaguely see
   that distinguished people occupied that spot.   72

"O glory of the sciences and arts,
   who are these souls enjoying special honor,
   dwelling apart from all the others here?"   75

And he to me: "The honored name they bear
   that still resounds above in your own world
   wins Heaven's favor for them in this place."   78

And as he spoke I heard a voice announce:
   "Now let us honor our illustrious poet,
   his shade that left is now returned to us."   81

And when the voice was silent and all was quiet
   I saw four mighty shades approaching us,
   their faces showing neither joy nor sorrow.   84

Then my good master started to explain:
   "Observe the one who comes with sword in hand,
   leading the three as if he were their master.   87

It is the shade of Homer, sovereign poet,
   and coming second, Horace, the satirist;
   Ovid is the third, and last comes Lucan.   90

Since they all share one name with me, the name
   you heard resounding in that single voice,
   they honor me and do well doing so."   93

So I saw gathered there the noble school
   of the master singer of sublimest verse
   who soars above all others like the eagle.   96

And after they had talked awhile together,
   they turned and with a gesture welcomed me,
   and at that sign I saw my master smile.   99

Greater honor still they deigned to grant me:
  they welcomed me as one of their own group,
  so that I numbered sixth among such minds.   *102*

We walked together towards the shining light,
  discussing things that here are best kept silent,
  as there they were most fitting for discussion.   *105*

We reached the boundaries of a splendid castle
  that seven times was circled by high walls
  · defended by a sweetly flowing stream.   *108*

We walked right over it as on hard ground;
  through seven gates I passed with those wise spirits,
  and then we reached a meadow fresh in bloom.   *111*

There people were whose eyes were calm and grave,
  whose bearing told of great authority;
  seldom they spoke and always quietly.   *114*

Then moving to one side we reached a place
  spread out and luminous, higher than before,
  allowing us to view all who were there.   *117*

And right before us on the lustrous green
  the mighty shades were pointed out to me
  (my heart felt glory when I looked at them).   *120*

There was Electra standing with a group,
  among whom I saw Hector and Aeneas,
  and Caesar, falcon-eyed and fully armed.   *123*

I saw Camilla and Penthesilea;
  across the way I saw the Latian King,
  with Lavinia, his daughter, by his side.   *126*

I saw the Brutus who drove out the Tarquin;
  Lucretia, Julia, Marcia and Cornelia;
  off, by himself, I noticed Saladin,   *129*

and when I raised my eyes a little higher
  I saw the master sage of those who know
  sitting with his philosophic family.   *132*

All gaze at him, all pay their homage to him;
  and there I saw both Socrates and Plato,
  each closer to his side than any other;   *135*

Democritus, who said the world was chance,
  Diogenes, Thales, Anaxagoras,
  Empedocles, Zeno, and Heraclitus;   138

I saw the one who classified our herbs:
  Dioscorides I mean. And I saw Orpheus,
  Tully, Linus, Seneca the moralist,   141

Euclid the geometer and Ptolemy,
  Hippocrates, Galen, Avicenna,
  and Averroës who made the Commentary.   144

I cannot tell about them all in full;
  my theme is long and urges me ahead,
  often I must omit things I have seen.   147

The company of six becomes just two;
  my wise guide leads me by another way
  out of the quiet into tempestuous air.   150

I come into a place where no light is.

NOTES

7. *and this is what I saw:* The passage across the Acheron, effected between cantos, remains a mystery to the Pilgrim. Unable to explain it, he can only describe the place where he now finds himself, beginning, "and this is what I saw. . . ."

20. *paints my face with pity:* Virgil's expression of pity indicates that he is thinking only of the souls in Limbo (where he himself dwells), for Reason cannot feel pity for the just punishment of sin; later he will rebuke Dante for taking pity on the sinners. Those virtuous shades in Limbo of course are not sinners and the absence there of the light of God is pitiable.

34. *they have not sinned:* According to Christian doctrine no one outside the Church (i.e. without baptism, the first Sacrament and, thus, the "gateway to the faith") can be saved. The souls suspended in Limbo, the First Circle of Hell, were on earth virtuous individuals who had no knowledge of Christ and His teachings (through no fault of their own since they preceded Him) or who, after His coming, died unbaptized. Here physical torment is absent; these shades suffer only mental anguish for, now cognizant of the Christian God, they have to "live on in desire" without any hope of beholding Him.

49–50. *did any ever leave here . . . ?:* The Pilgrim, remembering the Church's teaching concerning Christ's Harrowing of Hell, attempts to verify it by questioning Virgil, who should have been there at the time. Note the cautious presentation of the question (especially in the phrase "with another's help"), by means of which the Pilgrim, more than reassuring himself about Church doctrine, is subtly testing his guide. Virgil responds to the Pilgrim's "hidden question" in the terms of his classical culture. Unable to understand Christ in Christian terms, Virgil can only refer to Him as a "mighty lord . . . who wore the sign of victory as his crown."

66. *I say the woods, for souls were thick as trees:* This wood of souls is of course different from the "dark woods" of Canto I (l. 2). Nevertheless, this "woods" as well as several yet to come should remind us of the original "dark woods" and its symbolic suggestion of loss of salvation.

69. *a hemisphere of light that lit the dark:* The "hemisphere of light" emanates from a "splendid castle" (106), the dwelling place of the virtuous men of wisdom in Limbo. The light is the illumination of human intellect which those who dwell there had in such high measure on earth.

86–88. *Observe the one who comes with sword in hand:* Dante's inability to read Greek denied him access to Homer's works, with which he was acquainted only incidentally through Latin commentaries and redactions. Because his name was inseparably linked with the Trojan War, Homer is portrayed by Dante as a sword-bearing poet, one who sang of arms and martial heroes.

89. *Horace, the satirist:* In this limited reference to Horace Dante probably was thinking of the Roman poet's *Epistles* as well as of his *Satires*. It is possible that his *Odes* were unknown to Dante. Or he may have wished to stress Horace's role as a moralist.

90. *Ovid is the third, and last comes Lucan:* Ovid's major work, the *Metamorphoses*, was widely read and consulted as the principal source and authority for classical mythology during the Middle Ages. Lucan provided Dante with mythological material, and with much historical information on the civil war between Pompey and Caesar (*Pharsalia*).

91–93. *Since they all share one name with me:* This "one name" is that of "poet." The phrase "they honor me and do well doing so" is actually an expression of modesty, meaning that in "honoring me" they honor themselves as poets.

95–96. *the master singer of sublimest verse:* This may be Homer since Dante referred to him in line 87 as "leading the three as if he were their master" and in line 88 as "sovereign poet." But the words "master singer of sublimest verse" also make us think of Virgil, whom Dante referred to in Canto I as "light and honor of the other poets" (82); note also the comparison to an eagle (96), which could suggest the Roman Empire.

100–102. *Greater honor still they deigned to grant me:* In this passage Dante, equating himself with the famous poets of antiquity, acknowledges his art and talent. By this it should not be assumed that he is merely indulging in self-praise; rather, the reader should also interpret these lines as an indication of Dante's awareness of his role as a poet, of his purpose in writing, and of his unique position in the literary scene of his day.

104–105. *discussing things that here are best kept silent:* This phrase is a *topos* which Dante will frequently utilize in the *Divine Comedy*.

106–111. *We reached the boundaries of a splendid castle:* The allegorical construction of the castle is open to question. It may represent natural philosophy unilluminated by divine wisdom, in which case the seven walls serving to protect the castle would be the seven moral and speculative virtues (prudence, justice, fortitude, temperance, intellect, science, and knowledge); and the seven gates which provide access to the castle would be the seven liberal arts which formed the medieval school curriculum (music, arithmetic, geometry, astronomy—the *quadrivium*; and grammar, logic, and rhetoric—the *trivium*). The symbolic value of the stream also remains uncertain; it could signify eloquence, a "stream" which the eloquent Virgil and Dante should have no trouble crossing—and indeed, they "walked right over it as on hard ground" (109).

The inhabitants of the great castle are important pagan philosophers and poets, as well as famous warriors. Three of the shades named (Saladin, Avicenna, Averroës) lived only one or two hundred years before Dante. Modern readers might wonder at the inclusion of medieval non-Christians among the virtuous Pagans of antiquity, but the three just mentioned were among the non-Christians whom the Middle Ages, particularly, respected.

121. *There was Electra standing with a group:* Electra, daughter of Atlas, was the mother of Dardanus, the founder of Troy. Thus, her followers include all members of the Trojan race. She should not be confused with Electra, daughter of Agamemnon, the character in plays by Aeschylus, Sophocles, and Euripides.

122. *among whom I saw Hector and Aeneas:* Among Electra's descendants are: Hector, the eldest son of Priam, king of Troy, who after many battles was slain by Achilles; and Aeneas (cf. I, 73–75, and II, 13–24). The transition from Trojan to Roman hero is effected through the figure of Aeneas.

123. *and Caesar, falcon-eyed and fully armed:* Julius Caesar proclaimed himself the first Emperor of Rome after defeating numerous opponents in civil conflicts. Dante's source for the unusual description of Caesar ("falcon-eyed") is Suetonius; at the time "falcon-eyed" was occasionally used to describe a person with luminous or fiery eyes.

124–126. *I saw Camilla:* For Camilla, see I, n. 107. Penthesilea was the glamorous Queen of the Amazons who aided the Trojans against the Greeks and was slain by Achilles during the conflict. King Latinus commanded the central region of the Italian peninsula, the site where Aeneas founded Rome. He gave Lavinia to the Trojan conqueror in marriage.

127–129. *I saw the Brutus:* Outraged by the murder of his brother and the rape (and subsequent suicide) of his sister (Lucretia), Lucius Brutus incited the Roman populace to expel the Tarquins, the perpetrators of the offences. This accomplished, he was elected first consul and consequently became the founder of the Roman Republic. The four women were famous Roman wives and mothers. Lucretia: wife of Collatinus; Julia: daughter of Julius Caesar and wife of Pompey; Marcia: second wife of Cato of Utica (in the *Convivio* Dante makes her the symbol of the noble soul); Cornelia: daughter of Scipio Africanus Major and mother of the Gracchi, the tribunes Tiberius and Caius. A distinguished soldier, Saladin became sultan of Egypt in 1174. He launched many military campaigns and succeeded in expanding his empire. Although he won scattered victories over the Crusaders, he was soundly defeated by Richard the Lion-Hearted. A year after the truce he died (1193). Medieval opinion of Saladin was favorable; he was lauded for his generosity and his magnanimity. By including him among the virtuous souls in Limbo (although he is spatially isolated from the Trojan and Roman luminaries), Dante reflects this judgment of his age.

131. *I saw the master sage of those who know:* Aristotle was regarded as the "master sage" in the later Middle Ages. His widely known treatises were adapted to a Christian context by St. Thomas Aquinas. To Dante, Aristotle represented the summit of human reason, that point which man could reach on his own without the benefit of Christian revelation. With the exception of the Bible Dante draws most often from Aristotle.

134. *and there I saw both Socrates and Plato:* Acquainted with these Greek philosophers primarily through the works of Cicero, Dante considered them the initiators of the moral philosophy later perfected by Aristotle.

136. *Democritus, who said the world was chance:* A Greek philosopher (c. 460–c. 370 B.C.), born in Thrace, who formulated the theory that the universe was created from the random grouping of atoms.

137. *Diogenes, Thales, Anaxagoras:* Diogenes was the Cynic Philosopher who believed that the only good lies in virtue secured through self-control and abstinence. Anaxagoras was a Greek philosopher of the Ionian school (500–428 B.C.). Among his famous students were Pericles and Euripides. He introduced the theory that a spiritual presence gives life and form to material things. Thales (c. 635–c. 545 B.C.), an early Greek philosopher born at Miletus, founded the Ionian school of philosophy, and in his main doctrine maintained that water is the elemental principle of all things.

138. *Empedocles, Zeno, and Heraclitus:* Empedocles (c. 490–c. 430 B.C.), born at Agrigentum in Sicily, maintained that the four primal elements (fire, air, earth, water) joined together under the influence of Love to form the Universe whose union, then, is periodically destroyed by Hate, only to be formed anew. His works in verse later served as the model for Lucretius' *On the Nature of Things.* Heraclitus (c. 501 B.C.) was born at Ephesus; his ideas are couched in very obscure language. According to him, knowledge is based on sense perception, and man has the possibility of progressing toward the perfect knowledge possessed by the gods. Zeno, native of Citium in Cyprus (c. 336–c. 264 B.C.), founded the Stoic school of philosophy. It is, however, entirely possible that Dante was referring to Zeno of Elea (c. 490–c. 430 B.C.), one of Parmenides' disciples.

140. *Dioscorides I mean. And I saw Orpheus:* Dioscorides was a Greek natural scientist and physician of the first century A.D. His major work is *De Materia Medica* in which he discourses on the medicinal properties of plants. Orpheus was a mythical Greek poet and musician whose lyrical talent was such that it moved rocks and trees and tamed wild beasts. It is said that he descended into the Underworld, charmed Persephone with his song, and almost succeeded in bringing his wife, Eurydice, back to the world of the living.

141. *Tully, Linus, Seneca the moralist:* Tully is Marcus Tullius Cicero, celebrated Roman orator, writer, and philosopher (106–43 B.C.). Linus was a mythical Greek poet and musician who is credited with inventing the dirge. Lucius Annaeus Seneca (4 B.C.–A.D. 65) followed the philosophy of the Stoics in his moral treatises. Dante calls him "the moralist" to distinguish him from Seneca the tragedian who was thought (erroneously) during the Middle Ages to be another person.

142. *Euclid the geometer and Ptolemy:* Euclid, a Greek mathematician (c. 300 B.C.) who taught at Alexandria, wrote a treatise on geometry which was the first codification and exposition of mathematical principles. Ptolemy was a Greek mathematician, astronomer, and geographer, born in Egypt about the end of the first century A.D. The Ptolemaic system of the universe (which was accepted by the Middle Ages), so named although he did not invent it, presented the Earth as its fixed center encircled by nine spheres.

143. *Hippocrates, Galen, Avicenna:* Hippocrates was a Greek physician (c. 460–c. 377 B.C.) who founded the medical profession and introduced the scientific art of healing; his best known work was the *Aphorisms,* used as an authority in the Middle Ages. Galen was a celebrated physician (c. A.D. 130–c. 200) who practiced his art in Greece, Egypt, and Rome; he wrote about every branch of medicine known in his time. Like Hippocrates, he enjoyed the esteem of his contemporaries and later generations. Avicenna or Ibn-Sina (A.D. 980–1037), an Arab philosopher and physician, was a prolific writer; his works include commentaries on Galen and Aristotle.

144. *and Averroës who made the Commentary:* Ibn-Rushd, called Averroës (c. A.D. 1126–c. 1198) was the celebrated Arab scholar born in Spain whose interests ranged from medicine to philosophy and law. He was widely known in the Middle Ages for his commentary on Aristotle, which served as the basis for the work of St. Thomas Aquinas.

CANTO V

This way I went, descending from the first
  into the second circle, that holds less space
  but much more pain—stinging the soul to wailing.   *3*

There stands Minòs grotesquely, and he snarls,
  examining the guilty at the entrance;
  he judges and dispatches, tail in coils.   *6*

By this I mean that when the evil soul
  appears before him, it confesses all,
  and he who is the expert judge of sins   *9*

sees what place in Hell the soul belongs to;
  the times he wraps his tail around himself
  tells just how far the sinner must go down.   *12*

The damned keep crowding up in front of him:
  they pass along to judgment one by one;
  they speak, they hear, and then are hurled below.   *15*

"Oh you who come to the place where pain is host,"
  Minòs spoke out when he caught sight of me,
  putting aside the duties of his office,   *18*

"be careful how you enter and whom you trust:
  it is easy to get in, but don't be fooled!"
  And my guide to him: "Why do you keep on shouting?   *21*

Do not attempt to stop his fated journey;
  it is so willed there where the power is
  for what is willed; that's all you need to know."   *24*

And now the notes of anguish start to play
  upon my ears; and now I find myself
  where sounds on sounds of weeping pound at me.   *27*

I came to a place where no light shone at all,
　　bellowing like the sea racked by a tempest,
　　when warring winds attack it from both sides.　　　　　30

The infernal storm, eternal in its rage,
　　sweeps and drives the spirits with its blast:
　　it whirls them, lashing them with punishment.　　　　　33

When they are swept back past their place of judgment,
　　then come the shrieks, laments and anguished cries;
　　there they blaspheme the power of almighty God.　　　　36

I learned that to this place of punishment
　　all those who sin in lust have been condemned,
　　those who make reason slave to appetite;　　　　　　　39

and as the wings of starlings in the winter
　　bear them along in wide-spread, crowded flocks,
　　so does that wind propel the evil spirits:　　　　　　　42

here, then there, and up and down, it sweeps them
　　forever, without hope to comfort them
　　(hope, not of taking rest, but of suffering less).　　　　45

And just like cranes in flight, chanting their lays,
　　stretching an endless line in their formation,
　　I saw approaching, crying their laments,　　　　　　　48

spirits carried along by the battling winds.
　　And so I asked, "Teacher, tell me, what souls
　　are these punished in the sweep of the black wind?"　　51

"The first of those whose story you should know,"
　　my master wasted no time answering,
　　"was empress over lands of many tongues;　　　　　　54

her vicious tastes had so corrupted her,
　　she licensed every form of lust with laws
　　to cleanse the stain of scandal she had spread;　　　　57

she is Semiramis who, legend says,
　　was Ninus' wife and successor to his throne;
　　she governed all the land the Sultan rules.　　　　　　60

The next is she who killed herself for love
　　and broke faith with the ashes of Sichaeus;
　　and there is Cleopatra who loved men's lusting.　　　　63

See Helen there, the root of evil woe
    lasting long years, and see the great Achilles
    who lost his life to love, in final combat;   66

see Paris, Tristan"—then, more than a thousand
    he pointed out to me, and named them all,
    those shades whom love cut off from life on earth.   69

After I heard my teacher call the names
    of all these knights and ladies of ancient times,
    pity confused my senses, and I was dazed.   72

I began: "Poet, I would like, with all my heart,
    to speak to those two there who move together
    and seem to be so light upon the winds."   75

And he: "You'll see for yourself when they are closer;
    if you entreat them by that love of theirs
    that carries them along, they will come to you."   78

When the winds bent their course in our direction
    I raised my voice to them, "Oh, wearied souls,
    come speak with us if it be not forbidden."   81

As doves, called by desire to return
    to their sweet nest, with wings outstretched and poised,
    float downward through the air, guided by their will,   84

so these two left the flock where Dido is
    and came toward us through the malignant air,
    such was the tender power of my call.   87

"O living creature, gracious and so kind,
    who make your way here through this dingy air
    to visit us who stained the world with blood,   90

if we could claim as friend, the King of Kings,
    we would beseech him that he grant you peace,
    you who show pity for our atrocious plight.   93

Whatever pleases you to hear or speak
    we will hear and we will speak about with you
    as long as the wind, here where we are, is silent.   96

The place where I was born lies on the shore
    where the river Po with its attendant streams
    descends to seek its final resting place.   99

Love, that kindles quick in the gentle heart,
    seized this one for the beauty of my body,
    torn from me. (How it happened still offends me!)   102

Love, that excuses no one loved from loving,
    seized me so strongly with delight in him
    that, as you see, he never leaves my side.   105

Love led us straight to sudden death together.
    Caïna awaits the one who quenched our lives."
    These were the words that came from them to us.   108

When those offended souls had told their story,
    I bowed my head and kept it bowed until
    the poet said, "What are you thinking of?"   111

When finally I spoke, I sighed, "Alas,
    what sweet thoughts, and oh, how much desiring
    brought these two down into this agony."   114

And then I turned to them and tried to speak;
    I said, "Francesca, the torment that you suffer
    brings painful tears of pity to my eyes.   117

But tell me, in that time of your sweet sighing
    how, and by what signs, did love allow you
    to recognize your dubious desires?"   120

And she to me: "There is no greater pain
    than to remember, in our present grief,
    past happiness (as well your teacher knows)!   123

But if your great desire is to learn
    the very root of such a love as ours,
    I shall tell you, but in words of flowing tears.   126

One day we read, to pass the time away,
    of Lancelot, how he had fallen in love;
    we were alone, innocent of suspicion.   129

Time and again our eyes were brought together
    by the book we read; our faces flushed and paled.
    To the moment of one line alone we yielded: 132

it was when we read about those longed-for lips
    now being kissed by such a famous lover,
    that this one (who shall never leave my side)   135

then kissed my mouth, and trembled as he did.
    The book and its author was out Galehot!
    That day we read no further." And all the while   *138*

the one of the two spirits spoke these words,
    the other wept, in such a way that pity
    blurred my senses; I swooned as though to die,   *141*

and fell to Hell's floor as a body, dead, falls.

NOTES

1–72

    The fifth canto can be divided into two equal parts with a transitional tercet. The first part concerns Minòs and his activities, the band of souls being punished in the wind for their lust, and certain shades of royal figures seen in a formation that resembles that of flying cranes. The Pilgrim has learned (evidently from Virgil) the function of Minòs, and he will learn from him the type of sin being punished, the form of the punishment, and the names of many of those who are here. Chiefly, Virgil is trying to teach the Pilgrim three lessons in the first part of this canto, and each is concerned with the nature of lust—a heinous sin even if it is the least of those punished in Hell. The first lesson should come from the sight of Minòs exercising his function: the horror of this sight should shock the Pilgrim into an awareness of the true nature of all sin. The second lesson should come from the royal figures guilty of lust. Semiramis, who legalized lust because of her own incestuous activity (and to whom Virgil devotes three tercets, more lines than anyone else in this group receives), should be a particularly significant lesson to the Pilgrim as to the nature of carnal sins. And thirdly, the Pilgrim should come to despise the lustful because they blaspheme Divine Justice which has placed them here, and thereby show themselves to be totally unrepentant.

    But the Pilgrim learns nothing, as we see in the transitional tercet (70–72). Instead, pity for these sinners seizes his senses and he is "dazed." This tercet reveals the state of the Pilgrim's mind before meeting with Francesca da Rimini. Pity is precisely that side of the Pilgrim's character towards which Francesca will direct her carefully phrased speech. The Pilgrim has not learned his lesson, and in the direct encounter with one of the lustful (Francesca), he will fail his first "test."

    4. *There stands Minòs grotesquely:* Minòs was the son of Zeus and Europa. As king of Crete he was revered for his wisdom and judicial gifts. For these qualities he became chief magistrate of the Underworld in classical literature:

> Quaesitor Minos urnam movet: ille silentum
> Conciliumque vocat vitasque et crimina discit.
>   (Virgil, *Aeneid* VI, 432–33)

Although Dante did not alter Minòs' official function, he transformed him into a demonic figure, both in his physical characteristics and in his bestial activity. Minòs condemns souls to all parts of Hell, but Dante may well have placed him at the entrance to the Second Circle so that the reader, listening to the tragic tale of the sweet Francesca, would not be tempted to forget the hideous figure of Minòs who, with his tail, once pronounced sentence on Francesca as well as on Thaïs the whore (XVIII).

31–32. *The infernal storm, eternal in its rage:* The *contrapasso* or punishment suggests that lust (the "infernal storm") is pursued without the light of reason (in the darkness).

34. In Italian this line reads,

> Quando giungon davanti a la ruina

literally,

> When they come before the falling place

According to Busnelli (*Miscellanea dantesca,* Padova, 1922, 51–53) the *ruina* refers to the tribunal of Minòs, that is, to the place where the condemned sinners "fall" before him at the entrance to the Second Circle to be judged. Therefore I have translated *ruina* as "their place of judgment"; the entire tercet means that every time the sinners in the windstorm are blown near Minòs they shriek, lament, and blaspheme.

58. *she is Semiramis:* The legendary queen of Assyria who, although renowned for her military conquests and civic projects, fell prey to her passions and became dissolute to the extent of legalizing lust. Paulus Orosius, Dante's principal source for the story, also attributes the restoration of Babylon, built by Nimrod, to Semiramis. According to St. Augustine (*City of God*), one of the major conflicts of Christendom stems from the presence of two opposing civilizations: the city of God (*civitas dei,* founded by Abraham) and the city of man (*civitas mundi,* rejuvenated by Semiramis). Therefore, in a larger sense Dante conceived the Assyrian empress not only as the representative of libidinous passion in all its forms, but also as the motivating force of the degenerate society that ultimately opposes God's divine order.

60. *she governed all the land the Sultan rules:* During the Middle Ages the Sultan controlled the area which now contains Egypt and Syria .

61–62. *The next is she who killed herself for love:* According to Virgil (*Aeneid* I and IV), Dido, the Queen of Carthage swore faithfulness to the memory of her dead husband, Sichaeus. However, when the Trojan survivors of the war arrived in port, she fell helplessly in love with their leader, Aeneas, and they lived together as man and wife until the gods reminded Aeneas of his higher destiny: the founding of Rome and the Roman Empire. Immediately he set sail for Italy, and Dido, deserted, committed suicide.

63. *and there in Cleopatra who loved men's lusting:* Cleopatra was the daughter of Ptolemy Auletes, the last king of Egypt before it came under Roman domination. She was married to her brother in conformity with the incestuous practices of the Ptolemies, but with the assistance of Julius Caesar, whose child she bore, Cleopatra disposed of her brother and became Queen of Egypt. After Caesar's death her licentious charms captured Mark Antony, with whom she lived in debauchery until his death. Finally she attempted, unsuccessfully, to seduce Octavianus, the Roman governor of Egypt, and his refusal precipitated her suicide.

To the two great empires already mentioned, Assyria and Carthage, a third must be added, Egypt, which with its libidinous queen opposed the "*civitas dei.*"

64. *See Helen there, the root of evil woe:* Helen, wife of Menelaus, king of Sparta, was presented by Aphrodite to Paris in compensation for his judgment in the beauty contest of the goddesses. Paris carried Helen off to Troy and there married her, but her enraged husband demanded aid of the other Greek nobles to regain Helen. United, they embarked for Troy, and thus began the ten-year conflagration involving the two powerful nations.

65–66. *and see the great Achilles:* Dante's knowledge of the Trojan War came directly or indirectly from the early medieval accounts of Dares the Phrygian (*De Excidio Trojae Historia*) and Dictys of Crete (*De Bello Trojano*). In these versions

Achilles, the invincible Homeric warrior, had been transformed into an ordinary mortal who languished in the bonds of love. Enticed by the beauty of Polyxena, a daughter of the Trojan king, Achilles desired her to be his wife, but Hecuba, Polyxena's mother, arranged a counterplot with Paris so that when Achilles entered the temple for his presumed marriage, he was treacherously slain by Paris.

67. see Paris, Tristan: Paris was the son of Priam, king of Troy, whose abduction of Helen ignited the Trojan War. The classical Latin poets and the medieval redactors of the legend of Troy consistently depicted him more disposed to loving than to fighting. In the *Heroides* Ovid sums up Paris' essential nature in the words of Helen:

Quod bene te iactes et fortia facta loquaris,
a verbis facies dissidet ista tuis.
Apta magis Veneri, quam sunt tua corpora Marti.
Bella gerant fortes tu, Pari, semper ama!
    (XVII, 251–254)

Tristan is the central figure of numerous medieval French, German, and Italian romances. Sent as a messenger by his uncle, King Mark of Cornwall, to obtain Isolt for him in marriage, Tristan became enamored of her, and she of him. After Isolt's marriage to Mark, the lovers continued their love-affair, and in order to maintain its secrecy they necessarily employed many deceits and ruses. According to one version, however, Mark, growing continuously more suspicious of their attachment, finally discovered them together and ended the incestuous relationship by mortally wounding Tristan with a lance.

73–142

Having seen the shades of many "knights and ladies of ancient times" (71), the Pilgrim now centers his attention upon a single pair of lovers. The spotlight technique here employed emphasizes the essentially dramatic quality of the *Inferno*. Francesca recognizes the Pilgrim's sympathetic attitude and tells her story in a way that will not fail to win the Pilgrim's interest, even though she, like Semiramis, was the initiator in an act of incest. Her choice of words and phrases frequently reveals her gentility and her familiarity with the works of the *stilnovisti* poets (the school of poets which was contemporary with, and perhaps included, Dante). But beneath the superficial charm and grace the careful reader can see what Francesca really is—vain and accustomed to admiration. Francesca is also capable of lying, though whether her lies are intentional or the result of self-deception we do not know. For example her reference to the love of Lancelot in line 128 shows her technique of changing facts which would condemn her. In the medieval French romance, *Lancelot du Lac,* the hero, being quite bashful in love, is finally brought together in conversation with Queen Guinevere through the machinations of Galehot ("The book and its author was our Galehot," 137). Urged on by his words, Guinevere takes the initiative and, placing her hand on Lancelot's chin, kisses him. In order to fully understand Francesca's character, it is necessary to note that in our passage she has reversed the roles of the lovers: here she has Lancelot kissing Guinevere just as she had presented Paolo as kissing her. The distortion of this passage offered as a parallel to her own experience reveals the (at best) confusion of Francesca: if the passage in the romance inspired their kiss, it must have been she, as it was Guinevere, who was responsible. Like Eve, who tempted Adam to commit the first sin in the Garden of Eden, Francesca tempted Paolo, and thus she is perhaps an example of the common medieval view of women as "daughters of Eve." Francesca attempts to exculpate herself by blaming the romantic book that she and Paolo were reading (137); the Pilgrim is evidently convinced of her innocence for he is overcome ". . . in such a way that pity blurred [his] senses," and he faints.

Many critics, taken in like the Pilgrim by Francesca's smooth speech, have asserted that she and Paolo in their love have "conquered" Hell because they are still together. But their togetherness is certainly part of their punishment. The ever-silent, weeping Paolo is surely not happy with their state, and Francesca coolly alludes to Paolo with the impersonal "that one" (*costui*) or "this one" (*questi*). She never mentions his name. Line 102 indicates her distaste for Paolo: the manner of her death (they were caught and killed together in the midst of their lustful passion) *still* offends her because she is forever condemned to be together with her naked lover; he serves as a constant reminder of her shame and of the reason that they are in Hell ("he never leaves my side," 105). Their temporary pleasure together in lust has become their own particular torment in Hell.

74. *those two there who move together:* Francesca, daughter of Guido Vecchio da Polenta, lord of Ravenna, and Paolo Malatesta, third son of Malatesta da Verrucchio, lord of Rimini. Around 1275 the aristocratic Francesca was married for political reasons to Gianciotto, the physically deformed second son of Malatesta da Verrucchio. In time a love affair developed between Francesca and Gianciotto's younger brother, Paolo. One day the betrayed husband discovered them in an amorous embrace and slew them both.

82–84. *As doves:* Paolo and Francesca are compared to "doves, called by desire . . ." who "float downward through the air, guided by their will." The use of the words "desire" and "will" is particularly interesting, because it suggests the nature of lust as a sin: the subjugation of the will to desire.

97–99. *The place where I was born:* Ravenna, a city on the Adriatic coast.

100–108. *Love . . . Love . . . Love . . . :* These three tercets, each beginning with the word "Love," are particularly important as revealing the deceptive nature of Francesca. In lines 100 and 103 Francesca deliberately employs the style of *stilnovisti* poets such as Guinizelli and Cavalcanti in order to ensure the Pilgrim's sympathy, but she follows each of those lines with sensual and most un-*stilnovistic* ideas. For in the idealistic world of the *dolce stil nuovo* love would never "seize" a man for the beauty of the woman's body alone, nor would the sensual delight which "seized" Francesca be appropriate to *stilnovistic* love, which was distant, non-sexual, and ideal.

107. *Caïna awaits the one who quenched our lives:* Caïna is one of the four divisions of Cocytus, the lowest part of Hell, wherein are tormented those souls who treacherously betrayed their kin.

141–142. *I swooned as though to die:* To understand this reaction to Francesca, it is necessary to remember that Dante the Pilgrim is a fictional character who should not be equated with Dante the poet, author of the *Commedia*. Dante the Pilgrim is journeying through Hell as a man who must learn the true nature of sin, and since this is his first contact with those who are damned and punished in Hell proper, he is easily seduced into compassion for these souls. As the Pilgrim progresses he will learn the nature of sin and of evil souls, and his reaction to them will change (cf. XIX). But the extent of his failure in Canto V to recognize sin and treat it with proper disdain is symbolized here by his abject figure, unconscious (thus, without "reason") on the floor of Hell. Perhaps we should not blame the Pilgrim for being taken in by Francesca; dozens of critics, unaware of the wiles of sin, have also been seduced by her charm and the grace of her speech.

CANTO VI

When I regained my senses that had fainted
    at the sight of these two who were kinsmen lovers,
    a piteous sight confusing me to tears,   *3*

new suffering and new sinners suffering
    appeared to me, no matter where I moved
    or turned my eyes, no matter where I gazed.   *6*

I am in the third circle, in the round of rain
    eternal, cursèd, cold and falling heavy,
    unchanging beat, unchanging quality.   *9*

Thick hail and dirty water mixed with snow
    come down in torrents through the murky air,
    and the earth is stinking from this soaking rain.   *12*

Cerberus, a ruthless and fantastic beast,
    with all three throats howls out his dog-like sounds
    above the drowning sinners of this place.   *15*

His eyes are red, his beard is slobbered black,
    his belly swollen, and he has claws for hands;
    he rips the spirits, flays and mangles them.   *18*

Under the rain they howl like dogs, lying
    now on one side with the other as a screen,
    now on the other turning, these wretched sinners.   *21*

When the slimy Cerberus caught sight of us,
    he opened up his mouths and showed his fangs;
    his body was one mass of twitching muscles.   *24*

My master stooped and, spreading wide his fingers,
    he grabbed up heaping fistfuls of the mud
    and flung it down into those greedy gullets.   *27*

As a howling cur, hungering to get fed,
    quiets down with the first mouthful of his food,
    busy with eating, wrestling with that alone,   30

so it was with all three filthy heads
    of the demon Cerberus, used to barking thunder
    on these dead souls, who wished that they were deaf.   33

We walked across this marsh of shades beaten
    down by the heavy rain, our feet pressing
    on their emptiness that looked like human form.   36

Each sinner there was stretched out on the ground
    except for one who quickly sat up straight,
    the moment that he saw us pass him by.   39

"O you there being led through this inferno,"
    he said, "try to remember who I am,
    for you had life before I gave up mine."   42

I said: "The pain you suffer here perhaps
    disfigures you beyond all recognition:
    I can't remember seeing you before.   45

But tell me who you are, assigned to grieve
    in this sad place, afflicted by such torture
    that—worse there well may be, but none more foul."   48

"Your own city," he said, "so filled with envy
    its cup already overflows the brim,
    once held me in the brighter life above.   51

You citizens gave me the name of Ciacco;
    and for my sin of gluttony I am damned,
    as you can see, to rain that beats me weak.   54

And my sad sunken soul is not alone,
    for all these sinners here share in my pain
    and in my sin." And that was his last word.   57

"Ciacco," I said to him, "your grievous state
    weighs down on me, it makes me want to weep;
    but tell me what will happen, if you know,   60

to the citizens of that divided state?
    And are there any honest men among them?
    And tell me, why is it so plagued with strife?"   63

And he replied: "After much contention
   they will come to bloodshed; the rustic party
   will drive the other out by brutal means.   66

Then it will come to pass, this side will fall
   within three suns, and the other rise to power
   with the help of one now listing toward both sides.   69

For a long time they will keep their heads raised high,
   holding the others down with crushing weight,
   no matter how these weep or squirm for shame.   72

Two just men there are, but no one listens,
   for pride, envy, avarice are the three sparks
   that kindle in men's hearts and set them burning."   75

With this his mournful words came to an end.
   But I spoke back: "There's more I want to know;
   I beg you to provide me with more facts: 78

Farinata and Tegghiaio, who were so worthy,
   Jacopo Rusticucci, Arrigo, Mosca
   and all the rest so bent on doing good,   81

where are they? Tell me what's become of them;
   one great desire tortures me: to know
   whether they taste Heaven's sweetness or Hell's gall."   84

"They lie below with blacker souls," he said,
   "by different sins pushed down to different depths;
   if you keep going you may see them all.   87

But when you are once more in the sweet world
   I beg you to remind our friends of me.
   I speak no more; no more I answer you."   90

He twisted his straight gaze into a squint
   and stared awhile at me, then bent his head,
   falling to join his other sightless peers.   93

My guide then said to me: "He'll wake no more
   until the day the angel's trumpet blows,
   when the unfriendly Judge shall come down here;   96

each soul shall find again his wretched tomb,
   assume his flesh and take his human shape,
   and hear his fate resound eternally."   99

And so we made our way through the filthy mess
  of muddy shades and slush, moving slowly,
  talking a little about the afterlife.   *102*

I said, "Master, will these torments be increased,
  or lessened, on the final Judgment Day,
  or will the pain be just the same as now?"   *105*

And he: "Remember your philosophy:
  the closer a thing comes to its perfection,
  more keen will be its pleasure or its pain.   *108*

Although this cursèd race of punished souls
  shall never know the joy of true perfection,
  more perfect will their pain be then than now."   *111*

We circled round that curving road while talking
  of more than I shall mention at this time,
  and came to where the ledge begins descending;   *114*

there we found Plutus, mankind's arch-enemy.

N O T E S

7–21

The shades in this circle are the gluttons, and their punishment fits their sin.
Gluttony, like all the sins of Incontinence, subjects reason to desire; in this case
desire is a voracious appetite. Thus the shades howl like dogs—in desire, without
reason; they are sunk in slime, the image of their excess. The warm comfort their
gluttony brought them in life here has become cold, dirty rain and hail.

7–9. *I am in the third circle, in the round of rain:* Note the change in tense and
tone from the first two tercets. Suddenly Dante is writing in the present tense and
using the sharp staccato effect of one word pounding the other in order to rein-
force the immediacy of the image of cold rain and hail beating down on the
sinners.

13–22. *Cerberus, a ruthless and fantastic beast:* In classical mythology Cerberus
is a fierce three-headed dog which guards the entrance to the Underworld, per-
mitting admittance to all and escape to none. He is the prototype of the gluttons,
with his three howling, voracious throats that gulp down huge handfuls of muck.
He has become Appetite and as such he flays and mangles the spirits who reduced
their lives to a satisfaction of appetite. With his three heads, he appears to be a
prefiguration of Lucifer and thus another infernal distortion of the Trinity. In line
22 he is characterized as *il gran vermo* (literally, "the great worm") as Lucifer in
Canto XXXIV (108) is called *vermo reo* ("evil worm").

26–27. *he grabbed up heaping fistfuls of the mud:* With this action, Virgil imi-
tates the action of the Sibyl who, leading Aeneas through the Underworld,
placates Cerberus by casting honeyed cakes into his three throats (*Aeneid* VI,

417–423). By substituting "dirt" for the Virgilian cakes, Dante emphasizes Cerberus' irrational gluttony.

36. *their emptiness that looked like human form:* The shades in Hell bear only the appearance of their corporeal forms, although they can be ripped and torn and otherwise suffer physical torture—just as here they are able to bear the Pilgrim's weight. Yet they themselves evidently are airy shapes without weight (cf. VIII, 27) which will, after the Day of Judgment, be possessed of their actual bodies once more (see XIII, 103).

48. *worse there well may be, but none more foul:* At this early stage of his journey the Pilgrim, who will come to see the filth of excrements and dripping guts, can imagine nothing more foul than dirty water.

50. *its cup already overflows the brim:* The image used here by Ciacco to describe the envy in Florence, also reflects the sin of gluttony.

52. *You citizens gave me the name of Ciacco:* The only glutton whom the Pilgrim actually talks to is Ciacco, one of his Florentine contemporaries, whose true identity has never been determined. Several commentators believe him to be Ciacco dell'Anguillaia, a minor poet of the time and presumably the Ciacco of one of Boccaccio's stories (*Decameron* IX, 8). However, more than a proper name, "ciacco" is a derogatory Italian word for "pig," or "hog," and is also an adjective, "filthy," or "of a swinish nature."

59. *it makes me want to weep:* The Pilgrim, having learned very little from his experience in Canto V, feels pity again at the sight of Ciacco.

65–75. *they will come to bloodshed:* Ciacco's political prophecy reveals the fact that the shades in Hell are able to see the future; they also know the past, but they know nothing of the present (see X, 100–108). The prophecy itself can be interpreted in the following manner: in 1300 the Guelph party, having gained complete control over Florence by defeating the Ghibellines (1289), was divided into factions: the Whites (the "rustic party," 65), headed by the Cerchi family, and the Blacks ("the other," 66), led by the Donati. These two groups finally came into direct conflict on May 1, 1300, which resulted in the expulsion of the Blacks from the city (1301). However, they returned in 1302 ("within three suns," 68, i.e. within three years), and with the help of Pope Boniface VIII, sent the Whites (including Dante) into exile. Boniface VIII, the "one now listing toward both sides" (69), for a time did not reveal his designs on Florence, but rather steered a wavering course between the two factions, planning to aid the ultimate victor. The identity of the two honest men to whom no one listens (73) has not been established. The reader must of course realize that although the fictional date of the poem is 1300, the poem itself was written some years later, therefore most of what is "prophesied" in the *Inferno* had already taken place when Dante was writing.

73. *Two just men there are, but no one listens:* Although the two individuals remain unknown, it is probable that by "two" Dante simply intends to allude to the minimal few who are honest in corrupt Florence.

79–87. *Farinata and Tegghiaio, who were so worthy:* Ciacco informs the Pilgrim only that the men about whom he had inquired (79–81) are in Hell. But the Pilgrim will learn in the course of time that Farinata degli Uberti is in the Circle of the Heretics (X, 32); Tegghiaio Aldobrandini and Jacopo Rusticucci are among the Sodomites (XVI, n. 41 and n. 44); Mosca dei Lamberti is a Sower of Discord (XXVIII, n. 106). Arrigo is not mentioned again in the *Inferno* and has not been identified.

89. *I beg you to remind our friends of me:* In the upper regions of Hell, many of the damned are concerned with their worldly fame, because the perpetuation of their memory on earth by the living is their only means of remaining "alive." But as the sins become more heinous, the sinners seem less desirous of having their stories told on earth.

91–93. *He twisted his straight gaze into a squint:* The manner in which Ciacco takes leave is certainly odd: his eyes, fixed on the Pilgrim throughout their conversation, gradually lose their power to focus and can only stare blankly. The concentration required for the prophecy seems to have exhausted him.

106–111. *Remember your philosophy:* In answer to the Pilgrim's question (103–105), Virgil reminds him of the popular doctrine which states that the more a thing is perfect, the more it knows what pleasure is and pain. The perfected state of man from a "technical" point of view will be attained on Judgment Day, when the soul is reunited with the body. Therefore, the damned will feel more torment later than now; similarly, the blessed in Paradise will enjoy God's beatitude more.

115. *there we found Plutus, mankind's arch-enemy:* For Plutus see Canto VII, 2.

CANTO VII

"Pape Satàn, pape Satàn aleppe!"
   the voice of Plutus clucked these words at us,
   and that kind sage, to whom all things were known,   *3*

said reassuringly: "Pay no attention
   to your fear, for no matter what his power be
   he cannot stop our journey down this rock."   *6*

Then he turned toward that swollen face of rage
   crying, "Be quiet, cursèd wolf of Hell:
   feed on the burning bile that rots your guts.   *9*

This journey to the depths does have a reason,
   for it is willed on high, where Michael wrought
   a just revenge for the bold assault on God."   *12*

As sails swollen by wind when the ship's mast breaks,
   collapse, deflated, tangled in a heap,
   just so the savage beast fell to the ground.   *15*

And then we started down a fourth abyss,
   making our way along the dismal slope
   where all the evil of the world is dumped.   *18*

Ah, God's avenging justice! Who could heap up
   suffering and pain as strange as I saw here?
   How can we let our guilt bring us to this?   *21*

As every wave Charybdis whirls to sea
   comes crashing against its counter-current wave,
   so these folk here must dance their roundelay.   *24*

More shades were here than anywhere above,
   and from both sides, to the sound of their own screams,
   straining their chests, they rolled enormous weights.   *27*

And when they met and clashed against each other
    they turned to push the other way, one side
    screaming, "Why hoard?", the other side, "Why waste?"   *30*

And so they moved back round the gloomy circle
    returning on both sides to opposite poles
    to scream their shameful tune another time;   *33*

again they came to clash and turn and roll
    forever in their semi-circle joust.
    And I, my heart pierced through by such a sight,   *36*

spoke out, "My Master, please explain to me
    who are these people here? Were they all priests,
    these tonsured souls I see there to our left?"   *39*

He said, "In their first life all you see here
    had such myopic minds they could not judge
    with moderation when it came to spending;   *42*

their barking voices make this clear enough,
    when they arrive at the two points on the circle
    where opposing guilts divide them into two.   *45*

The ones who have the bald spot on their heads
    were priests and popes and cardinals, in whom
    avarice is most likely to prevail."   *48*

And I: "Master, in such a group as this
    I should be able to recognize a few
    who dirtied themselves by such crimes as these."   *51*

And he replied, "Yours is an empty hope:
    their undistinguished life that made them foul
    now makes it harder to distinguish them;   *54*

forever they will come to their two battles;
    then from the tomb they will be resurrected:
    these with tight fists, those without any hair.   *57*

It was squandering and hoarding that have robbed them
    of the lovely world, and got them in this brawl:
    I will not waste choice words describing it!   *60*

You see, my son, the short-lived mockery
    of all the wealth that is in Fortune's keep,
    over which the human race is bickering;   *63*

for all the gold that is or ever was
    beneath the moon won't buy a moment's rest
    for even one among these weary souls."   66

"Master, now tell me what this Fortune is
    you touched upon before. What is she like
    who holds all worldly wealth within her fists?"   69

And he to me, "Oh foolish race of man,
    how overwhelming is your ignorance!
    Now listen while I tell you what she means: 72

that One, whose wisdom knows infinity,
    made all the heavens and gave each one a guide,
    and each sphere shining shines on all the others,   75

so light is spread with equal distribution:
    for worldly splendors He decreed the same
    and ordained a guide and general ministress   78

who would at her discretion shift the world's
    vain wealth from nation to nation, house to house,
    with no chance of interference from mankind;   81

so while one nation rules, another falls
    according to whatever she decrees
    (her sentence hidden like a snake in grass).   84

Your knowledge has no influence on her;
    she provides for change, she judges, and she rules
    her domain as do the other gods their own.   87

Her changing changes never take a rest;
    necessity keeps her in constant motion,
    as men come and go to take their turn with her.   90

And thus is she so crucified and cursed;
    even those in luck who should be praising her,
    instead, revile her and condemn her acts.   93

But she is blest and in her bliss hears nothing;
    with all God's joyful first-created creatures
    she turns her sphere and, blest, turns it with joy.   96

Now let's move down to greater wretchedness;
    the stars that rose when I set out for you
    are going down—we cannot stay too long."   99

We crossed the circle to its other bank,
　　passing a spring that boils and overflows
　　into a ditch the spring itself cut out.　　　　　　　*102*

The water was a deeper dark than perse,
　　and we, with its grey waves for company,
　　made our way down along a rough, strange path.　　*105*

This dingy little stream, when it has reached
　　the bottom of the grey malignant slopes,
　　becomes a swamp that has the name of Styx.　　　*108*

And I, intent on looking as we passed,
　　saw muddy people moving in that marsh,
　　all naked, with their faces scarred by rage.　　　*111*

They fought each other, not with hands alone,
　　but struck with head and chest and feet as well,
　　with teeth they tore each other limb from limb.　　*114*

And the good teacher said: "My son, now see
　　the souls of those that anger overcame;
　　and I ask you to believe me when I say　　　　　*117*

beneath the slimy top are sighing souls
　　who make these waters bubble at the surface;
　　your eyes will tell you this—just look around.　　*120*

Bogged in this slime they say, 'Sluggish we were
　　in the sweet air made happy by the sun,
　　and the smoke of sloth was smoldering in our hearts;　*123*

now we lie sluggish here in this black muck!'
　　This is the hymn they gurgle in their throats
　　but cannot sing in words that truly sound."　　　*126*

Then making a wide arc we walked around
　　the pond between the dry bank and the slime,
　　our eyes still fixed on those who gobbled mud.　　*129*

We came, in time, to the foot of a high tower.

NOTES

1. *Pape Satàn, pape Satàn aleppe!:* This line, while it has never been interpreted satisfactorily, has certainly been interpreted variously. Critics as early as Boccaccio

have noted a relation of "pape" to "papa" (pope). Boccaccio implies that "pape" is a word expressive of great admiration, and Plutus applies it to Satan, "the prince of demons." Ciardi notes that "pape Satàn" would be the "opposite number" of "il papa santo," or the Pope. "Aleppe" has been connected with *aleph*, the first letter of the Hebrew alphabet, meaning either "prime"—or used as an expression of grief!

Some think that the line is addressed by Plutus to Dante; "Satàn" then is seen as the traditional, Biblical term for "enemy." But the main thrust of modern criticism is to accept the line as simple gibberish (cf. Nimrod's speech in XXXI, 67). However, considering the stress on the clergy throughout the canto, I think the equation "pape" = "pope" is probably most likely.

The hard sound of Plutus' voice onomatopoetically seconds the descriptive adjective "clucking" (*chioccia*).

2–15

Plutus, the god of wealth in classical mythology, appropriately presides over the Miserly and the Prodigal, those who did not use their material goods with moderation. In this canto his collapse like inflated sails "when the ship's mast breaks" (14) is interesting not only because it attests to the true, airy emptiness of wealth, but also because the simile prefigures an image Dante uses in describing Lucifer at the end of the *Inferno:* in XXXIV, 48, Lucifer's wings are compared to sails ("I never saw a ship with larger sails"). But Plutus is an empty satanic figure and his "sails" are empty.

8. *Be quiet, cursèd wolf of Hell:* Virgil's reference to the avaricious Plutus as a "cursèd wolf" recalls the She-Wolf of Canto I and lends more credence to the idea that the She-Wolf reigns over the circles of Incontinence. This opinion is further supported by Dante's words on the terrace of Avarice in the *Purgatory* (XX, 10) in reference to the sin: "Cursèd be you, age-old She-Wolf." Cf. line 43 of the present canto where the voices of the sinners are described as "barking," another wolfish trait (as in the previous canto, VI, 19).

11–12. *where Michael wrought / a just revenge:* The archangel Michael fought against and triumphed over the rebellious angels in Heaven.

22–66

The Miserly and the Prodigal, linked together as those who misused their wealth, suffer a joint punishment. Their material wealth has become a heavy weight which each group must shove against the other, since their attitudes toward wealth on earth were opposed to each other. Each of the two groups completes a semicircle (35) as they roll their weights at each other, therefore together they complete an entire circle (but whether there are many small circles or one huge one around the whole ledge is not clear). The image of a broken circle is surely related to the concept of Fortune mentioned by Virgil. Just as the Avaricious and the Prodigal believed they could outwit the turn of Fortune's wheel (see n. 73–96) by hoarding material goods or by wasting them on earth, so here the "short-lived mockery / of all the wealth that is in Fortune's keep" (61–62) is apparent, since part of their punishment is to complete the turn of the Wheel (circle) of Fortune against which they had rebelled during their short space of life on earth.

Because their total concern with wealth left them undistinguished in life, they are unrecognizable here, and the Pilgrim cannot pick out any one sinner in the teeming mass (49–54).

38–48. *who are these people here? Were they all priests:* The fact that most of the avaricious are tonsured priests ("the ones who have the bald spot on their heads,"

46) indicates a major abuse practiced by the priesthood in Dante's time; here we have the first of many criticisms in the *Inferno* of the materialistic clergy. See n. 1 of this canto.

57. *these with tight fists, those without any hair:* There is an old Italian proverb about prodigal individuals: "they spend even the hairs on their head" (*spendono fino i capelli*). After the resurrection even their hair appropriately will be missing.

70. *Oh foolish race of man:* Virgil's words are addressed not only to Dante but to every man.

73–96

Virgil's digression concerns Fortune, a major theme of medieval and renaissance writers such as Boethius, Petrarch, Boccaccio, Chaucer, and Machiavelli. Usually it was visualized as a female figure with a wheel, the revolutions of which symbolized the rise and fall of fortune in a man's life, but Dante deviates somewhat from the standard concept of Fortune (as related e.g. in Boethius' *Consolation of Philosophy*) by assigning to her the role of an angel. In Dante's world she is a minister of God who carries out the divine purpose among men; i.e., Dante has christianized a pagan goddess.

84. *her sentence hidden like a snake in grass:* This simile may seem comic to the reader, but it is not comic in Italian. Furthermore, it must be retained in translation because it is the pre-Christian Virgil who is speaking, and even though he knows the divine nature of Fortune for Christians, he cannot help but think of it in pre-Christian terms—as a monstrous and cunning evil force, and *not* a minister of God.

98–99. *the stars that rose when I set out for you:* The time is past midnight. The stars setting in the West were rising in the East when Virgil first met Dante on the evening of Good Friday in the "dark wood."

108. *a swamp that has the name of Styx:* The river Styx is the second of the rivers of Hell; Dante, following the *Aeneid*, refers to it here as a marsh or quagmire. Since we know from Canto XIV that all the rivers in Hell are joined, the spring (101) must be the point where the Acheron issues from an underground source.

116–126. *the souls of those that anger overcame:* The sinners in Circle Five present a problem. Virgil identifies those who are punished here as the wrathful. Yet there is evidently a difference between those on the surface of the Styx and those beneath the slime, whose sighing makes "these waters bubble at the surface." Aristotle (*Ethics* IV, 5) and St. Thomas (both in his commentary on Aristotle and in the *Summa Theologica*) distinguish three degrees of the wrathful: the *acuti* are the actively wrathful; the *amari*, those who are sullen because they keep their wrath locked within themselves; the *difficiles*, the vindictive. The *acuti* are probably those on the surface of the marsh; as for the other two categories, many commentators assume that those beneath the surface are the *amari* and perhaps the *difficiles* also. But Virgil says of the sinners gurgling beneath the mud that in life they were *tristi* or "sluggish" and here they remain so; and the words "smoke of sloth" (123) also indicate that those beneath the mire, whom Dante never sees, are really the Slothful. Some commentators believe that those being punished in the Vestibule of Hell (Canto III) are the Slothful, but in *Purgatory* XVIII the Slothful have a terrace to themselves, and it would seem likely that as souls guilty of one of the seven capital sins, they would be punished in Hell itself, not in the Vestibule!

Siegfried Wenzel, in his book *The Sin of Sloth: Acedia in Medieval Thought and Literature* (Chapel Hill, 1967), admits that it is difficult to reach a final conclusion concerning the identity of these sinners, but he also states that *acedia* (sloth) was equated with *tristitia* in early fourteenth-century scholastic teaching. It seems unlikely to me that Dante would have been unaware of such an equation when he had the figures beneath the mire gurgle *"tristi fummo"* ('sluggish we were', 121). Furthermore, it satisfies aesthetic balance to place both the Wrathful and Slothful in the Styx since the early part of the canto was also concerned with two opposite groups of sinners—the Prodigal and the Avaricious. Sloth, in fact, can be seen as the other side of the coin of Wrath.

CANTO VIII

I must explain, however, that before
  we finally reached the foot of that high tower,
  our eyes had been attracted to its summit   *3*

by two small flames we saw flare up just there;
  and, so far off the eye could hardly see,
  another burning torch flashed back a sign.   *6*

I turned to that vast sea of human knowledge:
  "What signal is this? And the other flame,
  what does it answer? And who's doing this?"   *9*

And he replied: "You should already see
  across the filthy waves what has been summoned,
  unless the marsh's vapors hide it from you."   *12*

A bowstring never shot an arrow off
  that cut the thin air any faster than
  a little boat I saw that very second   *15*

skimming along the water in our direction,
  with a solitary steersman, who was shouting,
  "Aha, I've got you now, you wretched soul!"   *18*

"Phlegyas, Phlegyas, this time you shout in vain,"
  my lord responded, "you will have us with you
  no longer than it takes to cross the muck."   *21*

As one who learns of some incredible trick
  just played on him, flares up resentfully—
  so, Phlegyas there, was seething in his anger.   *24*

My leader calmly stepped into the skiff
  and when he was inside, he had me enter,
  and only then it seemed to carry weight.   *27*

Soon as my guide and I were in the boat
   the ancient prow began to plough the water,
   more deeply, now, than any time before.   30

And as we sailed the course of this dead channel,
   before me there rose up a slimy shape
   that said: "Who are you, who come before your time?"   33

And I spoke back, "Though I come, I do not stay;
   but who are you, in all your ugliness?"
   "You see that I am one who weeps," he answered.   36

And then I said to him: "May you weep and wail
   stuck here in this place forever, you damned soul,
   for, filthy as you are, I recognize you."   39

With that he stretched both hands out toward the boat
   but, on his guard, my teacher pushed him back:
   "Away, get down there with the other curs!"   42

And then he put his arms around my neck
   and kissed my face and said, "Indignant soul,
   blessèd is she in whose womb you were conceived.   45

In the world this man was filled with arrogance,
   and nothing good about him decks his memory;
   for this, his shade is filled with fury here.   48

Many in life esteem themselves great men
   who then will wallow here like pigs in mud,
   leaving behind them their repulsive fame."   51

"Master, it certainly would make me happy
   to see him dunked deep in this slop just once
   before we leave this lake—it truly would."   54

And he to me, "Before the other shore
   comes into sight, you will be satisfied:
   a wish like that is worthy of fulfillment."   57

Soon afterwards, I saw the wretch so mangled
   by a gang of muddy souls that, to this day,
   I thank my Lord and praise Him for that sight: 60

"Get Filippo Argenti!" they all cried.
   And at those shouts the Florentine, gone mad,
   turned on himself and bit his body fiercely.   63

We left him there, I'll say no more about him.
　　A wailing noise began to pound my ears
　　and made me strain my eyes to see ahead.　　　　　　　66

"And now, my son," the gentle teacher said,
　　"coming closer is the city we call Dis,
　　with its great walls and its fierce citizens."　　　　　69

And I, "Master, already I can see
　　the clear glow of its mosques above the valley,
　　burning bright red, as though just forged, and left　72

to smoulder." And he to me: "Eternal fire
　　burns within, giving off the reddish glow
　　you see diffused throughout this lower Hell."　　　75

And then at last we entered those deep moats
　　that circled all of this unhappy city
　　whose walls, it seemed to me, were made of iron.　78

For quite a while we sailed around, until
　　we reached a place and heard our boatsman shout
　　with all his might, "Get out! Here is the entrance."　81

I saw more than a thousand fiendish angels
　　perching above the gates enraged, screaming:
　　"Who is the one approaching? Who, without death,　84

dares walk into the kingdom of the dead?"
　　And my wise teacher made some kind of signal
　　announcing he would speak to them in secret.　　87

They managed to suppress their great resentment
　　enough to say: "You come, but he must go
　　who thought to walk so boldly through this realm.　90

Let him retrace his foolish way alone,
　　just let him try. And you who led him here
　　through this dark land, you'll stay right where you are."　93

And now, my reader, consider how I felt
　　when those foreboding words came to my ears!
　　I thought I'd never see our world again!　　　　　96

"Oh my dear guide, who more than seven times
　　restored my confidence, and rescued me
　　from the many dangers that blocked my going on,　99

don't leave me, please," I cried in my distress,
    "and if the journey onward is denied us
    let's turn our footsteps back together quickly."   102

Then that lord who had brought me all this way
    said, "Do not fear, the journey we are making
    none can prevent: such power did decree it.   105

Wait here for me and feed your weary spirit
    with comfort and good hope; you can be sure
    I will not leave you in this underworld."   108

With this he walks away. He leaves me here,
    that gentle father, and I stay, doubting,
    and battling with my thoughts of "yes"—but "no."   111

I could not hear what he proposed to them,
    but they did not remain with him for long;
    I saw them race each other back for home.   114

Our adversaries slammed the heavy gates
    in my lord's face, and he stood there outside,
    then turned toward me and walked back very slowly   117

with eyes downcast, all self-assurance now
    erased from his forehead—sighing, "Who are these
    to forbid my entrance to the halls of grief!"   120

He spoke to me: "You need not be disturbed
    by my vexation, for I shall win the contest,
    no matter how they plot to keep us out!   123

This insolence of theirs is nothing new;
    they used it once at a less secret gate
    which is, and will forever be, unlocked;   126

you saw the words of death inscribed above it:
    already passing through, and with no guide,
    descending, through the circles, down the slope   129

comes one by whom the city will be opened."

NOTES

1–6. *I must explain, however, that before:* The opening words of this canto are,
in the original: "Io dico, seguitando, che. . . ." Many commentators interpret *se-*

guitando as evidence that Dante, having completed the first seven *canti* before his exile and now resuming work on the *Inferno*, would quite naturally begin: "I say, to continue (my story)." But a simple comparison of the opening lines with the last line of the preceding canto makes it unnecessary to look for the proper interpretation of the opening line of this canto in biographical data. Canto VII had concluded with the arrival of Virgil and the Pilgrim at the foot of a tower; now the flames flaring up at the top of the tower, mentioned for the first time in this canto, must have been seen while the two poets were on their way to the tower, and this is what Dante tells us ("before we reached the foot of that high tower"). That is, he must retrace his steps while continuing his story *(seguitando)* in order to establish the flames properly in the previous temporal context.

In my opinion the "biographical interpretation" is absurd for two reasons. That Dante, at the dramatic point represented by the last line of the previous canto (VII), knowing that at the beginning of the next he must recapitulate in order to introduce the correct timing of events—that precisely at this point Dante should have to put aside his writing is something less than probable. But even if this had been the case, why should Dante wish at this crucial point in his own narrative to drop a hint that he has taken a coffee break in exile!

18. *Aha, I've got you now, you wretched soul!:* Phlegyas, the son of Mars, set fire to Apollo's temple at Delphi, furiously enraged because Apollo raped his daughter Coronis. For this Apollo killed him and sent him to Tartarus. Dante makes Phlegyas the demonic guardian of the Styx. As a personification of great wrath he is well suited not only for guarding the Fifth Circle where the Wrathful are, but also for transporting the Pilgrim to the inner division of Hell, the City of Dis (68), whose gates are guarded by the rebellious angels (82–83).

32. *before me there rose up a slimy shape:* The befouled and indignant shade that rises from the marsh is Filippo Argenti (61), a member of the Adimari family.

36–63

The scene with Filippo Argenti is one of the most dramatic in the *Inferno*. The Pilgrim who had shown such pity for Francesca, and had even felt compassion for Ciacco, the swinish glutton, bursts into rage as soon as he recognizes Argenti. Filippo's self-identification as "one who weeps" (36) reminds us of Francesca's remark that she will speak "in words of flowing tears" (V, 126); but instead of being moved to pity (V, 117) the Pilgrim repulses Filippo with harsh words; later he expresses his wish to Virgil to see the sinner "dunked" in the mud; when he sees Filippo being attacked viciously he rejoices and thanks God for the sight. No one has been able to explain satisfactorily this new role assumed by the Pilgrim, and the extreme intensity of his anger with its suggestion of hatred. Many commentators believe his attitude can be explained as a personal reaction to a political adversary whom he hated. But if that had been the motivation for his outburst, this would surely not have won Virgil's encomium: "Indignant soul, / blessèd is she in whose womb you were conceived . . ." (44–45). Virgil's words must mean that he has sensed a core of righteous wrath in the Pilgrim's outburst, he sees that the hatred he has expressed is primarily a hatred of the sin of wrath. It is true that this moral anger expresses itself in a most unseemly way: there is something childishly vindictive in the taunting words he addresses to Filippo at the beginning of the scene; still more childish is his wish (52–54) to see the sinner "dunked." And when Filippo is made to suffer far greater pain, the Pilgrim's words suggest a hysterical condition. But we must remember that this is only the beginning of a spiritual development in the right direction, away from pity of the sinner toward hatred of his sin. Dante the Pilgrim has not yet learned to hate and at the same time show self-control and mastery of the situation, as he will later on (Canto XIX).

42. *Away, get down there with the other curs!:* For the reference to *curs* cf. VI, 19; VII, 8 and 43.

68. *coming closer is the city we call Dis:* Originally Dis was the name given by the Romans to Pluto, God of the Underworld. Dante applies the name to Lucifer, but he also applies the name to the pit-city at the base of which Lucifer is forever fixed. The walls of the City of Dis mark the division between upper Hell and "lower Hell" (75), and between the sins of Incontinence and those of Violence. In terms of the Seven Capital Sins, we have passed through circles punishing the five lesser ones (lust, gluttony, avarice, sloth, and wrath); beyond are sins occasioned specifically by envy and pride.

82–83. *I saw more than a thousand fiendish angels:* These are the rebellious angels who, with their leader Lucifer, were cast into Hell after their abortive attempt to gain control of Heaven.

97. *more than seven times:* That is to say, many times.

105. *such power did decree it:* Virgil hopes to allay the Pilgrim's fears by reminding him of the special nature of the journey, whose guarantor is God—although the "power" referred to could involve the three heavenly ladies of Canto II (Mary, Lucia, and Beatrice).

109–111. *With this he walks away. He leaves me here:* Dante's use of the present tense in this tercet is extraordinary. The desired effect, I believe, is to capture the reader completely, immersing him along with the Pilgrim in this terrible abandoned state, making him share the same doubts and questions. There is no longer any temporal separation between the Pilgrim's journey and the reader's awareness of its existence; in this tercet the two realities are joined. Then, suddenly, it is the Pilgrim's journey once again.

115. *Our adversaries slammed the heavy gates:* The Biblical designation "our adversary" for the Devil was quite common in the Middle Ages.

125–126. *they used it once at a less secret gate:* The rebellious angels tried to deny Christ entry into Hell, by barring the principal ("less secret") gate, but it was forced open by Him and will remain open for eternity.

127. *you saw the words of death inscribed above it:* For the "words of death," see Canto III, 1–9.

130. *comes one by whom the city will be opened:* The divine messenger, dispatched to open the gates of the City of Dis. See Canto IX, 61–105.

CANTO IX

The color of the coward on my face,
   when I realized my guide was turning back,
   made him quickly change the color of his own.   *3*

He stood alert, like one who strains to hear;
   his eyes could not see far enough ahead
   to cut the heavy fog of that black air.   *6*

"But surely we were meant to win this fight,"
   he began, "or else. . . . But, such help was promised!
   O how much time it's taking him to come!"   *9*

I saw too well how quickly he amended
   his opening words with what he added on!
   They were diffcrent from the ones he first pronounced;   *12*

but nonetheless his words made me afraid,
   perhaps because the phrase he left unfinished
   I finished with worse meaning than he meant.   *15*

"Has anyone before ever descended
   to this sad hollow's depths from that first circle
   whose pain is all in having hope cut off?"   *18*

I put this question to him. He replied,
   "It is not usual for one of us
   to make the journey I am making now.   *21*

But it happens I was down here once before,
   conjured by that heartless witch, Erichtho
   (who could recall the spirit to its body).   *24*

Soon after I had left my flesh in death
   she sent me through these walls, and down as far
   as the pit of Judas to bring a spirit out;   *27*

and that place is the lowest and the darkest
   and the farthest from the sphere that circles all;
   I know the road, and well, you can be sure.   30

This swamp that breathes with a prodigious stink
   lies in a circle round the doleful city
   that now we cannot enter without strife."   33

And he said other things, but I forget them,
   for suddenly my eyes were drawn above,
   up to the fiery top of that high tower   36

where in no time at all and all at once
   sprang up three hellish Furies stained with blood,
   their bodies and their gestures those of females;   39

their waists were bound in cords of wild green hydras,
   horned snakes and little serpents grew as hair,
   and twined themselves around the savage temples.   42

And he who had occasion to know well
   the handmaids of the queen of timeless woe
   cried out to me, "Look there! The fierce Erinyes!   45

That is Megaera, the one there to the left,
   and that one raving on the right, Alecto,
   Tisiphone, in the middle." He said no more.   48

With flailing palms the three would beat their breasts,
   then tear them with their nails, shrieking so loud
   I drew close to the poet, confused with fear.   51

"Call Medusa: we'll turn him into stone,"
   they shouted all together glaring down,
   "how wrong we were to let off Theseus lightly!"   54

"Now turn your back and cover up your eyes,
   for if the Gorgon comes and you should see her,
   there would be no returning to the world!"   57

These were my master's words. He turned me round
   and did not trust my hands to hide my eyes
   but placed his own on mine and kept them covered.   60

O all of you whose intellects are sound,
   look now and see the meaning that is hidden
   beneath the veil that covers my strange verses: 63

and then, above the filthy swell, approaching,
    a blast of sound, shot through with fear, exploded,
    making both shores of Hell begin to tremble;   66

it sounded like one of those violent winds,
    born from the clash of counter-temperatures,
    that tear through forests; raging on unchecked   69

it splits and rips and carries off the branches
    and proudly whips the dust up in its path
    and makes the beasts and shepherds flee its course!   72

He freed my eyes and said, "Now turn around
    and set your sight along the ancient scum,
    there where the marsh's mist is hovering thickest."   75

As frogs before their enemy, the snake,
    all scatter through the pond and then dive down
    until each one is squatting on the bottom,   78

so I saw more than a thousand fear-shocked souls
    in flight, clearing the path of one who came
    walking the Styx, his feet dry on the water.   81

From time to time with his left hand he fanned
    his face to push the putrid air away,
    and this was all that seemed to weary him.   84

I was certain now that he was sent from Heaven.
    I turned to my guide, but he made me a sign
    to keep my silence and bow low to this one.   87

Ah, the scorn that filled his holy presence!
    He reached the gate and touched it with a wand;
    it opened without resistance from inside.   90

"Oh Heaven's outcasts, despicable souls,"
    he started, standing on the dreadful threshold,
    "what insolence is this that breeds in you?   93

Why do you stubbornly resist that will
    whose end can never be denied and which,
    more than one time, increased your suffering?   96

What do you gain by locking horns with fate?
    If you remember well, your Cerberus
    still bears his chin and throat peeled for resisting!"   99

He turned then and retraced the squalid path
  without one word to us, and on his face
  the look of one concerned and spurred by things   102

that were not those he found surrounding him.
  And then we started moving toward the city
  in the safety of the holy words pronounced.   105

We entered there, and with no opposition.
  And I, so anxious to investigate
  the state of souls locked up in such a fortress,   108

once in the place, allowed my eyes to wander,
  and saw, in all directions spreading out,
  a countryside of pain and ugly anguish.   111

As at Arles where the Rhône turns to stagnant waters
  or as at Pola near Quarnero's Gulf
  that closes Italy and bathes her confines,   114

the sepulchers make all the land uneven,
  so they did here, strewn in all directions,
  except the graves here served a crueler purpose: 117

for scattered everywhere among the tombs
  were flames that kept them glowing far more hot
  than any iron an artisan might use.   120

Each tomb had its lid loose, pushed to one side,
  and from within came forth such fierce laments
  that I was sure inside were tortured souls.   123

I asked, "Master, what kind of shades are these
  lying down here, buried in the graves of stone,
  speaking their presence in such dolorous sighs?"   126

And he replied "There lie arch-heretics
  of every sect, with all of their disciples;
  more than you think are packed within these tombs.   129

Like heretics lie buried with their like
  and the graves burn more, or less, accordingly."
  Then turning to the right, we moved ahead   132

between the torments there and those high walls.

1. *The color of the coward on my face:* Extreme fear makes the Pilgrim pale.

17–18. *from that first circle:* Limbo, wherein are found those pagan shades who, now cognizant of the Christian God, are destined to remain in Hell, forever hoping for salvation but in vain. See Canto IV, 34–42.

22–30. *But it happens I was down here once before:* In answer to the Pilgrim's question Virgil states that, although such a journey is rarely made, he himself accomplished it once before at the command of Erichtho, a Thessalian necromancer who conjured up dead spirits (Lucan, *Pharsalia* VI, 508–830). To retrieve a spirit for her, Virgil descended to the lowest region of Hell ("the pit of Judas"), the center of the earth and, consequently, the farthest point from the Primum Mobile ("the sphere that circles all" according to Ptolemaic astronomy). Having no literary or legendary source, the story of Virgil's descent into Hell was probably Dante's invention.

38–48

The three Furies, Tisiphone, Megaera, and Alecto, were the traditional avengers of crime in classical mythology, but here in the *Inferno,* they would appear to be antitheses of the Heavenly Ladies (Mary, Lucia, and Beatrice) who form the chain of grace in Canto II; they are, therefore, another infernal distortion of the Trinity. See n. 61–105.

44. *the handmaids of the queen of timeless woe:* The Furies are "handmaids" to Persephone (Hecate), wife of Pluto, classical god of the Underworld.

52. *Call Medusa: we'll turn him into stone:* Medusa was in classical mythology one of the three Gorgons. Minerva, furious at Medusa for giving birth to two children in one of the former's temples, changed her beautiful hair into serpents, so that whoever gazed on her terrifying aspect was turned to stone.

It should be noted that the classical environment of this canto must have struck a familiar chord in Virgil's mind. Indeed, the Roman poet (and Dante refers to him as such in 51) is quite caught up in his world and sincerely believes that the Medusa could turn Dante into stone. In fact Virgil is described as "he who had occasion to know well / the handmaids of the queen of timeless woe" (43–44). See n. 61–105.

54. *how wrong we were to let off Theseus lightly!:* Theseus, the greatest Athenian hero, descended to Hades with his friend Pirithous, King of the Lapithae, in order to kidnap Proserpina for him. Pluto slew Pirithous, however, and kept Theseus a prisoner in Hades by having him sit on the Chair of Forgetfulness, which made his mind blank and thereby kept him from moving. Dante chooses a less common version of the myth which has Theseus set free by Hercules. See n. 61–105; also n. 98–99.

56. *for if the Gorgon comes:* The Gorgon is Medusa. See above, n. 52

61–105

The address to the reader (61–63) is arresting; most critics have assumed that the "meaning . . . hidden / beneath the veil that covers my strange verses" refers to the preceding lines concerning the Furies and Medusa, but I believe that it refers to the lines which follow, describing the arrival of the angel at the Gates of Dis. In order to fully understand the context of the address and the "meaning . . . hidden," it is necessary to compare the passage to its analogue in *Purgatory* VIII. There, as here, Dante the Poet interrupts the narrative to tell the reader to search beneath the literal level for the figurative meaning. If one accepts *Inferno* I as the introductory canto for the whole *Commedia*, then *Inferno* IX is really the eighth canto dealing with Hell and therefore occupies a position parallel to the eighth canto dealing with Purgatory. Moreover, as most critics admit, the address to the reader in *Purgatory* VIII (again to direct his vision to the truth beneath a veil "which is *now* easy to penetrate"; *Purg.* VIII, 20–21) refers to the section which follows—and which concerns the advent of two angels at the gates of Purgatory proper. The similarities of the passages are evident: an address to the reader and a description of the descent and action of angels before the gates of Inner Hell and Purgatory proper, respectively.

Symbolically, these passages, together with the coming of Beatrice at the top of the Mountain of Purgatory, are analogous to the medieval belief in the three Advents of Christ. St. Bernard (who appears in the *Paradise* to lead the Pilgrim to the ecstatic, beatific vision of God) expressed this concept in his *Sermons on the Advents:* there is the First Advent of Christ which culminates in his descent into Hell; the Second Advent is the daily coming of Christ into men's hearts, which is necessary to help them combat the daily temptation of sin; and the Third Advent will be the Last Judgment, when Christ shall come to judge the living and the dead. The coming of the angel in *Inferno* IX, then, is analogous to the first coming of Christ when He descended into Hell and opened the prime gate (Canto III) for all time in order to free the elect. That event, in fact, is referred to by Virgil at the end of the preceding canto (VIII) when he foretells the coming of the angel:

> This insolence of theirs is nothing new;
>   they used it once at a less secret gate
>   which is, and will forever be, unlocked;

> you saw the words of death inscribed above it:
>   already passing through, and with no guide,
>   descending, through the circles, down the slope

> comes one by whom the city will be opened.

The parallel between Christ's opening the Gate of Hell and the angel's opening the Gate of Dis is surely clear; as Christ came to free the innocent from Hell and provide salvation for Everyman, the angel comes, walking on the water of the Styx (without getting his feet wet) to free the Pilgrim (Everyman) from the powers of Hell so that he may continue his pre-ordained journey. The Second Advent, in Purgatory, is a daily one in which the guardian angels descend at the same time every day to drive the serpent of sin back from the gates of Purgatory. It is like Christ's daily descent into the heart of the Christian. The Third Advent, the Last Judgment, is symbolized by Beatrice's coming (*Purgatory* XXX) to pass judgment on her spiritual lover, whom she then leads to Paradise.

The three Advents comprise all of Christian time, from Christ's death and descent to Hell through his daily entrance into men's lives to his eventual judgment of all men. In this respect, the three Furies and Medusa should be seen, in part at least, as a segment of the allegorical drama played out before the Gates of Dis. Coming before the advent of the angel which symbolizes the beginning of Christian time, the classical female demons symbolize pagan time; the Furies' mention of the pre-Christian descent of Theseus (54) to the Underworld and his rescue by Hercules balances the coming *Christian* descent of the Angel of God to rescue Dante. Just as Dante wants to show allegorically that the journey of the *Divine Comedy* comprises all of Christian time through the three Advents, so too he wants to suggest that the journey looks back to and takes in its sweep all of pagan time. Virgil, in fact, as the prime representative of pre-Christian time, is so sure of the power of the pagan Medusa that he shields the Pilgrim's eyes. The *Divine Comedy* then, must not only be seen as the journey of the individual Everyman to God, but also as the entire scope of the life of mankind: from the mythological beliefs of the ancients (as well as their wisdom: Virgil is an example of both) through the life of man in the Christian age to the eventual Last Judgment.

Apart from its significance in the framework of the three Advents there is also a minor allegorical significance to be seen therein: that Reason (Virgil) can do much to instruct Everyman, but without Divine Grace (embodied in the Angel) the Pilgrim cannot hope to complete his journey and arrive at Purgatory.

94. *Why do you stubbornly resist that will:* The will of God.

98–99. *your Cerberus:* When Hercules descended into Hell to rescue Theseus, he chained the three-headed dog Cerberus and dragged him around and outside Hell so that the skin around his neck was ripped away.

112–117. *As at Arles where the Rhône turns to stagnant waters:* Arles, a city in Provence near the delta of the Rhône, is the site of the famous Roman (later Christian) cemetery of Aliscamps. There, as at Pola, a city in Istria (now Croatia) on the Quarnero Bay also famous for its ancient burying ground, great sarcophagi cover the landscape. Interestingly, according to tradition, Christ appeared to St. Trophimus when the latter consecrated Aliscamps as a Christian resting place, and promised that the souls of those buried there would be free from the sepulchral torments of the dead. Thus, Dante compares the sepulchers here to those at Pola and Arles, except that "the graves here served a crueler purpose" (117).

127–131. *There lie arch-heretics:* The Heretics are in a circle in Hell which is outside of the three main divisions of Incontinence, Violence and Fraud. Heresy is not due to weaknesses of the flesh or mind (Incontinence), nor is it a form of violence or of fraud; it is a clearly willed sin based on intellectual pride, and because it denies the Christian concept of reality, it is punished outside of the area allocated to the Christian categories of sin. The sin of Heresy is more serious than those caused by weaknesses of the flesh but somehow less serious than willed, premeditated sins of Violence and Fraud; it is a sin of the intellect and a state of being, not a source of sinful action (Fraud, Violence). Therefore it is between Incontinence and Violence.

There is great irony in the fact that those who believed that the death of the body meant the death of the soul suffer as their punishment the entombment of their living souls.

132. *Then turning to the right, we moved ahead:* Why Dante and Virgil, who have been circling always to the left, suddenly move off to the right remains a mystery; this will happen one other time in *Inferno* XVII, 31.

CANTO X

Now onward down a narrow path, between
   the city's ramparts and the suffering,
   my master walks, I following close behind.   *3*

"O lofty power who through these impious gyres
   lead me around as you see fit," I said,
   "I want to know, I want to understand: *6*

the people buried there in sepulchers,
   can they be seen? I mean, since all the lids
   are off the tombs and no one stands on guard."   *9*

And he: "They will forever be locked up,
   when they return here from Jehosaphat
   with the bodies that they left up in the world.   *12*

The private cemetery on this side
   serves Epicurus and his followers,
   who make the soul die when the body dies.   *15*

As for the question you just put to me,
   it will be answered soon, while we are here;
   and the wish you are keeping from me will be granted."   *18*

And I: "O my good guide, I do not hide
   my heart; I'm trying not to talk too much,
   as you have told me more than once to do."   *21*

"O Tuscan walking through our flaming city,
   alive, and speaking with such elegance,
   be kind enough to stop here for a while.   *24*

Your mode of speech identifies you clearly
   as one whose birthplace is that noble city
   with which in my time, perhaps, I was too harsh."   *27*

One of the vaults resounded suddenly
    with these clear words, and I, intimidated,
    drew up a little closer to my guide,   30

who said, "What are you doing? Turn around
    and look at Farinata who has risen,
    you will see him from the waist up standing straight."   33

I already had my eyes fixed on his face,
    and there he stood out tall, with chest and brow
    proclaiming his disdain for all this Hell.   36

My guide, with a gentle push, encouraged me
    to move among the sepulchers toward him:
    "Be sure you choose your words with care," he said.   39

And when I reached the margin of his tomb
    he looked at me, and half-contemptuously
    he asked, "And *who* would *your* ancestors be?"   42

And I who wanted only to oblige him
    held nothing back but told him everything.
    At this he lifted up his brows a little,   45

then said, "Bitter enemies of mine they were
    and of my ancestors and of my party;
    I had to scatter them not once but twice."   48

"They were expelled, but only to return
    from everywhere," I said, "not once but twice—
    an art your men, however, never mastered!"   51

Just then along that same tomb's open ledge
    a shade appeared, but just down to his chin,
    beside this other; I think he got up kneeling.   54

He looked around as though he hoped to see
    if someone else, perhaps, had come with me
    and, when his expectation was deceived,   57

he started weeping: "If it be great genius
    that carries you along through this blind jail,
    where is my son? Why is he not with you?"   60

"I do not come alone," I said to him,
    "that one waiting over there guides me through here,
    the one, perhaps, your Guido held in scorn."   63

(The place of pain assigned him, and what he asked,
 already had revealed his name to me
 and made my pointed answer possible).   66

Instantly, he sprang to his full height and cried,
 "What did you say? He *held*? Is he not living?
 The day's sweet light no longer strikes his eyes?"   69

And when he heard the silence of my delay
 responding to his question, he collapsed
 into his tomb, not to be seen again.   72

That other stately shade, at whose request
 I had first stopped to talk, showed no concern
 nor moved his head nor turned to see what happened;   75

he merely picked up where we had left off:
 "If that art they did not master," he went on,
 "that gives me greater pain than does this bed.   78

But the face of the queen who reigns down here will glow
 not more than fifty times before you learn
 how hard it is to master such an art;   81

and as I hope that you may once more know
 the sweet world, tell me, why should your party be
 so harsh to my clan in every law they make?"   84

I answered: "The massacre and butchery
 that stained the waters of the Arbia red
 now cause such laws to issue from our councils."   87

He sighed, shaking his head. "It was not I
 alone took part," he said, "nor certainly
 would I have joined the rest without good cause.   90

But I alone stood up when all of them
 were ready to have Florence razed. It was *I*
 who openly stood up in her defense."   93

"And now, as I would have your seed find peace,"
 I said, "I beg you to resolve a problem
 that has kept my reason tangled in a knot: 96

if I have heard correctly, all of you
 can see ahead to what the future holds
 but your knowledge of the present is not clear."   99

"Down here we see like those with faulty vision
   who only see," he said, "what's at a distance;
   this much the sovereign lord still grants us here. 102

When events are close to us, or when they happen,
   our mind is blank, and were it not for others
   we would know nothing of your living state. 105

Thus you can understand how all our knowledge
   will be completely dead at that time when
   the door to future things is closed forever." 108

Then I, moved by regret for what I'd done,
   said, "Now, will you please tell the fallen one
   his son is still on earth among the living; 111

and if, when he asked, silence was my answer,
   tell him: while he was speaking, all my thoughts
   were struggling with that point you solved for me." 114

My teacher had begun to call me back,
   so I quickly asked that spirit to reveal
   the names of those who shared the tomb with him. 117

He said, "More than a thousand lie with me,
   the Second Frederick is here and the Cardinal
   is with us. And the rest I shall not mention." 120

His figure disappeared. I made my way
   to the ancient poet, reflecting on those words,
   those words which were prophetic enemies. 123

He moved, and as we went along he said,
   "What troubles you? Why are you so distraught?"
   And I told him all the thoughts that filled my mind. 126

"Be sure your mind retains," the sage commanded,
   "those words you heard pronounced against yourself,
   and listen carefully now." He raised a finger: 129

"When at last you stand in the glow of her sweet ray,
   the one whose splendid eyes see everything,
   from her you'll learn your life's itinerary." 132

Then to the left he turned. Leaving the walls,
   he headed toward the center by a path
   that strikes into a vale, whose stench arose 135

disgusting us as high up as we were.

11–12. *When they return here from Jehosaphat:* According to the Old Testament prophet Joel (3:2, 12), the valley of Jehosaphat, situated between Jerusalem and the Mount of Olives, would be the site of the last Judgment, when the soul and the body would be reunited and thus returned to Heaven or Hell for eternity.

14–15. *Epicurus and his followers:* Epicurus was the Greek philosopher who in 306 B.C. organized in Athens the philosophical school named after him. The philosophy of the Epicureans taught that the highest good is temporal happiness, which is to be achieved by the practice of the virtues. In Dante's time Epicureans were considered heretics because they exalted temporal happiness, and therefore denied the immortality of the soul and the afterlife. Epicurus is among the heretics even though he was a pagan, because he denied the immortality of the soul, a truth known even to the ancients.

16–18. *As for the question you just put to me:* Dante's question was in lines 7–8; as for "the wish you are keeping from me" (18), many critics believe that it was the desire to know whether Farinata is among the heretics. But surely it is preferable to assume that the silent wish is rather to know the extent of the shades' knowledge, i.e., how much of the future they can foresee and whether they know the present. This "wish" which must have begun with Ciacco's prophecy in Canto VI will soon be the cause of Dante's silence before Cavalcante, and will be satisfied by Farinata (100–108).

22–27. *O Tuscan walking through our flaming city:* Having recognized Dante as a fellow Tuscan, Farinata bids him pause a moment. Born of an old and respected Florentine family, Farinata (Manente di Jacopo degli Uberti) took an active role in the political life of the Commune on the side of the Ghibelline party, whose head he became in 1239. He died in 1264, one year before Dante's birth.

42. *he asked, "And who would your ancestors be?":* Farinata's extremely proud character is reflected in these lines. The first thing noticed by this imposing and disdainful shade is the Pilgrim's elegance of speech (23), and his first question to him, delivered "half-contemptuously," concerns his lineage (42). His haughtiness is also apparent when he completely ignores the interruption of Cavalcante (52–72) and begins his speech again (77) as if nothing had happened. Further, when Dante asks him "the names of those who shared the tomb with him" (117), he deigns to give only two names, those of a king and a cardinal—whose lineage meets with his approval. Such haughtiness is symptomatic of the basis for Farinata's heresy: intellectual pride. Farinata in life was so self-centered (note his emphasis on "I") and self-assured that he disdained the truth of religion. Cavalcante, too, will reflect a kind of pride in his astonishment that his son is not accompanying the Pilgrim, "If it be great genius / that carries you along" (58–59).

48–51. *I had to scatter them not once but twice:* It happens that the Pilgrim's ancestors (along with other Guelphs) were twice (in 1248 and 1260) driven from the city (note the Pilgrim's appraisal of the action, revealed by his correcting Farinata's term "scatter" to "expel") by Farinata and his kinsmen (along with other Ghibellines), but they returned after both defeats (in 1251 and 1267). Dante's jibe, "an art your men, however, never mastered," refers to the expulsion of the Uberti family and other Ghibellines who never returned to Florence. See below n. 84.

53. *a shade appeared, but just down to his chin:* The shade is Cavalcante de' Cavalcanti, a member of an important Florentine family and father of Guido Cavalcanti. (Boccaccio, in his commentary on the *Divine Comedy*, states that both father and son were renowned Epicureans.) Cavalcante's son Guido, born about 1255, was one of the major poets of the day and was Dante's "first friend," as he says in the *Vita nuova*. A renowned thinker, Guido cultivated a highly philosophic poetic style and influenced Dante's own poetry. The Cavalcanti were well-known

Guelphs, and it was the marriage of Guido to Beatrice, daughter of the Ghibelline Farinata (see above, n. 22–27 and n. 42) that sealed the peace for a time between two factions. Guido died in August, 1300.

63. *the one, perhaps, your Guido held in scorn:* Some commentators, offering a different interpretation of the syntax of these two lines (to make the line mean that Virgil was leading the Pilgrim "to her whom" Guido perhaps held in scorn) believe that it is Beatrice whom Guido scorned. Most believe, however, that the object of Guido's attitude is Virgil. I agree with the latter critics, but not for the reasons usually offered: that Guido's pride was such that he would not submit to Reason's guidance or that he may have scorned Virgil as a symbol of Classicism or of religiosity. The first hypothesis is particularly absurd: no one loved Human Reason more ardently than did Guido Cavalcanti. Perhaps it could be said that Guido as a skeptic refused to allow Reason to fulfill its ultimate purpose (according to the teachings of the time): that of leading man to God.

68–72. *What did you say? He* held? *Is he not living?:* The use of the preterit "held" (*ebbe*) is ambiguous and occasions the misunderstanding of the father, who assumes, upon hearing the Pilgrim's words, that his son is now dead. The Pilgrim's silence, following Cavalcante's despairing outcry (68–69) is because he was puzzled by the old man's question: the Pilgrim is not yet aware that, although the souls of the damned can see into the future, they have no knowledge of the present. And this silence confirms Cavalcante's assumption that his son is dead.

Cavalcante's misunderstanding of Dante's use of the past tense, "held," and of his subsequent silence is a part of the aesthetic structure of Canto X, which is based on interruption and misunderstanding. Farinata interrupts the conversation of the Pilgrim and Virgil (22), Cavalcante interrupts Farinata and the Pilgrim (52) and misunderstands the latter's words. Such a structure indicates the self-centeredness and lack of understanding which Dante held to be typical of heretics.

79–81. *But the face of the queen who reigns down here will glow:* Hecate or Proserpina, the moon goddess, Queen of the Underworld (cf. IX, 44). Farinata makes the prophecy that Dante will know how difficult is the art of returning from exile before fifty months have passed. Dante was first exiled from Florence in January of 1302. The fiftieth month after Farinata's prediction (which, according to the fictional time element of the poem, took place in March of 1300) was May, 1304. By this time Dante had attempted repeatedly, together with the other exiles, to return to Florence, and it was in March of 1304 that Cardinal Niccolò da Prato, sent by Benedict XI to Florence to negotiate the return of the exiles, failed in his mission.

82. *and as I hope that you may once more know:* The lofty elegance of Farinata's character is evident in this formal, involved prelude to his request (83–84).

84. *so harsh to my clan in every law they make:* The Uberti, Farinata's family, were excluded, according to Villani, from all pardons conceded to the Ghibellines, including the pardon of 1280, when most of the Ghibellines were permitted to return to Florence.

85–86. *The massacre and butchery:* The hill of Montaperti, on the left bank of the Arbia, a small stream near Siena, was the scene of the fierce battle between the Florentine Guelphs and Ghibellines (September 4, 1260), in which the Guelphs were defeated. Farinata was a leader of the Ghibellines.

88–93. *It was not I . . . But I . . . It was I:* In rebuttal, Farinata states that he was not the only Ghibelline at the battle of Montaperti, and that he had good reason to fight; but that at the Council in Empoli after the victory at Montaperti, when the Ghibellines wanted to plan the destruction of Florence, Farinata was the only Ghibelline to oppose the plan. He proudly points out that the credit for the latter action is his alone, while, on the other hand, he is not willing to accept all the blame for the bloodshed at Montaperti.

100–108. *Down here we see like those with faulty vision:* In answer to the Pilgrim's wish (the "knot" of line 96) to know the shades' capacity for knowledge of the present, Farinata states that, while they have complete knowledge of things past and future, they are ignorant of the present (except, of course, for the news of current events brought them by the new arrivals in Hell, the "others," 104). Even this knowledge will be denied them after the Day of Judgment, when all will become absolute and eternal. The door of the future will be closed (108) and their remembrance of the past will fade away since there will no longer be any past, present or future.

119–120. *the Second Frederick . . . , the Cardinal:* The Emperor Frederick II (1194–1250) is in the circle of the Heretics because of the commonly held belief that he was an Epicurean.

Cardinal Ottaviano degli Ubaldini, a Ghibelline, was papal legate in Lombardy and Romagna until his death in 1273. He is reported to have once said: "If I have a soul, I have lost it for the Ghibellines"; it is presumably the doubt concerning the immortality of the soul implied in these words which led Dante to condemn the Cardinal as a heretic.

129–132. *He raised a finger:* The raised finger may indicate Virgil's role of teacher admonishing his student, or he may be pointing "up" to Beatrice, to her "whose splendid eyes see everything" (131). As it happens, however, Beatrice will not be the one to unveil the course of future events to the Pilgrim; that office will be granted to his ancestor Cacciaguida in *Paradise* XVII.

CANTO XI

We reached the curving brink of a steep bank
   constructed of enormous broken rocks;
   below us was a crueler den of pain.   *3*

And the disgusting overflow of stench
   the deep abyss was vomiting, forced us
   back from the edge. Crouched underneath the lid   *6*

of some great tomb, I saw it was inscribed:
   "Within lies Anastasius, the Pope
   Photinus lured away from the straight path."   *9*

"Our descent will have to be delayed somewhat
   so that our sense of smell may grow accustomed
   to these vile fumes; then we will not mind them,"   *12*

my master said. And I: "You will have to find
   some way to keep our time from being wasted."
   "That is precisely what I had in mind,"   *15*

he said, and then began the lesson: "My son,
   within these boulders' bounds are three more circles,
   concentrically arranged like those above,   *18*

all tightly packed with souls; and so that, later,
   the sight of them alone will be enough,
   I'll tell you how and why they are imprisoned.   *21*

All malice has injustice as its end,
   an end achieved by violence or by fraud;
   while both are sins that earn the hate of Heaven,   *24*

since fraud belongs exclusively to man,
   God hates it more and, therefore, far below,
   the fraudulent are placed and suffer most.   *27*

In the first of the circles below are all the violent;
　　since violence can be used against three persons,
　　into three concentric rounds it is divided:　　　　　　　　30

violence can be done to God, to self,
　　or to one's neighbor—to him or to his goods,
　　as my reasoned explanation will make clear.　　　　　　　33

By violent means a man can kill his neighbor
　　or wound him grievously; he can violate
　　his goods by arson, theft and devastation;　　　　　　　36

so, homicides and those who strike with malice,
　　those who destroy and plunder, are all punished
　　in the first round, but all in different groups.　　　　　39

Man can raise violent hands against himself
　　and his own goods; so in the second round,
　　paying the debt that never can be paid,　　　　　　　42

are suicides, self-robbers of your world,
　　or those who gamble all their wealth away
　　and weep up there when they should have rejoiced.　　45

One can use violence against the deity
　　by heartfelt disbelief and cursing Him,
　　or by despising Nature and God's bounty;　　　　　　48

therefore, the smallest round stamps with its seal
　　both Sodom and Cahors and all those souls
　　who hate God in their hearts and curse His name.　　　51

Fraud, that gnaws the conscience of its servants,
　　can be used on one who puts his trust in you
　　or else on one who has no trust invested.　　　　　　54

This latter sort seems only to destroy
　　the bond of love that Nature gives to man;
　　so in the second circle there are nests　　　　　　　57

of hypocrites, flatterers, dabblers in sorcery,
　　falsifiers, thieves and simonists,
　　panders, seducers, grafters and like filth.　　　　　60

The former kind of fraud both disregards
　　the love Nature enjoys and that extra bond
　　between men which creates a special trust;　　　　　63

thus, it is in the smallest of the circles,
    at the earth's center, around the throne of Dis,
    that traitors suffer their eternal pain."   66

And I, "Master, your reasoning runs smooth,
    and your explanation certainly makes clear
    the nature of this pit and of its inmates,   69

but what about those in the slimy swamp,
    those driven by the wind, those beat by rain,
    and those who come to blows with harsh refrains?   72

Why are they, too, not punished here inside
    the city of flame, if they have earned God's wrath?
    If they have not, why are they suffering?"   75

And he to me, "Why do you let your thoughts
    stray from the path they are accustomed to?
    Or have I missed the point you have in mind?   78

Have you forgotten how your *Ethics* reads,
    those terms it explicates in such detail:
    the three conditions that the heavens hate,   81

incontinence, malice and bestiality?
    Do you not remember how incontinence
    offends God least, and merits the least blame?   84

If you will reconsider well this doctrine
    and then recall to mind who those souls were
    suffering pain above, outside the walls,   87

you will clearly see why they are separated
    from these malicious ones, and why God's vengeance
    beats down upon their souls less heavily."   90

"O sun that shines to clear a misty vision,
    such joy is mine when you resolve my doubts
    that doubting pleases me no less than knowing!   93

Go back a little bit once more," I said
    "to where you say that usury offends
    God's goodness, and untie that knot for me."   96

"Philosophy," he said, "and more than once,
    points out to one who reads with understanding
    how Nature takes her course from the Divine   99

Intellect, from its artistic workmanship;
    and if you have your *Physics* well in mind
    you will find, not many pages from the start,   *102*

how your art too, as best it can, imitates
    Nature, the way an apprentice does his master;
    so your art may be said to be God's grandchild.   *105*

From Art and Nature man was meant to take
    his daily bread to live—if you recall
    the book of Genesis near the beginning;   *108*

but the usurer, adopting other means,
    scorns Nature in herself and in her pupil,
    Art—he invests his hope in something else.   *111*

Now follow me, we should be getting on;
    the Fish are shimmering over the horizon,
    the Wain is now exactly over Caurus,   *114*

and the passage down the bank is farther on."

NOTES

8–9. *Within lies Anastasius, the Pope:* Anastasius II, Pope from 496 to 498, was popularly believed for many centuries to be a heretic because, supposedly, he allowed Photinus, a deacon of Thessalonica who followed the heresy of Acacius, to take communion. This heresy denied Christ's divine birth, asserting that He was begotten by a mortal man; thus Anastasius II supposedly revealed his belief in the heretical doctrine. It has been proved, however, that this Pope was confused with the Byzantine Emperor Anastasius I (491–518) by Dante's probable sources. Emperor Anastasius was convinced by Photinus to accept the heretical doctrine.

14–15. *to keep our time from being wasted:* Note how the Pilgrim has become a student eager to learn. The *Inferno* consists to a great extent of action; Church doctrine is usually revealed first by the realistic panorama that confronts the student-pilgrim. But as he learns more and more by example (i.e. by action), a method any new student must use at first, he begins to hear more and more philosophical and theological doctrine from his teachers (Virgil, Beatrice, St. Bernard chiefly). The preponderance of doctrine increases in the *Purgatory* and grows even greater in the *Paradise*.

23. *by violence or by fraud:* The distinction between Violence and Fraud is taken from Cicero's *De Officiis* I, 13.

50. *both Sodom and Cahors:* Sodom is, of course, the Biblical city (Genesis 18–19) destroyed by God for its vicious sexual offenses. Cahors is a city in the south of France which was widely known in the Middle Ages as a thriving seat of usury. So notorious was Cahors for this sin that *Caorsino* came to be synonymous with "usurer" in medieval times. Dante uses the city names to indicate the Sodomites and Usurers who are punished in the smallest round of Circle VII.

65. *at the earth's center, around the throne of Dis:* Here the name refers to Lucifer. See Canto VIII, 68.

69. *the nature of this pit and of its inmates:* Virgil's explanation of the *Inferno* can be reduced to the following outline:

DIVISION OF HELL	INNER DIVISIONS	CIRCLE	CANTO
Limbo		I	IV
INCONTINENCE			
[sins of the She-Wolf]			
Lustful		II	V
Gluttonous		III	VI
Hoarders & Wasters		IV	VII
Wrathful & Slothful		V	VII–VIII
[City of Dis]			VIII–IX
Heretics		VI	IX–XI
VIOLENCE			
[sins of the Lion]			
Violent	1) Against Neighbors (murderers, destroyers)	VII	XII
	2) Against Self (suicides, self-robbers)		XIII
	3) Against God, Nature, Art (blasphemers, perverts, usurers)		XIV–XVII
FRAUD			
[sins of the Leopard]	*The Malebolge*		
	1) Panders and Seducers	VIII	XVIII
	2) Flatterers		XVIII
Against those	3) Simonists		XIX
who have no	4) Sorcerers (Soothsayers)		XX
special faith	5) Grafters (Barrators)		XXI–XXIII
in the deceiver	6) Hypocrites		XXIII–XXIV
	7) Thieves		XXIV–XXVI
	8) Like filth (Deceivers)		XXVI–XXVII
	9) Like filth (Sowers of Discord)		XXVIII–XXIX
	10) Falsifiers and counterfeiters		XXIX–XXX XXXI
Against those	Caina: Traitors to kindred	IX	XXXII
who have faith	Antenora: Traitors to country		XXXII–XXXIII
in the deceiver:			
Traitors	Ptolomea: Traitors to guests and hosts		XXXIII
	Judecca: Traitors against benefactors		XXXIV

70–75. *but what about those in the slimy swamp:* The sinners about whom Dante questions Virgil are those guilty of Incontinence. Virgil's answer (76–90) is that the Incontinent suffer a lighter punishment because their sins, being without malice, are less offensive to God.

79–84. *Have you forgotten how your* Ethics *reads?:* Virgil says "your *Ethics* in referring to Aristotle's *Ethica Nicomachea* because he realizes how thoroughly the Pilgrim studied this work (note his reference to "your *Physics*" in line 101).

While the distinction here offered between Incontinence and Malice is based on Aristotle (Book VII, Ch. 8) it should be clear that the overall classification of sins in the *Inferno* is not. Dante's is a twofold system, the main divisions of which may be illustrated as follows:

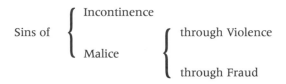

Aristotle, however, has a threefold classification: Incontinence, Malice and Bestiality (Book VII, Ch. 1), the third category having no correspondence with the outline offered by Virgil, in spite of many scholars' attempts to identify this with one of the subdivisions mentioned by him. Virgil's mention of the three sins treated by Aristotle is merely a device to introduce the work of the Greek philosopher and to indicate the exact book from which he will quote his distinction between Incontinence and Malice. For the threefold reference is found in the first sentence of Book VII of the *Nicomachean Ethics*.

It should be noted that Virgil makes no reference to the sinners in ante-Inferno, in Limbo and in the Sixth Circle; nor is it possible to fit their sins into the system presented in this canto: the Pusillanimous, the Unbaptized and the Heretics are guilty neither of Incontinence nor of Malice. With the last two groups we have to do with wrong beliefs rather than sinful acts; and with the first group it is the failure to act that is being punished. And Dante has indicated the tangential nature of their place within his moral system by the geographical location he has assigned them. The first two groups are not in Hell proper; the Heretics are within a kind of No-Man's-Land, between the sins of Incontinence and those of Malice, within the Gates of Dis but at the top of its abyss.

101–105. *and if you have your* Physics *well in mind:* Aristotle's *Physics* (Book II, part 2) concerns the doctrine that Art imitates Nature. Art, or human industry, is the child of Nature in the sense that it is the use to which man puts Nature, and thus is the grandchild of God. Usurers, who are in the third round of Circle VII, by doing violence to human industry are, in effect, doing violence to God.

108. *the book of Genesis near the beginning:* Man is to draw upon both Nature and human industry if he would thrive. This principle is stated in Genesis (3:17, 19), where man is commanded to work and earn his bread by the sweat of his brow.

113–115. *the Fish are shimmering over the horizon:* Virgil, as always, indicates the time by referring to the stars; how he knows of their position at any given moment Dante does not explain (the stars are not visible from Hell). Pisces, the Fish, is just appearing on the horizon, while the Great Bear, the Wain, is lying completely in the Northwestern quadrant of the heavens (Caurus is the Northwest Wind). The next sign of the Zodiac after Pisces is Aries; from Canto I we know that the sun is currently rising in Aries. Each sign of the Zodiac covers about two hours, thus it must be nearly two hours before sunrise.

CANTO XII

Not only was that place, where we had come
   to descend, craggy, but there was something there
   that made the scene appalling to the eye.   *3*

Like the ruins this side of Trent left by the landslide
   (an earthquake or erosion must have caused it)
   that hit the Adige on its left bank,   *6*

when, from the mountain's top where the slide began
   to the plain below, the shattered rocks slipped down,
   shaping a path for a difficult descent—   *9*

so was the slope of our ravine's formation.
   And at the edge, along the shattered chasm,
   there lay stretched out the infamy of Crete: *12*

the son conceived in the pretended cow.
   When he saw us he bit into his flesh,
   gone crazy with the fever of his rage.   *15*

My wise guide cried to him: "Perhaps you think
   you see the Duke of Athens come again
   who came once in the world to bring your death?   *18*

Begone you beast, for this one is not led
   down here by means of clues your sister gave him;
   he comes here only to observe your torments."   *21*

The way a bull breaks loose the very moment
   he knows he has been dealt the mortal blow,
   and cannot run but jumps and twists and turns,   *24*

just so I saw the Minotaur perform,
   and my guide, alert, cried out: "Run to the pass!
   While he still writhes with rage, get started down."   *27*

And so we made our way down through the ruins
　　of rocks, which often I felt shift and tilt
　　beneath my feet from weight they were not used to.　　　*30*

I was deep in thought when he began: "Are you,
　　perhaps, thinking about these ruins protected
　　by the furious beast I quenched in its own rage?　　　*33*

Now let me tell you that the other time
　　I came down to the lower part of Hell,
　　this rock had not then fallen into ruins;　　　*36*

but certainly, if I remember well,
　　it was just before the coming of that One
　　who took from Hell's first circle the great spoil,　　　*39*

that this abyss of stench, from top to bottom
　　began to shake, so I thought the universe
　　felt love—whereby, some have maintained, the world　　　*42*

has more than once renewed itself in chaos.
　　That was the moment when this ancient rock
　　was split this way—here, and in other places.　　　*45*

But now look down the valley. Coming closer
　　you will see the river of blood that boils the souls
　　of those who through their violence injured others."　　　*48*

(Oh blind cupidity and insane wrath,
　　spurring us on through our short life on earth
　　to steep us then forever in such misery!)　　　*51*

I saw a river—wide, curved like a bow—
　　that stretched embracing all the flatland there,
　　just as my guide had told me to expect.　　　*54*

Between the river and the steep came centaurs
　　galloping in single file equipped with arrows,
　　off hunting as they used to in the world;　　　*57*

then, seeing us descend, they all stopped short
　　and three of them departed from the ranks
　　with bows and arrows ready from their quivers.　　　*60*

One of them cried from his distant post: "You there,
　　on your way down here, what torture are you seeking?
　　Speak where you stand, if not, I draw my bow."　　　*63*

And then my master shouted back: "Our answer
   we will give to Chiron when we're at his side;
   as for you, I see you are as rash as ever!"   66

He nudged me saying: "That one there is Nessus
   who died from loving lovely Dejanira,
   and made of himself, of his blood, his own revenge.   69

The middle one who contemplates his chest
   is great Chiron who reared and taught Achilles;
   the last is Pholus, known for his drunken wrath.   72

They gallop, by the thousands round the ditch
   shooting at any daring soul emerging
   above the bloody level of his guilt."   75

When we came closer to those agile beasts,
   Chiron drew an arrow, and with its notch
   he parted his beard to both sides of his jaws,   78

and when he had uncovered his great mouth
   he spoke to his companions: "Have you noticed,
   how the one behind moves everything he touches?   81

This is not what a dead man's feet would do!"
   And my good guide, now standing by the torso
   at the point the beast's two natures joined, replied: 84

"He is indeed alive, and so alone
   that I must show him through this dismal valley;
   he travels by necessity, not pleasure.   87

A spirit came, from singing Alleluia,
   to give me this extraordinary mission;
   he is no rogue nor I a criminal spirit.   90

Now, in the name of that power by which I move
   my steps along so difficult a road,
   give us one of your troop to be our guide: 93

to lead us to the ford and, once we are there,
   to carry this one over on his back,
   for he is not a spirit who can fly."   96

Chiron looked over his right breast and said
   to Nessus, "You go, guide them as they ask,
   and if another troop protests, disperse them!"   99

So with this trusted escort we moved on
  along the boiling crimson river's bank
  where piercing shrieks rose from the boiling souls.   *102*

There I saw people sunken to their eyelids,
  and the huge centaur explained, "These are the tyrants
  who dealt in bloodshed and in plundered wealth.   *105*

Their tears are paying for their heartless crimes:
  here stand Alexander and fierce Dionysius
  who weighed down Sicily with years of pain;   *108*

and there, that forehead smeared with coal-black hair,
  is Azzolino; the other one, the blond,
  Opizzo d'Esti who, and this is true,   *111*

was killed by his own stepson in your world."
  With that I looked to Virgil, but he said
  "Let him instruct you now, don't look to me."   *114*

A little farther on, the centaur stopped
  above some people peering from the blood
  that came up to their throats. He pointed out   *117*

a shade off to one side, alone, and said:
  "There stands the one who, in God's keep, murdered
  the heart still dripping blood above the Thames."   *120*

Then I saw other souls stuck in the river
  who had their heads and chests above the blood,
  and I knew the names of many who were there.   *123*

The river's blood began decreasing slowly
  until it cooked the feet and nothing more,
  and here we found the ford where we could cross.   *126*

"Just as you see the boiling river here
  on this side getting shallow gradually,"
  the centaur said, "I would also have you know   *129*

that on the other side the riverbed
  sinks deeper more and more until it reaches
  the deepest meeting place where tyrants moan: *132*

it is there that Heaven's justice strikes its blow
  against Attila known as the scourge of earth,
  against Pyrrhus and Sextus; and forever   *135*

extracts the tears the scalding blood produces
    from Rinier da Corneto and Rinier Pazzo
    whose battlefields were highways where they robbed." 138

Then he turned round and crossed the ford again.

NOTES

4–10. *Like the ruins this side of Trent left by the landslide:* The way down the precipice to the Şeventh Circle is here compared to a great landslide, the *Slavini di Marco,* located near Trent in northern Italy; the event which took place about 883 diverted the Adige River from its course (6). In the *Inferno* the steep, shattered terrain was caused by the earthquake which shook Hell just before Christ descended there.

12–21. *there lay stretched out the infamy of Crete:* The Sins of Violence are also the Sins of Bestiality, and the perfect overseer of this circle is the half-man, half-bull known as the Minotaur. Called the "infamy of Crete," that creature was the result of an act of Violence against Nature (punished in the third round of this circle): Pasiphaë, wife of King Minos of Crete, conceived an unnatural desire for a bull, which she satisfied by creeping into a wooden cow and having intercourse with the bull. The Cretan labyrinth, designed by Daedalus, was the Minotaur's home. He was finally slain by Theseus (the Duke of Athens, 17) with the help of Ariadne (Pasiphaë's human daughter and, as such, a half-sister to the beast, 20). Note the continued appearance of the half-human, half-animal monsters, begun in Canto IX with the Furies.

30. *from weight they were not used to:* Cf. VIII, 27–30.

35–36. *I came down to the lower part of Hell:* For the account of Virgil's earlier descent into Hell see Canto IX, 22–30.

34–45

The "One" (38) is Christ, who, in the Harrowing of Hell, removed to Heaven the souls of the Elect (see Canto IV, 49–63). The great landslide whose origin is explained by Virgil is the means the poets use to descend to the Seventh Circle. Appropriately, it is described after the descent of the angel (analogous to Christ's descent) in Canto IX. Christ's life on earth, His descent into Hell and His Resurrection were given by the grace of God to save mankind from sin and death; and here too—as in Canto IX—Dante the Pilgrim (Everyman) going to God and salvation, is aided on his journey by a phenomenon caused ultimately by the grace of God. The description of the earthquake is the last reference to the Harrowing of Hell in this part of the *Inferno* and closes the drama of the angel's advent, which began in Canto VIII.

41–43. *so I thought the universe / felt love:* According to Empedoclean doctrine, Hate, by destroying pristine harmony (i.e. original chaos), occasions the creation of all things, and Love, by reunifying these disparate elements, re-establishes concord in the universe (see Canto IV, n. 138). Virgil describes Christ's descent into Hell in the only terms that he could conceive of, i.e. in terms of pagan philosophy.

47–48. *you will see the river of blood that boils the souls:* Phlegethon, the Virgilian river of fire, here one of boiling blood, in which are punished those shades who committed violence against their fellow men (see Canto XI, 34–39). Here are murderers and tyrants; men who through their violent deeds in life caused hot blood to flow are now themselves sunk in flowing boiling blood.

56. *centaurs / galloping in single file equipped with arrows:* Like the Minotaur, the Centaurs who guard the murderers and tyrants are men-beasts (half-horse, half-man) and thus appropriate to the sins of violence or bestiality. Some early commentators saw them as representing foreign mercenaries, who had begun to swarm over Italy.

65. *Chiron . . . :* Represented by the ancient poets as chief of the Centaurs, he was particularly noted for his wisdom. In mythology he was the son of Saturn (who temporarily changed himself into a horse to avoid the notice and anger of his wife) and Philyra. Chiron was particularly renowned in medicine and was reputedly the tutor of Achilles (71), Aesculapius, Hercules, and many others. In the *Inferno* he is represented in a reflective pose; and since he is the chief of the Centaurs, it is naturally to him that Virgil addresses himself.

67–69. *That one there is Nessus:* The Centaur who is the first to speak to the two travellers. He is later appointed by Chiron (98–99) to accompany them; he does so, pointing out various sinners along the way. Virgil refers to Dejanira, Hercules' wife, whom Nessus desired. In attempting to rape her, Nessus was shot by Hercules, but as he died he gave Dejanira a robe soaked in his blood which he said would preserve Hercules' love. Dejanira took it to her husband, whose death it caused, whereupon the distraught woman hanged herself.

72. *the last is Pholus, known for his drunken wrath:* Little is known about Pholus except that, during the wedding of Pirithous and Hippodamia, when the drunken Centaurs tried to rape the Lapithaen women, Pholus attempted to rape the bride herself.

82. *This is not what a dead man's feet would do!:* Cf. Canto VIII, 27–30, and lines 29–30 of this canto.

88. *a spirit came, from singing Alleluia:* Beatrice. See Canto II, 53–74

107–108. *here stand Alexander and fierce Dionysius:* The first is possibly Alexander the Great (356–323 B.C.), who is constantly referred to as a cruel and violent man by Orosius, Dante's chief source of ancient history. But many modern scholars believe this figure to be Alexander, tyrant of Pherae (368–359 B.C.), whose extreme cruelty is recorded by Cicero and Valerius Maximus. Both of these authors link Alexander of Pherae with the tyrant Dionysius of Syracuse, mentioned here, who may be Dionysius the Elder, tyrant of Syracuse (405–367 B.C.), known for his great cruelty. Or it is possible that the reference is to his son, Dionysius the Younger, who followed his father as a tyrant in 367 and who was also extremely cruel.

110. *Azzolino:* Ezzelino III da Romano (1194–1259) was a Ghibelline chief and tyrant of the March of Treviso. He was notoriously cruel and committed such inhuman atrocities that he was called a "son of Satan."

111–114. *Opizzo d'Esti . . . :* Obizzo d'Esti was Marquis of Ferrara and of the March of Ancona (1264–1293). He was a cruel tyrant, and it is said that he was murdered by his son Azzo, although the story is probably untrue. Dante uses the word *figliastro* (stepson) for his murderer, possibly to show the unnatural nature of the crime, possibly to suggest that Azzo's mother had been unfaithful to her husband, having borne the son of another man (*figliastro* here in this case would mean "bastard").

113–114. *With that I looked to Virgil:* When the Pilgrim turns to Virgil on hearing Nessus' account of the murder of Obizzo it was probably with a look of surprise at the reference to a "stepson," having thought that Azzo, the son, was the murderer.

Dante the Pilgrim, who had been warned by Virgil not to waste his words (see Canto X), and who kept faithfully to matters necessary for his education in Canto XI, is completely silent here in Canto XII. He is learning to observe more objectively and to ask only the questions that a more advanced pupil might ask, for he has learned much since he plied Virgil with questions in the early cantos. Virgil has already explained to Dante (Canto XI) who the sinners in this Round are, and so he has no need to ask. Moreover, he has learned (in Canto X) that Virgil knows even his unspoken questions; and therefore when Nessus begins to guide the poets, Dante does not speak but merely turns with surprise to Virgil, who answers the unspoken question with *Questi ti sia or primo, e io secondo* (114), literally "Let him be first for you and I second."

120. *the heart still dripping blood above the Thames:* In 1272 during Holy Mass at the church ("in God's keep") in Viterbo, Guy de Montfort (one of Charles d'Anjou's emissaries), in order to avenge his father's death at the hands of Edward I, King of England, stabbed to death the latter's cousin, Prince Henry, son of Richard, Earl of Cornwall. According to Giovanni Villani, the thirteenth-century chronicler, Henry's heart was placed in "a golden cup . . . above a column at the head of London bridge" where it still drips blood above the Thames (*Cronica* VII, xxxix). The dripping blood signifies that the murder has not yet been avenged.

124–126. *The river's blood began decreasing slowly:* The sinners are sunk in the river to a degree commensurate with the gravity of their crimes; tyrants, whose crimes of violence are directed against both man and his possessions are sunk deeper than murderers, whose crimes are against men alone. The river is at its shallowest at the point where the poets cross; from this ford, in both directions of its circle, it grows deeper.

134. *against Attila known as the scourge of earth:* Attila, King of the Huns (A.D. 434–453), was called the "scourge of God" (*Flagellum Dei*) because of his tyrannical cruelty. He conquered most of Italy in 452, but Pope Leo the Great went out to meet him as he was approaching Rome and persuaded him to turn back.

135. *against Pyrrhus and Sextus:* The first named is probably Pyrrhus (318–272 B.C.), King of Epirus, who fought the Romans three times between 280 and 276 B.C. before they finally defeated him. Some of the early commentators (like Boccaccio) favor the theory that Dante is referring to the famous ancestor of the King of Epirus, Pyrrhus the son of Achilles.

"Sextus" is probably the younger son of Pompey the Great. After the murder of Caesar he turned to piracy, causing near famine in Rome by cutting off the grain supply from Africa. He is condemned by Lucan (*Pharsalia* VI, 420–422) as being unworthy of his father. A few commentators believe that Dante is referring to Sextus Tarquinius Superbus, who raped and caused the death of Lucretia, the wife of his cousin.

137–138. *from Rinier da Corneto and Rinier Pazzo:* Two highway robbers famous in Dante's day. The latter, a powerful lord, was excommunicated because he particularly enjoyed robbing the clergy.

139. *Then he turned round and crossed the ford again:* The great speed of the Pilgrim's passage across the Phlegethon is evident when the reader realizes at this point that the river has already been crossed, though no mention of the crossing has been made.

CANTO XIII

Not yet had Nessus reached the other side
  when we were on our way into a forest
  that was not marked by any path at all.   *3*

No green leaves, but rather black in color,
  no smooth branches, but twisted and entangled,
  no fruit, but thorns of poison bloomed instead.   *6*

No thick, rough, scrubby home like this exists—
  not even between Cecina and Corneto—
  for those wild beasts that hate the run of farmlands.   *9*

Here the repulsive harpies twine their nests,
  who drove the Trojans from the Strophades
  with filthy forecasts of their close disaster.   *12*

Wide-winged they are, with human necks and faces,
  their feet are clawed, their bellies fat and feathered;
  perched in the trees they shriek their strange laments.   *15*

"Before we go on farther," my guide began,
  "remember, you are in the second round
  and shall be till we reach the dreadful sand;   *18*

now look around you carefully and see
  with your own eyes what I will not describe,
  for if I did, you wouldn't believe my words."   *21*

Around me wails of grief were echoing,
  and I saw no one there to make those sounds;
  bewildered by all this I had to stop.   *24*

I think perhaps he thought I might be thinking
  that all the voices coming fron those stumps
  belonged to people hiding there from us,   *27*

102

and so my teacher said, "If you break off
  a little branch of any of these plants,
    what you are thinking now will break off too."   30

Then slowly raising up my hand a bit
  I snapped the tiny branch of a great thorn,
    and its trunk cried: "Why are you tearing me?"   33

And when its blood turned dark around the wound,
  it started saying more: "Why do you rip me?
    Have you no sense of pity whatsoever?   36

Men were we once, now we are changed to scrub;
  but even if we had been souls of serpents,
    your hand should have shown more pity than it did."   39

Like a green log burning at one end only,
  sputtering at the other, oozing sap,
    and hissing with the air it forces out,   42

so from that splintered trunk a mixture poured
  of words and blood. I let the branch I held
    fall from my hand and stood there stiff with fear.   45

"O wounded soul," my sage replied to him,
  "if he had only let himself believe
    what he had read in verses I once wrote,   48

he never would have raised his hand against you,
  but the truth itself was so incredible
    I urged him on to do the thing that grieves me.   51

But tell him who you were; he can make amends,
  and will, by making bloom again your fame
    in the world above, where his return is sure."   54

And the trunk: "So appealing are your lovely words,
  I must reply. Be not displeased if I
    am lured into a little conversation.   57

I am that one who held both of the keys
  that fitted Frederick's heart; I turned them both,
    locking and unlocking, with such finesse   60

that I let few into his confidence.
  I was so faithful to my glorious office,
    I lost not only sleep but life itself.   63

That courtesan who constantly surveyed
   Caesar's household with her adulterous eyes,
   mankind's undoing, the special vice of courts,   66

inflamed the hearts of everyone against me,
   and these, inflamed, inflamed in turn Augustus,
   and my happy honors turned to sad laments.   69

My mind, moved by scornful satisfaction,
   believing death would free me from all scorn,
   made me unjust to me who was all just.   72

By these strange roots of my own tree I swear
   to you that never once did I break faith
   with my lord who was so worthy of all honor.   75

If one of you should go back to the world,
   restore the memory of me, who here
   remain cut down by the blow that Envy gave."   78

My poet paused awhile then said to me,
   "Since he is silent now, don't lose your chance,
   ask him, if there is more you wish to know."   81

"Why don't you keep on questioning," I said,
   "and ask him, for my part, what I would ask,
   for I cannot, such pity chokes my heart."   84

He began again: "That this man may fulfill
   generously what your words cry out for,
   imprisoned soul, may it please you to continue   87

by telling us just how a soul gets bound
   into these knots, and tell us, if you know,
   whether any soul might someday leave his branches."   90

At that the trunk breathed heavily, and then
   the breath changed to a voice that spoke these words:
   "Your question will be answered very briefly.   93

The moment that the violent soul departs
   the body it has torn itself away from,
   Minòs sends it down to the seventh hole;   96

it drops to the wood, not in a place allotted,
   but anywhere that fortune tosses it.
   There, like a grain of spelt, it germinates,   99

soon springs into a sapling, then a wild tree;
at last the harpies, feasting on its leaves,
create its pain, and for the pain an outlet.   *102*

Like the rest, we shall return to claim our bodies,
but never again to wear them—wrong it is
for a man to have again what he once cast off.   *105*

We shall drag them here and, all along the mournful
forest, our bodies shall hang forever more,
each one on a thorn of its own alien shade."   *108*

We were standing still attentive to the trunk,
thinking perhaps it might have more to say,
when we were startled by a rushing sound,   *111*

such as the hunter hears from where he stands:
first the boar, then all the chase approaching,
the crash of hunting dogs and branches smashing,   *114*

then, to the left of us appeared two shapes
naked and gashed, fleeing with such rough speed
they tore away with them the bushes' branches.   *117*

The one ahead: "Come on, come quickly, Death!"
The other, who could not keep up the pace,
screamed, "Lano, your legs were not so nimble   *120*

when you jousted in the tournament of Toppo!"
And then, from lack of breath perhaps, he slipped
into a bush and wrapped himself in thorns.   *123*

Behind these two the wood was overrun
by packs of black bitches ravenous and ready,
like hunting dogs just broken from their chains;   *126*

they sank their fangs in that poor wretch who hid,
they ripped him open piece by piece, and then
ran off with mouthfuls of his wretched limbs.   *129*

Quickly my escort took me by the hand
and led me over to the bush that wept
its vain laments from every bleeding sore: *132*

"O Giacomo da Sant' Andrea," it said,
"what good was it for you to hide in me?
What fault have I if you led an evil life?"   *135*

My master, standing over it, inquired:
  "Who were you once that now through many wounds
  breathes a grieving sermon with your blood?"   138

He answered us: "O souls who have just come
  in time to see this unjust mutilation
  that has separated me from all my leaves,   141

gather them round the foot of this sad bush.
  I was from the city that took the Baptist
  in exchange for her first patron, who, for this,   144

swears by his art she will have endless sorrow;
  and were it not that on the Arno's bridge
  some vestige of his image still remains,   147

those citizens who built anew the city
  on the ashes that Attila left behind
  would have accomplished such a task in vain;   150

I turned my home into my hanging place."

1–9
    The Wood of the Suicides is described in a series of negatives ("No green
leaves . . . No smooth branches . . . No fruit"), and in fact the first three tercets
begin with a negative. This device anticipates the negation inherent in suicide and
suggests the atmosphere in which the action of this canto will move: mistrust and
incredulity.

    8–9. *not even between Cecina and Corneto:* The vast swampland known as the
"Maremma toscana" lies between the towns of Cecina and Corneto, which mark
its northern and southern boundaries. The contorted syntax of these lines is in
accord with the aesthetic pattern of the canto (cf. n. 25 and 68–73) and may in
particular suggest the rugged topography of the uncultivated land.
    10–15. *Here the repulsive harpies twine their nests:* The Harpies were the daugh-
ters of Thaumas and Electra. Because of their malicious deeds they were banished
to the Strophades Islands, where, having encountered Aeneas and his followers
from Troy, they defiled their table and forecast future hardships for them
(11–12)—still another example of half-human, half-bestial creatures.
    25. *I think perhaps he thought I might be thinking:* The Pilgrim's "bewildered"
(24) state is reflected by the syntax, which imitates, in its own way, the action of
a confused mind.
    34. *And when its blood turned dark around the wound:* One aesthetic tie between
this Round and the previous one is the continuation of blood imagery.
    47–49. *if he had only let himself believe:* Virgil is referring to that section of the
Aeneid (III, 22–43), where Aeneas breaks a branch from a shrub, which then

begins to pour forth blood; at the same time a voice issues from the ground beneath the shrub where Polydorus is buried. See Canto XXX, 18.

52–54. *But tell him who you were:* Cf. VI, 88–89 and XVI, 82–85.

58–78

Born in the Southern Italian town of Capua (c. 1190), Pier delle Vigne studied at Bologna and, having attracted the attention of Frederick II, became attached to his court at Palermo, where he soon became the Emperor's most trusted minister ("I . . . held both of the keys / that fitted Frederick's heart," i.e., Pier's counsel of "Yes" opened the Emperor's heart and "No" closed it). Around 1248, however, he fell from the Emperor's grace and was placed in jail, where he committed suicide. Pier delle Vigne tells how Envy ("that courtesan," 64), ever present at Frederick's court ("Caesar's household," 65), inflamed everyone against him, Frederick ("Augustus," 68) becoming influenced by the attitude of others. The dishonor of the imprisonment and the envisaged self-justification through death led him to take his own life by dashing his head against the prison wall. He concludes by declaring his innocence (73–75) and expressing the desire for re-evaluation of his deeds, which will ensure his earthly fame (76–78).

68–72. *and these, inflamed, inflamed in turn Augustus:* Pier was also a renowned poet of the Sicilian School which flourished under Frederick's patronage and which is noted for its love of complex conceits and convoluted wordplay. Dante the Poet endows Pier with the type of poetic language for which he was well known (see particularly lines 68 and 72).

84. *for I cannot, such pity chokes my heart:* The Pilgrim feels pity for Pier because of the false accusation which precipitated his fall from favor, not because of the punishment meted out to this shade for having taken his own life. It is a completely different kind of pity from that which Dante felt for Francesca or Ciacco (V and VI). Even Pier himself recognized the justice of his punishment and the sinfulness of his suicide: "My mind . . . made me unjust to me who was all just" (70–72).

95–108. *the body it has torn itself away from:* Having denied the God-given sanctity of their bodies on earth, in Hell the Suicides are completely denied bodily form; their souls, thrown into this round by Minòs (96) fall at random and sprout like seeds in the same careless way in which they had treated their bodies (97–100). Even after the Last Judgment, when the Suicides, like all the other shades in Hell, will return to earth to reclaim their mortal flesh, each will be denied the use of its body, which will hang "on a thorn of its own alien shade" (103–108).

Part of the *contrapasso* inflicted on these sinners is the physical torment caused by the Harpies who rend the branches of the trees causing "pain, and for the pain an outlet" (101–102). It is only when part of the tree or bush is torn or broken that the shades can make sounds, thus the necessity for Dante to break a branch before Pier can speak.

115–121. *then, to the left of us appeared two shapes:* The second group of souls punished here are the Profligates, who did violence to their earthly goods by not valuing them as they should have, just as the Suicides did not value their bodies. They are represented by Lano (120), probably a member of the wealthy Maconi family of Siena, and by Giacomo da Sant'Andrea (133) from Padua. Both had the dubious honor of being incorrigible spendthrifts who squandered most of their wealth and property. The "tournament of Toppo" (121) recalls the disastrous defeat of the Sienese troops at the hands of the Aretines in 1287 at a river ford near Arezzo. Lano went into this battle to die because he had squandered his fortune; as legend has it, he remained to fight rather than escape on foot (hence Giacomo's reference to his "legs," 120), and was killed.

125–129. *by packs of black bitches ravenous and ready:* These dogs which pursue the Profligates have invited many interpretations (conscience, poverty, ruin and death, remorse, creditors), but I think that they probably represent that violent force which drove the Profligates to their end: they seem to be the dramatization of the act of violence itself. It is violence which distinguishes these Profligates from the Spendthrifts who are linked with the Misers in the Fourth Circle (Canto VII); these were merely wasteful, not *violent* in their wasting: the figures in the Seventh Circle on the other hand seem to have been driven by violent passions to consume their possessions as fast as possible, perhaps to outdo other profligates in the expense of magnificence. In fact, Giacomo da Sant'Andrea is reported to have set on fire several houses on his estate just for "kicks."

143–150. *I was from the city that took the Baptist:* The identity of this Florentine Suicide remains unknown. The "first patron" of Florence was Mars, the god of war (thus his "art" [145] is warfare); a fragment of his statue was to be found on the Ponte Vecchio ("the Arno's bridge," 146) until 1333. The Anonymous Suicide states that if this fragment of the statue were not still there, then Florence would have been completely destroyed after "those citizens . . . built anew the city / on the ashes that Attila left behind" (148–149). The reference to Attila, king of the Huns, is erroneous; Dante must have intended Totila, king of the Ostrogoths, who razed Florence in the sixth century. The confusion of Attila with Totila was common in the Middle Ages.

The second patron of the city was John the Baptist (143), whose image appeared on the florin, the principal monetary unit of the time. It has been suggested that Florence's change of patron indicates its transformation from a stronghold of martial excellence (under Mars) to one of servile money-making (under the Baptist).

151. *I turned my home into my hanging place:* The Florentine's anonymity corroborates his symbolic value as a representative of his city. Like the suicides condemned to this round, the city of Florence was killing itself, in Dante's opinion, through its internecine struggles (the revenge of Mars for having been abandoned as patron): she is making of herself a hanging place.

CANTO XIV

The love we both shared for our native city
  moved me to gather up the scattered leaves
  and give them back to the voice that now had faded.   *3*

We reached the confines of the woods that separate
  the second from the third round. There I saw
  God's justice in its dreadful operation.   *6*

Now to picture clearly these unheard-of things:
  we arrived to face an open stretch of flatland
  whose soil refused the roots of any plant;   *9*

the grieving forest made a wreath around it,
  as the sad river of blood enclosed the woods.
  We stopped right here, right at the borderline.   *12*

This wasteland was a dry expanse of sand,
  thick, burning sand, no different from the kind
  that Cato's feet packed down in other times.   *15*

O just revenge of God! how awesomely
  you should be feared by everyone who reads
  these truths that were revealed to my own eyes!   *18*

Many separate herds of naked souls I saw,
  all weeping desperately; it seemed each group
  had been assigned a different penalty: *21*

some were stretched out flat upon their backs,
  others were crouching there all tightly hunched,
  some wandered, never stopping, round and round.   *24*

Far more there were of those who roamed the sand
  and fewer were the souls stretched out to suffer,
  but their tongues were looser, for the pain was greater.   *27*

And over all that sandland, a fall of slowly
　　raining broad flakes of fire showered steadily
　　(a mountain snowstorm on a windless day),　　　　　　*30*

like those that Alexander saw descending
　　on his troops while crossing India's torrid lands:
　　flames falling, floating solid to the ground,　　　　　*33*

and he with all his men began to tread
　　the sand so that the burning flames might be
　　extinguished one by one before they joined.　　　　　*36*

Here too a never-ending blaze descended,
　　kindling the sand like tinder under flint-sparks,
　　and in this way the torment there was doubled.　　　　*39*

Without a moment's rest the rhythmic dance
　　of wretched hands went on, this side, that side,
　　brushing away the freshly fallen flames.　　　　　　*42*

And I: "My master, you who overcome
　　all opposition (except for those tough demons
　　who came to meet us at the gate of Dis),　　　　　　*45*

who is that mighty one that seems unbothered
　　by burning, stretched sullen and disdainful there,
　　looking as if the rainfall could not tame him?"　　　*48*

And that very one, who was quick to notice me
　　inquiring of my guide about him, answered:
　　"What I was once, alive I still am, dead!　　　　　　*51*

Let Jupiter wear out his smith, from whom
　　he seized in anger that sharp thunderbolt
　　he hurled, to strike me down, my final day;　　　　　*54*

let him wear out those others, one by one,
　　who work the soot-black forge of Mongibello
　　(as he shouts, 'Help me good Vulcan, I need your help,'　　*57*

the way he cried that time at Phlegra's battle),
　　and with all his force let him hurl his bolts at me,
　　no joy of satisfaction would I give him!"　　　　　　*60*

My guide spoke back at him with cutting force,
　　(I never heard his voice so strong before):
　　"O Capaneus, since your blustering pride　　　　　　*63*

will not be stilled, you are made to suffer more:
no torment other than your rage itself
could punish your gnawing pride more perfectly."   66

And then he turned a calmer face to me,
saying, "That was a king, one of the seven
besieging Thebes; he scorned, and would seem still   69

to go on scorning God and treat him lightly,
but, as I said to him, he decks his chest
with ornaments of lavish words that prick him.   72

Now follow me and also pay attention
not to put your feet upon the burning sand,
but to keep them well within the wooded line."   75

Without exchanging words we reached a place
where a narrow stream came gushing from the woods
(its reddish water still runs fear through me!);   78

like the one that issues from the Bulicame,
whose waters are shared by prostitutes downstream,
it wore its way across the desert sand.   81

This river's bed and banks were made of stone,
so were the tops on both its sides; and then
I understood this was our way across.   84

"Among the other marvels I have shown you,
from the time we made our entrance through the gate
whose threshold welcomes every evil soul,   87

your eyes have not discovered anything
as remarkable as this stream you see here
extinguishing the flames above its path."   90

These were my master's words, and I at once
implored him to provide me with the food
for which he had given me the appetite.   93

"In the middle of the sea there lies a wasteland,"
he immediately began, "that is known as Crete,
under whose king the world knew innocence.   96

There is a mountain there that was called Ida;
then happy in its verdure and its streams,
now deserted like an old, discarded thing;   99

Rhea chose it once as a safe cradle
    for her son, and, to conceal his presence better,
    she had her servants scream loud when he cried.   *102*

In the mountain's core an ancient man stands tall;
    he has his shoulders turned toward Damietta
    and faces Rome as though it were his mirror.   *105*

His head is fashioned of the finest gold;
    pure silver are his arms and hands and chest;
    from there to where his legs spread, he is brass;   *108*

the rest of him is all of chosen iron,
    except his right foot which is terra-cotta;
    he puts more weight on this foot than the other.   *111*

Every part of him, except the gold, is broken
    by a fissure dripping tears down to his feet
    where they collect to erode the cavern's rock;   *114*

from stone to stone they drain down here, becoming
    rivers: the Acheron, Styx, and Phlegethon
    then overflow down through this tight canal   *117*

until they fall to where all falling ends:
    they form Cocytus. What that pool is like
    I need not tell you. You will see, yourself."   *120*

And I to him: "If this small stream beside us
    has its source, as you have told me, in our world,
    why have we seen it only on this ledge?"   *123*

And he to me: "You know this place is round,
    and though your journey has been long, circling
    toward the bottom, turning only to the left,   *126*

you have not completed any circle's round;
    so you should never look surprised, as now,
    if you see something you have not seen before."   *129*

And I again: "Where, Master, shall we find
    Lethe and Phlegethon? You omit the first
    and say the other forms from the rain of tears."   *132*

"I am very happy when you question me,"
    he said, "but that the blood-red water boiled
    should answer certainly one of your questions.   *135*

And Lethe you shall see, but beyond this valley,
  at a place where souls collect to wash themselves
  when penitence has freed them of their guilt.   138

Now it is time to leave this edge of woods,"
  he added. "Be sure you follow close behind me:
  the margins are our road, they do not burn,   141

and all the flames above them are extinguished."

NOTES

3. *the voice that now had faded:* That of the anonymous Florentine suicide.

10. *the grieving forest:* The Wood of the grieving Suicides.

15. *that Cato's feet packed down in other times:* Cato of Utica (born 95 B.C.), a friend of Cicero, sided with Pompey in the Roman civil war. After Pompey was defeated at Pharsalia, Cato joined Metellus Scipio in Africa; and when it became apparent that he was about to be captured by Caesar, he killed himself (46 B.C.). The year before his death he led a march across the desert of Libya (recorded by Lucan in the *Pharsalia*)—hence the comparison between the arid plain of the Seventh Circle to the hot desert crossed by Cato.

22–24. *some . . . , others . . . , some . . . :* The shades in this third round of the Seventh Circle are divided into three groups: the Blasphemers lie supine on the ground (22), the Usurers are "crouching" (23), and the Sodomites wander "never stopping" (24). The sand they lie on perhaps suggests the sterility of their acts, just as the black leaves and lack of fruit on the trees in the Wood of the Suicides depicted their perversion of fruitful living.

33–36. *flames falling, floating solid to the ground:* Dante's source was probably Albertus Magnus' *De meteoris.* Albertus refers to an apocryphal letter from Alexander to Aristotle concerning the former's adventures in India. There, Alexander was said to have first encountered a heavy snowfall and later a rain of fire. According to the letter, Alexander had his soldiers trample the snow, but Albertus (and Dante after him) confuses the snow with the fire and has Alexander's legions trampling the flames.

41. *of wretched hands went on, this side, that side:* Note the expression "this side, that side" whose rhythm (in the original: *or quindi, or quinci*) imitates the ceaseless movements of the sinners' hands attempting to brush off the falling flames from their bodies. We will find this same effect also in line 55 ("one by one": *a muta a muta*), line 57 ("help me . . . I need your help": *aiuta, aiuta*) and even in the next canto, line 84 ("hour after hour": *ad ora ad ora*). In fact, this leitmotiv first appears before the sinners come in view, at the moment when the travellers reach the edge of the burning sand: "We stopped *right here, right at* the borderline": *a randa, a randa* (12).

44–45. *those tough demons:* The rebel angels of Canto IX who barred the travellers' entrance to the City of Dis. Note that the Pilgrim, in praising his guide, naively reminds him of his recent difficulty.

51–60. *What I was once, alive, I still am, dead!:* The representative of the Blasphemers is Capaneus, who, as Virgil will explain, was one of the seven kings who assaulted Thebes. Statius describes how Capaneus, when scaling the walls of Thebes, blasphemed against Jove, who then struck him with a thunderbolt (54).

Capaneus died with blasphemy on his lips and now, even in Hell, he is able to defy Jove's thunderbolts (59–60). At Phlegra Jove defeated the Titans who attempted to storm Olympus. Vulcan and the Cyclopes, of course, were the manufacturers of the thunderbolts. *Mongibello* (56), the Sicilian name for Mt. Aetna, was supposed to be Vulcan's furnace.

68–69. *one of the seven / besieging Thebes:* Thebes, the capital of Boeotia, was the scene of a great struggle for sovereignty between Eteocles and Polynices, the sons of Oedipus. Adrastus, King of Argos, on Polynices' behalf led an expedition of seven kings (including Capaneus) against Thebes and Eteocles. See the above note, 51–60.

79–80. *like the one that issues from the Bulicame:* Near Viterbo there was a hot spring called the Bulicame, whose sulphurous waters transformed the area into a watering place. Among the inhabitants were many prostitutes who were required to live in a separate quarter. A special stream channeled the hot spring water through their section, since they were denied use of the public baths. Here Dante compares the stream which flows from the river in Canto XII to the hot, steamy flow channeled for the prostitutes from the Bulicame—whose mineral-rich waters undoubtedly had a reddish cast.

86–87. *from the time we made our entrance through the gate:* The principal gate of Hell. Cf. Canto III, 1–11, and Canto VIII, 125–126.

94–119. *In the middle of the sea there lies a wasteland:* The island of Crete is given as the source of Acheron, Styx, and Phlegethon, the joined rivers of Hell whose course eventually leads to the "pool," Cocytus (119), at the bottom of Hell. Crete was probably chosen by Dante because, according to Virgil, it was the birthplace of Trojan—therefore Roman—civilization, the Trojan Aeneas being the founder of Rome (cf. I, 73–75, and II, 13–24). Crete was also at the center of the known world, the continents of Asia, Africa, and Europe. According to mythology, Mt. Ida on Crete was the place chosen by Rhea to protect her infant son, Jupiter, from his father, Saturn, who usually devoured his sons when they were born. Rhea, to keep him from finding Jupiter, "had her servants scream loud when he cried" (102) to drown out the infant's screams.

Within Mt. Ida Dante places the statue of the Old Man of Crete (certainly one of the most elaborate symbols in the *Inferno*), with his back to Damietta and gazing toward Rome (104–105). Damietta, an important Egyptian seaport, represents the East, the pagan world; Rome, of course, the modern, Christian world. The figure of the Old Man is drawn from the book of Daniel (2:32–35), but the symbolism is different, and more nearly (though not absolutely) reflects a poetic symbol utilized by Ovid (*Metamorphoses* I). The head of gold represents the Golden Age of man (that is, in Christian terms, before the Fall). The arms and breast of silver, the trunk of brass, and the legs of iron represent the three declining ages of man. The clay foot (the one made of *terra-cotta*) may symbolize the Church, weakened and corrupted by temporal concerns and political power struggles. Through the fissure which cracks every part of the figure but the golden head flow the Old Man's tears, the sins and sorrows of man through all ages except the Golden Age of Innocence. The tears bore their way down through the mountain, and eventually their course forms the rivers of Hell which are joined, evidently, by tributary streams (as we see here), since they are all circular. The Old Man, imprisoned in the darkness of Mt. Ida, certainly symbolizes from the neck down the fallen state of man due to the original sin in the Garden of Eden. Mt. Ida was once like Eden, "then happy in its verdure and its streams" (98), but now, devastated like man after the Fall, it is a "wasteland" (94). The fissure, through which flow the tears of sorrow caused by the Fall, represents an imperfection symbolic of original sin.

126. *turning only to the left:* As was pointed out in the note to Canto IX, 132, there are two exceptions to the usual procedure of circling to the left.

134–135. *that the blood-red water boiled:* To the Pilgrim's naive question (130–131) Virgil replies that he should have been able to recognize Phlegethon by its extreme heat. This property of the river is mentioned in the *Aeneid* (VI, 550–551):

Quae rapidus flammis ambit torrentibus amnis
Tartareus Phlegethon.

136–138. *And Lethe you shall see, but beyond this valley:* Dante places Lethe, the River of Forgetfulness, in the Earthly Paradise atop the mountain of Purgatory.

141. *the margins are our road, they do not burn:* The "margins" are the miraculously protected paths which run alongside the stream. See lines 82–84.

CANTO XV

Now one of those stone margins bears us on
   and the river's vapors hover like a shade,
   sheltering the banks and water from the flames.   *3*

As the Flemings, living with the constant threat
   of flood tides rushing in between Wissant
   and Bruges, build their dikes to force the sea back;   *6*

as the Paduans build theirs on the shores of Brenta
   to protect their town and homes before warm weather
   turns Chiarentana's snow to rushing water—   *9*

so were these walls we walked upon constructed,
   though the engineer, whoever he may have been,
   did not make them as high or thick as those.   *12*

We had left the wood behind (so far behind,
   by now, that if I had stopped to turn around,
   I am sure it could no longer have been seen)   *15*

when we saw a troop of souls come hurrying
   toward us beside the bank, and each of them
   looked us up and down as some men look   *18*

at other men, at night, when the moon is new.
   They strained their eyebrows, squinting hard at us,
   as an old tailor might at his needle's eye.   *21*

Eyed in such a way by this strange crew,
   I was recognized by one of them who grabbed
   my garment's hem and shouted: "How marvelous!"   *24*

And I, when he reached out his arm toward me,
   straining my eyes, saw through his face's crust,
   through his burned features that could not prevent   *27*

116

my memory from bringing back his name;
   and bending my face down to meet with his,
   I said: "Is this really you, here, Ser Brunetto?"   *30*

And he: "O my son, may it not displease you
   if Brunetto Latini lets his troop file on
   while he walks at your side for a little while."   *33*

And I: "With all my heart I beg you to,
   and if you wish me to sit here with you,
   I will, if my companion does not mind."   *36*

"My son," he said, "a member of this herd
   who stops one moment lies one hundred years
   unable to brush off the wounding flames,   *39*

so, move on; I shall follow at your hem
   and then rejoin my family that moves
   along, lamenting their eternal pain."   *42*

I did not dare step off the margin-path
   to walk at his own level but, with head
   bent low in reverence, I moved along.   *45*

He began: "What fortune or what destiny
   leads you down here before your final hour?
   And who is this one showing you the way?"   *48*

"Up there above in the bright living life
   before I reached the end of all my years,
   I lost myself in a valley," I replied;   *51*

"just yesterday at dawn I turned from it.
   This spirit here appeared as I turned back,
   and by this road he guides me home again."   *54*

He said to me: "Follow your constellation
   and you cannot fail to reach your port of glory,
   not if I saw clearly in the happy life;   *57*

and if I had not died just when I did,
   I would have cheered you on in all your work,
   seeing how favorable Heaven was to you.   *60*

But that ungrateful and malignant race
   which descended from the Fiesole of old,
   and still have rock and mountain in their blood,   *63*

will become, for your good deeds, your enemy—
   and right they are: among the bitter berries
   there's no fit place for the sweet fig to bloom.   66

They have always had the fame of being blind,
   an envious race, proud and avaricious;
   you must not let their ways contaminate you.   69

Your destiny reserves such honors for you:
   both parties shall be hungry to devour you,
   but the grass will not be growing where the goat is.   72

Let the wild beasts of Fiesole make fodder
   of each other, and let them leave the plant untouched
   (so rare it is that one grows in their dung-heap)   75

in which there lives again the holy seed
   of those remaining Romans who survived there
   when this new nest of malice was constructed."   78

"O, if all I wished for had been granted,"
   I answered him, "you certainly would not,
   not yet, be banished from our life on earth;   81

my mind is etched (and now my heart is pierced)
   with your kind image, loving and paternal,
   when, living in the world, hour after hour   84

you taught me how man makes himself eternal.
   And while I live my tongue shall always speak
   of my debt to you, and of my gratitude.   87

I will write down what you tell me of my future
   and save it, with another text, to show
   a lady who can interpret, if I can reach her.   90

This much, at least, let me make clear to you:
   if my conscience continues not to blame me,
   I am ready for whatever Fortune wants.   93

This prophecy is not new to my ears,
   and so let Fortune turn her wheel, spinning it
   as she pleases, and the peasant turn his spade."   96

My master hearing this looked to the right,
   then, turning round and facing me, he said:
   "He listens well who notes well what he hears."   99

But I did not answer him; I went on talking,
　walking with Ser Brunetto, asking him
　who of his company were the most distinguished.　*102*

And he: "It might be good to know who some are,
　about the rest I feel I should be silent,
　for the time would be too short, there are so many.　*105*

In brief, let me tell you, all here were clerics
　and respected men of letters of great fame,
　all befouled in the world by one same sin:　*108*

Priscian is travelling with that wretched crowd
　and Francesco d'Accorso too; and also there,
　if you could have stomached such repugnancy,　*111*

you might have seen the one the Servant of Servants
　transferred to the Bacchiglione from the Arno
　where his sinfully erected nerves were buried.　*114*

I would say more, but my walk and conversation
　with you cannot go on, for over there
　I see a new smoke rising from the sand:　*117*

people approach with whom I must not mingle.
　Remember my *Trésor*, where I live on,
　this is the only thing I ask of you."　*120*

Then he turned back, and he seemed like one of those
　who run in Verona's race across its fields
　to win the green cloth prize, and he was like　*123*

the winner of the group, not the last one in.

NOTES

1. *Now one of those stone margins bears us on:* Note the use of the present tense. Cf. VIII, n. 109–111.

4–6. *As the Flemings, living with the constant threat:* The cities of Wissant, between Boulogne and Calais, and Bruges, in eastern Flanders, were both centers of trade during the thirteenth century. Wissant was an important port city, and Bruges was famous for its extensive trade, especially with Italy.

It is not inconceivable that cities such as these, which counted a considerable number of itinerant tradesmen and sailors among their population, might have had a reputation for sodomy during Dante's time.

7. *as the Paduans build theirs on the shores of Brenta:* Although I know of no evidence which might support the theory that Padua was renowned for sodomy

during the Middle Ages, it is perhaps not mere coincidence that in the journals of William Lithgow, a seventeenth-century Scottish (?) traveler and writer, we find reference made to the propensity for sodomy he had noted among the Paduans ("for beastly Sodomy . . . [is] . . . a monstrous filthinesse, and yet to them a pleasant pastime, making songs, and singing sonets of the beauty and pleasure of their Bardassi, or buggered boyes").

9. *turns Chiarentana's snow to rushing water:* The Chiarentana is a mountainous district situated north of the Brenta River.

11. *the engineer:* God.

16–114

The sin of sodomy being punished in this Round is aesthetically mirrored in much of the imagery of the canto (the way in which the group of sodomites ogle the Pilgrim and Virgil, 17–22), and particularly in the language used by Brunetto Latini. He greets the Pilgrim with the exlamation "How marvelous!" (24), and in the metaphors of his prophecy (61–78), Dante is a "sweet fig" (66), whom "both parties shall be hungry to devour" (71); the next moment he is "grass" to be eaten by a "goat" (72). And it is difficult to be more explicit than Brunetto was in his description of Andrea de' Mozzi, who died in Vicenza, "where his sinfully erected nerves were buried" (114). The imagery used in connection with these scholarly or clerical sodomites should be compared to the more robust imagery used for the ones who were soldiers in Canto XVI, 22–27. The eternal wandering of the sodomites is comparable to the *contrapasso* of the lustful in Canto V, who are forever blown about aimlessly by a wind.

30. *I said: "Is this really you, here, Ser Brunetto?":* The Pilgrim addresses his fellow Florentine, Brunetto Latini (c. 1220–1294), with the respectful pronoun form '*voi*' (cf. Dante's use of '*voi*' with Farinata and Cavalcante in Canto X). The reverent tone of Dante's words bespeaks his admiration and affection for the famous Guelph statesman and writer, whose *Trésor* (see below, n. 119–120) and *Tesoretto*, an allegorical poem in Italian, greatly influenced Dante's own life and works. Brunetto was a notary, and Dante accordingly prefixes the title, "Ser," to his name. Forced into exile after the Guelph defeat at Montaperti (1260), he remained in France for six years. The Ghibelline defeat at Benevento (1266) ensured his safe return to Florence, where he took an active part in public affairs until his death.

48. *And who is this one showing you the way?:* The Pilgrim fails to answer Brunetto's second question, possibly because naming Virgil who has become his second "teacher" might offend Brunetto.

51. *I lost myself in a valley:* The "valley" is the "dark woods" of Canto I.

54. *and by this road he guides me home again:* That is, to God, man's true home. In the Middle Ages man's earthly existence was viewed as a pilgrimage, a preparation for the after-life.

61–78. *But that ungrateful and malignant race:* During a Roman power struggle, Cataline fled Rome and found sanctuary for himself and his troops in the originally Etruscan town of Fiesole. After Caesar's successful siege of that city, the survivors of both camps founded Florence, where those of the Roman camp were the elite.

Brunetto prophesies about Florence that both political parties will become Dante's enemies (61–64), for he will be the "sweet fig," (66) among the "bitter berries," (65) who are "an envious race, proud and avaricious" (68). They must hate the plant in which "there lives again the holy seed / of those remaining Romans who survived there . . . " (76–77).

The prophecy with its condemnation of the current state of Florence (and Italy) and its implied hope of a renascent empire continues the political theme, begun with the speech of the Anonymous Suicide in Canto XIII, and continued in the symbol of the Old Man of Crete in Canto XIV.

68. *an envious race, proud and avaricious:* Envy and pride are always the basis of the sins beyond the walls of Dis. See XXXI, n. 19–127.

85. *you taught me how man makes himself eternal:* Dante expresses his gratitude to Brunetto by saying that it was he who taught him how to become immortal through literary accomplishments.

89–90. *and save it, with another text, to show:* Again (as in X,130–132), Beatrice is referred to as the one who will reveal to the Pilgrim his future course. She will gloss the earlier prophecies ("another text") of Ciacco (VI, 64–75) and Farinata (X, 79–81), together with the one just related by Brunetto. However, in the *Paradise* this role is given to Dante's ancestor, Cacciaguida.

95–96. *let Fortune turn her wheel, . . . / . . . and the peasant turn his spade:* It is as right for Fortune to spin her wheel as it is for the peasant to turn his spade; and the Pilgrim will be as indifferent to the first as to the second.

Could there also be a suggestion in his reference to the peasant's spade of his indifference to those who might attempt to dig up the "plant . . . in which there lives again the holy seed . . ."?

99. *He listens well who notes well what he hears:* Virgil is certainly not rebuking the Pilgrim, as some think (for his supposed indifference to Brunetto's words), but rather praising him for remembering the other prophecies and for believing that they will eventually be interpreted by Beatrice. And surely, if the Pilgrim had considered himself rebuked by his guide, he would not have reacted as he did: "But I did not answer him; I went on talking."

110. *and Francesco d'Accorso:* A celebrated Florentine lawyer (1225–1294) who taught law at the University of Bologna and later at Oxford at the request of King Edward I.

112–114. *you might have seen the one the Servant of Servants:* Andrea de' Mozzi was Bishop of Florence from 1287 to 1295, when, by order of Pope Boniface VIII (the "Servant of Servants": i.e. the servant of the servants of God), he was transferred to Vicenza (on the Bacchiglione River), where he died that same year or the next. The early commentators make reference to his naive and inept preaching and to his general stupidity. Dante, by mentioning his "sinfully erected nerves" calls attention to his major weakness: unnatural lust or sodomy. See n. 16–114.

119–120. *Remember my* Trésor, *where I live on:* The *Livres dou Tresor,* Brunetto's most significant composition, was written during his exile in France and is an encyclopedic work written in French prose.

123–124. *to win the green cloth prize:* The first prize for the footrace, which was one of the games held annually on the first Sunday of Lent in Verona during the thirteenth century, was a green cloth. Ironically, the Pilgrim's last view of his elderly and dignified teacher is the sight of him, naked, racing off at top speed to catch up with his companions in sin. This image of the race in Verona (which was, appropriately for its aesthetic function in this canto, run naked) prepares the reader for the athletic imagery of the next canto.

CANTO XVI

Already we were where I could hear the rumbling
  of the water plunging down to the next circle,
  something like the sound of beehives humming,   *3*

when three shades with one impulse broke away,
  running, from a group of spirits passing us
  beneath the rain of bitter suffering.   *6*

They were coming toward us shouting with one voice:
  "O, you there, stop! From the clothes you wear, you seem
  to be a man from our perverted city."   *9*

Ah, the wounds I saw covering their limbs,
  some old, some freshly branded by the flames!
  Even now, when I think back to them, I grieve.   *12*

Their shouts caught the attention of my guide,
  and then he turned to face me saying, "Wait,
  for these are shades that merit your respect.   *15*

And were it not the nature of this place
  to rain with piercing flames, I would suggest
  you run toward *them*, for it would be more fitting."   *18*

When we stopped, they resumed their normal pace
  and when they reached us, then they started circling;
  the three together formed a turning wheel,   *21*

just like professional wrestlers stripped and oiled
  eyeing one another for the first, best grip
  before the actual blows and thrusts begin.   *24*

And circling in this way each kept his face
  pointed up at me, so that their necks and feet
  moved constantly in opposite directions.   *27*

122

"And if the misery along these sterile sands,"
    one of them said, "and our charred and peeling flesh
    makes us, and what we ask, repulsive to you,   *30*

let our great worldly fame persuade your heart
    to tell us who you are, how you can walk
    safely with living feet through Hell itself.   *33*

This one in front whose footsteps I am treading,
    even though he runs his round naked and skinned,
    was of noble station, more than you may think: *36*

he was the grandson of the good Gualdrada;
    his name was Guido Guerra, and in his life
    he accomplished much with counsel and with sword.   *39*

This other one who pounds the sand behind me
    is Tegghiaio Aldobrandi whose wise voice
    the world would have done well to listen to.   *42*

And I who share this post of pain with them
    was Jacopo Rusticucci, and for sure
    my reluctant wife first drove me to my sin."   *45*

If I could have been sheltered from the fire,
    I would have thrown myself below with them,
    and I think my guide would have allowed me to;   *48*

but, knowing well I would be burned and seared,
    my fear won over my first good intention
    that made me want to put my arms around them.   *51*

And then I spoke: "Repulsion, no, but grief
    for your condition spread throughout my heart
    (and years will pass before it fades away),   *54*

as soon as my lord here began to speak
    in terms that led me to believe a group
    of such men as yourselves might be approaching.   *57*

I am from your city, and your honored names
    and your accomplishments I have always heard
    rehearsed, and have rehearsed, myself, with fondness.   *60*

I leave the bitter gall, and journey toward
    those sweet fruits promised me by my true guide,
    but first I must go down to the very center."   *63*

"So may your soul remain to guide your body
    for years to come," that same one spoke again,
    "and your fame's light shine after you are gone,   66

tell us if courtesy and valor dwell
    within our city as they used to do,
    or have they both been banished from the place?   69

Guglielmo Borsiere, who joined our painful ranks
    of late, and travels there with our companions,
    has given us reports that make us grieve."   72

"A new breed of people with their sudden wealth
    have stimulated pride and unrestraint
    in you, O Florence, made to weep so soon."   75

These words I shouted with my head strained high,
    and the three below took this to be my answer
    and looked, as if on truth, at one another.   78

"If you always answer questions with such ease,"
    they all spoke up at once, "O happy you
    to have this gift of ready, open speech;   81

therefore, if you survive these unlit regions
    and return to gaze upon the lovely stars,
    when it pleases you to say 'I was down there,'   84

do not fail to speak of us to living men."
    They broke their man-made wheel and ran away,
    their nimble legs were more like wings in flight.   87

"Amen" could not have been pronounced as quick
    as they were off, and vanished from our sight;
    and then my teacher thought it time to leave.   90

I followed him, and we had not gone far
    before the sound of water was so close
    that if we spoke we hardly heard each other.   93

As that river on the Apennines' left slope
    first springing from its source at Monte Veso
    then flowing eastward holding its own course   96

(called Acquacheta at its start above
    before descending to its lower bed
    where, at Forlì, it has another name),   99

reverberates there near San Benedetto
    dell'Alpe (plunging in a single bound)
    where at least a thousand vassals could be housed,   *102*

so down a single rocky precipice
    we found the tainted waters falling, roaring
    sound loud enough to deafen us in seconds.   *105*

I wore a cord that fastened round my waist
    with which I once had thought I might be able
    to catch the leopard with the gaudy skin.   *108*

As soon as I removed it from my body
    just as my guide commanded me to do,
    I gave it to him looped into a coil.   *111*

Then taking it and turning to the right,
    he flung it quite a distance past the bank
    and down into the deepness of the pit.   *114*

"Now surely something strange is going to happen,"
    I thought to myself, "to answer the strange signal
    whose course my master follows with his eyes."   *117*

How cautious a man must be in company
    with one who can not only see his actions
    but read his mind and understand his thoughts!   *120*

He spoke: "Soon will rise up what I expect;
    and what you are trying to imagine now
    soon must reveal itself before your eyes."   *123*

It is always better to hold one's tongue than speak
    a truth that seems a bold-face lie when uttered,
    since to tell this truth could be embarrassing;   *126*

but I shall not keep quiet; and by the verses
    of my *Comedy*—so may they be received
    with lasting favor, Reader—I swear to you   *129*

I saw a figure coming, it was swimming
    through the thick and murky air, up to the top
    (a thing to startle even stalwart hearts),   *132*

like one returning who has swum below
    to free the anchor that has caught its hooks
    on a reef or something else the sea conceals,   *135*

spreading out his arms, and doubling up his legs.

1–3. *I could hear the rumbling / of the water:* The action of this canto begins and ends with the waterfall of the tributary of the Phlegethon; in the first tercet it is distant, and the Pilgrim hears "something like the sound of beehives humming," but by the end of the canto, when the poets stand beside the precipice, the roaring water is "loud enough to deafen us in seconds" (105).

9. *from our perverted city:* Florence. The three shades in question are all Florentines.

20–45

Dante now comes upon a group of warrior-sodomites, and the language and imagery, though changed, still reflects the sin. Jacopo Rusticucci uses bold, masculine language (in contrast to the delicate and rather precious diction of Brunetto Latini in the previous canto) to question Dante and to identify himself and his companions (28–45). But the dance-like image of the turning wheel formed by the three shades is perfectly suited to describe these sinners (24–27).

37–39. *he was the grandson of the good Gualdrada:* The good Gualdrada was the daughter of Bellincione Berti of Florence. According to a story well known in medieval Italy, she was married to Guido Guerra IV at the suggestion of the Emperor Otto IV, who had been impressed with her great beauty, wit, and modesty. The legend is discredited by the fact that she married Guido Guerra IV in 1180, twenty years before Otto IV became Emperor. Her grandson was the Guido Guerra (1220–1272) mentioned here. This Guido was a Guelph leader in several battles, hence his nickname (*guerra*—'war'). His wisdom (*counsel,* 39) is exemplified by his advice to the Florentine Guelphs not to undertake the campaign against Siena in 1260; they ignored his words, and that battle destroyed the Guelph party in Florence.

41–42. *Tegghiaio Aldobrandi:* He, like Guido Guerra, was a leader of the Guelph party in Florence (d. before 1266). He, too, tried to dissuade the Guelphs from attacking the Sienese in 1260; in fact, he was the spokesman for the group of Guelph soldiers headed by Guido Guerra. The fact that his advice was disregarded probably accounts for Dante's saying that "the world would have done well to listen to" his voice.

44–45. *Jacopo Rusticucci:* Little is known of this spokesman for the three Sodomites. He is occasionally mentioned in Florentine records between 1235 and 1266 and was probably a rich merchant. The early Dante commentary of the "Anonimo Fiorentino" relates that he "was a man of the people, of lowly origin, a knight, a valorous and pleasing man." The source also states that his argumentative wife was sent home to her parents.

48. *and I think my guide would have allowed me to:* In essence Virgil gave his consent in lines 16–18.

52–54. *Repulsion, no, but grief:* It is worth noting that Dante once again feels grief (a step removed from pity) for those sinners, presumably because they were Florentines whose ". . . accomplishments I have always heard / rehearsed, and have rehearsed, myself, with fondness" (59–60). They recall the flourishing times of Florence, and Dante is grieved over their suffering.

63. *but first I must go down to the very center:* The "center" is the center of the earth and, consequently, the lowest part of Hell (Cocytus).

70–72. *Guglielmo Borsiere:* Little is known of him except that he must have died about 1300, as is evident from lines 70–71. Boccaccio says that he was a knight of the Court, a matchmaker, and a peacemaker.

73–75. A new breed of people with their sudden wealth: Dante attributes the ills of Florence to the infiltration by the rural population of the established Florentine gentry. His rhetorical condemnation of Florence here may be linked with his picture of Profligates (Lano and Giacomo da Sant'Andrea), with the words of the anonymous suicide in Canto XIII, with the symbolism of the Old Man of Crete in Canto XIV, and with Brunetto Latini's prophecy in Canto XV. All suggest the decay of the city and loss of its golden age through violent squandering—personally and socially—of the gifts of God: the perversion of the shades in Circle VII reflects the "perverted city" (9) from which Dante comes.

85. do not fail to speak of us to living men: Many of the infernal shades are concerned with their memory on earth through which they continue to "live." Cf. Ciacco's last words to the Pilgrim (VI, 88–89).

94–101. As that river on the Apennines' left slope: Dante compares the descent of the tributary of the Phlegethon River in Hell with the plummeting fall of the Montone River near the San Benedetto dell'Alpe monastery. Evidently, in Dante's time the river was called the Acquacheta as far as Forlì, where it became the Montone. Today the entire river is known as the Montone.

102. where at least a thousand vassals could be housed: According to Boccaccio one of the Conti Guidi, who ruled over this region, had planned to construct, near the waterfall, lodgings for a large number of his vassals; he died, however, before his plan could be put into effect.

If this sudden allusion to something so irrelevant, dropped, in passing, at the end of a long description of the course of a river, should seem puzzling—the reader need only remember the reference in Canto XIV (79–81) to the stream issuing from the Bulicame, whose waters, we are told, were shared by prostitutes.

106–108. I wore a cord that fastened round my waist: There are many interpretations for the cord which Virgil takes from the Pilgrim and throws over the edge of the steep. Some have seen in this passage evidence that Dante the Poet became a Franciscan friar, the cord being a sign of that order. However that may be, I feel that the cord here has a purely symbolic meaning. It represents self-confidence; for with that cord, he tells us here, he had once thought he could catch the Leopard (whom we met in Canto I). Thus he would be deliberately confessing here the weakness of foolish self-confidence. It is at the command of his guide, Reason, that he frees himself of the cord, to rely on him fully in the coming encounter with Fraud. Fraud, personified by the monster Geryon, is naturally attracted by this symbol of confidence and comes swimming to the top; but against Reason, Fraud cannot prevail. The Pilgrim will now go without a cord until Cato in Purgatory instructs him to gird himself with a reed in order to be able to ascend the Mount of Purgatory (*Purg.* I); the reed symbolizes humility, the opposite of self-confidence, and another step forward in the growth of the Pilgrim.

The mention of the Leopard (108) at the moment when the Pilgrim is about to enter into a new division (the third and final one) of Hell is to me clear evidence that of the three great beasts belonging to the "nowhere" landscape of Canto I, it is the Leopard that reigns over this last division, where Fraud is punished (some commentators believe that the Leopard reigns over the circles of the Incontinent).

CANTO XVII

"And now, behold the beast with pointed tail
    that passes mountains, annulling walls and weapons,
    behold the one that makes the whole world stink!"   *3*

These were the words I heard my master say
    as he signaled for the beast to come ashore,
    up close to where the rocky levee ends.   *6*

And that repulsive spectacle of fraud
    floated close, maneuvering head and chest
    on to the shore, but his tail he let hang free.   *9*

His face was the face of any honest man,
    it shone with such a look of benediction;
    and all the rest of him was serpentine;   *12*

his two clawed paws were hairy to the armpits,
    his back and all his belly and both flanks
    were painted arabesques and curlicues: *15*

the Turks and Tartars never made a fabric
    with richer colors intricately woven,
    nor were such complex webs spun by Arachne.   *18*

As sometimes fishing boats are seen ashore,
    part fixed in sand and part still in the water;
    and as the beaver, living in the land   *21*

of drunken Germans, squats to catch his prey,
    just so that beast, the worst of beasts, hung waiting
    on the bank that bounds the stretch of sand in stone.   *24*

In the void beyond he exercises his tail,
    twitching and twisting-up the venomed fork
    that armed its tip just like a scorpion's stinger.   *27*

My leader said: "Now we must turn aside
   a little from our path, in the direction
   of that malignant beast that lies in wait."   30

Then we stepped off our path down to the right
   and moved ten paces straight across the brink
   to keep the sand and flames at a safe distance.   33

And when we stood by Geryon's side, I noticed,
   a little farther on, some people crouched
   in the sand quite close to the edge of emptiness.   36

Just then my master spoke: "So you may have
   a knowledge of this round that is complete,"
   he said, "go and see their torment for yourself.   39

But let your conversation there be brief;
   while you are gone I shall speak to this one
   and ask him for the loan of his strong back."   42

So I continued walking, all alone,
   along the seventh circle's outer edge
   to where the group of sufferers were sitting.   45

The pain was bursting from their eyes; their hands
   went scurrying up and down to give protection
   here from the flames, there from the burning sands.   48

They were, in fact, like a dog in summertime
   busy, now with his paw, now with his snout,
   tormented by the fleas and flies that bite him.   51

I carefully examined several faces
   among this group caught in the raining flames
   and did not know a soul, but I observed   54

that around each sinner's neck a pouch was hung
   each of a different color, with a coat of arms,
   and fixed on these they seemed to feast their eyes.   57

And while I looked about among the crowd,
   I saw something in blue on a yellow purse
   that had the face and bearing of a lion;   60

and while my eyes continued their inspection
   I saw another purse as red as blood
   exhibiting a goose more white than butter.   63

And one who had a blue sow, pregnant-looking,
   stamped on the whiteness of his moneybag
   asked me: "What are you doing in this pit?   66

Get out of here! And since you're still alive,
   I'll tell you that my neighbor Vitaliano
   will come to take his seat on my left side.   69

Among these Florentines I sit, one Paduan:
   time after time they fill my ears with blasts
   of shouting: 'Send us down the sovereign knight   72

who will come bearing three goats on his pouch.'"
   As final comment he stuck out his tongue—
   as far out as an ox licking its nose.   75

And I, afraid my staying there much longer
   might anger the one who warned me to be brief,
   turned my back on these frustrated sinners.   78

I found my guide already sitting high
   upon the back of that fierce animal;
   he said: "And now, take courage and be strong.   81

From now on we descend by stairs like these.
   Get on up front. I want to ride behind,
   to be between you and the dangerous tail."   84

A man who feels the shivers of a fever
   coming on, his nails already dead of color,
   will tremble at the mere sight of cool shade;   87

I was that man when I had heard his words.
   But then I felt those stabs of shame that make
   a servant brave before his valorous master.   90

As I squirmed around on those enormous shoulders,
   I wanted to cry out, "Hold on to me,"
   but I had no voice to second my desire.   93

Then he who once before had helped me out
   when I was threatened, put his arms around me
   as soon as I was settled, and held me tight;   96

and then he cried: "Now Geryon, start moving,
   descend with gentle motion, circling wide:
   remember you are carrying living weight."   99

Just as a boat slips back away from shore,
  back slowly, more and more, he left that pier;
  and when he felt himself all clear in space,   *102*

to where his breast had been he swung his tail
  and stretched it undulating like an eel,
  as with his paws he gathered in the air.   *105*

I doubt if Phaëthon feared more—that time
  he dropped the sun-reins of his father's chariot
  and burned the streak of sky we see today—   *108*

or if poor Icarus did—feeling his sides
  unfeathering as the wax began to melt,
  his father shouting: "Wrong, your course is wrong"—   *111*

than I had when I felt myself in air
  and saw on every side nothing but air;
  only the beast I sat upon was there.   *114*

He moves along slowly, and swimming slowly,
  descends a spiral path—but I know this
  only from a breeze ahead and one below;   *117*

I hear now on my right the whirlpool roar
  with hideous sound beneath us on the ground;
  at this I stretch my neck to look below,   *120*

but leaning out soon made me more afraid,
  for I heard moaning there and saw the flames;
  trembling I cowered back, tightening my legs,   *123*

and I saw then what I had not before:
  the spiral path of our descent to torments
  closing in on us, it seemed, from every side.   *126*

As the falcon on the wing for many hours,
  having found no prey, and having seen no signal
  (so that his falconer sighs: "Oh, he falls already"),   *129*

descends, worn out, circling a hundred times
  (instead of swooping down), settling at some distance
  from his master, perched in anger and disdain,   *132*

so Geryon brought us down to the bottom
  at the foot of the jagged cliff, almost against it,
  and once he got our bodies off his back,   *135*

he shot off like a shaft shot from a bowstring.

1–27

In classical mythology Geryon was a three-bodied giant who ruled Spain, and was slain by Hercules in the course of his Twelve Labors. Here in the *Inferno* he is the personification of Fraud, whose face ("the face of any honest man," 10) deceives his victim long enough for his poisoned tail ("like a scorpion's stinger," 27) to strike. The triune nature of Geryon, as Dante presents him here, is an adaptation and modification of passages from the Bible (Revelation 9:7–11) and from Pliny (*Historia naturalis* VIII, 30). Because of his three-fold nature Geryon assumes a place alongside other Dantean monsters which are perversions of the Trinity.

We should note that, by answering Virgil's signal, Geryon himself has been deceived: the symbol of Fraud has been defrauded.

16–17. *the Turks and tartars never made a fabric:* The Tartars and the Turks were often considered the best weavers of the Middle Ages. Their highly colored and ornate fabrics were very fashionable and much in demand.

18. *nor were such complex webs spun by Arachne:* Arachne, a legendary Lydian maiden, was so skilled in the art of weaving that she challenged the goddess Minerva to a contest. Minerva, furious because her opponent's cloth was perfect, tore it to shreds; Arachne hanged herself, but Minerva loosened the rope, turning it into a web and Arachne into a spider.

21–22. *and as the beaver:* According to medieval bestiaries the beaver, squatting on the ground at the edge of the water, catches fish with its tail hanging in the water. Geryon assumes a similar pose.

31. *down to the right:* See IX, n. 132.

35–36. *some people crouched:* The Usurers, described in Canto XI as those who scorn "Nature in herself and in her pupil / Art" (110–111), are the last group in the third round of the Seventh Circle. Having introduced Geryon, Dante the Poet then brings in these sinners who, crouching very close to the edge of the abyss, serve as the artistic and spatial connection between the sins of Violence and those of Fraud. Similarly Geryon, who at this moment rests partly in Circle Seven and partly (his tail, 25) in Circle Eight, links the two sins. Earlier Dante effected the transition from Incontinence to Violence via the sin of Anger (crossing the river of the Wrathful); here he accomplishes the transition to Fraud through usury.

48. *here from the flames, there from the burning sands:* Compare the similar construction used to describe the movement of the Sodomites' hands (XIV, 41).

55–56. *that around each sinner's neck a pouch was hung:* The identity (or rather the family connection) of the usurers, who "feast their eyes" (57) on the purses dangling from their necks, is revealed to the Pilgrim by the different coats of arms visible on the pouches. Apparently the usurers are unrecognizable through facial characteristics because their total concern with their material goods has caused them to lose their individuality. The yellow purse with the blue lion (59–60) indicates the Gianfigliazzi family of Florence; the red purse with the "goose more white than butter" (62–63), the Ubriachi family, also of Florence; the one with the "blue sow, pregnant-looking" (64–65), the Scrovegni family of Padua.

68–69. *I'll tell you that my neighbor Vitaliano:* Referred to as "my neighbor" by one of the Scrovegni family, the Vitaliano who will join the company of usurers is undoubtedly from Padua, but beyond this nothing certain is known.

70. *Among these Florentines I sit, one Paduan:* The theme of the decadence and materialism of Florence is continued to the very edge of the circle of Violence.

72–73. *Send us down the sovereign knight:* This is generally considered to be Giovanni Buiamonte, one of the Florentine Becchi family. He took part in public affairs and was honored with the title of "knight" in 1298. His business, money-lending, made his family one of the wealthiest in Florence; however, after going bankrupt he died in abject poverty in 1310.

82. *From now on we descend by stairs like these:* The Pilgrim and Virgil will descend from the Eighth Circle to the Ninth with the help of the giant Antaeus (XXXI, 130–145), and from Cocytus to Purgatory by climbing up Lucifer's legs (XXXIV, 70–87). By the phrase "stairs like these," Virgil is simply alluding to methods of getting from one circle to another, methods as terrifying as their ride on Geryon's back.

106–108. *I doubt if Phaëthon more feared that time:* Phaëthon, son of Apollo, was told by Epaphus that Apollo was not his father. Thereupon the boy begged Apollo to allow him to drive the Chariot of the Sun for one day to prove himself the offspring of the God of the Sun. The request was granted, but Phaëthon, unable to control the Chariot, let loose the reins. The Chariot raced wildly through the heavens, burning the "streak of sky" which today we call the Milky Way, and at one point dipping so close to the Earth that it almost set the planet afire. But Jupiter, hearing the Earth's prayer, killed the youthful charioteer with a thunderbolt and hurled him to his death. The story was familiar to Dante from Ovid's *Metamorphoses* II, 1–324.

109–111. *or if poor Icarus did—feeling his sides:* Daedalus, father of Icarus, in order to escape from Crete, fashioned wings for himself and his son. Because the feathers were fastened with wax, Daedalus warned his son not to fly too close to the sun. But Icarus, ignoring his father's words, flew too high, and when the sun had melted the wax, he plunged to his death in the Aegean Sea.

The stories of Phaëthon and Icarus were often used in the Middle Ages as examples of pride, thus giving more support to the theory that Pride and Envy underlie the sins punished in Lower Hell. See Canto XXXI, n. 19–127.

136. *he shot off like a shaft shot from a bowstring:* The metaphor used to describe Geryon's rapid departure (arrow shot from the bow) is the same as that found in the description of Phlegyas' swift approach in Canto VIII (13–15). The wrath of the swiftly moving Phlegyas was clearly indicated by his words; I think we are meant to assume that the mute Geryon was also moved by anger (and had been sulking all the while), because he had been outwitted by Reason. Moreover, in the description of Geryon's descent there are two indications of his hostility: the falcon to whose descending movement his own is compared shows anger and disdain (132) towards his master; and the way in which Geryon lands, bringing the Pilgrim and his guide almost up against the jagged cliff (134), suggests a futile final gesture of sulkiness.

CANTO XVIII

There is a place in Hell called Malebolge
  cut out of stone the color of iron ore,
  just like the circling cliff that walls it in.   3

Right at the center of this evil plain
  there yawns a very wide, deep well, whose structure
  I will talk of when the place itself is reached.   6

That belt of land remaining, then, runs round
  between the well and cliff, and all this space
  is divided into ten descending valleys,   9

just like a ground-plan for successive moats
  that in concentric circles bind their center
  and serve to protect the ramparts of the castle.   12

This was the surface image they presented;
  and as bridges from a castle's portal stretch
  from moat to moat to reach the farthest bank,   15

so, from the great cliff's base, jut spokes of rock
  crossing from bank to bank, intersecting ditches
  until the pit's hub cuts them off from meeting.   18

This is the place in which we found ourselves,
  once shaken from the back of Geryon.
  The poet turned to the left, I walked behind him.   21

There, on our right, I saw new suffering souls,
  new means of torture, and new torturers,
  crammed into the depths of the first ditch.   24

Two files of naked souls walked on the bottom,
  the ones on our side faced us as they passed,
  the others moved as we did but more quickly.   27

The Romans, too, in the year of the Jubilee
  took measures to accommodate the throngs
  that had to come and go across their bridge: 30

they fixed it so on one side all were looking
  at the castle, and were walking to St. Peter's;
  on the other, they were moving toward the mount.   33

On both sides, up along the deadly rock,
  I saw horned devils with enormous whips
  lashing backs of shades with cruel delight.   36

Ah, how they made them skip and lift their heels
  at the very first crack of the whip! Not one of them
  dared pause to take a second or a third!   39

As I walked on my eyes met with the glance
  of one down there; I murmured to myself:
  "I know this face from somewhere, I am sure."   42

And so I stopped to study him more closely;
  my leader also stopped, and was so kind
  as to allow me to retrace my steps;   45

and that whipped soul thought he would hide from me
  by lowering his face—which did no good.
  I said, "O you, there, with your head bent low,   48

if the features of your shade do not deceive me,
  you are Venedico Caccianemico, I'm sure.
  How did you get yourself in such a pickle?"   51

"I'm not so keen on answering," he said,
  "but I feel I must; your plain talk is compelling,
  it makes me think of old times in the world.   54

I was the one who coaxed Ghisolabella
  to serve the lusty wishes of the Marquis,
  no matter how the sordid tale is told;   57

I'm not the only Bolognese who weeps here—
  hardly! This place is packed with us; in fact,
  there are more of us here than there are living tongues,   60

between Savena and Reno, saying 'Sipa';
  I call on your own memory as witness:
  remember we have avaricious hearts."   63

Just at that point a devil let him have
　　the feel of his tailed whip and cried: "Move on,
　　you pimp, you can't cash in on women here!"　　　66

I turned and hurried to rejoin my guide;
　　we walked a few more steps and then we reached
　　the rocky bridge that juts out from the bank.　　　69

We had no difficulty climbing up,
　　and turning right, along the jagged ridge,
　　we left those shades to their eternal circlings.　　　72

When we were where the ditch yawned wide below
　　the ridge, to make a passage for the scourged,
　　my guide said: "Stop and stand where you can see　　　75

these other misbegotten souls whose faces
　　you could not see before, for they were moving
　　in the same direction we were, over there."　　　78

So from the ancient bridge we viewed the train
　　that hurried toward us along the other tract—
　　kept moving, like the first, by stinging whips.　　　81

And the good master, without my asking him,
　　said, "Look at that imposing one approaching,
　　who does not shed a single tear of pain:　　　84

what majesty he still maintains down there!
　　He is Jason, who by courage and sharp wits,
　　fleeced the Colchians of their golden ram.　　　87

He later journeyed through the isle of Lemnos
　　whose bold and heartless females, earlier,
　　had slaughtered every male upon the island;　　　90

there with his words of love, and loving looks,
　　he succeeded in deceiving young Hypsipyle
　　who had in turn deceived the other women.　　　93

He left her there, with child, and all alone:
　　such sin condemns him to such punishment,
　　and Medea, too, gets her revenge on him.　　　96

With him go all deceivers of this type,
　　and let this be enough to know concerning
　　the first valley and the souls locked in its jaws."　　　99

We were already where the narrow ridge
   begins to cross the second bank, to make it
   an abutment for another ditch's arch.   *102*

Now we could hear the shades in the next *bolgia*
   whimpering, making snorting grunting sounds,
   and sounds of blows, slapping with open palms.   *105*

From a steaming stench below, the banks were coated
   with a slimy mould that stuck to them like glue,
   disgusting to behold and worse to smell.   *108*

The bottom was so hollowed out of sight,
   we saw it only when we climbed the arch
   and looked down from the ridge's highest point: *111*

there we were, and from where I stood I saw
   souls in the ditch plunged into excrement
   that might well have been flushed from our latrines;   *114*

my eyes were searching hard along the bottom,
   and I saw somebody's head so smirched with shit
   you could not tell if he were priest or layman.   *117*

He shouted up: "Why do you feast your eyes
   on me more than these other dirty beasts?"
   And I replied: "Because, remembering well,   *120*

I've seen you with your hair dry once or twice.
   You are Alessio Interminei from Lucca,
   that's why I stare at you more than the rest."   *123*

He beat his slimy forehead as he answered:
   "I am stuck down here by all those flatteries
   that rolled unceasing off my tongue up there."   *126*

He finished speaking, and my guide began:
   "Lean out a little more, look hard down there
   so you can get a good look at the face   *129*

of that repulsive and dishevelled tramp
   scratching herself with shitty fingernails,
   spreading her legs while squatting up and down: *132*

it is Thaïs the whore who gave this answer
   to her lover when he asked: 'Am I very worthy
   of your thanks?': 'Very, nay, incredibly so!'   *135*

I think our eyes have had their fill of this."

1–20. There is a place in Hell called Malebolge: This detailed description of the Eighth Circle with its ten ditches (*Malebolge*) may surprise the reader coming as it does before the Pilgrim has as much as landed at the edge of its beginning. Are we supposed to imagine we are hearing the voice of Dante the Poet supplying us with information that the Pilgrim himself could not have known? Surely not: Dante the Poet never intervenes for such practical (and inartistic) considerations. It is the Pilgrim who offers the description of the Eighth Circle, as he has seen it from the air, when descending in a slow gyre on Geryon's back (see XVII, 115–126). The picture presented here can be only an aerial view.

26–27. the ones on our side faced us as they passed: The First *Bolgia* accommodates two classes of sinners, each filing by rapidly, but in separate directions. The Pimps are those walking toward the Pilgrim and his guide; the Seducers go in the same direction with them.

28–33. The Romans, too, in the year of the Jubilee: Dante compares the movement of the sinners in the First *Bolgia* to that of the many pilgrims who, having come to Rome for the Jubilee in 1300, were herded across the bridge, half going toward the Castel Sant'Angelo and St. Peter's and the other half going toward Monte Giordano (the "mount," 33), a small knoll on the opposite side of the Tiber River.

50–57. Venedico Caccianemico: This person (born c. 1228) was head of the Guelphs in Bologna from 1260 to 1297; he was at various times *podestà* (mayor) of Pistoia, Modena, Imola, and Milan. He was accused, among other things, of murdering his cousin, but he is placed in this *bolgia* because, according to popular report, he acted as a procurer, turning his own sister, Ghisolabella, over to the Marquis of Este (either Obizzo II or his son, Azzo VIII) to curry favor.

51. How did you get yourself in such a pickle: Dante is undoubtedly punning on the word *salse* (pickle) which characterizes the torments suffered in this *bolgia* and also is the name of a certain ravine (a *bolgia*, if you will) near Bologna (Venedico's city) into which the bodies of criminals were thrown.

61. saying "Sipa": Venedico reveals that he is not the only Bolognese punished in this *bolgia* and further states that there are more pimps here from that city than there are present-day inhabitants of the region between the Savena and Reno Rivers (i.e. Bolognese, indicated by the word *sipa*, dialect for *sì*, 'yes.' Cf. XXXIII, 80, and note).

86–96. He is Jason, who by courage and sharp wits: Jason, leader of the Argonauts, when a child, had been deprived of the throne of Iolcus by his half-brother Pelias. When Jason grew up, Pelias promised him the kingdom if he could secure the golden fleece of King Aeëtes of Colchis. Jason agreed to make the attempt, and on the way to Colchis stopped at Lemnos, where he seduced and abandoned Hypsipyle (92), the daughter of the King of Lemnos. At Colchis King Aeëtes agreed to give Jason the fleece if he would yoke two fire-breathing oxen to a plow and sow the teeth of the dragon that guarded the fleece. Medea (96), who was a sorceress and the daughter of the King, fell in love with Jason and with magic helped him fulfill her father's conditions and obtain the fleece. The two returned to Greece where Jason married her, but later he fell in love with Creusa, daughter of Creon, King of Corinth, and deserted Medea to marry her. Medea, mad with rage, killed Creusa by sending her a poisoned coat as a wedding gift, and then murdered her own children; Jason himself died of grief.

Hypsipyle "deceived the other women" (93) of Lemnos by swearing that she had slain her father Thoas, the King, when the Lemnian women massacred all the males on that island. Instead she hid him, saving his life.

104–105. whimpering, making snorting grunting sounds: The sinners found in the excrement of the Second *Bolgia* are the Flatterers. Note the "teeming" nature of the language, different from that of the First *Bolgia,* a change indicative of the nature of the sin of flattery and its punishment.

122. *You are Alessio Interminei from Lucca:* The Interminei family was prominent in the White Party at Lucca. But of Alessio almost nothing is known save that his name is recorded in several documents of the second half of the thirteenth century, the last in 1295, when apparently he was still alive.

135. *Very, nay, incredibly so!:* This Thaïs is not the historical person by the same name (the most famous courtesan of all time) but a character in Terence's *Eunuchus.* Dante was probably unfamiliar with the play, but he knew of this Thaïs from Cicero's *De amicitia,* where her reply to her lover is presented as an example of the exaggeration used by flatterers. In the play a lover sends Thaïs a slave, and later sends a servant to inquire if he is worthy of her thanks. Dante attributes the exaggerated reply, "Very, nay, incredibly so!" to Thaïs, although in the play it is the servant Gnatho who thus exaggerates her response.

CANTO XIX

O Simon Magus! O scum that followed him!
   Those things of God that rightly should be wed
   to holiness, you, rapacious creatures,   *3*

for the price of gold and silver, prostitute.
   Now, in your honor, I must sound my trumpet
   here in the third *bolgia* where you are packed.   *6*

We had already climbed to see this tomb,
   and were standing high above it on the bridge,
   exactly at the mid-point of the ditch.   *9*

O Highest Wisdom, how you demonstrate
   your art in Heaven, on earth, and here in Hell!
   How justly does your power make awards!   *12*

I saw along the sides and on the bottom
   the livid-colored rock all full of holes;
   all were the same in size, and each was round.   *15*

To me they seemed no wider and no deeper
   than those inside my lovely San Giovanni,
   made for priests to stand in or baptize from;   *18*

and one of these, not many years ago,
   I smashed for someone who was drowning in it:
   let this be mankind's picture of the truth!   *21*

From the mouth of every hole were sticking out
   a single sinner's feet, and then the legs
   up to the calf—the rest was stuffed inside.   *24*

The soles of every sinner's feet were flaming;
   their naked legs were twitching frenziedly—
   they would have broken any chain or rope.   *27*

Just as a flame will only move along
  an object's oily outer peel, so here
  the fire slid from heel to toe and back.   30

"Who is that one, Master, that angry wretch,
  who is writhing more than any of his comrades,"
  I asked, "the one licked by a redder flame?"   33

And he to me, "If you want to be carried down
  along that lower bank to where he is,
  you can ask him who he is and why he's here."   36

And I, "My pleasure is what pleases you:
  you are my lord, you know that from your will
  I would not swerve. You even know my thoughts."   39

When we reached the fourth bank, we began to turn
  and, keeping to the left, made our way down
  to the bottom of the holed and narrow ditch.   42

The good guide did not drop me from his side
  until he brought me to the broken rock
  of that one who was fretting with his shanks.   45

"O whatever you are, holding your upside down,
  wretched soul, stuck in the ground like a stake,
  make some sound," I said, "that is, if you can."   48

I stood there like a priest hearing confession
  from a vile assassin who, once fixed in his ditch,
  calls him back again to put off dying.   51

He cried: "Is that *you*, here, already, upright?
  Is that you here already upright, Boniface?
  By many years the book has lied to me!   54

Are you fed up so soon with all that wealth
  for which you did not fear to take by guile
  the beautiful lady, then tear her asunder?"   57

I stood there like a person just made fun of,
  dumbfounded by a question for an answer,
  not knowing how to answer the reply.   60

Then Virgil said: "Quick, hurry up and tell him:
  'I'm not the one, I'm not the one you think!' "
  And I answered just the way he told me to.   63

The spirit heard, and twisted both his feet,
  then, sighing with a grieving, tearful voice
  he said: "Well then, what do you want of me?   66

If it concerns you so to learn my name
  that for this reason you came down the bank,
  know that I once was dressed in the great mantle.   69

But actually I was the she-bear's son,
  so greedy to advance my cubs, that wealth
  I pocketed in life, and here, myself.   72

Beneath my head are pushed down all the others
  who came, sinning in simony, before me,
  squeezed tightly in the fissures of the rock.   75

I, in my turn, shall join the rest below
  as soon as *he* comes, the one I thought you were
  when, all too quick, I put my question to you.   78

But already my feet have baked a longer time
  (and I have been stuck upside-down like this)
  than he will stay here planted with feet aflame: 81

soon after him shall come one from the West,
  a lawless shepherd, one whose fouler deeds
  make him a fitting cover for us both.   84

He shall be another Jason, like the one
  in Maccabees: just as his king was pliant,
  so France's king shall soften to this priest."   87

I do not know, perhaps I was too bold here,
  but I answered him in tune with his own words:
  "Well tell me now: what was the sum of money   90

that holy Peter had to pay our Lord
  before He gave the keys into his keeping?
  Certainly He asked no more than 'Follow me.'   93

Nor did Peter or the rest extort gold coins
  or silver from Matthias when he was picked
  to fill the place the evil one had lost.   96

So stay stuck there, for you are rightly punished,
  and guard with care the money wrongly gained
  that made you stand courageous against Charles.   99

And were it not for the reverence I have
   for those highest of all keys that you once held
   in the happy life—if this did not restrain me, 102

I would use even harsher words than these,
   for your avarice brings grief upon the world,
   crushing the good, exalting the depraved. 105

You shepherds it was the Evangelist had in mind
   when the vision came to him of her who sits
   upon the waters playing whore with kings: 108

that one who with the seven heads was born
   and from her ten horns managed to draw strength
   so long as virtue was her bridegroom's joy. 111

You have built yourselves a God of gold and silver!
   How do you differ from the idolator,
   except he worships one, you worship hundreds? 114

Oh, Constantine, what evil did you sire,
   not by your conversion, but by the dower
   that the first wealthy Father got from you!" 117

And while I sang these very notes to him,
   his big flat feet kicked fiercely out of anger,
   —or perhaps it was his conscience gnawing him. 120

I think my master liked what I was saying,
   for all the while he smiled and was intent
   on hearing the ring of truly spoken words. 123

Then he took hold of me with both his arms,
   and when he had me firm against his breast,
   he climbed back up the path he had come down. 126

He did not tire of the weight clasped tight to him,
   but brought me to the top of the bridge's arch,
   the one that joins the fourth bank to the fifth. 129

And here he gently set his burden down—
   gently, for the ridge, so steep and rugged,
   would have been hard even for goats to cross. 132

From here another valley opened up.

NOTES

1–6

As related in Acts (8:9–24), Simon the magician, having observed the descent of the Holy Spirit upon the Apostles John and Peter, desired to purchase this power for himself. Whereupon Peter harshly admonished him for even thinking that the gift of God might be bought. Derived from this sorcerer's name, the word "simony" refers to those offences involving the sale or fraudulent possession of ecclesiastical offices.

Note the dramatic effect achieved by the opening six-line invective following immediately upon the quiet words of Virgil with which Canto XVIII closed, and followed immediately by the calm tone of the narrative, with which we might have expected the canto to open. The emotional force of this apostrophe (the words certainly are those of Dante the Poet, for the Pilgrim could neither have known what sin is being punished in the Third *Bolgia*, to which he has not as yet been formally introduced, nor could he have consciously thought in terms of the originator of the sin) has no equal in the *Inferno;* the initial position of the outburst in the canto shocks the reader and prepares him to read with greater awareness, while its passion is intended to arouse his hatred for the sin a priori.

4. *for the price of gold and silver, prostitute:* In spite of the fact that the opening invective seems to make a clear break between this canto and the previous one, the connection is aesthetically achieved through the image of prostitution. Thus the final figure of Canto XVIII, Thaïs the whore, provides the link to the Simonists who prostitute "those things of God . . . for the price of gold and silver" (2–4). Other echoes of this image are found in this canto: see 56–57, 108.

5–6. *Now, in your honor, I must sound my trumpet:* Dante in announcing the nature of the sin being punished in the Third *Bolgia* is comparing himself to the medieval town-crier whose announcements were preceded by a blast from his trumpet.

10–12. *O Highest Wisdom, how you demonstrate:* Again Dante the Poet interrupts his narrative, this time to praise the workings of Divine Justice (as yet unobserved in this canto!). The rapid succession of the interruptive apostrophes enhances the effectiveness of Dante's moral indignation at the sin of Simony.

21. *let this be mankind's picture of the truth:* Most commentators interpret these lines as an attempt on Dante's part to exonerate himself from the charge of sacrilege which technically could have been leveled at him in consequence of this (obviously humanitarian) act. But surely the interpolation of such a highly personal element, completely irrelevant to the aesthetic structure of the canto, was not Dante's intention. Rather, he considered the breakage of a baptismal implement as a symbol of the practice of Simony, though the former was done out of love and the latter out of lust for material gain. Dante, then, by incorporating this simile hoped to reveal to his reader the true nature of Simony: an act that results in the destruction of Christ's Church, symbolized by the Font.

25. *The soles of every sinner's feet were flaming:* Just as the Simonists' perversion of the Church is symbolized by their "perverted" immersion in holes resembling baptismal fonts, so their "baptism" is perverted: instead of the head being moistened with water, the feet are "baptized" with oil and fire.

45. *of that one who was fretting with his shanks:* Note the pejorative word shanks (*zanche*) applied to the conspicuous legs of Nicholas. The only other appearance of this word in the *Divine Comedy* is in Canto XXXIV, 79 of the *Inferno* where it is used to refer to the legs of Lucifer.

48. *"make some sound," I said, "that is, if you can":* Confronted with the grotesque spectacle of two gesticulating legs, Dante the Pilgrim addresses them in a

manner that certainly reveals his confused, uncertain state of mind. His invocation, "O whatever you are," reveals his doubts concerning the "human" nature of the soul. The closing imperative, "make some sound . . . if you can," suggests his belief that the object in front of him may not be able even to do that.

53. *Is that you here already upright, Boniface?:* From the foreknowledge granted to the infernal shades, the speaker knows that Pope Boniface VIII, upon his death in 1303, will take his place in that very receptacle wherein he himself is now being tormented. The Pilgrim's voice, so close at hand, has caused the sinner to believe that his successor has arrived unexpectedly before his time (three years, in fact) and, consequently, that the Divine Plan of Events, the Book of Fate (54), has lied to him.

Having obtained the abdication of Pope Celestine V, Boniface gained the support of Charles II of Naples and thus was assured of his election to the Papacy (1294). In addition to misusing the Church's influence in his dealings with Charles, Boniface VIII freely distributed ecclesiastical offices among his family and confidants. As early as 1300 he was plotting the destruction of the Whites, the Florentine political faction to which Dante belonged (cf. VI, 67–69). Thus, he was ultimately responsible for the Poet's exile in 1302, which is mentioned in a "prophetic" passage in the *Paradise,* XVII, 49–51.

57. *the beautiful lady:* The Church.

67–72. *If it concerns you so to learn my name:* Gian Gaetano degli Orsini (lit. "of the little bears," hence the designation "she-bear's son," and the reference to "my cubs") became Pope Nicholas III in 1277. As a Cardinal he won renown for his integrity; however, in the short three years between ascent to the Papal throne and his death he became notorious for his simoniacal practices. He furthered his dynastic aspirations by the ecclesiastical advancement of many relatives, the acquisition of lands, the channeling of public power into the hands of his kinsmen, and the arrangement of political marriages with other ruling families of Europe.

The famous pun in line 72 signifies Nicholas' *contrapasso:* as he "pocketed" wealth in life, in Hell he himself is in a "pocket."

74. *sinning in simony:* The Italian verb, *simoneggiare* (here used in the gerund by Nicholas III—'sinning in simony'), was invented by Dante, doubtless to anticipate the parallel form *puttaneggiando* ('playing whore'), 108, employed by the Pilgrim.

77. *as soon as* he *comes, the one I thought you were:* Boniface VIII. See above, n. 53.

82–84. *soon after him shall come one from the West:* Pope Clement V of Gascony, upon his death in 1314, will join Nicholas and Boniface in eternal torment. In exchange for his election to the Papacy, Clement promised to engage in numerous secret intrigues with Philip the Fair, King of France. In Philip's hands he was no more than a puppet, constrained by his pledges to carry out the King's devious plans, among them the suppression and plunder of the Templars. During Clement's rule the Holy See was transferred from Rome to Avignon.

85–87. *He shall be another Jason, like the one:* Having obtained the high priesthood of the Jews by bribing King Antiochus of Syria, Jason neglected the sacrifices and sanctuary of the Temple and introduced Greek modes of life into his community. As Jason had fraudulently acquired his position, so had Menelaus, who offered more money to the king, supplanted Jason (2 Maccabees 4:7–27). As Jason obtained his office from King Antiochus fraudulently, so shall Clement acquire his from Philip.

94–96. *Nor did Peter or the rest extort gold coins:* After the treachery and subsequent expulsion of Judas, the Apostles cast lots in order to replenish their number. Thus, by the will of God, not through monetary payment, was Matthias elected to the vacated post (Acts 1:15–26).

98–99. *and guard with care the money wrongly gained:* The thirteenth-century Florentine chronicler, Giovanni Villani, alludes to a plot against Charles d'Anjou, King of Naples and Sicily, promoted by Nicholas III and supported by the "money wrongly gained" of Michael Palaeologus, Emperor of Greece. The Pope transferred his aid and influence to Giovanni da Procida in Sicily, who, it is supposed, was a motive force behind the Sicilian Vespers, a bloody insurrection in which the Sicilian people liberated themselves from French domination.

106–111. *You shepherds it was the Evangelist had in mind:* St. John the Evangelist relates his vision of the dissolute Imperial City of Rome. To Dante, she "who sits / upon the waters" represents the Church which has been corrupted by the simoniacal activities of many Popes (the "shepherds" of the Church). The seven heads symbolize the seven Holy Sacraments; the ten horns represent the Ten Commandments.

115–117. *Oh, Constantine, what evil did you sire:* Constantine the Great, Emperor of Rome (306–337), was converted to Christianity in the year 312. Having conquered the eastern Mediterranean lands, he transferred the capital of the Roman Empire to Constantinople (330). This move, according to tradition, stemmed from Constantine's decision to place the western part of the Empire under the jurisdiction of the Church in order to repay Pope Sylvester ("the first wealthy Father") for healing him of leprosy. The so called "Donation of Constantine," though it was proved in the fifteenth century to be a complete fabrication on the part of the clergy, was universally accepted as the truth in the Middle Ages. Dante the Pilgrim reflects this tradition in his sad apostrophe to the individual who first would have introduced wealth to the Church and who, unknowingly, would be ultimately responsible for its present corruption. Cf. *De Monarchia* III, 10.

The entire *Divine Comedy* is, of course, the story of the Pilgrim's learning process and spiritual development, and here in *Inferno* XIX Dante has chosen to present us with a picture of that process in miniature. Virgil tells the Pilgrim that he will carry him to the bottom of the *bolgia* so that he can learn for himself about the sinner who has stirred his curiosity (36). And the Pilgrim does learn; Nicholas becomes his teacher, describing his sin and his punishment and announcing the next two Popes who will come after him to push him deeper into his hole. The Pilgrim also learns from the lofty tone of Nicholas' discourse, and responds, for the first time in the *Inferno*, with a full-fledged rhetorical "speech":

> I do not know, perhaps I was too bold here,
> but I answered him in tune with his own words. . . .
> (88–89)

The last part of the "speech," moreover, is aimed not just at Nicholas, but at all the Simonists in this *bolgia*, a fact signified by the change in the Italian text from the singular pronoun *tu*, used when Dante is speaking only to Nicholas, to the plural pronoun *voi* from line 104 on. Dante has not only learned the nature of the sin of Simony, but he recognizes that the sin is more important than is an individual sinner like Nicholas. And just as Dante the Poet had opened the canto with an auctorial apostrophe-invective against Simon Magus, so Dante the Pilgrim, having reached the Poet's state of knowledge, ends the segment dealing with the Simonists with an apostrophe-invective against Constantine. Thus the Pilgrim's learning process is aesthetically "imitated" in his speech—beginning with his speechlessness.

Virgil is quite pleased by the Pilgrim's accomplishments and he takes him "with both his arms, / and when he had [him] firm against his breast, / he climbed back up the path he had come down" (124–126). When Virgil carried his ward down into the *bolgia*, he clasped him to his side (43), but now he carries him up against his breast, showing his pleasure, and bringing the circle of movement to a close.

That Dante the Poet set great importance on his Pilgrim's learning thoroughly the base nature of Simony is evident not only from the didactic invectives within the canto, but also from the way the picture of the Simonists in their holes is recalled in the final canto of the *Inferno* (XXXIV, 79): after the two travellers have completed their journey along a portion of Lucifer's huge body, during which they have passed the midpoint of the earth, Dante pauses and looks up to see the raised legs of Lucifer protruding from the crevice in which he is frozen, like a magnification of the legs of Nicholas. Just as Nicholas defrauded God's Church, so Lucifer tried to defraud God himself.

CANTO XX

Now I must turn strange torments into verse
   to form the matter of the twentieth canto
   of the first chant, the one about the damned.   *3*

Already I was where I could look down
   into the depths of the ditch: I saw its floor
   was wet with anguished tears shed by the sinners,   *6*

and I saw people in the valley's circle,
   silent, weeping, walking at a litany pace
   the way processions push along in our world.   *9*

And when my gaze moved down below their faces,
   I saw all were incredibly distorted,
   the chin was not above the chest, the neck   *12*

was twisted—their faces looked down on their backs;
   they had to move ahead by moving backwards,
   for they never saw what was ahead of them.   *15*

Perhaps there was a case of someone once
   in a palsy fit becoming so distorted,
   but none that *I* know of! I doubt there could be!   *18*

So may God grant you, Reader, benefit
   from reading of my poem, just ask yourself
   how I could keep my eyes dry when, close by,   *21*

I saw the image of our human form
   so twisted—the tears their eyes were shedding
   streamed down to wet their buttocks at the cleft.   *24*

Indeed I did weep, as I leaned my body
   against a jut of rugged rock. My guide:
   "So you are still like all the other fools?   *27*

In this place piety lives when pity is dead,
    for who could be more wicked than that man
    who tries to bend divine will to his own!   *30*

Lift your head up, lift it, see him for whom
    the earth split wide before the Thebans' eyes,
    while they all shouted, 'Where are you rushing off to,   *33*

Amphiaraus? Why do you quit the war?'
    He kept on rushing downwards through the gap
    until Minòs, who gets them all, got him.   *36*

You see how he has made his back his chest:
    because he wished to see too far ahead,
    he sees behind and walks a backward track.   *39*

Behold Tiresias who changed his looks:
    from a man he turned himself into a woman,
    transforming all his body, part for part;   *42*

then later on he had to take the wand
    and strike once more those two snakes making love
    before he could get back his virile parts.   *45*

Backing up to this one's chest comes Aruns
    who, in the hills of Luni, worked by peasants
    of Carrara dwelling in the valley's plain,   *48*

lived in white marble cut into a cave,
    and from this site where nothing blocked his view
    he could observe the sea and stars with ease.   *51*

And that one, with her hair loose, flowing back
    to cover both her breasts you cannot see,
    and with her hairy parts in front behind her,   *54*

was Manto who had searched through many lands
    before she came to dwell where I was born;
    now let me tell you something of her story.   *57*

When her father had departed from the living,
    and Bacchus' sacred city fell enslaved,
    she wandered through the world for many years.   *60*

High in fair Italy there spreads a lake,
    beneath the mountains bounding Germany
    beyond the Tyrol, known as Lake Benaco;   *63*

by a thousand streams and more, I think, the Alps
    are bathed from Garda to the Val Camonica
    with the waters flowing down into that lake;   *66*

at its center is a place where all three bishops
    of Trent and Brescia and Verona could,
    if they would ever visit there, say Mass;   *69*

Peschiera sits, a handsome well-built fortress,
    to ward off Brescians and the Bergamese,
    along the lowest point of that lake's shore   *72*

where all the water that Benaco's basin
    cannot hold must overflow to make a stream
    that winds its way through countrysides of green;   *75*

but when the water starts to flow, its name
    is not Benaco but Mencio, all the way
    to Governol where it falls into the Po;   *78*

but before its course is run it strikes a lowland
    on which it spreads and turns into a marsh
    that can become unbearable in summer.   *81*

Passing this place one day the savage virgin
    saw land that lay in the center of the mire,
    untilled and empty of inhabitants.   *84*

There, to escape all human intercourse,
    she stopped to practice magic with her servants;
    there she lived, and there she left her corpse.   *87*

Later on, the men who lived around there gathered
    on that very spot, for it was well-protected
    by the bog that girded it on every side.   *90*

They built a city over her dead bones,
    and for her, the first to choose that place, they named it
    Mantua, without recourse to sorcery.   *93*

Once, there were far more people living there,
    before the foolish Casalodi listened
    to the fraudulent advice of Pinamonte.   *96*

And so, I warn you, should you ever hear
    my city's origin told otherwise,
    let no false tales adulterate the truth."   *99*

And I replied: "Master, your explanations
　　are truth for me, winning my faith entirely;
　　any others would be just like burned-out coals.　　　　　*102*

But speak to me of these shades passing by,
　　if you see anyone that is worth noting;
　　for now my mind is set on only that."　　　　　*105*

He said: "That one whose beard flows from his cheeks
　　and settles on his back and makes it dark,
　　was (when the war stripped Greece of all its males　　　　　*108*

so that the few there were still rocked in cradles)
　　an augur who, with Calchas, called the moment
　　to cut the first ship's cable free at Aulis:　　　　　*111*

he is Eurypylus. I sang his story
　　this way, somewhere in my high tragedy:
　　you should know where—you know it, every line.　　　　　*114*

That other one whose thighs are scarcely fleshed
　　was Michael Scot, who most assuredly
　　knew every trick of magic fraudulence.　　　　　*117*

See there Guido Bonatti; see Asdente,
　　who wishes now he had been more devoted
　　to making shoes—too late now for repentance.　　　　　*120*

And see those wretched hags who traded in
　　needle, spindle, shuttle, for fortune-telling,
　　and cast their spells with image-dolls and potions.　　　　　*123*

Now come along. Cain with his thorn-bush straddles
　　the confines of both hemispheres already
　　and dips into the waves below Seville;　　　　　*126*

and the moon last night already was at full;
　　and you should well remember that at times
　　when you were lost in the dark wood she helped you."　　　　　*129*

And we were moving all the time he spoke.

NOTES

　　1–3. *Now I must turn strange torments into verse:* This canto has the most prosaic
opening of all those in the *Inferno.* And the second part (61–99) contains the pro-

saic description of the founding of Mantua. Perhaps this undramatic canto is meant to serve as a rest for the reader from the action-filled cantos with their elaborate poetic openings that have preceded (and that will follow). Also, the prosaic nature of this canto with its stress on facts and the truth may be a device to entice the reader to suspend his disbelief and accept the truth of the fantastic cantos to come—in which Dante will always be at pains to emphasize the "truthful" nature of the fiction.

15. *for they never saw what was ahead of them:* Note the appropriate nature of the punishment: the augurs who, when living, looked into the future are here in Hell denied any forward vision. See lines 38–39.

28. *In this place piety lives when pity is dead:* In the original there is a play on words: the word *pietà* means both 'piety' and 'pity'.

The Pilgrim has once again felt pity for the torments of the sinners, and Virgil rebukes him with some exasperation. This rebuke is the climax of the important theme of the Pilgrim's pity. Cf. V, 139–142; VI, 58–59, etc.

34–36. *Amphiaraus? Why do you quit the war?:* Amphiaraus was a seer, and one of the seven kings who led the expedition against Thebes (see XIV, 68–69). He foresaw that he would die during the siege, and to avoid his fate he hid himself so that he would not have to fight. But his wife Eriphyle revealed his hiding place to Polynices, and Amphiaraus was forced to go to battle. He met his death when the earth opened up and swallowed him. Dante's source was Statius' *Thebaid* VII and VIII.

40–45. *Behold Tiresias who changed his looks:* Tiresias was the famous soothsayer of Thebes referred to by Ovid (*Metamorphoses* III, 316–338). According to Ovid, Tiresias with his rod once separated two serpents which were coupled together, whereupon he was transformed into a woman. Seven years later he found the same two serpents, struck them again, and became a man once more. Later Jupiter and Juno asked Tiresias, who had had the experience of belonging to both sexes, which sex enjoyed love-making more. When Tiresias answered "woman," Juno struck him blind. However, Jupiter, in compensation, gave him the gift of prophecy.

46–51. *Backing up to this one's chest comes Aruns:* Aruns, the Etruscan diviner who forecast the Roman civil war and its outcome (Caesar's triumph over Pompey [Lucan, *Pharsalia* I, 584–638]), made his home "in the hills of Luni" (47), the area now known as Carrara and renowned for its white marble.

52–60. *And that one, with her hair loose, flowing back:* Manto, upon the death of her father Tiresias, fled Thebes ("Bacchus' sacred city," 59) and its tyrant Creon. She finally arrived in Italy and there founded the city of Mantua, Virgil's birthplace (56).

61–99

Virgil's account of the founding of Mantua seems to have been offered to provide the true version of an apparently controversial issue. In Canto XIX the Pilgrim had revealed the true nature of Simony, and the line (20) containing the first reference to "breaking" is followed by the words "Let this be mankind's picture of the truth." Now, in Canto XX, Virgil tells the "true" story of the founding of Mantua ("without recourse to sorcery," 93) and reveals the "true" nature of augury, i.e. that it is a fraudulent practice, adding "let no false tales adulterate the truth," 99. (Perhaps Virgil is here, by implication, defending himself against his medieval reputation as a magician.) Thus, Cantos XIX and XX are linked by these correlative investigations and interpretations of the true nature of the respective sins.

63. *beyond the Tyrol, known as Lake Benaco:* Lake Benaco is today Lake Garda, which lies in northern Italy at the center of the triangle formed by the cities of Trent, Brescia, and Verona (68).

64–66. *by a thousand streams and more, I think, the Alps:* Here, the "Alps" means that range between the Camonica valley, west of Lake Garda, and the city of Garda, on the lake's eastern shore, that is watered by many streams which ultimately flow into Lake Garda.

67–69. *at its center is a place where all three bishops:* On an island in Lake Garda (Benaco) the boundaries of the dioceses of Trent, Brescia, and Verona met, thereby making it possible for all three bishops to hold services or "say Mass" there. It is quite possible that Dante in the phrase "if they would ever visit there" (69), intends to criticize the practice of non-resident clergy taking money from their parishes.

70–72. *Peschiera sits, a handsome well-built fortress:* The fortress of Peschiera and the town of the same name are on the southeast shore of Lake Garda.

78. *to Governol where it falls into the Po:* Governol, now called Governolo, is twelve miles from Mantua and situated at the junction of the Mincio and the Po rivers.

82. *the savage virgin:* Manto.

93. *without recourse to sorcery:* The customs of ancient peoples dictated that the name of a newly founded city be obtained through sorcery. Such was not the case with Mantua.

95–96. *before the foolish Casalodi listened:* In 1272 Alberto da Casalodi, one of the Guelph counts of Brescia, was lord of Mantua. Having encountered public opposition, he was duped by the Ghibelline Pinamonte de' Bonaccolsi into thinking that he could remain in power only by exiling the nobles. Having faithfully followed Pinamonte's false counsel, he found himself bereft of his supporters and protectors, and consequently Pinamonte was able to take command; he banished the Guelphs, and ruled until 1291.

106–112. *That one whose beard flows from his cheeks:* At the time of the Trojan War ("when the war stripped Greece of all its males," 108), Eurypylus, whom Dante thought to be a Greek augur (as was Calchas, 110), was asked to divine the most opportune time to launch the Greek fleet ("to cut the first ship's cable free," 111) from the port at Aulis.

113. *this way, somewhere in my high tragedy:* The "high tragedy" is, of course, the *Aeneid* (Book II,114–119). In this work, however, Eurypylus is not an augur, but a soldier sent to the oracle to discover Apollo's predictions as to the best time to set sail from Troy.

116–117. *Michael Scot:* A Scottish philosopher attached to Frederick II's court at Palermo (see X, 119) who translated the works of Aristotle from the Arabic of his commentator, Avicenna (see IV, 143). By reputation he was a magician and augur. Cf. Boccaccio, *Decameron* VIII, 9.

118–120. *See there Guido Bonatti; see Asdente:* A native of Forlì, Guido Bonatti was a well-known astrologer and diviner in the service of many lords, among whom were Frederick II, Ezzelino (see XII, 110), and Guido da Montefeltro (see XXVII).

Benvenuto (or Asdente, "toothless," as he was called) was a cobbler from Parma who supposedly possessed certain magical powers. According to Dante, he would have fared better had he "been more devoted then / to making shoes" (119–120). See the *Convivio* IV, xvi, 6.

124–126. *Now come along. Cain with his thorn-bush straddles:* By some mysterious power Virgil is able to reckon time in the depths of Hell. The moon (referred to as "Cain with his thorn-bush," 124, the medieval Italian counterpart of our "Man in the Moon") is directly over the line of demarcation between the Northern (land) and the Southern (water) Hemispheres and is setting on the western horizon (the "waves below Seville," 126). The time is approximately six A.M.

129. *when you were lost in the dark wood, she helped you:* See Canto I, 2. The literal significance of this line defies explanation, since in the beginning of the *Inferno* describing the Pilgrim's wanderings in the "dark woods" no mention is made of the moon. Most commentators would see an allegorical significance intended, but their interpretations vary and I find none of them convincing.

CANTO XXI

From this bridge to the next we walked and talked
  of things my Comedy does not care to tell;
  and when we reached the summit of the arch,   3

we stopped to see the next fosse of Malebolge
  and to hear more lamentation voiced in vain:
  I saw that it was very strangely dark!   6

In the vast and busy shipyard of the Venetians
  there boils all winter long a tough, thick pitch
  that is used to caulk the ribs of unsound ships.   9

Since winter will not let them sail, they toil:
  some build new ships, others repair the old ones,
  plugging the planks come loose from many sailings;   12

some hammer at the bow, some at the stern,
  one carves the oars while others twine the ropes,
  one mends the jib, one patches up the mainsail;   15

here, too, but heated by God's art, not fire,
  a sticky tar was boiling in the ditch
  that smeared the banks with viscous residue.   18

I saw it there, but I saw nothing in it,
  except the rising of the boiling bubbles
  breathing-in air to burst and sink again.   21

I stood intently gazing there below,
  my guide, shouting to me: "Watch out, watch out!"
  took hold of me and drew me to his side.   24

I turned my head like one who can't resist
  looking to see what makes him run away
  (his body's strength draining with sudden fear),   27

but, looking back, does not delay his flight;
and I saw coming right behind our backs,
rushing along the ridge, a devil, black!   30

His face, his look, how frightening it was!
With outstretched wings he skimmed along the rock,
and every single move he made was cruel;   33

on one of his high-hunched and pointed shoulders
he had a sinner slung by both his thighs,
held tightly clawed at the tendons of his heels.   36

He shouted from our bridge: "Hey, Malebranche,
here's one of Santa Zita's elders for you!
You stick him under—I'll go back for more;   39

I've got that city stocked with the likes of him,
they're all a bunch of grafters, save Bonturo!
You can change a 'no' to 'yes' for cash in Lucca."   42

He flung him in, then from the flinty cliff
sprang off. No hound unleashed to chase a thief
could have taken off with greater speed than he.   45

That sinner plunged, then floated up stretched out,
and the devils underneath the bridge all shouted:
"You shouldn't imitate the Holy Face!   48

The swimming's different here from in the Serchio!
We have our grappling hooks along with us—
don't show yourself above the pitch, or else!"   51

With a hundred prongs or more they pricked him, shrieking:
"You've got to do your squirming under cover,
try learning how to cheat beneath the surface."   54

They were like cooks who make their scullery boys
poke down into the caldron with their forks
to keep the meat from floating to the top.   57

My master said: "We'd best not let them know
that you are here with me; crouch down behind
some jutting rock so that they cannot see you;   60

whatever insults they may hurl at me,
you must not fear, I know how things are run here;
I have been caught in as bad a fix before."   63

He crossed the bridge and walked on past the end;
   as soon as he set foot on the sixth bank
   he forced himself to look as bold as possible. 66

With all the sound and fury that breaks loose
   when dogs rush out at some poor begging tramp,
   making him stop and beg from where he stands— 69

the ones who hid beneath the bridge sprang out
   and blocked him with a flourish of their pitchforks,
   but he shouted: "All of you behave yourselves! 72

Before you start to jab me with your forks,
   let one of you step forth to hear me out,
   and then decide if you still care to grapple." 75

They all cried out: "Let Malacoda go!"
   One stepped forward—the others stood their ground—
   and moving, said, "What good will this do him?" 78

"Do you think, Malacoda," said my master,
   "that you would see me here, come all this way,
   against all opposition, and still safe, 81

without propitious fate and God's permission?
   Now let us pass, for it is willed in Heaven
   that I lead another by this savage path." 84

With this the devil's arrogance collapsed,
   his pitchfork, too, dropped right down to his feet,
   as he announced to all: "Don't touch this man!" 87

"You, hiding over there," my guide called me,
   "behind the bridge's rocks, curled up and quiet,
   come back to me, you may return in safety." 90

At his words I rose and then I ran to him
   and all the devils made a movement forward;
   I feared they would not really keep their pact. 93

(I remember seeing soldiers under truce,
   as they left the castle of Caprona, frightened
   to be passing in the midst of such an enemy.) 96

I drew up close to him, as close as possible,
   and did not take my eyes from all those faces
   that certainly had nothing good about them. 99

Their prongs were aimed at me, and one was saying:
  "Now do I let him have it in the rump?"
  They answered all for one: "Sure, stick him good!"   102

But the devil who had spoken with my guide
  was quick to spin around and scream an order:
  "At ease there, take it easy, Scarmiglione!"   105

Then he said to us: "You cannot travel straight
  across this string of bridges, for the sixth arch
  lies broken at the bottom of its ditch;   108

if you have made your mind up to proceed,
  you must continue on along this ridge;
  not far, you'll find a bridge that crosses it.   111

Five hours more and it will be one thousand,
  two hundred sixty-six years and a day
  since the bridge-way here fell crumbling to the ground.   114

I plan to send a squad of mine that way
  to see that no one airs himself down there;
  go along with them, they will not misbehave.   117

Front and center, Alichino, Calcabrina,"
  he shouted his commands, "you too, Cagnazzo;
  Barbariccia, you be captain of the squad.   120

Take Libicocco with you and Draghignazzo,
  toothy Ciriatto and Graffiacane,
  Farfarello and our crazy Rubicante.   123

Now tour the ditch, inspect the boiling tar;
  these two shall have safe passage to the bridge
  connecting den to den without a break."   126

"O master, I don't like the looks of this,"
  I said, "let's go, just you and me, no escort,
  you know the way. I want no part of them!   129

If you're observant as you usually are,
  why is it you don't see them grind their teeth
  and wink at one another?—we're in danger!"   132

And he to me: "I will not have you frightened;
  let them do all the grinding that they want,
  they do it for the boiling souls, not us."   135

Before they turned left-face along the bank
  each one gave their good captain a salute
  with farting tongue pressed tightly to his teeth,   138

and he blew back with his bugle of an ass-hole.

N O T E S

7–15. *In the vast and busy shipyard of the Venetians:* During the Middle Ages the
shipyard at Venice, built in 1104, was one of the most active and productive in all
Europe. The image of the busy shipyard with its activity revolving around a vat of
viscous pitch establishes the tone for this canto (and the next) as one of tense and
excited movement. Also we once again see Dante imitating the action with his
language: the busy syntax reflects the activity of the shipyard.

20–21. *except the rising of the boiling bubbles:* The repetition of "b" sounds (and
"p's" in the Italian) audibly represents the bubbling, bursting action of the boiling
pitch.

37. *Hey, Malebranche:* The *Malebranche* ("Evil Claws") are the overseer-devils
of this *bolgia* wherein are punished the Barrators (grafters, 41), those swindlers in
public office whose sin against the state is comparable to that of the Simonists
against the Church (XIX).

38–42. *here's one of Santa Zita's elders for you!:* Santa Zita, who lived and was
canonized in the thirteenth century, is the patron saint of Lucca. The "elders" (38)
are the Luccan government officials; and one of them, Bonturo Dati (41), is iron-
ically referred to here as being guiltless when in reality he was the worst barrator
of them all.

46–51. *You shouldn't imitate the Holy Face!:* The "Holy Face" was a wooden cru-
cifix at Lucca. The sinner surfaces stretched out (46) on his back with arms flung
wide like the figure on a crucifix—and this gives rise to the devil's remark that
here in Hell one does not swim the same way as in the Serchio (a river near
Lucca). In other words, in the Serchio people swim for pleasure, often floating on
their backs (in the position of a crucifix). The use of a crucifixion image to suggest
swimming for pleasure is in keeping with the grotesque humor of XXI–XXIII.

55–57. *They were like cooks who make their scullery boys:* The "cooking" imagery
begun here is continued in XXII, 150, and is one of several images which unifies
these cantos.

76. *They all cried out: "Let Malacoda go!":* Malacoda is the leader of the devils in
this *bolgia*. It is significant that a devil whose name means "Evil-Tail" ends this
canto with a fart (139).

94–96. *I remember seeing soldiers under truce:* Dante's personal recollection con-
cerns the siege of Caprona (a fortress on the Arno River near Pisa) by Guelph
troops from Lucca and Florence in 1289. Having surrendered, the Pisan soldiers
"under truce" issued forth, having to pass through the rank of the enemy. The Pil-
grim's present state is similar to that of the frightened soldiers. The military
imagery begun here will continue in the next canto.

112–114. *Five hours more and it will be . . .:* Christ's death on Good Friday,
A.D. 34, would in five hours, according to Malacoda, have occurred 1266 years ago
yesterday—"today" being the morning of Holy Saturday, 1300. Although the
bridge across the next *bolgia* was shattered by the earthquake following Christ's
crucifixion, Malacoda tells Virgil and the Pilgrim that there is another bridge that

crosses this *bolgia*. This lie, carefully contrived by the spokesman for the devils, sets the trap for the overly confident, trusting Virgil and his wary charge, who—at least in these cantos—appears more intelligent than his guide. See lines 127–132; also Canto XXIII, n. 140–141.

118–123. *Front and center, Alichino, Calcabrina:* The significance of the devils' names reinforces their ambivalent nature, both comic and fearful. While they inspire fear in Virgil and the Pilgrim, their words and gestures are for the most part light and playful. Many of the names could be translated, but they would lose much of their grotesque appearance. (Malacoda, for instance, means "Evil-Tail," Barbariccia means "Curly-Beard.") Some critics have suggested that Dante might be mocking Florentine or Lucchese magistrates of the early 1300s through the devils. Manno Branca, for example, was mayor of Florence in 1300 and his followers might easily have been called *Male branche* ('Bad Brancas'); one of the priors of Florence at the time was named Raffacani—which is quite close to the devil-name, Graffiacane.

139. *and he blew back with his bugle of an ass-hole:* The canto closes on this vulgar, but comic note, which is indicative of the essentially farcical nature of this *bolgia,* so different from the remainder of the *Inferno.* In the next canto we see the devils and sinners amusing themselves with bizarre sports which we must assume are the rule rather than the exception.

CANTO XXII

I have seen troops of horsemen breaking camp,
  opening the attack, or passing in review,
  I have even seen them fleeing for their lives;   *3*

I have seen scouts ride exploring your terrain,
  O Aretines, and I have seen raiding-parties
  and the clash of tournaments, the run of jousts—   *6*

to the tune of trumpets, to the ring of clanging bells,
  to the roll of drums, to the flash of flares on ramparts,
  to the accompaniment of every known device;   *9*

but I never saw cavalry or infantry
  or ships that sail by landmarks or by stars
  signaled to set off by such strange bugling!   *12*

So, on our way we went with those ten fiends.
  What savage company! But—in church, with saints—
  with rowdy good-for-nothings, in the tavern!   *15*

My attention now was fixed upon the pitch
  to see the operations of this *bolgia,*
  and how the cooking souls got on down there.   *18*

Much like the dolphins that are said to surface
  with their backs arched to warn all men at sea
  to rig their ships for stormy seas ahead,   *21*

so now and then a sinner's back would surface
  in order to alleviate his pain,
  then dive to hide as quick as lightning strikes.   *24*

Like squatting frogs along the ditch's edge,
  with just their muzzles sticking out of water,
  their legs and all the rest concealed below,   *27*

these sinners squatted all around their pond;
　　but as soon as Barbariccia would approach
　　they quickly ducked beneath the boiling pitch. 　　　　30

I saw (my heart still shudders at the thought)
　　one lingering behind—as it sometimes happens
　　one frog remains while all the rest dive down— 　　　　33

and Graffiacane, standing in front of him,
　　hooked and twirled him by his pitchy hair
　　and hoisted him. He looked just like an otter! 　　　　36

By then I knew the names of all the fiends:
　　I had listened carefully when they were chosen,
　　each of them stepping forth to match his name. 　　　　39

"Hey, Rubicante, dig your claws down deep,
　　into his back and peel the skin off him,"
　　this fiendish chorus egged him on with screams. 　　　　42

I said: "Master, will you, if you can, find out
　　the name of that poor wretch who has just fallen
　　into the cruel hands of his adversaries?" 　　　　45

My guide walked right up to the sinner's side
　　and asked where he was from, and he replied:
　　"I was born and bred in the kingdom of Navarre; 　　　　48

my mother gave me to a lord to serve,
　　for she had me by some dishonest spendthrift
　　who ran through all he owned and killed himself. 　　　　51

Then I became a servant in the household
　　of good King Thibault. There I learned my graft,
　　and now I pay my bill by boiling here." 　　　　54

Ciriatto who had two tusks sticking out
　　on both sides of his mouth, just like a boar's,
　　let him feel how just one tusk could rip him open. 　　　　57

The mouse had fallen prey to evil cats,
　　but Barbariccia locked him with his arms
　　shouting: "Get back while I've got hold of him!" 　　　　60

Then toward my guide he turned his face and said:
　　"If you want more from him, keep questioning
　　before he's torn to pieces by the others." 　　　　63

My guide went on: "Then tell me, do you know
of some Italian stuck among these sinners
beneath the pitch?" And he, "A second ago   66

I was with one who lived around those parts.
Oh, I wish I were undercover with him now!
I wouldn't have these hooks or claws to fear."   69

Libicocco cried: "We've waited long enough,"
then with his fork he hooked the sinner's arm
and, tearing at it, he pulled out a piece.   72

Draghignazzo, too, was anxious for some fun;
he tried the wretch's leg, but their captain quickly
spun around and gave them all a dirty look.   75

As soon as they calmed down a bit, my master
began again to interrogate the wretch
who still was contemplating his new wound: 78

"Who was it, you were saying, that unluckily
you left behind you when you came ashore?"
"Gomita," he said, "the friar from Gallura,   81

receptacle for every kind of fraud:
when his lord's enemies were in his hands,
the treatment they received delighted them: 84

he took their cash, and as he says, hushed up
the case and let them off; none of his acts
was petty grafting, all were of sovereign order.   87

He spends his time with don Michele Zanche
of Logodoro, talking on and on
about Sardinia—their tongues no worse for wear!   90

Oh, but look how that one grins and grinds his teeth;
I could tell you so much more, but I am afraid
he is going to grate my scabby hide for me."   93

But their master-sergeant turned to Farfarello,
whose wild eyes warned he was about to strike,
shouting, "Get away, you filthy bird of prey."   96

"If you would like to see Tuscans or Lombards,"
the frightened shade took up where he left off,
"and have a talk with them, I'll bring some here;   99

but the Malebranche must back up a bit,
    or else those shades won't risk a surfacing;
    I, by myself, will bring you up a catch   *102*

of seven, without moving from this spot,
    just by whistling—that's our signal to the rest
    when one peers out and sees the coast is clear."   *105*

Cagnazzo raised his snout at such a story,
    then shook his head and said: "Listen to the trick
    he's cooked up to get off the hook by jumping!"   *108*

And he, full of tricks his trade had taught him,
    said: "Tricky, I surely am, especially
    when it comes to getting friends into worse trouble."   *111*

But Alichin could not resist the challenge,
    and in spite of what the others thought, cried out:
    "If you jump, I won't come galloping for you,   *114*

I've got my wings to beat you to the pitch.
    We'll clear this ledge and wait behind that slope.
    Let's see if one of you can outmatch us!"   *117*

Now listen, Reader, here's a game that's strange:
    they all turned toward the slope, and first to turn
    was the fiend who from the start opposed the game.   *120*

The Navarrese had perfect sense of timing:
    feet planted on the ground, in a flash he jumped,
    the devil's plan was foiled, and he was free.   *123*

The squad was stung with shame but most of all
    the one who brought this blunder to perfection;
    he swooped down howling, "Now I've got you caught!"   *126*

Little good it did, for wings could not outstrip
    the flight of terror: down the sinner dived
    and up the fiend was forced to strain his chest   *129*

like a falcon swooping down on a wild duck:
    the duck dives quickly out of sight, the falcon
    must fly back up dejected and defeated.   *132*

In the meantime, Calcabrina, furious,
    also took off, hoping the shade would make it,
    so he could pick a fight with his companion.   *135*

And when he saw the grafter hit the pitch
　he turned his claws to grapple with his brother,
　and they tangled in mid-air above the ditch;　　　　　　　　*138*

but the other was a full-fledged hawk as well
　and used his claws on him, and both of them
　went plunging straight into the boiling tar.　　　　　　　　*141*

The heat was quick to make them separate,
　but there seemed no way of getting out of there;
　their wings were clogged and could not lift them up.　　　　*144*

Barbariccia, no less peeved than all his men,
　sent four fiends flying to the other shore
　with their equipment at top speed; instantly,　　　　　　　*147*

some here, some there, they took the posts assigned them.
　They stretched their hooks to reach the pitch-dipped pair
　who were by now deep-fried within their crusts.　　　　　　*150*

And we left them messed up in their occupation.

NOTES

1–12. *I have seen troops of horsemen breaking camp:* Continuing the military imagery, Dante elaborates in mock-epic style on the effect of the vulgar signal (the "strange bugling" of 12) given at the close of Canto XXI. The reference to the Aretines (5) recalls Dante's presence at their defeat in the battle of Campaldino (1289) at the hands of the Florentine and Luccan troops.

14–15. *But—in church, with saints:* The proverbial nature of this phrase is characteristic of the flippant manner of speech found throughout Cantos XXI and XXII and, moreover, is indicative of the playful atmosphere wherein all participants (the Pilgrim, Virgil, the Devils, and the sinners) seem to operate on the same plane as equal agents.

19. *Much like the dolphins that are said to surface:* Consistent with the playful and grotesque nature of this canto is Dante's use of animal imagery. The grafters are compared successively to dolphins, frogs (25–33), an otter (36), a mouse (58), a wild duck (130); the devils are compared to falcons (130) and hawks (139). All of these animals are depicted in grotesque poses or are described as playing games.

48–54. *I was born and bred in the kingdom of Navarre:* Early commentators have given the name of Ciampolo or Giampolo to this native of Navarre who, after being placed in the service of a Spanish nobleman, later served in the court of Thibault II. Exploiting the court duties with which he was entrusted, he took to barratry. One commentator suggests that were it not for the tradition which attributes the name of Ciampolo to this man, one might identify him with the seneschal Goffredo di Beaumont who took over the government of Navarre during Thibault's absence.

53. *good King Thibault:* Thibault II, the son-in-law of Louis IX of France, was Count of Champagne and later King of Navarre during the mid-thirteenth century.

58. *The mouse had fallen prey to evil cats:* This image, together with the references to frogs (25–34) and to the "games" of the Malebranche and Ciampolo, anticipates the reference to Aesop's fable which begins Canto XXIII (4–6).

81–87. *"Gomita," he said, "the friar from Gallura":* Fra Gomita was a Sardinian friar, chancellor of Nino Visconti, governor of Pisa, whom Dante places in *Purgatory* VIII (53). From 1275–1296 Nino Visconti was judge of Gallura, one of the four districts into which Sardinia, a Pisan possession during the thirteenth century, was divided. Profiting by his position and the good faith of Nino Visconti, who refused to listen to the complaints raised against him, Fra Gomita indulged in the sale of public offices. When Nino learned, however, that he had accepted bribes to let prisoners escape, he promptly had him hanged.

88–89. *He spends his time with don Michele Zanche:* Although no documents mentioning the name of Michele Zanche have been found, he is believed to have been the governor of Logodoro, another of the four districts into which Sardinia was divided in the thirteenth century (see n. 81–87) during the period when King Enzo of Sardinia, the son of Frederick II, was engaged in war. After King Enzo was captured and subsequently divorced from the Queen, Michele married her and took over the government of the Sardinian provinces. Around 1275 he was murdered by his son-in-law, Branca d'Oria, whose shade Dante will see in the lowest region of Hell (see XXXIII, 134–147).

97–132

The second lie of Cantos XXI–XXII is Ciampolo's device to escape the claws of the *Malebranche:* if the devils will hide, he will whistle and thus summon his fellow sinners from below the pitch in order to get his friends into worse trouble than he himself is in. Thus he tells the devils that he will lie to his friends (by whistling to let them know that the coast is clear), but actually he is lying to the devils. They are suspicious but they agree to hide and play the game and Ciampolo escapes. In Ciampolo, for the first time in the *Inferno,* we see a sinner actually performing his sin: for the clever way in which Ciampolo constructs his lie (using Virgil and Dante), his admission that he is "tricky" (110), and his well-timed leap into the pitch all show the sin of fraud in action. Just as Malacoda joined his lie with a very minute and truthful description of the time since the bridge had fallen (XXI, 112–114), so Ciampolo leads up to his lie with a precise and truthful statement of the major facts of his life (48–54). The admixture of precise truth and falsehood gives, in both cases, an aura of unquestioned truth to what is ultimately a fraud, and that method too comes, of course, from experience in the sin of barratry. Cf. XXI, 109–111; also XXIII, n. 140–141.

There is possibly a third, implicit, lie in this canto, this time perpetrated by the devils again. Cagnazzo from the start is suspicious of Ciampolo's proposal, but when Alichino cannot resist the challenge, Cagnazzo is the first to turn to go and hide ("first to turn / was the fiend who from the start opposed the game," 119–120). The Pilgrim calls this "a game that's strange" (118), and indeed it is, because each of the devils is silently "lying" to his brother by agreeing to what they must realize is a fraud on the part of Ciampolo; the real reason for their ready acceptance of Ciampolo's proposal is, of course, that when he escapes they can "pick a fight" with the responsible devil—Alichino. That is exactly what happens when Calcabrina, "furious, / also took off, hoping the shade would make it, / so he could pick a fight with his companion" (133–135). The deceit involved in this "game" strikes the Pilgrim as "strange," but we must assume that it represents the normal daily fare in this *bolgia,* where there is a free interchange of roles between devils and sinners, and a continuous activity that is grotesquely comic.

CANTO XXIII

In silence, all alone, without an escort,
  we moved along, one behind the other,
  like minor friars bent upon a journey.   *3*

I was thinking over one of Aesop's fables
  that this recent skirmish had brought back to mind,
  where he tells the story of the frog and mouse;   *6*

for "yon" and "there" could not be more alike
  than the fable and the fact, if one compares
  the start and finish of both incidents.   *9*

As from one thought another often rises,
  so this thought gave quick birth to still another,
  and then the fear I first had felt was doubled.   *12*

I was thinking: "Since these fiends, on our account,
  were tricked and mortified by mockery,
  they certainly will be more than resentful;   *15*

with rage now added to their evil instincts,
  they will hunt us down with all the savagery
  of dogs about to pounce upon the hare."   *18*

I felt my body's skin begin to tighten—
  I was so frightened!—and I kept looking back:
  "O master," I said, "if you do not hide   *21*

both of us, and very quick, I am afraid
  of the Malebranche—right now they're on our trail—
  I feel they're there, I think I hear them now."   *24*

And he replied: "Even if I were a mirror
  I could not reflect your outward image faster
  than your inner thoughts transmit themselves to me.   *27*

In fact, just now they joined themselves with mine,
and since they were alike in birth and form,
I decided to unite them toward one goal: 30

if the right-hand bank should slope in such a way
as to allow us to descend to the next *bolgia,*
we could escape that chase we have imagined."   33

He had hardly finished telling me his plan
when I saw them coming with their wings wide-open
not too far off, and now they meant to get us!   36

My guide instinctively caught hold of me,
like a mother waking to some warning sound,
who sees the rising flames are getting close   39

and grabs her son and runs—she does not wait
the short time it would take to put on something;
she cares not for herself, only for him.   42

And over the edge, then down the stony bank
he slid, on his back, along the sloping rock
that walls the higher side of the next *bolgia.*   45

Water that turns a mill wheel never ran
the narrow sluice at greater speed, not even
at the point before it hits the paddle-blades,   48

than down that sloping border my guide slid
bearing me with him, clasping me to his chest
as though I were his child, not his companion.   51

His feet had hardly touched rock bottom, when
there they were, the ten of them, above us
on the height; but now there was no need to fear: 54

High Providence that willed for them to be
the ministers in charge of the fifth ditch
also willed them powerless to leave their realm.   57

And now, down there, we found a painted people,
slow-motioned: step by step, they walked their round
in tears, and seeming wasted by fatigue.   60

All were wearing cloaks with hoods pulled low
covering the eyes (the style was much the same
as those the Benedictines wear at Cluny),   63

dazzling, gilded cloaks outside, but inside
    they were lined with lead, so heavy, that the capes
    King Frederick used, compared to these, were straw.   66

O cloak of everlasting weariness!
    We turned again, as usual, to the left
    and moved with them, those souls lost in their mourning;   69

but with their weight that tired-out race of shades
    paced on so slowly that we found ourselves
    in new company with every step we took;   72

and so I asked my guide: "Would you look around
    and see, as we keep walking, if you find
    someone here whose name or deeds are known."   75

And one who overheard me speaking Tuscan
    cried out somewhere behind us: "Not so fast,
    you there, rushing ahead through this heavy air,   78

perhaps from me you can obtain an answer."
    At this my guide turned toward me saying, "Stop,
    and wait for him, then match your pace with his."   81

I paused and saw two shades with straining faces
    revealing their mind's haste to join my side,
    but the weight they bore and the crowded road delayed them.   84

When they arrived, they looked at me sideways
    and for some time, without exchanging words;
    then they turned to one another and were saying: 87

"He seems alive, the way his throat is moving,
    and if both are dead, what privilege allows them
    to walk uncovered by the heavy cloak?"   90

Then they spoke to me "O Tuscan who has come
    to visit the college of the sullen hypocrites,
    do not disdain to tell us who you are."   93

I answered them: "I was born and I grew up
    in the great city on the lovely Arno's shore,
    and I have the body I have always had.   96

But who are you, distilling tears of grief,
    so many I see running down your cheeks?
    And what kind of pain is this that it can glitter?"   99

One of them answered: "The orange-gilded cloaks
  are thick with lead so heavy that it makes us,
  who are the scales it hangs on, creak as we walk.   102

Jovial Friars we were, both from Bologna.
  My name was Catalano, his, Loderingo,
  and both of us were chosen by your city,   105

that usually would choose one man alone,
  to keep the peace. Evidence of what we were
  may still be seen around Gardingo's parts."   108

I began: "O Friars, all your wretchedness . . ."
  but said no more; I couldn't, for I saw
  one crucified with three stakes on the ground.   111

And when he saw me all his body writhed,
  and through his beard he heaved out sighs of pain;
  then Friar Catalano, who watched the scene,   114

remarked: "That impaled figure you see there
  advised the Pharisees it was expedient
  to sacrifice one man for all the people.   117

Naked he lies stretched out across the road,
  as you can see, and he must feel the load
  of every weight that steps on him to cross.   120

His father-in-law and the other council members,
  who were the seed of evil for all Jews,
  are racked the same way all along this ditch."   123

And I saw Virgil staring down amazed
  at this body stretching out in crucifixion,
  so vilely punished in the eternal exile.   126

Then he looked up and asked one of the friars:
  "Could you please tell us, if your rule permits:
  is there a passageway on the right, somewhere,   129

by which the two of us may leave this place   ·
  without summoning one of those black angels
  to come down here and raise us from this pit?"   132

He answered: "Closer than you might expect,
  a ridge jutting out from the base of the great circle
  extends, and bridges every hideous ditch   135

except this one whose arch is totally smashed
   and crosses nowhere; but you can climb up
   its massive ruins that slope against this bank."   *138*

My guide stood there awhile, his head bent low,
   then said: "He told a lie about this business,
   that one who hooks the sinners over there."   *141*

And the friar: "Once, in Bologna, I heard discussed
   the devil's many vices; one of them is
   that he tells lies and is father of all lies."   *144*

In haste, taking great strides, my guide walked off,
   his face revealing traces of his anger.
   I turned and left the heavy-weighted souls   *147*

to make my way behind those cherished footprints.

NOTES

3. *like minor friars bent upon a journey:* The image of the "minor friars" (Franciscans) who walk in single file is preparatory to the presentation of the Hypocrites whose clothing is compared to that of monks (61–66).

4–9. *I was thinking over one of Aesop's fables:* Dante incorrectly attributes the fable of the frog and the mouse to Aesop, to whom during the Middle Ages all such tales were attributed. The fable concerns a mouse who, arriving at a stream, asks a frog to carry him across; the frog agrees and ties the mouse to his leg, but once they are in the water the frog attempts to drown the mouse by diving. But while the mouse is fighting to stay afloat, a hawk swoops down and carries them away, and (in most versions) frees the mouse and eats the frog. Dante restricts the comparison to the "start and finish of both incidents" (9). Most critics have equated the frog to Ciampolo and the mouse with Alichino, since the former attempts to (and does) deceive the latter, and they see the end of the fable—the hawk swooping down on frog and mouse—as the rescue of the two stuck devils by their fellows. Although apparently no exact equation between the fable and the "recent skirmish" was intended by Dante, it seems to me that the beginning of the fable (the deception of the mouse by the frog) better suggests the attempted deception of Dante and Virgil (who are looking for a way to cross *Bolgia* Six) by the *Malebranche,* and that the end of the fable which Dante refers to (9) is not the end of the story itself, but the moral which was inevitably appended to such fables in the Middle Ages: in this case that divine justice punishes the guilty (the frog is caught, and two of the *Malebranche* fall into the pitch)—and the innocent "mice," Dante and Virgil, get away.

7. *for "yon" and "there" could not be more alike:* The words *mo* and *issa* of the Italian text, which I have translated as 'yon' and 'there' are synonymous in the Lucchese dialect, both meaning 'now.'

25–27. *Even if I were a mirror:* Cf. Proverbs 27:19.

37–42. *My guide instinctively caught hold of me:* Note the instinctive reaction of Virgil, who, at this moment, is not acting in the capacity of Reason. Cf. n. 140–141.

61–63. *All were wearing cloaks with hoods pulled low:* The vestments of the monks at Cluny were particularly famous for their fullness and elegance. St. Bernard wrote sarcastically that if the elegance of the dress indicated holiness, he too would become a Benedictine at Cluny. Perhaps Dante is using the comparison to criticize the hypocrisy of these monks in their choice of habit.

64–66. *dazzling, gilded cloaks outside, but inside:* Dante's image of the gilded exterior concealing a leaden interior is perhaps drawn from Matthew 23:27: "Woe unto you, scribes and Pharisees, hypocrites! For ye are like unto whited sepulchres, which indeed appear beautiful outwardly but are within full of dead men's bones, and of all uncleanness."

Probably also known to Dante was the *Magnae Derivationes* of Uguccione da Pisa, who says that *ypocrita* coming from the Greek meant *superauratus* or 'gilded.'

The "capes / King Frederick used" (65–66) refers to a mode of punishment for traitors reportedly instituted by Frederick II, grandson of Frederick Barbarossa. The condemned were dressed in leaden capes which were then melted on their bodies. It is uncertain whether or not Frederick actually used this punishment.

103–108. *Jovial Friars we were, both from Bologna:* The Order of the *Cavalieri di Beata Santa Maria,* or "Jovial Friars" (*frati gaudenti*) as they were called, was founded at Bologna in 1261 and was dedicated to the maintenance of peace between political factions and families, and to the defense of the weak and poor. However, because of its rather liberal rules, this high-principled organization gained the nickname of "Jovial Friars"—which, no doubt, impaired its serious function to some degree. The Bolognese friars Catalano de' Malavolti (c. 1210–1285) and Loderingo degli Andalò (c. 1210–1293) were elected jointly to the office of *Podestà* (mayor) in Florence because it was thought that the combination of the former, a Guelph, and the latter, a Ghibelline, would ensure the peace of the city. In reality their tenure, short though it was, was characterized by strife, which culminated in the expulsion of the Ghibellines from Florence in 1266. Gardingo (108) is the name of the section of Florence around the Palazzo Vecchio; in this area the Uberti family, the heads of the Florentine Ghibelline party, had their palace, which was razed during the uprisings of 1266. Modern historians have proved that Pope Clement IV controlled both the election and actions of Catalano and Loderingo, in order to overthrow the Ghibellines and establish the Guelphs in power.

115–124. *That impaled figure you see there:* Caiaphas, the High Priest of the Jews, maintained that it was better that one man (Jesus) die than for the Hebrew nation to be lost (John 11:49–50). Annas, Caiaphas' father-in-law (121), delivered Jesus to him for judgment. For their act against God these men and the other evil counselors who judged Christ were the "seed of evil for all Jews" (122); in retaliation God caused Jerusalem to be destroyed and the Hebrew people dispersed to all parts of the world. It is, then, a fitting punishment for Caiaphas, Annas, and the rest to bear the weight of all the Hypocrites for their crime, and to be crucified on the ground with "three stakes" (111).

It should be noted that these crucified Hypocrites are also evil counselors.

124–127. *And I saw Virgil staring down amazed:* Most commentators seem to think that Virgil's amazement at seeing the crucified Caiaphas is due to the fact that he was not there when Virgil first descended into Hell. However, many of the shades seen by Dante and Virgil were not there on Virgil's first descent and the Roman poet expresses no amazement at seeing them; it seems more likely that Virgil is struck by the unusual form which the *contrapasso* takes—crucifixion.

140–141. *He told a lie about this business:* Aesthetically, the action of the Fifth *Bolgia* ends here with Virgil's recognition that Malacoda's words (XXI, 110–111) about the unbroken bridge were false. The events, in fact, of Cantos XXI–XXIII revolve around a series of lies which show the general sin of Fraud in action. First

Malacoda and the other *Malebranche* deceive Dante and Virgil by making them think that although the "primary" bridge over *Bolgia* Six is smashed, there is another farther on which is whole; next, Ciampolo the Navarrese deceives Dante and Virgil into thinking that he is going to summon up Italians from beneath the pitch for them to speak with, and he tricks the *Malebranche* into leaving him free for a moment with the promise that he will call up new sinners for them to torment (XXII, 97–132); then the *Malebranche* subtly deceive each other by agreeing to Ciampolo's lying proposal so that they might have a fight among themselves should Ciampolo escape—as he does (XXII, 106–141); and finally the sin of Hypocrisy which we see in Canto XXIII reflects all of the lies which have gone before. In fact the method of telling lies portrayed by Malacoda and Ciampolo—a precise truth followed by a false statement (see XXI, n. 112–114; XXII, n. 97–132) is depicted in a larger sense by the punishment of the Hypocrites with their appearance of truth (gilded exterior) cloaking a false substance.

It is interesting that Virgil, too, is taken in by the lies, and is almost a weaker figure in these cantos than the Pilgrim. In XXI he belittles the Pilgrim's fear, who is suspicious of the *Malebranche* (127–135), and in XXIII he waits for his warning (21–24) before grabbing him up and sliding into the next *bolgia*. Virgil's failure to cope with the lies perhaps indicates Reason's inability to immediately recognize Fraud, which is always disguised in reasonable phrases (the precise truths preceding the lies); and in this light it should be noted that Virgil's escape from the lying devils of *Bolgia* Six is instinctive and not reasoned (XXIII, 37–45).

146–148. *his face revealing traces of his anger:* Virgil is angry, of course, because he had trusted Malacoda and had been deceived, and also because of the friar's slightly taunting rebuke at his naiveté (142–144). That Virgil's temporary failure has not lessened the Pilgrim's respect and love in any way is evident in the concluding line: "to make my way behind those cherished footprints" (148).

*   *   *   *

Dante shows complete mastery of techniques which unify these last three cantos. First, of course, Barratry and Hypocrisy, the sins punished in the Fifth and Sixth *Bolge* are closely related, and the lies told by the characters in the Fifth *Bolgia* (XXI and XXII) are revealed as falsehoods in the Sixth *Bolgia* (XXIII). The *Malebranche* themselves are figures continued through all three cantos, and the humor, often grotesque, comes through in the flippant language and Keystone-Cop-like actions of the devils. The humor perhaps comes to an end with the sarcastic remark of the friar to Virgil that "Once, in Bologna, I heard discussed / the devil's many vices; one of them is / that he tells lies and is father of all lies" (XXIII, 142–144). The imagery too binds the cantos together. The opening image of XXI (the Venice shipyard) forecasts the coming busy, semimilitary activity of the *Malebranche* around the pitch; the mock epic opening of XXII continues the comic military imagery in its reference back to the fart that ended XXI; and Aesop's fable, of which the Pilgrim is reminded at the beginning of XXIII by the skirmish at the end of XXII, is also foreshadowed in XXII by animal similes involving frogs, a mouse, and a hawk. Finally Dante deftly alternates speed and slowness in his poetry to reflect the activity described and to link the cantos. The rapid busyness of the Venetian shipyard simile is soon reflected in the busyness of the *Malebranche's* speech:

> . . . "Hey Malebranche,
> here's one of Santa Zita's elders for you!
> You stick him under—I'll go back for more. . . ."
> (XXI, 37–39)

The busy language is continued through XXII, but the first tercets of XXIII are by contrast slow and ponderous:

> In silence, all alone, without an escort,
> we moved along, one behind the other,
> like minor friars bent upon a journey.
>
> (1–3)

These lines of course foreshadow the heavy, slow movement of the Hypocrites to come, but soon the pace is picked up again as Virgil and Dante escape the *Malebranche*, and it reaches its frenetic climax as the poets' sliding down the bank is compared to water rushing down a mill-sluice (46–51). But as soon as they are safely on the ground of the Sixth *Bolgia*, they see the Hypocrites, and the pace slows to a crawl again:

> And now, down there, we found a painted people,
> slow-motioned: step by step, they walked their round.
>
> (58–59)

These three cantos are linked by aesthetic devices of particular effectiveness.

CANTO XXIV

In the season of the newborn year, when the sun
　　renews its rays beneath Aquarius
　　and nights begin to last as long as days,　　　　　　　　　*3*

at the time the hoarfrost paints upon the ground
　　the outward semblance of his snow-white sister
　　(but the color from his brush soon fades away),　　　　　*6*

the peasant wakes, gets up, goes out and sees
　　the fields all white. No fodder for his sheep!
　　He smites his thighs in anger and goes back　　　　　　*9*

into his shack and, pacing up and down,
　　complains, poor wretch, not knowing what to do;
　　once more he goes outdoors, and hope fills him　　　*12*

again when he sees the world has changed its face
　　in so little time, and he picks up his crook
　　and out to pasture drives his sheep to graze—　　　*15*

just so I felt myself lose heart to see
　　my master's face wearing a troubled look,
　　and as quickly came the salve to heal my sore:　　　*18*

for when we reached the shattered heap of bridge,
　　my leader turned to me with that sweet look
　　of warmth I first saw at the mountain's foot;　　　　*21*

he opened up his arms (but not before
　　he had carefully studied how the ruins lay
　　and found some sort of plan) to pick me up.　　　　*24*

Like one who works and thinks things out ahead,
　　always ready for the next move he will make,
　　so while he raised me up toward one great rock,　　*27*

he had already singled out another,
  saying, "Now get a grip on that rock there,
  but test it first to see it holds your weight."   *30*

It was no road for one who wore a cloak!
  Even though I had his help and he weighed nothing,
  we could hardly lift ourselves from crag to crag.   *33*

And had it not been that the bank we climbed
  was lower than the one we had slid down—
  I cannot speak for him—but I for one   *36*

surely would have quit. But since the Evil Pits
  slope toward the yawning well that is the lowest,
  each valley is laid out in such a way   *39*

that one bank rises higher than the next.
  We somehow finally reached the point above
  where the last of all that rock was shaken loose.   *42*

My lungs were so pumped out of breath by the time
  I reached the top, I could not go on farther,
  and instantly I sat down where I was.   *45*

"Come on, shake off the covers of this sloth,"
  the master said, "for sitting softly cushioned,
  or tucked in bed, is no way to win fame;   *48*

and without it man must waste his life away,
  leaving such traces of what he was on earth
  as smoke in wind and foam upon the water.   *51*

Stand up! Dominate this weariness of yours
  with the strength of soul that wins in every battle
  if it does not sink beneath the body's weight.   *54*

Much steeper stairs than these we'll have to climb;
  we have not seen enough of sinners yet!
  If you understand me, act, learn from my words."   *57*

At this I stood up straight and made it seem
  I had more breath than I began to breathe,
  and said: "Move on, for I am strong and ready."   *60*

We climbed and made our way along the bridge
  which was jagged, tight and difficult to cross,
  and steep—far more than any we had climbed.   *63*

Not to seem faint I spoke while I was climbing;
    then came a voice from the depths of the next chasm,
    a voice unable to articulate.   66

I don't know what it said, even though I stood
    at the very top of the arch that crosses there;
    to me it seemed whoever spoke, spoke running.   69

I was bending over, but no living eyes
    could penetrate the bottom of that darkness;
    therefore I said: "Master, why not go down   72

this bridge onto the next encircling bank,
    for I hear sounds I cannot understand,
    and I look down but cannot see a thing."   75

"No other answer," he replied, "I give you
    than doing what you ask, for a fit request
    is answered best in silence and in deed."   78

From the bridge's height we came down to the point
    where it ends and joins the edge of the eighth bank,
    and then the *bolgia* opened up to me: 81

down there I saw a terrible confusion
    of serpents, all of such a monstrous kind
    the thought of them still makes my blood run cold.   84

Let all the sands of Libya boast no longer,
    for though she breeds chelydri and jaculi,
    phareans, cenchres and head-tailed amphisbenes,   87

she never bred so great a plague of venom,
    not even if combined with Ethiopia
    or all the sands that lie by the Red Sea.   90

Within this cruel and bitterest abundance
    people ran terrified and naked, hopeless
    of finding hiding-holes or heliotrope.   93

Their hands were tied behind their backs with serpents
    which pushed their tails and heads around the loins
    and coiled themselves in knots around the front.   96

And then—at a sinner running by our bank
    a snake shot out and, striking, hit his mark:
    right where the neck attaches to the shoulder.   99

No *O* or *I* was ever quicker put
  by pen to paper than he flared up and burned,
  and turned into a heap of crumbled ash;   *102*

and then, these ashes scattered on the ground
  began to come together on their own
  and quickly take the form they had before: *105*

precisely so, philosophers declare
  the phoenix dies to be reborn again
  as she approaches her five-hundredth year;   *108*

alive she does not feed on herbs or grain,
  but on teardrops of frankincense and balm,
  and wraps herself to die in nard and myrrh.   *111*

As a man in a fit will fall, not knowing why
  (perhaps some hidden demon pulls him down,
  or some oppilation chokes his vital spirits),   *114*

then, struggling to his feet, will look around,
  confused and overwhelmed by the great anguish
  he has suffered, moaning as he stares about—   *117*

so did this sinner when he finally rose.
  Oh, how harsh the power of the Lord can be,
  raining in its vengeance blows like these!   *120*

My guide asked him to tell us who he was,
  and he replied: "It's not too long ago
  I rained from Tuscany to this fierce gullet.   *123*

I loved the bestial life more than the human,
  like the bastard that I was; I'm Vanni Fucci,
  the beast! Pistoia was my fitting den."   *126*

I told my guide: "Tell him not to run away;
  ask him what sin has driven him down here,
  for I knew him as a man of bloody rage."   *129*

The sinner heard and did not try to feign;
  directing straight at me his mind and face,
  he reddened with a look of ugly shame,   *132*

and said: "That you have caught me by surprise
  here in this wretched *bolgia*, makes me grieve
  more than the day I lost my other life.   *135*

Now I am forced to answer what you ask:
  I am stuck so far down here because of theft:
  I stole the treasure of the sacristy—   138

a crime falsely attributed to another.
  I don't want you to rejoice at having seen me,
  if ever you escape from these dark pits,   141

so open your ears and hear my prophecy:
  Pistoia first shall be stripped of all its Blacks,
  and Florence then shall change its men and laws;   144

from Valdimagra Mars shall thrust a bolt
  of lightning wrapped in thick, foreboding clouds,
  then bolt and clouds will battle bitterly   147

in a violent storm above Piceno's fields
  where rapidly the bolt will burst the cloud,
  and no White will escape without his wounds.   150

And I have told you this so you will suffer!"

NOTES

1–18. *In the seaon of the newborn year when the sun:* The striking image which opens Canto XXIV has been taken by most critics to be a *tour de force* which has little or no relation to the canto as a whole; I believe, however, that in its shifting imagery it sets the tone for the fantastic metamorphoses of this canto and the next. In the simile, a peasant, erroneously believing the hoarfrost to be snow, first becomes angry, then, discovering that he has been deceived, regains his composure and drives his sheep out to pasture. From one point of view the peasant is like Dante the Pilgrim and Virgil is like the countryside:

  just so I felt myself lose heart to see
  my master's face wearing a troubled look,
  and as quickly came the salve to heal my sore.
                (16–18)

So Dante, when he sees that Virgil has regained his composure, is glad like the peasant "when he sees the world has changed its face / in so little time . . ." (13–14). But from another point of view the peasant is like Virgil because he believed the hoarfrost to be snow, just as Virgil had believed Malacoda's lie; just as the angry peasant recovers his composure "in so little time" so Virgil does. The Pilgrim, in this case, is like the sheep which the peasant drives out to pasture, for Virgil, having regained his composure, urges the Pilgrim up the rocky slope.

Thus the two figures compared to the elements of the simile undergo a shifting metamorphosis just as the thieves in the Seventh *Bolgia* will. But Dante's subtle foreshadowing of metamorphosis does not stop there; within the simile itself the countryside undergoes a metamorphosis as the white hoarfrost melts away. Even in the rhyme itself, in Italian, there are words which suggest the same process, for here Dante makes extensive use of equivocal rhyme: two words rhyming with each other, which are spelled the same way but mean different things. One example (out of at least three instances in the first twenty-four lines) occurs in lines 11 and 13:

Come 'l tapin che non sa che si faccia;

. . . .

veggendo il mondo aver cangiata faccia.
(11 and 13)

'Che si faccia' in line 11 means 'what to do' (from *fare*, v. 'to do') while 'aver cangiata faccia' in line 13 means 'has changed its face' (*la faccia*, n. 'face'). Thus words themselves in this passage undergo metamorphosis.

The simile is indeed a *tour de force*, but a *tour de force* foreshadowing the complex and fantastic transformations to come.

21. *at the mountain's foot:* The mountain of Canto I, a reference which reminds the reader of the entire journey.

31. *It was no road for one who wore a cloak!:* Such as the Hypocrites of the previous *bolgia*.

38. *slope toward the yawning well that is the lowest:* That is, toward Cocytus, the lowest part of Hell.

47–48. *for sitting softly cushioned:* Note the rustic, proverbial tone of Virgil's words. He is talking like the peasant to whom he is compared in the opening simile.

55. *Much steeper stairs than these we'll have to climb:* Virgil is referring to the ascent up Lucifer's legs and beyond. See XXXIV, 82–84.

85–90. *Let all the sands of Libya boast no longer:* Libya and the other lands near the Red Sea (Ethiopia and Arabia) were renowned for producing several types of dreadful reptiles. All of these mentioned by Dante were described in the Pharsalia (IX, 700 ff). The *chelydri*, according to Lucan, leave smoking paths; the *jaculi* dart through the air and pierce whatever they encounter. The *phareans* make paths in the earth with their tails; the *cenchres* leave a wavering course in the sand; and the *amphisbenes* have two heads, one at each end.

92. *people ran terrified and naked, hopeless:* The Thieves.

93. *of finding hiding-holes or heliotrope:* According to folk tradition, heliotrope was believed to be a stone of many virtues. It could cure snakebites and make the man who carried it on his person invisible. Boccaccio relates a tale of a man who thought himself invisible through the power of the heliotrope (*Decameron* VIII, 3).

100. *No O or I was ever quicker put:* The letter *o* and the undotted *i* can be written with one stroke of the pen; thus, the action described is very rapid.

108–111. *as she approaches her five-hundredth year:* Dante compares the complex metamorphosis of Vanni Fucci to that of the phoenix which, according to legend, consumes itself in flames every five hundred years. From the ashes is born a worm which in three days develops into the bird again. The "philosophers" (*savi*, which can also be translated as "poets") are probably Ovid and Brunetto Latini, both of whom wrote about the phoenix.

112–117. *As a man in a fit will fall, not knowing why:* It was a popular belief that during an epileptic fit, the victim was possessed by the devil; in addition to this, Dante presents a more rational explanation: that some blockage of his veins inhibits the proper functioning of a man's body.

125–129. *like the bastard that I was; I'm Vanni Fucci:* Vanni Fucci, the illegitimate son of Fuccio de' Lazzari, was a militant leader of the Blacks in Pistoia. His notoriety "as a man of bloody rage" (129) was widespread; in fact, the Pilgrim is surprised to find him here and not immersed in the Phlegethon together with the other shades of the Violent (Canto XII).

138–139. *I stole the treasure of the sacristy:* Around 1293 the treasury of San Iacopo in the church of San Zeno at Pistoia was robbed. The person unjustly accused (139) of the theft (and almost executed for it) was Rampino Foresi. Later, the true facts came to light, and Vanni della Monna, one of the conspirators, was sentenced to death. Vanni Fucci, however, escaped, and although he received a sentence in 1295 for murder and other acts of violence, he managed to remain free until his death in 1300.

143–150. *Pistoia first shall be stripped of all its Blacks:* Vanni Fucci's prophecy remains somewhat obscure, but the best explanation for it seems to be as follows. Members of the White Party in Pistoia forced the Blacks to leave after May, 1301. The Pistoian Blacks fled to Florence and, together with the Florentine Blacks, took over the government of the city with the aid of Charles of Valois in November, 1301; the Whites were then banished from the city. The Valdimagra of line 145 was the territory of Moroello Malaspina (the "bolt of lightning"), who as captain led a force of Florentines and Lucchesi (Blacks?) against Pistoia in 1302. The "thick, foreboding clouds" in which he is "wrapped" are the Pistoians who surprised Moroello and surrounded him at the battle of Serravalle, a town near "Piceno's fields." Although surrounded, Moroello managed to rally his forces and disperse the enemy.

The use of meteorological imagery is typical of the science of Dante's time.

CANTO XXV

When he had finished saying this, the thief
  shaped his fists into figs and raised them high
  and cried: "Here, God, I've shaped them just for you!"   *3*

From then on all those snakes became my friends,
  for one of them at once coiled round his neck
  as if to say, "That's all you're going to say,"   *6*

while another twisted round his arms in front;
  it tied itself into so tight a knot,
  between the two he could not move a muscle.   *9*

Pistoia, ah Pistoia! why not resolve
  to burn yourself to ashes, ending all,
  since you have done more evil than your founders?   *12*

Throughout the circles of this dark inferno
  I saw no shade so haughty toward his God,
  not even he who fell from Thebes' high walls.   *15*

Without another word he fled, and then
  I saw a raging centaur gallop up
  roaring: "Where is he, where is that untamed beast?"   *18*

I think that all Maremma does not have
  as many snakes as he had on his back,
  right up to where his human form begins.   *21*

Upon his shoulders, just behind the nape,
  a dragon with its wings spread wide was crouching
  and spitting fire at whoever came its way.   *24*

My master said to me: "That one is Cacus,
  who more than once in the grotto far beneath
  Mount Aventine spilled blood to fill a lake.   *27*

He does not go the same road as his brothers
    because of the cunning way he committed theft
    when he stole his neighbor's famous cattle herd;   *30*

and then his evil deeds came to an end
    beneath the club of Hercules, who struck
    a hundred blows, and he, perhaps, felt ten."   *33*

While he was speaking Cacus galloped off;
    at the same time three shades appeared below us;
    my guide and I would not have seen them there   *36*

if they had not cried out: "Who are you two?"
    At this we cut our conversation short
    to give our full attention to these three.   *39*

I didn't know who they were, but then it happened,
    as often it will happen just by chance,
    that one of them was forced to name another: *42*

"Where did Cianfa go off to?" he asked. And then,
    to keep my guide from saying anything,
    I put my finger tight against my lips.   *45*

Now if, my reader, you should hesitate
    to believe what I shall say, there's little wonder,
    for I, the witness, scarcely can believe it.   *48*

While I was watching them, all of a sudden
    a serpent—and it had six feet—shot up
    and hooked one of these wretches with all six.   *51*

With the middle feet it hugged the sinner's stomach
    and, with the front ones, grabbed him by the arms,
    and bit him first through one cheek then the other;   *54*

the serpent spread its hind feet round both thighs
    then stuck its tail between the sinner's legs,
    and up against his back the tail slid stiff.   *57*

No ivy ever grew to any tree
    so tight entwined, as the way that hideous beast
    had woven in and out its limbs with his;   *60*

and then both started melting like hot wax
    and, fusing, they began to mix their colors
    (so neither one seemed what he was before),   *63*

just as a brownish tint, ahead of flame,
　　creeps up a burning page that is not black
　　completely, even though the white is dying.　　　　　　66

The other two who watched began to shout:
　　"Oh Agnèl! If you could see how you are changing!
　　You're not yourself, and you're not both of you!"　　69

The two heads had already fused to one
　　and features from each flowed and blended into
　　one face where two were lost in one another;　　　72

two arms of each were four blurred strips of flesh;
　　and thighs with legs, then stomach and the chest
　　sprouted limbs that human eyes have never seen.　75

Each former likeness now was blotted out:
　　both, and neither one it seemed—this picture
　　of deformity. And then it sneaked off slowly.　　78

Just as a lizard darting from hedge to hedge,
　　under the stinging lash of the dog-days' heat,
　　zips across the road, like a flash of lightning,　　81

so, rushing toward the two remaining thieves,
　　aiming at their guts, a little serpent,
　　fiery with rage and black as pepper-corn,　　　　84

shot up and sank its teeth in one of them,
　　right where the embryo receives its food,
　　then back it fell and lay stretched out before him.　87

The wounded thief stared speechless at the beast,
　　and standing motionless began to yawn
　　as though he needed sleep, or had a fever.　　　90

The snake and he were staring at each other;
　　one from his wound, the other from its mouth
　　fumed violently, and smoke with smoke was mingling.　93

Let Lucan from this moment on be silent,
　　who tells of poor Nasidius and Sabellus,
　　and wait to hear what I still have in store;　　　96

and Ovid, too, with his Cadmus and Arethusa—
　　though he metamorphosed one into a snake,
　　the other to a fountain, I feel no envy,　　　　99

for never did he interchange two beings
    face to face so that both forms were ready
    to exchange their substance, each one for the other's,   *102*

an interchange of perfect symmetry:
    the serpent split its tail into a fork,
    and the wounded sinner drew his feet together;   *105*

the legs, with both the thighs, closed in to join
    and in a short time fused, so that the juncture
    didn't show signs of ever having been there,   *108*

the while the cloven tail assumed the features
    that the other one was losing, and its skin
    was growing soft, the other's getting scaly;   *111*

I saw his arms retreating to the armpits,
    and the reptile's two front feet, that had been short,
    began to stretch the length the man's had shortened;   *114*

the beast's hind feet then twisted round each other
    and turned into the member man conceals,
    while from the wretch's member grew two legs.   *117*

The smoke from each was swirling round the other,
    exchanging colors, bringing out the hair
    where there was none, and stripping off the other's.   *120*

The one rose up, the other sank, but neither
    dissolved the bond between their evil stares,
    fixed eye to eye, exchanging face for face;   *123*

the standing creature's face began receding
    toward the temples; from the excess stuff pulled back,
    the ears were growing out of flattened cheeks,   *126*

while from the excess flesh that did not flee
    the front, a nose was fashioned for the face,
    and lips puffed out to just the normal size.   *129*

The prostrate creature strains his face out long
    and makes his ears withdraw into his head,
    the way a snail pulls in its horns. The tongue,   *132*

that once had been one piece and capable
    of forming words, divides into a fork,
    while the other's fork heals up. The smoke subsides.   *135*

The soul that had been changed into a beast
  went hissing off along the valley's floor,
  the other close behind him, spitting words.   *138*

Then he turned his new-formed back on him and said
  to the shade left standing there: "Let Buoso run
  the valley on all fours, the way I did."   *141*

Thus I saw the cargo of the seventh hold
  exchange and interchange; and let the strangeness
  of it all excuse me, if my pen has failed.   *144*

And though this spectacle confused my eyes
  and stunned my mind, the two thieves could not flee
  so secretly I did not recognize   *147*

that one was certainly Puccio Sciancato
  (and he alone, of that company of three
  that first appeared, did not change to something else),   *150*

the other, he who made you mourn, Gaville.

NOTES

2. *shaped his fists into figs and raised them high:* An obscene gesture still current in Italy. The gesture is made by closing the hand to form a fist with the thumb inserted between the first and second fingers. It means "Up yours!" or "Fuck you!"

10–12. *Pistoia, ah Pistoia! why not resolve:* Pistoia was supposedly founded by the remnants of the defeated army of Catiline (cf. XV, 61–78), composed primarily of evil-doers and brigands. Note that Dante calls upon Pistoia to destroy itself in the same manner that Vanni Fucci, its native son, was destroyed in the previous canto (10–117).

15. *he who fell from Thebes' high walls:* Capaneus, whom Dante placed among the Blasphemers in the Seventh Circle (XIV, 63). Like Vanni Fucci, Capaneus continues to blaspheme and rebel against God even in Hell.

19–20. *I think that all Maremma does not have:* Maremma was a swampy area along the Tuscan coast which was infested with snakes. Cf. XIII, 8–9; also XXIX, 48–49.

25–33. *That one is Cacus:* Cacus, a centaur, was the son of Vulcan; he was a fire-belching monster who lived in a cave beneath Mt. Aventine and pillaged the inhabitants of the area. But when he stole several cattle of Hercules, the latter went to Cacus' cave and killed him. "His brothers" (28) are the centaurs who serve as guardians in the first round of the Seventh Circle (Canto XII).

43. *"Where did Cianfa go off to?" he asked:* Cianfa was a member of the Florentine Donati family. He makes his appearance in line 50 in the form of a serpent.

68. *Oh Agnèl!:* Besides the indication that Agnèl is Florentine (except for Vanni Fucci, the thieves in this canto are all Florentines), and possibly is one of the Brunelleschi family, nothing more is known of him.

86. *right where the embryo receives its food:* The navel.

94–102. *Let Lucan from this moment on be silent:* In the *Pharsalia* (IX, 763 and 790) Lucan tells of the physical transformations undergone by Sabellus and Nasidius, both soldiers in Cato's army who, being bitten by snakes, turned respectively into ashes (cf. Vanni Fucci's metamorphosis, XXIV, 100–117) and into a formless mass. Ovid relates (*Metamorphoses* IV, 576) how Cadmus took the form of a serpent and how Arethusa became a fountain (V, 572).

In these rather boastful verses Dante declares the superiority of his art, at least in this case, to that of Lucan and Ovid. Theirs was a "one-way" transformation; his transformation will be reciprocal, and therein lies its uniqueness.

140–141. *Let Buoso run:* The identity of Buoso, the newly formed serpent, is uncertain; some commentators think him to be Buoso degli Abati and others, Buoso Donati (see XXX, 44).

142. *Thus I saw the cargo of the seventh hold:* Dante, by referring to the inhabitants of the Seventh *Bolgia* as "cargo" (*zavorra*), sets up the ship imagery for Ulysses in the next canto.

145–151

That the Pilgrim's eyes are confused and his mind is stunned at this point is easily understandable in terms merely of the spectacle he has witnessed. He has seen three types of metamorphosis undergone by the thieves in Cantos XXIV–XXV. First, a sinner (Vanni Fucci) is struck by a serpent at the base of the neck, burns to ashes and reshapes himself from the pile of ashes; more complicated is the next transformation, caused when another sinner is attacked by a six-footed serpent—who merges with him as the two grow together into one hideous creature; finally, the attacking serpent shares again in the metamorphosis, in a still more complicated way: the snake becomes a man and the man becomes a snake. As for the symbolism involved in these metamorphoses, I agree with Dorothy Sayers' interpretation: "In this canto we see how the Thieves, who made no distinction between *meum* and *tuum* . . . cannot call their forms or their personalities their own. . . ."

But there is still a greater reason for the Pilgrim's confusion, given the problems of identification involved in the last two metamorphoses. We are told beforehand that the one who imitates the birth and death of the phoenix is Vanni Fucci; but it takes careful reading and re-reading (and some guessing) to establish the roles played by three of the five sinners alluded to in this canto: Cianfa, Buoso and "he who made you mourn, Gaville" (Francesco Cavalcanti, see n. 151). Cianfa's name is mentioned by one of the three thieves appearing in line 35, who seems surprised at Cianfa's disappearance ("Where did Cianfa go off to?" 43). But if Cianfa has disappeared we must assume it is because he has just been transformed into the six-footed serpent who attacks Agnèl ("Oh Agnèl! If you could see how you are changing!" 68), to fuse with him into one monstrous form. From the words "Let Buoso run / the valley on all fours, the way I did" (140–141) spoken after the next metamorphosis by the serpent-become-man about the man-become-serpent we learn that Buoso must have also been one of the three thieves seen by the Pilgrim. Finally, the speaker himself must have been Francesco Cavalcanti alluded to in the last line of the canto.

Surely the blurry presentation of identities offered to the reader represents an artistic device on the part of Dante to enhance the fluctuation of identity given by metamorphosis itself.

148. *that one was certainly Puccio Sciancato:* Puccio Sciancato (the only one of the original three Florentine thieves who does not assume a new shape) was a

member of the Galigai family and a supporter of the Ghibellines. He was exiled from Florence in 1268.

151. *the other, he who made you mourn, Gaville:* Francesco Cavalcanti, known as Guercio, was slain by the inhabitants of Gaville, a small town near Florence in Valdarno (Arno Valley). The Cavalcanti family avenged his death by decimating the populace; thus, he was Gaville's reason to mourn.

CANTO XXVI

Be joyful, Florence, since you are so great
    that your outstretched wings beat over land and sea,
    and your name is spread throughout the realm of Hell!   *3*

I was ashamed to find among the thieves
    five of your most eminent citizens,
    a fact which does you very little honor.   *6*

But if early morning dreams have any truth,
    you will have the fate, in not too long a time,
    that Prato and the others crave for you.   *9*

And were this the day, it would not be too soon!
    Would it had come to pass, since pass it must!
    The longer the delay, the more my grief.   *12*

We started climbing up the stairs of boulders
    that had brought us to the place from where we watched;
    my guide went first and pulled me up behind him.   *15*

We went along our solitary way
    among the rocks, among the ridge's crags,
    where the foot could not advance without the hand.   *18*

I know that I grieved then, and now again
    I grieve when I remember what I saw,
    and more than ever I restrain my talent   *21*

lest it run a course that virtue has not set;
    for if a lucky star or something better
    has given me this good, I must not misuse it.   *24*

As many fireflies (in the season when
    the one who lights the world hides his face least,
    in the hour when the flies yield to mosquitoes)   *27*

189

as the peasant on the hillside at his ease
   sees, flickering in the valley down below,
   where perhaps he gathers grapes or tills the soil—   *30*

with just so many flames all the eighth *bolgia*
   shone brilliantly, as I became aware
   when at last I stood where the depths were visible.   *33*

As he who was avenged by bears beheld
   Elijah's chariot at its departure,
   when the rearing horses took to flight toward Heaven,   *36*

and though he tried to follow with his eyes,
   he could not see more than the flame alone
   like a small cloud once it had risen high—   *39*

so each flame moves itself along the throat
   of the abyss, none showing what it steals
   but each one stealing nonetheless a sinner.   *42*

I was on the bridge, leaning far over—so far
   that if I had not grabbed some jut of rock
   I could easily have fallen to the bottom.   *45*

And my guide who saw me so absorbed, explained:
   "There are souls concealed within these moving fires,
   each one swathed in his burning punishment."   *48*

"O master," I replied, "from what you say
   I know now I was right; I had guessed already
   it might be so, and I was about to ask you: *51*

Who's in that flame with its tip split in two,
   like that one which once sprang up from the pyre
   where Eteocles was placed beside his brother?"   *54*

He said: "Within, Ulysses and Diomed
   are suffering in anger with each other,
   just vengeance makes them march together now.   *57*

And they lament inside one flame the ambush
   of the horse become the gateway that allowed
   the Romans' noble seed to issue forth.   *60*

Therein they mourn the trick that caused the grief
   of Deidamia who still weeps for Achilles;
   and there they pay for the Palladium."   *63*

"If it is possible for them to speak
   from within those flames," I said, "master, I pray
   and repray you—let my prayer be like a thousand—   66

that you do not forbid me to remain
   until the two-horned flame comes close to us;
   you see how I bend toward it with desire!"   69

"Your prayer indeed is worthy of highest praise,"
   he said to me, "and therefore I shall grant it;
   but see to it your tongue refrains from speaking.   72

Leave it to me to speak, for I know well
   what you would ask; perhaps since they were Greeks
   they might not pay attention to your words."   75

So when the flame had reached us, and my guide
   decided that the time and place were right,
   he addressed them and I listened to him speaking: 78

"O you who are two souls within one fire,
   if I have deserved from you when I was living,
   if I have deserved from you much praise or little,   81

when in the world I wrote my lofty verses,
   do not move on; let one of you tell where
   he lost himself through his own fault, and died."   84

The greater of the ancient flame's two horns
   began to sway and quiver, murmuring
   just like a flame that strains against the wind;   87

then, while its tip was moving back and forth,
   as if it were the tongue itself that spoke,
   the flame took on a voice and said: "When I   90

set sail from Circe who, more than a year,
   had kept me occupied close to Gaëta
   (before Aeneas called it by that name),   93

not sweetness of a son, not reverence
   for an aging father, not the debt of love
   I owed Penelope to make her happy,   96

could quench deep in myself the burning wish
   to know the world and have experience
   of all man's vices, of all human worth.   99

So I set out on the deep and open sea
   with just one ship and with that group of men,
   not many, who had not deserted me.   *102*

I saw as far as Spain, far as Morocco,
   both shores; I had left behind Sardinia,
   and the other islands which that sea encloses.   *105*

I and my mates were old and tired men.
   Then finally we reached the narrow neck
   where Hercules put up his signal-pillars   *108*

to warn men not to go beyond that point.
   On my right I saw Seville, and passed beyond;
   on my left, Ceuta had already sunk behind me.   *111*

'Brothers,' I said, 'who through a hundred thousand
   perils have made your way to reach the West,
   during this so brief vigil of our senses   *114*

that is still reserved for us do not deny
   yourself experience of what there is beyond,
   behind the sun, in the world they call unpeopled.   *117*

Consider what you came from: you are Greeks!
   You were not born to live like mindless brutes
   but to follow paths of excellence and knowledge.'   *120*

With this brief exhortation I made my crew
   so anxious for the way that lay ahead,
   that then I hardly could have held them back;   *123*

and with our stern turned toward the morning light,
   we made our oars our wings for that mad flight,
   gaining distance, always sailing to the left.   *126*

The night already had surveyed the stars
   the other pole contains; it saw ours so low
   it did not show above the ocean floor.   *129*

Five times we saw the splendor of the moon
   grow full and five times wane away again
   since we had entered through the narrow pass—   *132*

when there appeared a mountain shape, darkened
   by distance, that arose to endless heights.
   I had never seen another mountain like it.   *135*

Our celebrations soon turned into grief:
  from the new land there rose a whirling wind
  that beat against the forepart of the ship   *138*

and whirled us round three times in churning waters;
  the fourth blast raised the stern up high, and sent
  the bow down deep, as pleased Another's will.   *141*

And then the sea was closed again, above us."

NOTES

1–6. *Be joyful, Florence, since you are so great:* Dante's invective against Florence, inspired by the presence of five of her citizens in the *bolgia* of the Thieves, also serves an artistic function. Depicted as a great bird that spreads its wings, the proud city of Florence prefigures Lucifer (cf. XXXIV, 46–48) and, more immediately, the "mad flight" (126) of Ulysses, whose ship's oars were like wings. But as Lucifer was cast down into Hell in defeat by God, so Ulysses was cast into the depths of the sea by a force he refers to as "Another's will" (141). The implication is that some day Florence, by adhering to her present course, will also be destroyed.

7–9. *But if early morning dreams have any truth:* According to the ancient and medieval popular tradition, the dreams that men have in the early morning hours before daybreak will come true.

Dante's dream-prophecy concerns impending strife for Florence and can be interpreted in several ways. It could refer to the malediction placed on the city by Cardinal Niccolò da Prato, who was sent (1304) by Pope Benedict XI to reconcile the opposing political factions, and who, having failed in his mission, decided to lay a curse on the city. Or we may have an allusion to the expulsion of the Blacks from Prato in 1309. However, it seems most plausible, given the phrase "and the others" (9) that Prato is to be interpreted here in a generic sense to indicate all the small Tuscan towns subjected to Florentine rule, which will soon rebel against their master.

34–39 *As he who was avenged by bears beheld:* The prophet Elisha saw Elijah transported to Heaven in a fiery chariot.

When Elisha on another occasion cursed, in the name of the Lord, a group of children who were mocking him, two bears came out of the forest and devoured them (2 Kings 2:9–12, 23–24).

52–54. *who's in that flame with its tip split in two:* Here the attention of the Pilgrim, is captured by a divided flame, as it was in Canto XIX by the flaming, flailing legs of Nicholas III. Dante compares this flame with that which rose from the funeral pyre of Eteocles and Polynices, twin sons of Oedipus and Jocasta, who, contesting the throne of Thebes, caused a major conflict known as the Seven Against Thebes (see XIV, 68–69). The two brothers met in single combat and slew each other. They were placed together on the pyre, but because of their great mutual hatred, the flame split.

55–57. *Within, Ulysses and Diomed:* Ulysses, the son of Laertes, was a central figure in the Trojan War. Although his deeds are recounted by Homer, Dictys of Crete, and many others, the story of his last voyage presented here by Dante (90–142), has no literary or historical precedent. His story, being an invention of Dante's, is unique in the *Divine Comedy*.

Diomed, the son of Tydeus and Deipyle, ruled Argos. He was a major Greek figure in the Trojan War and was frequently associated with Ulysses in his exploits.

In Italian, lines 56–57 are: ". . . e così 'nseme / a la vendetta vanno come a l'ira." Most commentators interpret the lines to mean that Ulysses and Diomed go together toward punishment ("vendetta") now, as in life they went together in anger (they fought together?). But because of the parallel construction *a la vendetta . . . a l'ira*, both parts of which depend on the verb *vanno* ("go") in the present tense, and because of the comparison Dante makes between Ulysses and Diomed and Eteocles and Polynices, I believe that these two figures in the flames are angry *now*; that it is part of their punishment, since they were close companions in sin on earth, to suffer ". . . in anger with each other" in Hell. "Togetherness" in punishment suffered by those who were once joined in sin has been suggested in the case of Paolo and Francesca (Canto V).

58–60. *And they lament inside one flame the ambush:* The Trojans mistakenly believed the mammoth wooden horse, left outside the city's walls, to be a sign of Greek capitulation. They brought it through the gates of the city amid great rejoicing. Later that evening the Greek soldiers hidden in the horse emerged and sacked the city. The Fall of Troy occasioned the journey of Aeneas and his followers ("noble seed") to establish a new nation on the shores of Italy which would become the heart of the Roman Empire. See Cantos I (73–75) and II (13–21).

61–62. *the grief / of Deidamia:* Thetis brought her son Achilles, disguised as a girl, to the court of King Lycomedes on the island of Scyros, so that he would not have to fight in the Trojan War. There Achilles seduced the king's daughter Deidamia, who bore him a child and whom he later abandoned, encouraged by Ulysses (who in company with Diomed had come in search of him) to join the war. Achilles' female disguise was unveiled by a "trick": bearing gifts for Lycomedes' daughters, Ulysses had smuggled in among them a shield and lance; Achilles betrayed his real sex by manifesting an inordinate interest in the two weapons.

63. *and there they pay for the Palladium:* The sacred Palladium, a statue of the goddess Pallas Athena, guaranteed the integrity of Troy as long as it remained in the citadel. Ulysses and Diomed stole it and carried it off to Argos, thereby securing victory for the Greeks over the Trojans.

75. *they might not pay attention to your words:* No one has yet offered a convincing explanation for Virgil's reluctance to allow the Pilgrim to address the two Greek warriors.

Perhaps Virgil felt that it was more fitting for him to speak because he represented the same world of antiquity as they. (See XXVII, n. 33.)

90–92. *When I / set sail from Circe:* On his return voyage to Ithaca from Troy Ulysses was detained by Circe, the daughter of the Sun, for more than a year. She was an enchantress who transformed Ulysses' men into swine.

92–93. *close to Gaëta:* Along the coast of Southern Italy above Naples there is a promontory (and now on it there is a city) then called Gaëta. Aeneas named it to honor his nurse who had died there. See *Aeneid* VII, 1 ff. and Ovid's *Metamorphoses* XIV, 441 ff.

94–96. *not sweetness of a son, not reverence:* In his quest for knowledge of the world Ulysses puts aside his affection for his son, Telemachus, his duty towards his father, Laertes, and the love of his devoted wife Penelope; that is, he sinned against the classical notion of *pietas*.

108. *where Hercules put up his signal-pillars:* The Strait of Gibraltar, referred to in ancient times as the Pillars of Hercules. The two "pillars" are Mt. Abyla on the North African coast and Mt. Calpe on the European side, which, originally one

mountain, were separated by Hercules to designate the farthest reach of the inhabited world, beyond which no man was permitted to venture.

110–111. *On my right I saw Seville, and passed beyond:* In other words Ulysses has passed through the Strait of Gibraltar and is now in the Atlantic Ocean. Ceuta is a town on the North African coast opposite Gibraltar; in this passage Seville probably represents the Iberian Peninsula and, as such, the boundary of the inhabited world.

126. *we made our oars our wings for that mad flight:* Note Ulysses' *present* judgment in Hell of his past action. (See XXVII, final note.)

130–131. *Five times we saw the splendor of the moon:* Five months had passed since they began their voyage.

133. *when there appeared a mountain shape, darkened:* In Dante's time the Southern Hemisphere was believed to be composed entirely of water; the mountain that Ulysses and his men see from afar is the Mount of Purgatory which rises from the sea in the Southern Hemisphere, the polar opposite of Jerusalem. For the formation of the mountain see XXXIV, 112–126.

* * * *

In the list of sins punished in the Eighth Circle of Hell (those of Simple Fraud) which Virgil offers in Canto XI, two categories are left unspecified, summed up in the phrase "and like filth." When the sins specified in this list are assigned to their respective *bolge* (and all commentators are agreed as to their localization), two *bolge* are left open: the Eighth and the Ninth—which must be those where the sins of "like filth" are punished. As for the specific variety of Fraud being punished in the Ninth *Bolgia*, the sinners there are clearly identified when we meet them in Canto XXVIII, as "sowers of scandal and schism." As for our canto, all scholars have assumed that the sin for which Ulysses and Diomed are being punished is that of Fraudulent Counseling, not because of what is said about them here but what is said about Guido da Montefeltro in the next canto: the Black Cherub in claiming Guido's soul says (XXVII, 115–116): "He must come down to join my other servants for the false counsel he gave." Since Guido is in the same *bolgia*, and suffers the same punishment as Ulysses and Diomed, critics have evidently assumed (as is only logical) that they must have committed the same sin; they also assume that the sin they share in common must be that of Fraudulent Counseling.

But as for Ulysses and Diomed, their sins are specifically mentioned and in none of the three instances involved is any act of "fraudulent counseling" recorded. If these two are not in Hell for this sin, then, in spite of the Black Cherub's words, it must follow that neither is Guido. (See final note to Canto XXVII.)

CANTO XXVII

By now the flame was standing straight and still;
   it said no more and had already turned
   from us, with sanction of the gentle poet,   *3*

when another, coming right behind it,
   attracted our attention to its tip,
   where a roaring of confusing sounds had started.   *6*

As the Sicilian bull—that bellowed first
   with cries of that one (and it served him right)
   who with his file had fashioned such a beast—   *9*

would bellow with the victim's voice inside
   so that, although the bull was only brass,
   the effigy itself seemed pierced with pain: *12*

so, lacking any outlet to escape
   from the burning soul that was inside the flame,
   the suffering words became the fire's language.   *15*

But after they had made their journey upward
   to reach the tip, giving it that same quiver
   the sinner's tongue inside had given them,   *18*

we heard the words: "O you to whom I point
   my voice, who spoke just now in Lombard, saying:
   'you may move on, I won't ask more of you,'   *21*

although I have been slow in coming to you,
   be willing, please, to pause and speak with me.
   You see how willing I am—and I burn!   *24*

If you have just now fallen to this world
   of blindness, from that sweet Italian land
   where I took on the burden of my guilt,   *27*

tell me, are the Romagnols at war or peace?
  For I come from the hills between Urbino
  and the mountain chain that lets the Tiber loose."   *30*

I was still bending forward listening
  when my master touched my side and said to me:
  "*You* speak to him; *this* one is Italian."   *33*

And I, who was prepared to answer him,
  began without delaying my response:
  "O soul who stands concealed from me down there,   *36*

your Romagna is not now and never was
  without war in her tyrants' hearts, although
  there was no open warfare when I came here.   *39*

Ravenna's situation has not changed:
  the eagle of Polenta broods up there,
  covering all of Cervia with its pinions;   *42*

the land that stood the test of long endurance
  and left the French piled in a bloody heap
  is once again beneath the verdant claws.   *45*

Verrucchio's Old Mastiff and its New One,
  who both were bad custodians of Montagna,
  still sink their fangs into their people's flesh;   *48*

the cities by Lamone and Santerno
  are governed by the Lion of the White Lair
  who changes parties every change of season.   *51*

As for the town whose side the Savio bathes:
  just as it lies between the hills and plains,
  it lives between freedom and tyranny.   *54*

And now I beg you tell us who you are—
  grant me my wish as yours was granted you—
  so that your fame may hold its own on earth."   *57*

And when the fire, in its own way, had roared
  a while, the flame's sharp tip began to sway
  to and fro, then released a blow of words: *60*

"If I thought that I were speaking to a soul
  who someday might return to see he world,
  most certainly this flame would cease to flicker;   *63*

but since no one, if I have heard the truth,
   ever returns alive from this deep pit,
   with no fear of dishonor I answer you: 66

I was a man of arms and then a friar,
   believing with the cord to make amends;
   and surely my belief would have come true   69

were it not for that High Priest (his soul be damned!)
   who put me back among my early sins;
   I want to tell you why and how it happened.   72

While I still had the form of the bones and flesh
   my mother gave me, all my actions were
   not those of a lion, but those of a fox;   75

the wiles and covert paths, I knew them all,
   and so employed my art that rumor of me
   spread to the farthest limits of the earth.   78

When I saw that the time of life had come
   for me, as it must come for every man,
   to lower the sails and gather in the lines,   81

things I once found pleasure in then grieved me;
   repentant and confessed, I took the vows
   a monk takes. And, oh, to think it could have worked!   84

And then the Prince of the New Pharisees
   chose to wage war upon the Lateran
   instead of fighting Saracens or Jews,   87

for all his enemies were Christian souls,
   (none among the ones who conquered Acri,
   none a trader in the Sultan's kingdom).   90

His lofty Papal Seat, his sacred vows
   were no concern to him, nor was the cord
   I wore (that once made those it girded leaner).   93

As Constantine once had Silvestro brought
   from Mount Soracte to cure his leprosy,
   so this one sought me out as his physician   96

to cure his burning fever caused by pride.
   He asked me to advise him. I was silent,
   for his words were drunken. Then he spoke again: 99

'Fear not, I tell you: the sin you will commit,
    it is forgiven. Now you will teach me how
    I can level Palestrina to the ground.   *102*

Mine is the power, as you cannot deny,
    to lock and unlock Heaven. Two keys I have,
    those keys my predecessor did not cherish.'   *105*

And when his weighty arguments had forced me
    to the point that silence seemed the poorer choice,
    I said: 'Father, since you grant me absolution   *108*

for the sin I find I must fall into now:
    ample promise with a scant fulfillment
    will bring you triumph on your lofty throne.'   *111*

Saint Francis came to get me when I died,
    but one of the black Cherubim cried out:
    'Don't touch him, don't cheat me of what is mine!   *114*

He must come down to join my other servants
    for the false counsel he gave. From then to now
    I have been ready at his hair, because   *117*

one cannot be absolved unless repentant,
    nor can one both repent and will a thing
    at once—the one is cancelled by the other!'   *120* ˙

O wretched me! How I shook when he took me,
    saying: 'Perhaps you never stopped to think
    that I might be somewhat of a logician!'   *123*

He took me down to Minòs, who eight times
    twisted his tail around his hardened back,
    then in his rage he bit it, and announced: *126*

'He goes with those the thievish fire burns.'
    And here you see me now, lost, wrapped this way,
    moving, as I do, with my resentment."   *129*

When he had brought his story to a close,
    the flame, in grievous pain, departed from us
    gnarling and flickering its pointed horn.   *132*

My guide and I moved farther on; we climbed
    the ridge until we stood on the next arch
    that spans the fosse where penalties are paid   *135*

by those who, sowing discord, earned Hell's wages.

7–15. *As the Sicilian bull—that bellowed first:* Phalaris, despotic ruler of Agrigentum in Sicily, commissioned Perillus to construct a bronze bull intended to be used as an instrument of torture; it was fashioned so that, once it was heated, the victim roasting within would emit cries which sounded without like those of a bellowing bull. To test the device, Phalaris made the artisan himself its first victim, and thus he received his just reward for creating such a cruel instrument.

20. *who spoke just now in Lombard:* Evidently the words overheard by Guido were contained in Virgil's dismissal of Ulysses (3), which means that Virgil from the beginning had spoken to him in that dialect (or possibly only with a Lombard accent). Although some commentators have suggested that "Lombard" simply means "Italian," it would be quite fitting for Virgil to speak the dialect of his native region.

28. *tell me, are the Romagnols at war or peace?:* The Romagnols are the inhabitants of Romagna, the area bounded by the Po and the Reno Rivers, the Apennines, and the Adriatic Sea.

29–30. *For I come from the hills between Urbino:* Between the town of Urbino and Mount Coronaro (one of the Tuscan Apennines where the Tiber River originates) lies the region known as Montefeltro. The speaker is Guido da Montefeltro, the Ghibelline captain whose wisdom and skill in military strategy won him fame. In a later passage (73–78) he refers to his martial talent and activity as more fox-like than lion-like.

33. You *speak to him*; this *one is Italian:* After having prevented the Pilgrim from addressing Ulysses and Diomed (because they were Greeks?), he now, in the case of the Italian Guido, urges his ward to do the talking.

41–42. *the eagle of Polenta broods up there:* In 1300 Guido Vecchio, head of the Polenta family (whose coat of arms bears an eagle) and father of Francesca da Rimini, governed Ravenna and the surrounding territory which included Cervia, a small town on the Adriatic.

43–45. *the land that stood the test of long endurance:* Besieged for many months by French and Guelph troops, the Ghibelline city of Forlì emerged victorious. In May, 1282, her inhabitants led by Guido da Montefeltro broke the siege and massacred the opposing army. However, in 1300 Forlì was dominated by the tyrannical Ordelaffi family, whose insignia bore a green lion ("beneath the verdant claws," 45).

46–48. *Verrucchio's Old Mastiff and its New One:* In return for their services the city of Rimini gave her ruling family the castle of Verrucchio. Malatesta, lord of Rimini from 1295–1312, and his first born son, Malatestino, are respectively the "Old" and "New" Mastiffs. Having defeated the Ghibellines of Rimini in 1295, Malatesta captured Montagna de' Parcitati, the head of the party, who was subsequently murdered in prison by Malatestino.

49–51. *the cities by Lamone and Santerno:* The cities of Faenza (situated on the Lamone River) and Imola (near the Santerno) were governed by Maghinardo Pagani da Susinana whose coat of arms bore a blue lion on a white field. He was noted for his political instability (Ghibelline in Romagna and Guelph in Tuscany).

52–54. *As for the town whose side the Savio bathes:* Unlike the other cities mentioned by Guido, Cesena was not ruled by a despot; rather, her government, although not completely determined by the people, was in the hands of an able ruler, Galasso da Montefeltro, a cousin of Guido.

67–71. *I was a man of arms and then a friar:* In 1296 Guido joined the Franciscan order. The reason for his harsh condemnation of Pope Boniface VIII ("that High Priest") is found in lines 85–111.

81. *to lower the sails and gather in the lines:* Guido's use of the metaphor of the voyage to describe his arrival at old age certainly invites us to think of Ulysses' voyage, also undertaken when Ulysses was an old man; and the two voyages underscore the nature of the central metaphor of the *Divine Comedy,* the "voyage" of Dante the Pilgrim. As a pagan, Ulysses, of course, could not have reached the Mount of Purgatory; but even in pagan terms he committed two serious sins in undertaking the voyage: he failed to honor his commitments to his family as son, husband, and father (XXVI, 94–96), and he sailed past the limits allowed to pagan man (the pillars Hercules "put up . . . / to warn men not to go beyond that point," XXVI, 108–109). This voyage could only end in failure.

Guido's "voyage" is his whole life, and when he becomes an old man, he gives the *appearance* of doing what is right in Christian terms: "repentant and confessed, I took the vows / a monk takes" (XXVII, 83–84). But his repentance could not have been sincere, since Guido breaks his vows with his sinful advice to Pope Boniface. Thus Guido's "voyage" too, can only end in failure, and in thinking that appearance is enough, he only deceives himself.

The Pilgrim, however, will be successful in his "voyage" because he undertakes it for the right reason (to learn the nature of sin, that he may repent past sins and avoid future ones, and ultimately to reach God) and because he goes in a spirit of humility and love of God; also the Pilgrim does not wait until old age to repent of his sinful past (he is "midway in the journey of . . . life," I, l) and the success of his journey is vouchsafed by the grace of God. Unlike Ulysses and Guido, who were also men of great genius and excellence, Dante uses his *virtù* in the right way: in the service of God. See the final note to this canto.

85–90. *And then the Prince of the New Pharisees:* In 1297 the struggle between Boniface VIII ("the Prince of the New Pharisees") and the Colonna family (who lived near the Lateran palace, the Pope's residence, and who did not consider the resignation of Celestine V valid) erupted into open conflict. Boniface did not launch his crusade against the traditional rivals—Saracens and Jews (87)— but rather against his fellow Christians, faithful warriors of the Church who neither aided the Saracens during the conquest of Acre in 1291 (the last Christian stronghold in the Holy Land), nor disobeyed the interdict on commerce with Mohammedan lands (89–90).

92–93. *nor was the cord / I wore:* In earlier, less corrupt times the friars of the Franciscan order ("those it [the cord] girded") were faithful to their founder's example of poverty and abstinence.

94–95. *As Constantine once had Silvestro brought:* See Canto XIX, n. 115–117.

102. *I can level Palestrina to the ground:* The Colonna family, excommunicated by Boniface, took refuge in their fortress at Palestrina (twenty-five miles east of Rome) which was able to withstand the onslaughts of papal troops. Acting on Guido's counsel (110–111), Boniface promised (but without serious intentions) to grant complete pardon to the Colonna family, who then surrendered and, consequently, lost everything.

104–105. *Two keys I have:* Deceived by Boniface who was to be his successor, Celestine V renounced the Papacy ("those two keys") in 1294. See Canto III, n. 60, and XIX, n. 53.

108–109. *Father, since you grant me absolution:* Guido's principal error was self-deception: a man cannot be absolved from a sin before he commits it, and moreover, he cannot direct his will towards committing a sin and repent it at the same time (118–120).

113. *one of the black Cherubim:* Some of the Cherubim (the *eighth* order of angels) were transformed into demons for their rebellion against God; appropriately they appear in the *eighth* circle and the *eighth* "bolgia" of Hell.

* * * *

In the final note to Canto XXVI it was stated that there is no record of Ulysses having used fraudulent counseling in the three sins attributed to him by Virgil and that, if Ulysses is not being punished for that sin, the same must be true of Guido. But Guido confesses to having given fraudulent counsel, in one case at least, at the urging of Pope Boniface; and when the Black Cherub comes to claim his soul from St. Francis, he says of Guido: "He must come down to join my other servants / for the false counsel he gave."

But Guido's advice to the Pope was not only a sin committed at a given moment but also, and in a far more important way, a revelation about his past, his whole past: in the scene between Guido and Boniface we see that the wily strategist has not truly repented of the sins committed during his military career. Yes, Guido is in Hell because he gave the fraudulert counsel—that is, because he was capable of such an act; and he was capable of it because he had not repented for the sins committed during his life as a soldier, sins which we have no reason to believe were those of counseling ("I was a man of arms . . ."). His "repentance" itself was fraudulent: "believing to make amends with the cord."

If, then, both Ulysses and Guido are in Hell for having committed a sin other than that of fraudulent counseling, what is that sin? The only clear-cut subdivision of simple fraud that could fit the two sinners would be that of military fraud, since both of them were men of arms who were famous for their guile. Perhaps military fraud could be on a level with simony which is ecclesiastical fraud: one would involve the abuse of a noble profession, the other of a sacred office. But there is something else in common between Ulysses and Guido which is far more important than the profession they shared in life, and that is their exceptional sharpness of intellect and powers of invention. And so, instead of a clear-cut subdivision, determined by the professional goal toward which the fraud is directed, I prefer to think, in a more general way, of fraud unspecified—except in terms of the talents that characterize its practitioners. While all fraud involves in some way the abuse of the intellect, the intellect that Ulysses and Guido abused was exceptionally brilliant. If all men are endowed with reason, they had received a special gift from God, but they had used it—these brilliant sinners who shine in flames— for deception and the creation of snares.

CANTO XXVIII

Who could, even in the simplest kind of prose
   describe in full the scene of blood and wounds
   that I saw now—no matter how he tries!   *3*

Certainly any tongue would have to fail:
   man's memory and man's vocabulary
   are not enough to comprehend such pain.   *6*

If one could bring together all the wounded
   who once upon the fateful soil of Puglia
   grieved for their life's-blood spilled by the Romans,   *9*

and spilled again in the long years of the war
   that ended in great spoils of golden rings
   (as Livy's history tells, that does not err),   *12*

and pile them with the ones who felt the blows
   when they stood up against great Robert Guiscard,
   and with those others whose bones are still in heaps   *15*

at Ceprano (there where every Puglian
   turned traitor), and add those from Tagliacozzo
   where old Alardo conquered, weaponless—   *18*

if all these maimed with limbs lopped off or pierced
   were brought together, the scene would be nothing
   to compare with the foul ninth *bolgia's* bloody sight.   *21*

No wine cask with its stave or cant-bar sprung
   was ever split the way I saw someone
   ripped open from his chin to where we fart.   *24*

Between his legs his guts spilled out, with the heart
   and other vital parts, and the dirty sack
   that turns to shit whatever the mouth gulps down.   *27*

While I stood staring into his misery,
  he looked at me and with both hands he opened
  his chest and said: "See how I tear myself!   30

See how Mahomet is deformed and torn!
  In front of me, and weeping, Ali walks,
  his face cleft from his chin up to the crown.   33

The souls that you see passing in this ditch
  were all sowers of scandal and schism in life,
  and so in death you see them torn asunder.   36

A devil stands back there who trims us all
  in this cruel way, and each one of this mob
  receives anew the blade of the devil's sword   39

each time we make one round of this sad road,
  because the wounds have all healed up again
  by the time each one presents himself once more.   42

But who are you there gawking from the bridge
  and trying to put off, perhaps, fulfillment
  of the sentence passed on you when you confessed?"   45

"Death does not have him yet, he is not here
  to suffer for his guilt," my master answered;
  "but that he may have full experience;   48

I, who am dead, must lead him through this Hell
  from round to round, down to the very bottom,
  and this is as true as my presence speaking here."   51

More than a hundred in that ditch stopped short
  to look at me when they had heard his words,
  forgetting in their stupor what they suffered.   54

"And you, who will behold the sun, perhaps
  quite soon, tell Fra Dolcino that unless
  he wants to follow me here quick, he'd better   57

stock up on food, or else the binding snows
  will give the Novarese their victory,
  a conquest not won easily otherwise."   60

With the heel of one foot raised to take a step
  Mahomet said these words to me, and then
  stretched out and down his foot and moved away.   63

Another, with his throat slit, and his nose
   cut off as far as where the eyebrows start
   (and he only had a single ear to show),   66

who had stopped like all the rest to stare in wonder,
   stepped out from the group and opened up his throat
   that ran with red from all sides of his wound,   69

and spoke: "O you whom guilt does not condemn,
   whom I have seen in Italy up there,
   unless I am deceived by similarity,   72

recall to mind Pier da Medicina,
   should you return to see the gentle plain
   declining from Vercelli to Marcabò,   75

and inform the two best citizens of Fano—
   tell Messer Guido and tell Angiolello—
   that, if our foresight here is no deception,   78

from their ship they shall be hurled bound in a sack
   to drown in the water near Cattolica,
   the victims of a tyrant's treachery;   81

between the isles of Cyprus and Mallorca
   so great a crime Neptune never witnessed
   among the deeds of pirates or the Argives.   84

That traitor, who sees only with one eye
   and rules the land that someone with me here
   wishes he'd never fed his eyes upon,   87

will have them come to join him in a parley,
   then see to it they do not waste their breath
   on vows or prayers to escape Focara's wind."   90

And I to him: "If you want me to bring back
   to those on earth your message—who is the one
   sated with the bitter sight? Show him to me."   93

At once he grabbed the jaws of a companion
   standing near by, and squeezed his mouth half-open,
   announcing, "Here he is, and he is mute.   96

This man, in exile, drowned all Caesar's doubts
   and helped him cast the die, when he insisted:
   'a man prepared, who hesitates, is lost.'"   99

How helpless and bewildered he appeared,
　　his tongue hacked off as far down as the throat,
　　this Curio, once so bold and quick to speak! 　　　　　　*102*

And one who had both arms but had no hands,
　　raising the gory stumps in the filthy air
　　so that the blood dripped down and smeared his face, 　　*105*

cried: "You, no doubt, also remember Mosca,
　　who said, alas, 'What's done is over with,'
　　and sowed the seed of discord for the Tuscans." 　　　　*108*

"And of death for all your clan," I quickly said,
　　and he, this fresh wound added to his wound,
　　turned and went off like one gone mad from pain. 　　　*111*

But I remained to watch the multitude,
　　and saw a thing that I would be afraid
　　to tell about without more evidence, 　　　　　　　　　*114*

were I not reassured by my own conscience—
　　that good companion enheartening a man
　　beneath the breastplate of its purity. 　　　　　　　　*117*

I saw it, I'm sure, and I seem to see it still:
　　a body with no head that moved along,
　　moving no differently from all the rest; 　　　　　　　*120*

he held his severed head up by its hair,
　　swinging it in one hand just like a lantern,
　　and as it looked at us it said: "Alas!" 　　　　　　　　*123*

Of his own self he made himself á light
　　and they were two in one and one in two.
　　How could this be? He who ordained it knows. 　　　　*126*

And when he had arrived below our bridge,
　　he raised the arm that held the head up high
　　to let it speak to us at closer range. 　　　　　　　　*129*

It spoke: "Now see the monstrous punishment,
　　you there still breathing, looking at the dead,
　　see if you find anything else like this; 　　　　　　　*132*

and that you may report on me up there,
　　know that I am Bertran de Born, the one
　　who evilly encouraged the young king. 　　　　　　　*135*

Father and son I set against each other:
  Achitophel with his wicked instigations
  did not do more with Absalom and David.   *138*

Because I cut the bonds of persons joined
  I bear my head cut off from its life-source
  which is back there, alas, within its trunk.   *141*

In me you see the perfect *contrapasso*!"

NOTES

7–12. *If one could bring together all the wounded:* In order to introduce the great number of maimed and dismembered shades which will present themselves in the Ninth *Bolgia,* Dante "piles" together references to a number of bloody battles which took place in Puglia, the southeastern section of the Italian peninsula. The first of the series, in which the Pugliese "grieved for their life's-blood spilled by the Romans" (9), is the long war between the Samnites and the Romans (343–290 B.C.). The next, "the long years of the war / that ended in great spoils of golden rings" (10–11), is the Second Punic War which Hannibal's legions fought against Rome (218–201 B.C.). Livy writes that after the battle of Cannae (where Hannibal defeated the Romans, 216 B.C.), the Carthaginians gathered three bushels of rings from the fingers of dead Romans.

14. *when they stood up against great Robert Guiscard:* In the eleventh century Robert Guiscard (c. 1015–1085), a noble Norman adventurer, gained control of most of Southern Italy and became Duke of Apulia and Calabria, as well as Gonfalonier of the Church (1059). For the next two decades he battled the schismatic Greeks and the Saracens for the Church in the South of Italy. Later he fought for the Church in the East, raised a siege against Pope Gregory VII (1084), and died at the age of seventy, still engaged in warfare. Dante places him with the warriors for the Faith in the Heaven of Mars (*Paradise XVIII,* 48).

15–18 *and with those others whose bones are still in heaps:* A further comparison between bloody battles in Puglia and the Ninth *Bolgia:* in 1266 Charles of Anjou marched against the armies of Manfred, King of Sicily. Manfred blocked the passes leading to the south, but the pass at Ceprano was abandoned by its traitorous defenders. Charles then advanced unhindered and defeated the Sicilians at Benevento, killing Manfred. In reality, then, the battle did not take place at Ceprano, but at Benevento.

The final example in the lengthy series of battles, was a continuation of the hostilities between Charles of Anjou and the followers of Manfred. In 1268 at the battle of Tagliacozzo Charles adopted the suggestions of his general Erard de Valéry (*Alardo*) and won the encounter. Although Erard's strategy was one of wit rather than force (a "hidden" reserve troop entered the battle at the last minute when Manfred's nephew Conradin seemed to have won), it can hardly be said that "old Alardo" conquered without arms.

31. *See how Mahomet is deformed and torn!:* Mahomet, founder of the Mohammedan religion, was born at Mecca about 570 and died in 632. His punishment, to be split open from the crotch to the chin, together with the complementary punishment of Ali, represents Dante's belief that they were initiators of the great schism between the Christian Church and Mohammedanism. Many

of Dante's contemporaries thought that Mahomet was originally a Christian and a Cardinal who wanted to become Pope.

32. *In front of me, and weeping, Ali walks:* Ali (c. 600–661) was the first of Mahomet's followers, and married the prophet's daughter Fatima. Mahomet died in 632, and Ali assumed the Caliphate in 656.

45. *of the sentence passed on you when you confessed:* That is, confessed before Minòs. Cf. V, 8.

56–60 *tell Fra Dolcino:* Fra Dolcino (d. 1307), though not a monk as his name would seem to indicate, was the leader of a religious sect banned as heretical by Pope Clement V in 1305. Dolcino's sect, the Apostolic Brothers, preached the return of religion to the simplicity of apostolic times, and among their tenets was community of property and sharing of women. When Clement V ordered the eradication of the Brothers, Dolcino and his followers retreated to the hills near Novara, where they withstood the papal forces for over a year until starvation conquered them. Dolcino and his companion, Margaret of Trent, were burned at the stake in 1307. Mahomet's interest in Dolcino may stem from their similar views on marriage and women.

73. *recall to mind Pier da Medicina:* Although nothing certain is known about the life of this sinner, we do know that his home was in Medicina, a town in the Po River Valley ("the gentle plain," which lies between the towns of Vercelli and Marcabò, 74) near Bologna. According to the early commentator Benvenuto da Imola, Pier da Medicina was the instigator of strife between the Polenta and Malatesta families.

77–90. *tell Messer Guido and tell Angiolello:* Guido del Cassero and Angiolello di Carignano, leading citizens of Fano, a small town on the Adriatic, south of Rimini, were invited by Malatestino (the "traitor, who sees only with one eye," 85) to meet on a ship off the coastal city of Cattolica, which lies between Rimini and Fano. There Malatestino, Lord of Rimini from 1312 to 1317, ordered them thrown overboard in order that he might gain control of Fano. Already dead, the two victims of Malatestino's treachery will not have to pray to escape "Focara's wind," (90), the terribly destructive gale which preyed on vessels passing by the promontory of Focara near Cattolica.

92–93. *who is the one / sated with the bitter sight?:* The Pilgrim refers to what Pier da Medicina said earlier about "someone" who "wishes he'd never fed his eyes upon" Rimini (86–87).

97–102. *This man, in exile, drowned all Caesar's doubts:* Caius Scribonius Curio wishes he had never seen Rimini, the city near which the Rubicon River empties into the Adriatic. Once a Roman tribune under Pompey, Curio defected to Caesar's side, and, when the Roman general hesitated to cross the Rubicon, Curio convinced him to cross and march on Rome. At that time the Rubicon formed the boundary between Gaul and the Roman Republic; Caesar's decision to cross it precipitated the Roman Civil War.

106–108. *You, no doubt, also remember Mosca:* Mosca, about whom the Pilgrim earlier had asked Ciacco (VI, 80), was a member of the Lamberti family of Florence. His counsel ("What's done is over with," 107) was the cause of the division of Florence into the feuding Guelph and Ghibelline parties. As tradition has it, Buondelmonte de' Buondelmonti was engaged to the daughter of Lambertuccio degli Amidei; however, Aldruda, of the Donati family, offered him her daughter and promised to pay the penalty for the broken engagement. Buondelmonte accepted, thus enraging Oderigo, who demanded revenge. The powerful Uberti family, at the instigation of Mosca, declared that Buondelmonte should be killed (and he was), because a milder form of revenge (a simple beating, for example) would incur as much hatred as the most severe form (murder).

134–136. *know that I am Bertran de Born, the one:* One of the greatest of the Provençal troubadours, Bertran de Born lived in the second half of the twelfth century. His involvement in the politics of the time is reflected in his poetry, which is almost entirely of a political character. He suffers here in Hell for having caused the rebellion of Prince Henry (the "young king," 135) against his father Henry II, King of England.

137–138. *Achitophel with his wicked instigations:* Dante compares Bertran de Born's evil counsel with that of Achitophel. Once the aide of David, Achitophel the Gilonite provoked Absalom's rebellion against David, his father and king. See 2 Samuel 15–17.

142. *In me you see the perfect* contrapasso!: The decapitated figure of Bertran de Born perhaps best illustrates the law of divine retribution, the *contrapasso,* at work in the Dantean *Inferno.* In a manner of speaking, it is identical with the Old Testament God's form of vengeance: "An eye for an eye, a tooth for a tooth." Bertran de Born's *contrapasso* may have been suggested to Dante by a passage in the Provençal *vida* (biography) affixed to Bertran's poetry. Having once boasted to King Henry that he had more intelligence than he needed, he was later reminded of this boast after the death of the "young king" and after his own imprisonment by Henry. In the *vida* we read that "when King Henry took him prisoner he asked him whether he had not need of all his wits then; and Bertran answered that he lost all his wits when the young king died." In this canto, of course, Bertran's "wits" are physically separated from his body.

Bertran's most famous poem, in fact, was a lament (*planh*) for the death of the young Henry, the first stanza of which may well have suggested the opening imagery of this canto with its piling up of the miseries of war:

> If all the grief and bitterness and woe
> And all the pain and hurt and suffering
> That in this world of misery men know,
> Were massed in one, it would seem but a light thing
> Beside the death of the Young English King.

So Dante says:

> If one could bring together all the wounded
> who once upon the fateful soil of Puglia
> grieved for their life's-blood . . .
> [it] would be nothing
> to compare with the foul ninth *bolgia's* bloody sight.

Dante knew Bertran's poetry well, and in the *De Vulgari Eloquentia* II, ii, 9, he asserts that Bertran was the paragon of martial poets.

CANTO XXIX

The crowds, the countless different mutilations
   had stunned my eyes and left them so confused
   they wanted to keep looking and to weep,   3

but Virgil said: "What are you staring at?
   Why do your eyes insist on drowning there
   below, among those wretched, broken shades?   6

You did not act this way in other *bolge*.
   If you hope to count them one by one, remember
   the valley winds some twenty-two miles around;   9

and already the moon is underneath our feet;
   the time remaining to us now is short—
   and there is more to see than you see here."   12

"If you had taken time to find out what
   I was looking for," I started telling him,
   "perhaps you would have let me stay there longer."   15

My guide was moving on, with me behind him
   answering as I did while we went on,
   and adding: "Somewhere down along this ditch   18

that I was staring at a while ago,
   I think there is a spirit of my family
   mourning the guilt that's paid so dear down there."   21

And then my master said: "From this time on
   you should not waste another thought on him;
   think on ahead, and let him stay behind,   24

for I saw him standing underneath the bridge
   pointing at you, and threatening with his gesture,
   and I heard his name called out: Geri del Bello.   27

That was the moment you were so absorbed
    with him who was the lord of Altaforte
    that you did not look his way before he left."   30

"Alas, my guide," I answered him, "his death
    by violence which has not yet been avenged
    by anyone who shares in his disgrace,   33

made him resentful, and I suppose for this
    he went away without a word to me,
    and because he did I feel great piety."   36

We spoke of this until we reached the start
    of the bridge across the next *bolgia,* from which
    the bottom, with more light, might have been seen.   39

Having come to stand above the final cloister
    of Malebolge, we saw it spreading out
    revealing to our eyes its congregation.   42

Weird shrieks of lamentation pierced through me
    like arrow-shafts whose tips are barbed with pity,
    so that my hands were covering my ears.   45

Imagine all the sick in the hospitals
    of Maremma, Valdichiana and Sardinia
    between the months of July and September,   48

crammed altogether rotting in one ditch—
    such was the misery here; and such a stench
    was pouring out as comes from flesh decaying.   51

Still keeping to our left we made our way
    down the long bridge on to the final bank,
    and now my sight was clear enough to find   54

the bottom where the High Lord's ministress,
    Justice infallible, metes out her punishment
    to falsifiers she registers on earth.   57

I doubt if all those dying in Aegina
    when the air was blowing sick with pestilence
    and the animals, down to the smallest worm,   60

all perished (later on this ancient race,
    according to what the poets tell as true,
    was born again from families of ants),   63

offered a scene of greater agony
    than was the sight spread out in that dark valley
    of heaped-up spirits languishing in clumps.   *66*

Some sprawled out on others' bellies, some
    on others' backs, and some, on hands and knees,
    dragged themselves along that squalid alley.   *69*

Slowly, in silence, slowly we moved along
    looking, listening to the words of all those sick
    who had no strength to raise their bodies up.   *72*

I saw two sitting, leaning against each other
    like pans propped back to back against a fire,
    and they were blotched from head to foot with scabs.   *75*

I never saw a curry-comb applied
    by a stable-boy who is harried by his master,
    or simply wants to finish and go to bed,   *78*

the way those two applied their nails and dug
    and dug into their flesh, crazy to ease
    the itching that can never find relief.   *81*

They worked their nails down, scraping off the scabs
    the way one works a knife to scale a bream
    or some other fish with larger, tougher scales.   *84*

"O you there scraping off your scabs of mail
    and even making pincers of your fingers,"
    my guide began to speak to one of them,   *87*

"so may your fingernails eternally
    suffice their task, tell us: among the many
    packed in this place is anyone Italian?"   *90*

"Both of us whom you see disfigured here,"
    one answered through his tears, "we are Italians.
    But you, who ask about us, who are you?"   *93*

"I am one accompanying this living man
    descending bank from bank," my leader said,
    "and I intend to show him all of Hell."   *96*

With that each lost the other back's support
    and each one, shaky, turned to look at me,
    as others did who overheard these words.   *99*

My gentle master came up close to me
  and said: "Now ask them what you want to know,"
  and since he wanted me to speak, I started: 102

"So may the memory of you not fade
  from the minds of men up there in the first world,
  but rather live on under many suns,   105

tell me your names and where it was you lived;
  do not let your dreadful, loathsome punishment
  discourage you from speaking openly."   108

"I'm from Arezzo," one of them replied,
  "and Albert of Siena had me burned,
  but I'm not here for what I died for there;   111

it's true I told him, jokingly, of course:
  'I know the trick of flying through the air,'
  and he, eager to learn and not too bright,   114

asked me to demonstrate my art; and only
  just because I didn't make him Daedalus,
  he had me burned by one whose child he was.   117

But here, to the last *bolgia* of the ten,
  for the alchemy I practiced in the world
  I was condemned by Minòs, who cannot err."   120

I said to my poet: "Have you ever known
  people as silly as the Sienese?
  Even the French cannot compare with them!"   123

With that the other leper who was listening
  feigned exception to my quip: "Excluding,
  of course, Stricca, who lived so frugally,   126

and Niccolo, the first to introduce
  the luxury of the clove for condiment
  into that choice garden where the seed took root,   129

and surely not that fashionable club
  where Caccia squandered all his woods and vineyards
  and Abbagliato flaunted his great wit!   132

That you may know who this is backing you
  against the Sienese, look sharply at me
  so that my face will give you its own answer,   135

and you will recognize Capocchio's shade,
  betrayer of metals with his alchemy;
  you'll surely recall—if you're the one I think—   *138*

how fine an ape of nature I once was."

10. *and already the moon is underneath our feet:* The sun, then, is directly over-head, indicating that it is midday in Jerusalem.

27–35. *and I heard his name called out: Geri del Bello:* Geri del Bello was a first cousin of Dante's father. Little is known about him except that he was among those to whom reparation was made in 1269 for damages suffered at the hands of the Ghibellines in 1260, and that he was involved in a blood feud with the Sac-chetti family. It was probably one of the Sacchetti who murdered him. Vengeance by kinsmen for a slaying was considered obligatory at the time, and apparently Geri's murder was still unavenged by the Alighieri in 1300.

29. *the lord of Altaforte:* Bertran de Born. See XXVIII, 130–142 and n. 142.

40. *Having come to stand above the final cloister:* Cantos XXVIIIXXX seem to be all part of one unit, indicating perhaps that the frauds are becoming more difficult to separate from each other the deeper the Pilgrim goes. Links between *Bolge* Nine and Ten include the similarities in the punishment (dismembered, diseased, and disfigured bodies and minds), and the fact that the Ninth *Bolgia* is carried over into Canto XXIX (the Tenth *Bolgia* actually begins here, at line 40).

47–49. *of Maremma, Valdichiana and Sardinia:* Valdichiana and Maremma are swampy areas in Tuscany. Along with the swamps of Sardinia they were famous for breeding malaria and other diseases. Dante mentioned Maremma in XXV, 19, in connection with the snakes which infested the swamp. The "hospital" image introduces the diseased shades of the Tenth *Bolgia*.

58–66. *I doubt if all those dying in Aegina:* This comparison with the sufferers of the Tenth *Bolgia* concerns the island of Aegina in the Saronic Gulf. Juno sent a plague to the island which killed all the inhabitants except Aeacus. Aeacus prayed to Jupiter to repopulate the island, and Jupiter did so by turning ants into men. See Ovid, *Metamorphoses* VII, 523.

The confusion of this image, which piles one phrase on top of another, imi-tates stylistically the confusion of the pile of diseased bodies which are described immediately afterwards.

67–139

In the last of the *Malebolge*, at the end of the largest segment of the *Inferno* (*Malebolge* began in Canto XVIII), Dante stylistically summarizes much of the jour-ney so far. Here, for instance, we have a return of the grotesque humor of the *bolgia* of the Barrators presided over by the *Malebranche* (XXI, XXII): there is what we would call "sick" humor in Virgil's remark to the alchemists (88–89), there is the comedy of crude sarcasm in Capocchio's words (125–132), and even the "cooking" imagery in the *bolgia* of the Barrators is repeated in his words (128–129) and in the picture of Griffolino and Capocchio (74). Other examples of the condensation in this canto of elements from the journey up to this point in-clude Virgil's summary of the journey's purpose (94–96). The *largo* movement of the *bolgia* of the Hypocrites is found here, too (70–71), and the comparison to monks in a cloister which Dante had used for the Hypocrites is also in evidence (40–42). This summarizing technique continues in the next canto (note for instance, the immobility of the Counterfeiters and the speed of the Impersonators, and compare it with the scene in the Wood of Suicides [XIII] where the immobility of Pier delle Vigne is in contrast to the mad dash of Lano and Giacomo da Sant'Andrea).

109–117. *"I'm from Arezzo," one of them replied:* Most of the commentators identify this man as Griffolino da Arezzo. The story was that Griffolino had led the doltish Alberto da Siena to believe that he could teach him how to fly. Alberto paid him well but, upon discovering the fraud, he denounced Griffolino to the Bishop of Siena as a magician, and the Bishop had him burned. The expression "the one whose child he [Alberto] was," applied to the Bishop, could mean either that he was Alberto's father or his protector.

122. *people as silly as the Sienese:* The Florentines made the citizens of rival Siena the butt of many jokes.

124–126. *With that the other leper who was listening:* Capocchio (see below, 136) makes several ironic comments here about the foolishness of the Sienese. Stricca (probably Stricca di Giovanni dei Salimbeni of Siena) was evidently renowned as a spendthrift. The old commentators hold that he was a member of the "Spendthrifts' Brigade" (see line 130), a group of young Sienese who wasted their fortunes carelessly. Cf. XIII, 115–121.

127–129. *and Niccolo, the first to introduce:* Niccolò de' Salimbeni was another member of the "Spendthrifts' Club" and was possibly the brother of Stricca. He introduced to Siena the use of cloves, then a very expensive spice. Some of the early commentators claim that he roasted pheasants on beds of flaming cloves. In any case Capocchio is referring to Niccolò's careless extravagance as another example of the silliness of the Sienese. The "choice garden" is Siena itself, where any fashionable custom, no matter how foolish, could gain acceptance.

131. *where Caccia squandered all his woods and vineyards:* Caccia d'Asciano was another member of the "Spendthrifts' Brigade" (that "fashionable club," 130), who squandered his inheritance.

132. *and Abbagliato flaunted his great wit!:* Abbagliato has been identified as one Bartolomeo dei Folcacchieri, who held office in Siena up to 1300. He was another member of this "fashionable club."

136. *and you will recognize Capocchio's shade:* Capocchio is the name (or nickname) of a man who in 1293 was burned alive in Siena for alchemy. Apparently Dante had known him; according to the early commentators, it was in their student days.

CANTO XXX

In ancient times when Juno was enraged
   against the Thebans because of Semele
   (she showed her wrath on more than one occasion)   *3*

she made King Athamas go raving mad:
   so mad that one day when he saw his wife
   coming with his two sons in either arm,   *6*

he cried: "Let's spread the nets, so I can catch
   the lioness with her lion-cubs at the pass!"
   Then he spread out his insane hands, like talons   *9*

and, seizing one of his two sons, Learchus,
   he whirled him round and smashed him on a rock.
   She drowned herself with the other in her arms.   *12*

And when the wheel of Fortune brought down low
   the immeasurable haughtiness of Trojans,
   destroying in their downfall king and kingdom,   *15*

Hecuba sad, in misery, a slave
   (after she saw Polyxena lie slain,
   after this grieving mother found her son   *18*

Polydorus left unburied on the shore),
   now gone quite mad, went barking like a dog—
   it was the weight of grief that snapped her mind.   *21*

But never in Thebes or Troy were madmen seen
   driven to acts of such ferocity
   against their victims, animal or human,   *24*

as two shades I saw white with rage and naked,
   running, snapping crazily at things in sight,
   like pigs, directionless, broken from their pen.   *27*

One, landing on Capocchio sank his teeth
   into his neck, and started dragging him
   along, scraping his belly on the rocky ground.   *30*

The Aretine spoke, shaking where he sat:
   "You see that batty shade? He's Gianni Schicchi!
   He's rabid and he treats us all that way."   *33*

"Oh," I answered, "so may that other shade
   never sink its teeth in you—if you don't mind,
   please tell me who it is before it's gone."   *36*

And he to me: "That is the ancient shade
   of Myrrha, the depraved one, who became,
   against love's laws, too much her father's friend.   *39*

She went to him, and there she sinned in love,
   pretending that her body was another's—
   just as the other there fleeing in the distance,   *42*

contrived to make his own the 'queen of studs',
   pretending that he was Buoso Donati,
   making his will and giving it due form."   *45*

Now that the rabid pair had come and gone
   (from whom I never took my eyes away),
   I turned to watch the other evil shades.   *48*

And there I saw a soul shaped like a lute,
   if only he'd been cut off from his legs
   below the belly, where they divide in two.   *51*

The bloating dropsy, disproportioning
   the body's parts with unconverted humors
   so that the face, matched with the paunch, was puny,   *54*

forced him to keep his parched lips wide apart,
   as a man who suffers thirst from raging fever
   has one lip curling up, the other sagging.   *57*

"O you who bear no punishment at all
   (I can't think why) within this world of sorrow,"
   he said to us, "pause here and look upon   *60*

the misery of one Master Adamo:
   in life I had all that I could desire,
   and now, alas, I crave a drop of water.   *63*

The little streams that flow from the green hills
  of Casentino, descending to the Arno
  keeping their banks so cool and soft with moisture   66

forever flow before me, haunting me;
  and the image of them leaves me far more parched
  than the sickness that has dried my shriveled face.   69

Relentless Justice, tantalizing me,
  exploits the countryside that knew my sin,
  to draw from me ever new sighs of pain: 72

I still can see Romena where I learned
  to falsify the coin stamped with the Baptist,
  for which I paid with my burned body there;   75

but if I could see down here the wretched souls
  of Guido or Alexander or their brother,
  I would not exchange the sight for Branda's fountain.   78

One is here already, if those maniacs
  running around this place have told the truth,
  but what good is it, with my useless legs?   81

If only I were lighter, just enough
  to move one inch in every hundred years,
  I would have started on my way by now   84

to find him somewhere in this gruesome lot,
  although this ditch winds round eleven miles
  and is at least a half a mile across.   87

It's their fault I am here with this choice family:
  they encouraged me to turn out florins
  whose gold contained three carats' worth of alloy."   90

And I to him: "Who are those two poor souls
  lying to the right, close to your body's boundary,
  steaming like wet hands in wintertime?"   93

"When I poured into this ditch, I found them here,"
  he answered, "and they haven't budged since then,
  and I doubt they'll move through all eternity.   96

One is the false accuser of young Joseph;
  the other is false Sinon, the Greek in Troy:
  it's their burning fever makes them smell so bad."   99

And one of them, perhaps somewhat offended
    at the kind of introduction he received,
    with his fist struck out at the distended belly,   102

which responded like a drum reverberating;
    and Master Adam struck him in the face
    with an arm as strong as the fist he had received,   105

and he said to him: "Although I am not free
    to move around, with swollen legs like these,
    I have a ready arm for such occasions."   108

"*But* it was *not* as free and ready, was it,"
    the other answered, "when you went to the stake?
    Of course, when you were coining, it was readier!"   111

And he with the dropsy: "*Now* you tell the truth,
    but you were not as full of truth that time
    when you were asked to tell the truth at Troy!"   114

"My words were false—so were the coins you made,"
    said Sinon, "and *I* am here for one false act
    but *you* for more than any fiend in hell!"   117

"The horse, recall the horse, you falsifier,"
    the bloated paunch was quick to answer back,
    "may it burn your guts that all the world remembers!"   120

"May your guts burn with thirst that cracks your tongue,"
    the Greek said, "may they burn with rotting humors
    that swell your hedge of a paunch to block your eyes!"   123

And then the money-man: "So there you go,
    your evil mouth pours out its filth as usual;
    for if *I* thirst, and humors swell me up,   126

you burn more, and your head is fit to split,
    and it wouldn't take much coaxing to convince you
    to lap the mirror of Narcissus dry!"   129

I was listening, all absorbed in this debate,
    when the master said to me: "Keep right on looking,
    a little more, and I shall lose my patience."   132

I heard the note of anger in his voice
    and turned to him; I was so full of shame
    that it still haunts my memory today.   135

Like one asleep who dreams himself in trouble
　　and in his dream he wishes he were dreaming,
　　longing for that which is, as if it were not,　　　　　　　　*138*

just so I found myself: unable to speak,
　　longing to beg for pardon and already
　　begging for pardon, not knowing that I did.　　　　　　　　*141*

"Less shame than yours would wash away a fault
　　greater than yours has been," my master said,
　　"and so forget about it, do not be sad.　　　　　　　　　　*144*

If ever again you should meet up with men
　　engaging in this kind of futile wrangling,
　　remember I am always at your side;　　　　　　　　　　　　*147*

to have a taste for talk like this is vulgar!"

1–12. *In ancient times when Juno was enraged:* Jupiter's predilection for mortal women always enraged Juno, his wife. In this case her ire was provoked by her husband's dalliance with Semele, the daughter of Cadmus, King of Thebes, who bore him Bacchus. Having vowed to wreak revenge on her and her family, Juno not only had Semele struck by lightning, but also caused King Athamas, the husband of Ino (Semele's sister), to go insane. In his demented state he killed his son Learchus. Ino drowned herself and her other son, Melicertes.

16–21. *Hecuba sad, in misery, a slave:* Having triumphed over the Trojans, the Greeks returned to their homeland bearing with them as a slave Hecuba, wife of Priam, King of Troy. She was also to make some tragic discoveries: she saw Polyxena, her daughter, slain on the grave of Achilles (17) and she discovered her son Polydorus dead and unburied on the coast of Thrace (18–19). So great was her grief that she became insane.

25. *as two shades I saw white with rage and naked:* See below, n. 32 and n. 37–41.

31. *And the Aretine:* He is Griffolino d'Arezzo. See XXIX, 109–120.

32. *You see that batty shade? He's Gianni Schicchi!:* A member of the Florentine Cavalcanti family, Gianni Schicchi was well known for his mimetic virtuosity. Simone Donati, keeping his father's death a secret in order that he might change the will to his advantage, engaged Gianni to impersonate his dead father (Buoso Donati, 44) and alter the latter's will. The plan was carried out to perfection, and in the process Gianni willed himself, among other things, a prize mare ("the 'queen of studs'," 43).

33. *He's rabid and he treats us all that way:* Gianni Schicchi, then, is insane as must be also his companion in the mad flight through this *bolgia*. These are the only two sinners in the *Divine Comedy* who are mentally deranged, so that it is most fitting that the canto should open with a reminder of two famous cases of insanity in classical mythology.

37–41. *That is the ancient shade / of Myrrha:* The other self-falsifier darting about the *bolgia* with Gianni Schicchi is Myrrha, who, overpowered by an incestuous desire for her father, King Cinyras of Cyprus, went *incognita* to his bed where they made love. Discovering the deception, Cinyras vowed to kill her; however, Myrrha escaped and wandered about until the gods took pity on her and transformed her into a myrrh tree, from which Adonis, the child conceived in the incestuous union, was born. See Ovid's *Metamorphoses* X.

52–53. *The bloating dropsy, disproportioning:* In other words, Adamo's dropsy was caused by the failure of the humors in his body to follow a natural course of change.

61–75

Although the early commentators disagree concerning Master Adamo's birthplace (Brescia? Casentino? Bologna?), it is now generally believed that he was not an Italian. He plied his art, the falsifying of gold florins ("the coin stamped with the Baptist," 74, i.e., with the image of John the Baptist, the patron saint of Florence), throughout Northern Italy, encouraged to do so by the Conti Guidi, the lords of Romena (73). He was arrested by the Florentine authorities and burned to death in 1281.

64–66. *the green hills / of Casentino:* The Casentino is a hilly region southeast of Florence where the headwaters of the Arno river spread out.

76–78. *I would not exchange the sight for Branda's fountain:* Master Adamo, as much as he craves a "drop of water" (63), would forego that pleasure if only he could see here in Hell the Conti Guidi (Guido, Alexander, Aghinolfo, and Ildebrando), who encouraged him in crime. "Branda's fountain" (78) is the name of a spring which once flowed near Romena. Often confused with it is the still-functioning fountain of the same name at Siena.

79. *One is here already:* Guido (d. 1292) is the only one of the four Conti Guidi who died before 1300.

90. *whose gold contained three carats' worth of alloy:* The florin was supposed to contain twenty-four carat gold; those of Master Adamo had twenty-one carats.

92. *close to your body's boundary:* Note the dehumanization suggested by this phrase which accords well with the advanced state of bodily deterioration in the *bolgia;* Master Adamo is more a land mass than a human being.

97. *One is the false accuser of young Joseph:* Potiphar's wife falsely accused Joseph, son of Jacob and Rachel, of trying to seduce her, while in reality it was she who made improper amorous advances. See Genesis 39.

98. *the other is false Sinon, the Greek in Troy:* Sinon was left behind by his fellow Greek soldiers in accordance with the master plan for the capture of Troy. Taken prisoner by the Trojans, and misrepresenting his position with the Greeks, he persuaded them to bring the wooden horse (XXVI, 59) into the city.

100. *And one of them, perhaps somewhat offended:* Sinon.

129. *the mirror of Narcissus:* Water. According to the myth, Narcissus, enamoured with his own reflection in a pond, continued to gaze at it until he died.

*　　*　　*　　*

Canto XXX is unique in that the suffering undergone by the sinners is caused not by something outside of them, some factor in this physical environment, but by something within them, by their own disease—mental or physical. The Alchemists are afflicted with leprosy, the Impersonators are mad, the Counterfeiters suffer from dropsy and the Liars are afflicted with a fever that makes them stink.

In this, the last of the *Malebolge*, we see Simple Fraud at its most extreme; and because of the miscellaneous nature of the sins of the Falsifiers, we see perhaps the essence of the sin of Simple Fraud in general. In that case, Dante would be telling us that Fraud in general is a disease: the corrupt sense of values of the Fraudulent is here symbolized, in the case of the Falsifiers, by the corrupt state of their minds and bodies.

CANTO XXXI

The very tongue that first spoke—stinging me,
  making the blood rush up to both my cheeks—
  then gave the remedy to ease the pain,   3

just as, so I have heard, Achilles' lance,
  belonging to his father, was the source
  of pain, and then of balm, to him it struck.   6

Turning our backs on that trench of misery,
  gaining the bank again that walls it in,
  we cut across, walking in dead silence.   9

Here it was less than night and less than day,
  so that my eyes could not see far ahead;
  but then I heard the blast of some high horn   12

which would have made a thunder-clap sound dim;
  it drew my eyes directly to one place,
  as they retraced the sound's path to its source.   15

After the tragic rout when Charlemagne
  lost all his faithful, holy paladins,
  the sound of Roland's horn was not as ominous.   18

Keeping my eyes still turned that way, I soon
 . made out what seemed to be high, clustered towers.
  "Master," I said, "what city lies ahead?"   21

"Because you try to penetrate the shadows,"
  he said to me, "from much too far away,
  you confuse the truth with your imagination.   24

You will see clearly when you reach that place
  how much the eyes may be deceived by distance,
  and so, just push ahead a little more."   27

Then lovingly he took me by the hand
  and said: "But now, before we go on farther,
  to prepare you for the truth that could seem strange,   30

I'll tell you these aren't towers, they are giants;
  they're standing in the well around the bank—
  all of them hidden from their navels down."   33

As, when the fog begins to thin and clear,
  the sight can slowly make out more and more
  what is hidden in the mist that clogs the air,   36

so, as I pierced the thick and murky air,
  approaching slowly, closer to the well,
  confusion cleared and my fear took on more shape.   39

For just as Montereggion is crowned with towers
  soaring high above its curving ramparts,
  so, on the bank that runs around the well,   42

towering with only half their bodies out,
  stood the terrible giants, forever threatened
  by Jupiter in the heavens when he thunders.   45

And now I could make out one of the faces,
  the shoulders, the chest and a good part of the belly
  and, down along the sides, the two great arms.   48

Nature, when she cast away the mold
  for shaping beasts like these, without a doubt
  did well, depriving Mars of more such agents.   51

And if she never did repent of whales
  and elephants, we must consider her,
  on sober thought, all the more just and wary: 54

for when the faculty of intellect
  is joined with brute force and with evil will,
  no man can win against such an alliance.   57

His face, it seemed to me, was about as long
  and just as wide as St. Peter's cone in Rome,
  and all his body's bones were in proportion,   60

so that the bank which served to cover him
  from his waist down showed so much height above
  that three tall Frisians on each other's shoulders   63

could never boast of stretching to his hair,
    for downwards from the place men clasp their cloaks
    I saw a generous thirty hand-spans of him.   66

"Raphel may amech zabi almi!"
    He played these sputtering notes with prideful lips
    for which no sweeter psalm was suitable.   69

My guide called up to him: "Blathering idiot,
    stick to your horn and take it out on that
    when you feel a fit of anger coming on;   72

search round your neck and you will find the strap
    it's tied to, you poor muddle-headed soul,
    and there's the horn so pretty on your chest."   75

And then he turned to me: "His words accuse him.
    He is Nimrod, through whose infamous device
    the world no longer speaks a common language.   78

But let's leave him alone and not waste breath,
    for he can no more understand our words
    than anyone can understand his language."   81

We had to walk still farther than before,
    continuing to the left, a full bow's-shot,
    to find another giant, huger and more fierce.   84

What engineer it took to bind this brute
    I cannot say, but there he was, one arm
    pinned to his back, the other locked in front,   87

with a giant chain winding around him tight
    which, starting from his neck, made five great coils—
    and that was counting only to his waist.   90

"This beast of pride decided he would try
    to pit his strength against almighty Jove,"
    my leader said, "and he has won this prize.   93

He's Ephialtes who made his great attempt,
    when the giants arose to fill the Gods with panic;
    the arms he lifted then, he moves no more."   96

And I to him: "If it were possible,
    I would really like to have the chance to see
    the fantastic figure of Briareus."   99

His answer was: "Not far from here you'll see
  Antaeus who can speak and is not chained;
  he will set us down in the very pit of sin.   102

The one you want to see is farther off;
  he too is bound and looks just like this one,
  except for his expression, which is fiercer."   105

No earthquake of the most outrageous force
  ever shook a tower with such violence
  as, suddenly, Ephialtes shook himself.   108

I never feared to die as much as then,
  and my fear might have been enough to kill me,
  if I had not already seen those chains.   111

We left him and continued moving on
  and came to where Antaeus stood, extending
  from the well a good five ells up to his head.   114

"O you who in the celebrated valley
  (that saw Scipio become the heir of glory,
  when Hannibal with all his men retreated)   117

once captured a thousand lions as your quarry
  (and with whose aid, had you chosen to take part
  in the great war with your brothers, the sons of earth 120

would, as many still think, have been the victors),
  do not disdain this modest wish: take us,
  and put us down where ice locks in Cocytus.   123

Don't make us go to Tityus or Typhon;
  this man can give you what all long for here,
  and so bend down, and do not scowl at us.   126

He still can spread your legend in the world,
  for he yet lives, and long life lies before him,
  unless Grace summons him before his time."   129

Thus spoke my master, and the giant in haste
  stretched out the hands whose formidable grip
  great Hercules once felt, and took my guide.   132

And Virgil, when he felt the grasping hands,
  called out: "Now come and I'll take hold of you."
  Clasped together, we made a single burden.   135

As the Garisenda looks from underneath
    its leaning side, at the moment when a cloud
    comes drifting over against the tower's slant,   *138*

just so the bending giant Antaeus seemed
    as I looked up, expecting him to topple.
    I wished then I had gone another way.   *141*

But he, most carefully, handed us down
    to the pit that swallows Lucifer with Judas.
    And then, the leaning giant immediately   *144*

drew himself up as tall as a ship's mast.

NOTES

4–6. just as, so I have heard, Achilles' lance: Dante aptly compares the nature of
Virgil's words at the end of Canto XXX (first rebuking then comforting) to the
spear of Achilles and his father, Peleus, which reputedly could heal the wounds it
had inflicted.

16–18. After the tragic rout when Charlemagne: In the medieval French epic *La
Chanson de Roland*, the title character, one of Charlemagne's "holy paladins" (17),
was assigned to the rear guard on the return from an expedition in Spain. At Ron-
cevalles in the Pyrenees the Saracens attacked, and Roland, proud to the point of
foolishness, refused to sound his horn until total extermination was imminent.

19–127

From afar, the Pilgrim who has mistaken the great giants for towers, asks
Virgil, what city lies ahead?"—a question which should recall the scene before the
gates of the walled City of Dis in Cantos VIII and IX. By this device not only are
we introduced to a new division of Hell (the Pit of the Giants and Cocytus: Com-
plex Fraud), but also the unifed nature of Lower Hell (i.e. from the City of Dis to
Cocytus) is underscored. And the Fallen Angels perched on the wall who shut the
gate to the City in Virgil's face (VIII) are analogous to the Giants here, who stand
at the boundary of the lowest part of Hell. The fact that the Giants—in terms of
pagan mythology—and the Fallen Angels—in terms of the Judeo-Christian tradi-
tion—both rebelled against their respective gods, not only links the parts of Lower
Hell together, but also suggests that the bases for all the sins punished in Lower
Hell (Heresy, Violence, and Fraud) are Envy and Pride, the sins of both groups of
rebels.

Canto XXXI revolves around the pride of the Giants exemplified by Nimrod
mumbling gibberish through his "prideful lips" (68), and even by Virgil's flatter-
ing Antaeus about his hunting exploits (115–118), in order to persuade him to
transport Dante and himself down to the pit's floor. Of course the greatest evi-
dence of Envy and Pride on the part of the Giants is their rebellion against their
gods. Nimrod, envious of God's dominion, tried, in his pride, to build a tower to
Heaven, and the Titans (save Antaeus who took no active part) rebelled against
Jove. The Fallen Angels, of course (spurred on by their pride and envy), also re-
belled against God.

In lines 55–57 is described the terrible combination of qualities represented by the extreme evil of the Giants as well as of the others in the Ninth Circle:

for when the faculty of intellect
is joined with brute force and with evil will,
no man can win against such an alliance.

The difference between the sins of Incontinence (the first five of the Seven Capital Sins) and the sins punished in the Lower Hell is that the former are sins of the appetite, not the product of an "evil will," while the sins of Heresy, Violence, and Fraud are all inspired by a will to do evil. (That Heresy is caused by intellectual pride and its inseparable companion, envy, seems obvious; see IX, note 127–131.) Violence is an alliance of "evil will" and "brute force," while Simple Fraud (in the *Malebolge*) is the product of "evil will" allied with "the faculty of intellect." But Complex Fraud, exemplified by the Giants, the Fallen Angels, Lucifer, and the other figures in the Ninth Circle, is a combination of simple frauds and violence (all of the figures in this circle are here for violent rebellion or treacherous murder), that is, of "the faculty of intellect . . . joined with brute force and with evil will." It can be seen that the key to the sins in Lower Hell is the "evil will," that is, an active willing of evil ends; and of all the capital sins, only pride and envy could cause such a will to evil.

40–41. *For just as Montereggion is crowned with towers:* In 1213 the Sienese constructed Montereggioni, a fortress on the crest of a hill eight miles from their city. The specific allusion here is to the fourteen high towers which stood on its perimeter like giant sentries.

44–45. *forever threatened / by Jupiter:* When the Titans rebelled against Heaven, Jupiter struck them down with lightning bolts (see XIV, 51–60). Here in Hell they continue to fear his vengeance, suggested by his thundering.

49–57. *Nature, when she cast away the mold:* Dante praises the wisdom that Nature showed in discontinuing the race of giants, for Mars (51), the god of war, with the help of the giants could have effectively destroyed mankind. A clear distinction is made between brute animals ("whales / and elephants," 52–53), which Nature rightly allows to live, and giants, whom she made extinct, in that the former do not possess a rational faculty, and therefore are easily subjugated by man.

59. *and just as wide as St. Peter's cone in Rome:* This bronze pine cone measuring over seven feet in height, which now stands in an inner courtyard of the Vatican was, at Dante's time, in the courtyard of St. Peter's.

63. *that three tall Frisians on each other's shoulders:* The inhabitants of Friesland, a northern province of the Netherlands, were renowned for their height.

67. *"Raphel may amech zabi almi!":* Although there have been numerous attempts to interpret these words, I, along with most modern commentators, believe that they are gibberish—the perfect representation of Nimrod's role in the confusion of languages caused by his construction of the Tower of Babel (the "infamous device," 77).

77. *He is Nimrod, through whose infamous device:* Orosius, St. Augustine, and other early Christians believed Nimrod to be a giant; and his "infamous device," the Tower of Babel, through which he tried to ascend to Heaven, certainly equates him with the giants who besieged Jupiter. In both cases the dominant sin is pride; this, in addition to their gigantic proportions, makes them prefigurations of Lucifer.

78. *the world no longer speaks a common language:* Before the construction of the Tower of Babel all men spoke a common language; it was as a punishment for

building the Tower that God confused their tongues. See Genesis 11:1 (where, however, Nimrod is not mentioned).

94. *He's Ephialtes who made his great attempt:* Ephialtes was the son of Neptune and Iphimedia. At the age of nine, together with his brother Otus, he attempted to put Mt. Pelion on top of Ossa in order to ascend to the gods and make war on them. But Apollo slew the brothers.

99. *the fantastic figure of Briareus:* The son of Uranus and Gaea (Earth), the Titan Briareus joined the rebellion against the Olympian deities.

101. *Antaeus who can speak and is not chained:* See below, n. 123.

102. *he will set us down in the very pit of sin:* Cocytus, the ninth and last circle of the Inferno.

123. *and put us down where ice locks in Cocytus:* Antaeus was the son of Neptune and Gaea (Earth) and consequently one of the Titans; but since he did not take part in the insurrection against the gods (119–120) he is not chained (101). Had he taken part, it is quite possible that the Titans ("sons of the earth," 120) would have conquered the Olympians. An inhabitant of Libya, he performed great feats of hunting in the valley of the Bagradas, where Scipio later defeated Hannibal (115–117).

124. *Don't make us go to Tityus or Typhon:* Also members of the race of Titans, Tityus and Typhon were slain by Jupiter, the former for his attempted rape of Diana and the latter for his rebellion against the gods. Both were cast down to Earth and buried under Mt. Aetna.

131–132. *stretched out the hands whose formidable grip:* Antaeus derived his great strength from constant contact with the earth (Gaea, his mother). In a wrestling match with Hercules, the latter lifted him off the ground, thus killing him.

136–138. *As the Garisenda looks from underneath:* Of the two leaning towers in Bologna, the Garisenda, built c. 1110, is the shorter. The passage of a cloud "against the tower's slant" (138) would make the tower appear to be falling.

CANTO XXXII

If I had words grating and crude enough
   that really could describe this horrid hole
   supporting the converging weight of Hell,   *3*

I could squeeze out the juice of my memories
   to the last drop. But I don't have these words,
   and so I am reluctant to begin.   *6*

To talk about the bottom of the universe
   the way it truly is, is no child's play,
   no task for tongues that gurgle baby-talk.   *9*

But may those heavenly ladies aid my verse
   who aided Amphion to wall-in Thebes,
   that my words may tell exactly what I saw.   *12*

O misbegotten rabble of all rabble
   who crowd this realm, hard even to describe,
   it were better you had lived as sheep or goats!   *15*

When we reached a point of darkness in the well
   below the giant's feet, farther down the slope,
   and I was gazing still at the high wall,   *18*

I heard somebody say: "Watch where you step!
   Be careful that you do not kick the heads
   of this brotherhood of miserable souls."   *21*

At that I turned around and saw before me
   a lake of ice stretching beneath my feet,
   more like a sheet of glass than frozen water.   *24*

In the depths of Austria's wintertime, the Danube
   never in all its course showed ice so thick,
   nor did the Don beneath its frigid sky,   *27*

as this crust here; for if Mount Tambernic
  or Pietrapana would crash down upon it
  not even at its edges would a crack creak.   30

The way the frogs (in the season when the harvest
  will often haunt the dreams of the peasant girl)
  sit croaking with their muzzles out of water,   33

so these frigid, livid shades were stuck in ice
  up to where a person's shame appears;
  their teeth clicked notes like storks' beaks snapping shut.   36

And each one kept his face bowed toward the ice:
  the mouth bore testimony to the cold,
  the eyes, to sadness welling in the heart.   39

I gazed around a while and then looked down,
  and by my feet I saw two figures clasped
  so tight that one's hair could have been the other's.   42

"Tell me, you two, pressing your chests together,"
  I asked them, "who are you?" Both stretched their necks
  and when they had their faces raised toward me,   45

their eyes, which had before been only glazed,
  dripped tears down to their lips, and the cold froze
  the tears between them, locking the pair more tightly.   48

Wood to wood with iron was never clamped
  so firm! And the two of them like billy-goats
  were butting at each other, mad with anger.   51

Another one with both ears frozen off,
  and head still bowed over his icy mirror,
  cried out: "What makes you look at us so hard?   54

If you're interested to know who those two are:
  the valley where Bisenzio's waters flow
  belonged to them and to their father, Albert;   57

the same womb bore them both, and if you scour
  all of Caïna, you will not turn up one
  who's more deserving of this frozen aspic—   60

not him who had his breast and shadow pierced
  with one thrust of the lance from Arthur's hand;
  not Focaccia; not even this one here   63

whose head gets in my way and blocks my view,
  known in the world as Sassol Mascheroni,
  and if you're Tuscan you must know who he was.   66

To save me from your asking for more news:
  I was Camicion de' Pazzi, and I await
  Carlin whose guilt will make my own seem less."   69

Farther on I saw a thousand dog-like faces
  purple from the cold. That's why I shudder,
  and always will, when I see a frozen pond.   72

While we were getting closer to the center
  of the universe where all weights must converge
  and I was shivering in the eternal chill—   75

by fate or chance or willfully perhaps,
  I do not know—but stepping among the heads,
  my foot kicked hard against one of those faces.   78

Weeping he screamed: "Why are you kicking me?
  You have not come to take revenge on me
  for Montaperti, have you? Why bother me?"   81

And I: "My master, please wait here for me,
  let me clear up a doubt concerning this one,
  then I shall be as rapid as you wish."   84

My leader stopped, and to that wretch who still
  had not let up in his barrage of curses,
  I said: "Who are you, insulting other people?"   87

"And you, who are *you* who march through Antenora
  kicking other people in their faces?
  No living man could kick as hard!" he answered.   90

"I am a living man," was my reply,
  "and it might serve you well, if you seek fame,
  for me to put your name down in my notes."   93

And he said: "That's the last thing I would want!
  That's not the way to flatter in these lowlands!
  Stop pestering me like this—get out of here!"   96

At that I grabbed him by his hair in back
  and said: "You'd better tell me who you are
  or else I'll not leave one hair on your head."   99

And he to me: "Go on and strip me bald
    and pound and stamp my head a thousand times,
    you'll never hear my name or see my face."   102

I had my fingers twisted in his hair
    and already I'd pulled out more than one fistful,
    while he yelped like a cur with eyes shut tight,   105

when someone else yelled: "What's the matter, Bocca?
    It's bad enough to hear your shivering teeth;
    now you bark! What the devil's wrong with you?"   108

"There's no need now for you to speak," I said,
    "you vicious traitor! Now I know your name
    and I'll bring back the shameful truth about you."   111

"Go away!" he answered, "Tell them what you want;
    but if you do get out of here, be sure
    you also tell about that blabber-mouth   114

who's paying here what the French silver cost him:
    'I saw,' you can tell the world, 'the one from Duera
    stuck in with all the sinners keeping cool.'   117

And if you should be asked: 'Who else was there?'
    Right by your side is the one from Beccheria
    whose head was chopped off by the Florentines.   120

As for Gianni Soldanier I think you'll find him
    farther along with Ganelon and Tibbald
    who opened up Faenza while it slept."   123

Soon after leaving him I saw two souls
    frozen together in a single hole
    so that one head used the other for a cap.   126

As a man with hungry teeth tears into bread,
    the soul with capping head had sunk his teeth
    into the other's neck, just beneath the skull.   129

Tydeus in his fury did not gnaw
    the head of Menalippus with more relish
    than this one chewed that head of meat and bones.   132

"O you who show with every bestial bite
    your hatred for the head you are devouring,"
    I said, "tell me your reason, and I promise   135

if you are justified in your revenge,
  once I know who you are and this one's sin,
  I'll repay your confidence in the world above

unless my tongue dry up before I die."

N O T E S

1. *If I had words grating and crude enough:* Dante fulfills his wish with the very words he speaks in uttering it ("grating and crude").

10–12. *But may those heavenly ladies aid my verse:* The Muses ("those heavenly ladies," 10) helped Amphion, the son of Jupiter and Antiope, construct a wall around Thebes. As the legend has it, Amphion played upon his lyre and so charmed the stones on Mt. Cithaeron that they came of their own accord and formed the wall.

27. *nor did the Don beneath its frigid sky:* The river Don which has its source in the heart of Russia would naturally be icebound in the frigid Russian winter. In the Italian, Dante uses the classical name for the Don, the *Tanai.*

28–30. *Mount Tambernic / or Pietrapana:* Tambernic has never been successfully identified. The older commentators place it in the Balkans. Pietrapana is probably a rocky peak in the northwest corner of Tuscany, today called Pania della Croce.

35. *up to where a person's shame appears:* The face.

55–58. *If you're interested to know who these two are:* The two brothers were Napoleone and Alessandro, sons of Count Alberto of Mangona, who owned part of the valley of the Bisenzio near Florence. The two quarrelled often and eventually killed each other in a fight concerning their inheritance.

59. *all of Caïna:* The icy outer ring of Cocytus is named Caïna after Cain, who slew his brother Abel. Thus, in the first division of this, the Ninth Circle, are punished those treacherous shades who murderously violated family bonds.

61–62. *not him who had his breast and shadow pierced:* Mordred, the wicked nephew of King Arthur, tried to kill the king and take his kingdom. But Arthur pierced him with such a mighty blow that when the lance was pulled from the dying traitor a ray of sunlight traversed his body and interrupted Mordred's shadow. The story is told in the Old French romance *Lancelot du Lac,* the book which Francesca claims led her astray with Paolo in *Inferno* V, 127.

63. *not Focaccia:* He was one of the Cancellieri family of Pistoia and a member of the White party. His treacherous murder of his cousin, Detto de' Cancellieri (a Black), was possibly the act which led to the Florentine intervention in Pistoian affairs.

65. *known in the world as Sassol Mascheroni:* The early commentators say that Sassol Mascheroni was a member of the Toschi family in Florence who murdered his nephew in order to gain his inheritance.

68–69. *I was Camicion de' Pazzi, and I await:* Nothing is known of Camicion de' Pazzi except that he murdered one Ubertino, a relative. Another of Camicion's kin, Carlino de' Pazzi (69) from Valdarno, was still alive when the Pilgrim's conversation with Camicion was taking place. But Camicion already knew that Carlino, in July, 1302, would accept a bribe to surrender the castle of Piantravigne to the Blacks of Florence.

80–81. *You have not come to take revenge on me:* See below, n. 106.

88. *And you, who are you who march through Antenora:* Dante and Virgil have passed into the second division of Cocytus, named Antenora after the Trojan warrior who, according to one legend, betrayed his city to the Greeks. In this round are tormented those who committed acts of treachery against country, city, or political party.

106. *What's the matter, Bocca?:* Bocca degli Abati was a Ghibelline who appeared to side with the Florentine Guelphs. However, while fighting on the side of the Guelphs at the battle of Montaperti in 1260, he is said to have cut off the hand of the standard bearer. The disappearance of the standard led to panic among the Florentine Guelphs, who were then decisively defeated by the Sienese Ghibellines and their German allies under Manfred.

116–117. *the one from Duera:* Buoso da Duera, a chief of the Ghibelline party of Cremona, was a well-known traitor. When Charles of Anjou marched against Naples in 1265, Manfred sent troops under the command of Buoso to stop them. But Buoso accepted a bribe from Charles (the "French silver," 115) and allowed the French troops to pass unmolested.

119–120. *Right by your side is the one from Beccheria:* Tesauro dei Beccheria of Pavia was an Abbot of Vallombrosa and a Papal Legate to Alexander IV in Tuscany. He was tortured and finally beheaded in 1258 by the Guelphs of Florence for carrying on secret intercourse with Ghibellines who had been exiled.

121. *As for Gianni Soldanier I think you'll find him:* Gianni de' Soldanier was an important Ghibelline of Florence who, when the Florentines (mostly Guelph) began to chafe under Ghibelline rule, deserted his party and went over to the Guelphs.

122-123. *farther along with Ganelon and Tibbald:* Ganelon is the treacherous knight who betrayed Roland (and the rear guard of Charlemagne's army) to the Saracens. See XXXI, 16–18.

Tibbald is one of the Zambrasi family of Faenza. In order to avenge himself on the Ghibelline Lambertazzi family (who had been exiled from Bologna in 1274 and had taken refuge in Faenza), he opened his city to their Bolognese Guelph enemies on the morning of November 13, 1280.

130–131. *Tydeus in his fury did not gnaw:* Tydeus, one of the Seven against Thebes (see XIV, 68–70), slew Menalippus in combat—who, however, managed to wound him fatally. Tydeus called for his enemy's head, which, when brought to him by Amphiaraus, he proceeded to gnaw in rage.

CANTO XXXIII

Lifting his mouth from his horrendous meal,
  this sinner first wiped off his messy lips
  in the hair remaining on the chewed-up skull,   *3*

then spoke: "You want me to renew a grief
  so desperate that just the thought of it,
  much less the telling, grips my heart with pain;   *6*

but if my words can be the seed to bear
  the fruit of infamy for this betrayer
  who feeds my hunger, then I shall speak—in tears.   *9*

I do not know your name, nor do I know
  how you have come down here, but Florentine
  you surely seem to be, to hear you speak.   *12*

First you should know I was Count Ugolino
  and my neighbor here, Ruggieri the Archbishop;
  now I'll tell you why I'm so unneighborly.   *15*

That I, trusting in him, was put in prison
  through his evil machinations, where I died,
  this much I surely do not have to tell you.   *18*

What you could not have known, however, is
  the inhuman circumstances of my death.
  Now listen, then decide if he has wronged me!   *21*

Through a narrow slit of window high in that mew
  (which is called the tower of hunger, after me,
  and I'll not be the last to know that place)   *24*

I had watched moon after moon after moon go by,
  when finally I dreamed the evil dream
  which ripped away the veil that hid my future.   *27*

I dreamed of this one here as lord and huntsman,
  pursuing the wolf and the wolf-cubs up the mountain
  (which blocks the sight of Lucca from the Pisans)   30

with skinny bitches, well trained and obedient;
  he had out front as leaders of the pack
  Gualandi with Sismondi and Lanfranchi.   33

A short run, and the father with his sons
  seemed to grow tired, and then I thought I saw
  long fangs sunk deep into their sides, ripped open.   36

When I awoke before the light of dawn,
  I heard my children sobbing in their sleep
  (you see they, too, were there) asking for bread.   39

If the thought of what my heart was telling me
  does not fill you with grief, how cruel you are!
  If you are not weeping now—do you ever weep?   42

And then they awoke. It was around the time
  they usually brought our food to us. But now
  each one of us was full of dread from dreaming;   45

then from below I heard them driving nails
  into the dreadful tower's door; with that,
  I stared in silence at my flesh and blood.   48

I did not weep, I turned to stone inside;
  they wept, and my little Anselmuccio spoke:
  'What is it, father? Why do you look that way?'   51

For them I held my tears back, saying nothing,
  all of that day, and then all of that night,
  until another sun shone on the world.   54

A meager ray of sunlight found its way
  to the misery of our cell, and I could see
  myself reflected four times in their faces;   57

I bit my hands in anguish. And my children,
  who thought that hunger made me bite my hands
  were quick to draw up closer to me, saying: 60

'O father, you would make us suffer less,
  if you would feed on us: you were the one
  who gave us this sad flesh; you take it from us!'   63

I calmed myself to make them less unhappy.
That day we sat in silence, and the next day.
O pitiless earth! You should have swallowed us!   66

The fourth day came, and it was on that day
my Gaddo fell prostrate before my feet,
crying: 'Why don't you help me? Why, my father?'   69

There he died. Just as you see me here,
I saw the other three fall one by one,
as the fifth day and the sixth day passed. And I,   72

by then gone blind, groped over their dead bodies.
Though they were dead, two days I called their names.
Then hunger proved more powerful than grief."   75

He spoke these words; then, glaring down in rage,
attacked again the live skull with his teeth
sharp as a dog's, and as fit for grinding bones.   78

O Pisa, blot of shame upon the people
of that fair land where the sound of "sì" is heard!
Since your neighbors hesitate to punish you,   81

let Capraia and Gorgona move and join,
damming up the River Arno at its mouth,
and let every Pisan perish in its flood!   84

For if Count Ugolino was accused
of turning traitor, trading-in your castles,
you had no right to make his children suffer.   87

Their new-born years (O new-born Thebes!) made them
all innocents: Brigata, Uguiccione
and the other two soft names my canto sings.   90

We moved ahead to where the frozen water
wraps in harsh wrinkles another sinful race,
with faces not turned down but looking up.   93

Here, the weeping puts an end to weeping,
and the grief that finds no outlet from the eyes
turns inward to intensify the anguish: 96

for the tears they first wept knotted in a cluster
and like a visor made for them in crystal,
filled all the hollow part around their eyes.   99

Although the bitter coldness of the dark
    had driven all sensation from my face,
    as though it were not tender skin but callous,   *102*

I thought I felt the air begin to blow,
    and I: "What causes such a wind, my master?
    I thought no heat could reach into these depths."   *105*

And he to me: "Before long you will be
    where your own eyes can answer for themselves,
    when they will see what keeps this wind in motion."   *108*

And one of the wretches with the frozen crust
    screamed out at us: "O wicked souls, so wicked
    that you have been assigned the ultimate post,   *111*

break off these hard veils covering my eyes
    and give relief from the pain that swells my heart—
    at least until the new tears freeze again."   *114*

I answered him: "If this is what you want,
    tell me your name; and if I do not help you,
    may I be forced to drop beneath this ice!"   *117*

He answered then: "I am Friar Alberigo,
    I am he who offered fruit from the evil orchard:
    here dates are served me for the figs I gave."   *120*

"Oh, then!" I said, "Are you already dead?"
    And he to me: "Just how my body is
    in the world above, I have no way of knowing.   *123*

This zone of Tolomea is very special,
    for it often happens that a soul falls here
    before the time that Atropos should send it.   *126*

And that you may more willingly scrape off
    my cluster of glass tears, let me tell you:
    whenever a soul betrays the way I did,   *129*

a demon takes possession of the body,
    controlling its maneuvers from then on,
    for all the years it has to live up there,   *132*

while the soul falls straight into this cistern here;
    and the shade in winter quarters just behind me
    may well have left his body up on earth.   *135*

But you should know, if you've just come from there:
   he is Ser Branca D'Oria; and many years
   have passed since he first joined us here, ice-bound." 138

"I think you're telling me a lie," I said,
   "for Branca D'Oria is not dead at all;
   he eats and drinks, he sleeps and wears out clothes." 141

"The ditch the Malebranche watch above,"
   he said, "the ditch of clinging, boiling pitch,
   had not yet caught the soul of Michel Zanche, 144

when Branca left a devil in his body
   to take his place, and so did his close kinsman,
   his accomplice in this act of treachery. 147

But now, at last, give me the hand you promised.
   Open my eyes." I did not open them.
   To be mean to him was a generous reward. 150

O all you Genovese, you men estranged
   from every good, at home with every vice,
   why can't the world be wiped clean of your race? 153

For in company with Romagna's rankest soul
   I found one of your men whose deeds were such
   that his soul bathes already in Cocytus 156

but his body seems alive and walks among you.

NOTES

13–14. *First you should know I was Count Ugolino:* Ugolino della Gherardesca, the Count of Donoratico, belonged to a noble Tuscan family whose political affiliations were Ghibelline. In 1275 he conspired with his son-in-law, Giovanni Visconti, to raise the Guelphs to power in Pisa. Although exiled for this subversive activity, Ugolino, together with his grandson, Nino Visconti, took over the Guelph government of the city in 1285. Three years later, Ugolino plotted with Archbishop Ruggieri degli Ubaldini to rid Pisa of the Visconti. Ruggieri, however, had other plans, and with the aid of the Ghibellines, he seized control of the city and imprisoned Ugolino, together with his sons and grandsons, in the "tower of hunger" (23). The two were evidently just at the boundary between Antenora and Ptolomea, for Ugolino is being punished for betraying his country (in Antenora), and Ruggieri for betraying his associate, Ugolino (in Ptolomea).

25. *I had watched moon after moon after moon go by:* Imprisoned in June of 1288, they finally starved to death in February, 1289.

28–36. *I dreamed of this one here as lord and huntsman:* Ugolino's dream was indeed prophetic. The "lord and huntsman" (28) is Archbishop Ruggieri, who, with the leading Ghibelline families of Pisa ("Gualandi . . . Sismondi and Lanfranchi," 33) and the populace ("skinny bitches," 31), runs down Ugolino and his offspring ("the wolf and the wolf-cubs," 29) and finally kills them; the phrase, "up the mountain" (i.e., up San Giuliano, which lies between Pisa and Lucca) is probably meant to suggest the high tower in which they were imprisoned.

50. *they wept, and my little Anselmuccio spoke:* Anselmuccio was the younger of Ugolino's grandsons who, according to official documents, must have been fifteen at the time.

68. *my Gaddo fell prostrate before my feet:* Gaddo was one of Ugolino's sons.

75. *Then hunger proved more powerful than grief:* Whether in this line Ugolino is confessing to an act of cannibalism or whether it simply relates the cause of his death (hunger instead of grief)—Dante has left this to the reader's imagination. It cannot be denied that he has made it possible for us to think in terms of the first possibility; moreover, he has chosen to present Ugolino as chewing on the skull of Ruggieri.

79–90

Dante inveighs against Pisa for having killed the four innocent offspring of Count Ugolino, not for having punished him as he deserved. He calls upon the islands of Capraia and Gorgona, both of which lie in the Tyrrhenian Sea not far from the mouth of the Arno River, to come block the Arno, thereby flooding Pisa and killing its evil inhabitants (82–84). By referring to Pisa as the "new-born Thebes" (88), Dante evokes the horrendous and scandalous events which characterized the history of that Greek city. For previous allusions to Thebes see XIV, 69; XX, 59; XXV, 15; XXX, 22; XXXII, 11.

80. *of that fair land where the sound of "sì" is heard!:* Italy. It was customary in Dante's time to indicate a language area by the words signifying "yes." Cf. XVIII, 61 and note.

89–90. *Brigata, Uguiccione / and the other two:* Brigata was Ugolino's second grandson and Uguiccione his fifth son. For the "other two" (90) see above, n. 50 and n. 68. Dante, in mentioning "their new-born years," departs from historical fact—which reports that all except Anselmuccio were grown men.

91–93. *We moved ahead to where the frozen water:* Virgil and the Pilgrim have now entered the third division of Cocytus, called Tolomea (124) after Ptolemy, the captain of Jericho, who had Simon, his father-in-law, and two of his sons killed while dining (see 1 Maccabees 16:11–17). Or possibly this zone of Cocytus is named after Ptolemy XII: the Egyptian king who, having welcomed Pompey to his realm, slew him. In Tolomea are punished those who have betrayed their guests.

105. *I thought no heat could reach into these depths:* Wind, according to the science of Dante's time, is produced by varying degrees of heat; thus, Cocytus, being completely icebound, lacks all heat, and should be free of winds. In the next canto the Pilgrim will see for himself that Lucifer's giant wings cause the wind. See XXXIV, 46–51.

115–117. *may I be forced to drop beneath this ice!:* The Pilgrim, fully aware that his journey will indeed take him below the ice, carefully phrases his treacherous promise to the treacherous shade, and successfully deceives him (149–150). The Pilgrim betrays a sinner in this circle, as the latter does one of his companions there with him in the ice (by naming him).

118–120. *I am Friar Alberigo:* One of the Jovial Friars (see XXIII, 103–108), Alberigo di Ugolino dei Manfredi was a native of Faenza. In 1285, in the midst of a family feud, Alberigo invited his principal opponents, Manfred (close relative) and Alberghetto (Manfred's son), to dinner as a gesture of good will. During the course of the meal, Alberigo, using a pre-arranged signal, called for the fruit, at which his men murdered the dinner guests. Continuing the "fruit" imagery, Alberigo laments his present anguish by saying ironically that "here dates are served me for the figs I gave" (120), which is to say that he is suffering more than his share (since a date is more valuable than a fig).

124–135. *This zone of Tolomea is very special:* According to Church doctrine, under certain circumstances a living person may, through acts of treachery, lose possession of his soul before he dies ("before the time that Atropos [the Fate who cuts man's thread of life] should send it," 126). Then, on earth, a devil inhabits the body until its natural death.

137–147. *he is Ser Branca D'Oria:* A prominent resident of Genoa, Branca D'Oria murdered his father-in-law, Michel Zanche (see XXII, 88), after having invited him to dine with him. Although this treacherous act occurred in 1275, Branca (or at least his earthly body) did not die until 1325. Alberigo tells Dante that the soul of Branca, together with a close relative who helped him carry out his acts of treachery, fell here, to Tolomea, even before Michel Zanche's soul reached the *bolgia* of the Barrators (142–147).

154. *For in company with Romagna's rankest soul:* Friar Alberigo. Faenza, his home town, was in the region of Romagna (now called Emilia).

155. *I found one of your men whose deeds were such:* Branca D'Oria.

CANTO XXXIV

"Vexilla regis prodeunt Inferni,"
  my master said, "closer to us, so now
  look ahead and see if you can make him out."   *3*

A far-off windmill turning its huge sails
  when a thick fog begins to settle in,
  or when the light of day begins to fade,   *6*

that is what I thought I saw appearing.
  And the gusts of wind it stirred made me shrink back
  behind my guide, my only means of cover.   *9*

Down here, I stood on souls fixed under ice
  (I tremble as I put this into verse),
  to me they looked like straws worked into glass.   *12*

Some lying flat, some perpendicular,
  either with their heads up or their feet,
  and some bent head to foot, shaped like a bow.   *15*

When we had moved far enough along the way
  that my master thought the time had come to show me
  the creature who was once so beautiful,   *18*

he stepped aside, and stopping me, announced:
  "This is he, this is Dis; this is the place
  that calls for all the courage you have in you."   *21*

How chilled and nerveless, Reader, I felt then;
  do not ask me—I cannot write about it—
  there are no words to tell you how I felt.   *24*

I did not die—I was not living either!
  Try to imagine, if you can imagine,
  me there, deprived of life and death at once.   *27*

The king of the vast kingdom of all grief
    stuck out with half his chest above the ice;
    my height is closer to the height of giants   30

than theirs is to the length of his great arms;
    consider now how large all of him was:
    this body in proportion to his arms.   33

If once he was as fair as now he's foul
    and dared to raise his brows against his Maker,
    it is fitting that all grief should spring from him.   36

Oh, how amazed I was when I looked up
    and saw a head—one head wearing three faces!
    One was in front (and that was a bright red),   39

the other two attached themselves to this one
    just above the middle of each shoulder,
    and at the crown all three were joined in one: 42

The right face was a blend of white and yellow,
    the left the color of those people's skin
    who live along the river Nile's descent.   45

Beneath each face two mighty wings stretched out,
    the size you might expect of this huge bird
    (I never saw a ship with larger sails):   48

not feathered wings but rather like the ones
    a bat would have. He flapped them constantly,
    keeping three winds continuously in motion   51

to lock Cocytus eternally in ice.
    He wept from his six eyes, and down three chins
    were dripping tears all mixed with bloody slaver.   54

In each of his three mouths he crunched a sinner
    with teeth like those that rake the hemp and flax,
    keeping three sinners constantly in pain;   57

the one in front—the biting he endured
    was nothing like the clawing that he took:
    sometimes his back was raked clean of its skin.   60

"That soul up there who suffers most of all,"
    my guide explained, "is Judas Iscariot:
    the one with head inside and legs out kicking.   63

As for the other two whose heads stick out,
the one who hangs from that black face is Brutus—
see how he squirms in silent desperation,   66

the other one is Cassius, he still looks sturdy.
But soon it will be night. Now is the time
to leave this place, for we have seen it all."   69

I held on to his neck, as he told me to,
while he watched and waited for the time and place,
and when the wings were stretched out just enough,   72

he grabbed on to the shaggy sides of Satan;
then downward, tuft by tuft, he made his way
between the tangled hair and frozen crust.   75

When we had reached the point exactly where
the thigh begins, right at the haunch's curve,
my guide with strain and force of every muscle,   78

turned his head toward the shaggy shanks of Dis
and grabbed the hair as if about to climb—
I thought that we were heading back to Hell.   81

"Hold tight, there is no other way," he said,
panting, exhausted, "only by these stairs
can we leave behind the evil we have seen."   84

When he had got me through the rocky crevice,
he raised me to its edge and set me down,
then carefully he climbed and joined me there.   87

I raised my eyes expecting I would see
the half of Lucifer I saw before.
Instead I saw his two legs stretching upward.   90

If at that sight I found myself confused,
so will those simple-minded folk who still
don't see what point it was I must have passed.   93

"Get up," my master said, "get to your feet,
the way is long, the road a rough climb up,
already the sun approaches middle tierce!"   96

It was no palace promenade we came to,
but rather like some dungeon Nature built:
it was paved with broken stone and poorly lit.   99

"Before we start to struggle out of here,
  O master," I said when I was on my feet,
  "I wish you would explain some things to me.   102

Where is the ice? And how can he be lodged
  upside-down? And how, in so little time
  could the sun go all the way from night to day?"   105

"You think you're still on the center's other side,"
  he said, "where I first grabbed the hairy worm
  of rottenness that pierces the earth's core;   108

and you *were* there as long as I moved downward
  but, when I turned myself, you passed the point
  to which all weight from every part is drawn.   111

Now you are standing beneath the hemisphere
  which is opposite the side covered by land,
  where at the central point was sacrificed   114

the Man whose birth and life were free of sin.
  You have both feet upon a little sphere
  whose other side Judecca occupies;   117

when it is morning here, there it is evening.
  And he whose hairs were stairs for our descent
  has not changed his position since his fall.   120

When he fell from the heavens on this side,
  all of the land that once was spread out here,
  alarmed by his plunge, took cover beneath the sea   123

and moved to our hemisphere; with equal fear
  the mountain-land, piled up on this side, fled
  and made this cavern here when it rushed upward.   126

Below somewhere there is a space, as far
  from Beelzebub as the limit of his tomb,
  known not by sight but only by the sound   129

of a little stream that makes its way down here
  through the hollow of a rock that it has worn
  gently winding in gradual descent."   132

My guide and I entered that hidden road
  to make our way back up to the bright world.
  We never thought of resting while we climbed.   135

We climbed, he first and I behind, until,

through a small round opening ahead of us
I saw the lovely things the heavens hold,   *138*

and we came out to see once more the stars.

1. *"Vexilla regis prodeunt Inferni":* The opening lines of the hymn "Vexilla regis prodeunt"—"The banners of the King advance" (written by Venantius Fortunatus, sixth-century Bishop of Poitiers; this hymn belongs to the liturgy of the Church) is here parodied by the addition of the word *Inferni* "of Hell" to the word *regis* "of the King." Sung on Good Friday, the hymn anticipates the unveiling of the Cross; Dante, who began his journey on the evening of Good Friday, is prepared by Virgil's words for the sight of Lucifer, who will appear like a "windmill" in a "thick fog." The banners referred to are Lucifer's wings. The ironic nature of the parodied line and its effect are evident: with the first three words the reader is prepared to think in terms of the Cross, the symbol of man's redemption through Christ; but with the fourth he is abruptly recalled to the present reality of Hell and, moreover, to the immediate presence of Lucifer, the personification of Evil and the antithesis of Christian Love.

10. *Down here, I stood on souls fixed under ice:* These sinners in various positions fixed rigidly in the ice present a picture of complete immobility and incommunicability, as though they have been entombed a second time. Silence reigns in this fourth division of Cocytus (named Judecca, 117, after the traitor Judas), the gelid abode of those souls in whom all warmth of love for God and for their fellow man has been extinguished.

18. *the creature who was once so beautiful:* Before his fall Lucifer was held by God to be the fairest of the angels. Pride caused Lucifer's rebellion against his Maker and precipitated his expulsion from Heaven. The arch-traitor is, like the other sinners, fixed and suffering in the ice. He weeps.

20. *This is he, this is Dis; this is the place:* In antiquity Pluto, god of the Underworld, was often referred to as "Dis," a name here applied to Lucifer.

38–45. *and saw a head—one head wearing three faces!:* Dante presents Lucifer's head as a perverted parallel of the Trinity. The symbolic value of the three single faces has been much debated. Although many commentators believe that the colors (red, yellow, black) represent the three known continents (Europe, Asia, Africa), it seems more logical that they should be antithetically analogous to the qualities attributed to the Trinity (see Canto III, 5–6). Therefore, Highest Wisdom would be opposed by ignorance (black), Divine Omnipotence by impotence (yellow), Primal Love by hatred or envy (red).

46. *Beneath each face two mighty wings stretched out:* The entire figure of Lucifer is a parody of the angelic. Originally belonging to the order of the Cherubim, he retains his six wings even in Hell, though here, devoid of their heavenly plumage, they appear as those of a bat (the standard depiction of the devil's wings in the Middle Ages). Satan's huge but impotent figure in the darkness might also be contrasted with the image of God (in the *Paradise*) as a small, indivisible point of light in movement.

61–63. *That soul up there who suffers most of all:* Having betrayed Christ for thirty pieces of silver Judas endures greater punishment than the other two souls.

His position in Lucifer's mouth recalls that of the Simonists in Canto XIX. Moreover, Lucifer himself will appear in the same manner ("his two legs stretching upward," 90), when Dante and Virgil have passed the center of the earth and are about to leave Hell. The Simonists, then, prefigure the principal traitors against God and Christ, both in act (treachery to Christ's Church) and spatial disposition of their bodies. See XIX, final note.

65. *the one who hangs from that black face is Brutus:* Marcus Brutus, who was deceitfully persuaded by Cassius (67) to join the conspiracy, aided in the assassination of Julius Caesar. It is fitting that in his final vision of the Inferno the Pilgrim should see those shades who committed treacherous acts against Divine and worldly authorities: the Church and the Roman Empire. This provides the culmination, at least in this canticle, of these basic themes: Church and Empire.

67. *the other one is Cassius, he still looks sturdy:* Caius Cassius Longinus was another member of the conspiracy against Caesar. By describing Cassius as "still looking sturdy," Dante shows he has evidently confused him with Lucius Cassius, whom Cicero calls *adeps,* "corpulent."

79–81. *turned his head toward the shaggy shanks of Dis:* Virgil, carrying the Pilgrim on his back, slowly makes his way down Lucifer's hairy body and, upon reaching a certain point (the center of the universe and, consequently, of terrestrial gravity), where Lucifer's thighs begin, he must turn his head in the direction of Lucifer's legs and begin to climb "upward"—thus confusing the Pilgrim on his back. The way in which Virgil executed his own shift of position on Lucifer's body must have been as follows: when he reached the thigh he moved his head to the side and downwards until (still holding on with one hand to the hair of the chest) he could reach with his other hand to grasp the hair on the thigh—then (aided now by the shift of gravitational pull) to free the first hand and complete the half-circle he had initiated, proceeding henceforth as a man climbing.

Incidentally, of all the translations of this passage which I have read (including not only translations in English but also those in French, Spanish, Portuguese, German, Dutch, Latin, Greek, Welsh) none translates line 79 as I do, attributing the "shanks" to Lucifer; all give them to Virgil, presenting him as turning his head towards his own shanks. This is not because the line is difficult (*Volse la testa ov' elli avea le zanche* "he turned the head to where *he* had the shanks"); in fact, it is not even ambiguous, if the translator bears in mind the use of subject pronouns in Italian. What must have happened is that every translator has copied unthinkingly translations that have preceded. As it is, by attributing the *zanche* "shanks" to Virgil they have not only sinned on aesthetic grounds (this derisive, pejorative term applied to the noble body of Virgil!), but have blurred the clear symbolism here intended: *zanche* is used only twice in the *Divine Comedy,* once in reference to the legs of Nicholas (Canto XIX) and once in this canto. Surely, the two pairs of legs thus verbally linked must be those not of Nicholas and Virgil but those of Nicholas and Lucifer—both of whom present to the Pilgrim's eyes their legs protruding from the ground.

96. *already the sun approaches middle tierce!:* The time is approximately halfway between the canonical hours of Prime and Tierce, i.e. 7:30 A.M. The rapid change from night ("But soon it will be night," 68) to day (96) is the result of the travellers' having passed the earth's center, thus moving into the Southern Hemisphere which is twelve hours ahead of the northern.

107–108. *The hairy worm of rottenness:* Cf. VI, 22; n. 13–22.

112–115. *Now you are standing beneath the hemisphere:* Lucifer's body, falling head first from Heaven to the Southern Hemisphere, bored through to the earth's center where he remains imprisoned. Before he fell through the Southern Hemisphere ("this side," 121), it was covered with land, but the land, "alarmed by his plunge," sank beneath the sea and shifted to the Northern Hemisphere ("our hemisphere," 124). But the land at the center of the earth rushed upward, at once leaving the "cavern" above Lucifer's legs and forming the Mount of Purgatory, the only land in the Southern Hemisphere.

127–132. *Below somewhere there is a space:* Somewhere below the land which rushed upward to form the Mount of Purgatory "there is a space" (127) through which a stream runs, and it is through this space that Virgil and Dante will climb to reach the base of the Mount. The "space" is "as far / from Beelzebub [Lucifer] as the limit of his tomb" (127–128); that is, at the edge of the natural dungeon that constitutes Lucifer's "tomb," there is an opening, a "space," serving as the entrance to the passage from the earth's center to its circumference, created by Lucifer in his fall from Heaven to Hell.

139. *and we came out to see once more the stars:* The Pilgrim, denied sight of the celestial bodies in Hell, now looks up at them again. The direction his journey will now take is upward, toward that Divine Realm of which the stars are the signal for us on earth. That all three canticles end with the word "stars," symmetrically reinforces the concept of movement upward toward God, the central theme and motive force of the *Divine Comedy*.

Critical
Essays

Read It and (Don't) Weep: Textual Irony in the *Inferno*

LAWRENCE BALDASSARO

Readers approaching the *Inferno* for the first time will face any number of questions regarding both the poem itself (theme, structure, language, imagery) and its cultural context (medieval history, theology, politics, even astronomy). Among the many questions raised by the text, one of the first to confront readers head-on at the outset is that of the identity of the protagonist of the poem; whose voice is it that we hear narrating the journey? The question of narrative voice must be addressed in reading any work of fiction, but it is of particular significance in an autobiographical narrative such as the *Divine Comedy*.

On the literal level, the *Comedy* is the story of Dante's journey through the afterlife, a journey that leads him from the brink of despair to enlightened awareness culminating in a direct vision of God. But the voice that speaks in the past tense—"I woke to find myself in some dark woods" (*Inf.* I, 2)—tells the story of a journey already completed. The poet who recalls and transcribes the events of that journey is somehow different from the protagonist, or pilgrim, who experiences the journey firsthand.[1] In other words, the fiction of the poem asks us to accept a diachronic distinction between the experience and its representation. But the poem, of necessity, creates a oneness out of the fictional duality, and therein lies the dilemma for the poem's readers.

The distinction between author and protagonist is made more complex by the autobiographical nature of the *Comedy;* in some ways the poet and pilgrim are obviously one and the same Dante Alighieri. Even in a retrospective narrative such as the *Divine Comedy*, which recounts the protagonist's conversion from a former self to a new, different self, the protagonist cannot be completely "other" than the author. Whatever corrective vision the author applies to his past, the duality of writer and protagonist remains relative, not absolute. Be that as it may, we as readers need to keep in mind that the protagonist is a character in a work of fiction, and therefore we must listen carefully to the voice of the poet who does establish a difference between his perspective and that of his less informed protagonist. Unless we are aware that there are two voices speaking in the poem, and unless we pay attention to the difference, we are likely to confuse fiction and biography. In so doing we confuse the voice of the protagonist, who is caught up in the immediate drama of his journey, with that of the poet, who creates and orders the whole with specific aesthetic and structural strategies that lead the pilgrim, and perhaps the reader, to the desired end.

Dante would have us believe that the protagonist is what he, the poet, once was but no longer is, thanks to the redemptive journey depicted in the poem. The poet has been to the mountain top and has been shown the truth; his vision has been clarified by knowledge and divine grace. What, then, is the nature of the protagonist as created by the poet? What is the starting point, or ground zero, that necessitates the pilgrim's difficult journey through Hell?

A narrative of conversion and redemption such as the *Divine Comedy* obviously requires a protagonist in need of radical transformation. Such is the nature of Dante's pilgrim at the beginning of the poem. Lost and alone in a dark wood, he finds temporary hope when he emerges to see a hill whose summit is bathed in the rays of the sun. But he sinks back into hopelessness when three beasts block his attempt to ascend the hill and drive him back to the bottom of the slope. The pilgrim's startling situation in a mysterious setting begs for interpretation, setting the tone for a poem which will challenge its readers throughout to come to terms with its meaning.

The universality of Dante's poem becomes evident in this opening scene. At the outset we find a terrified man who is without direction in his life, somehow cut off from the path that leads to truth and serenity. In the terminology of contemporary psychology, we might define his condition as a mid-life crisis; the story takes place when Dante is "midway upon the journey of our life" (*Inf.* I, 1). A Jungian archetypal analysis might see the pilgrim's condition as suggestive of the individual's struggle to come to grips with the dark side of his consciousness. But in terms of the poet's medieval cultural context, the figure we encounter in the first canto of the *Inferno* is in a state of sin which threatens to cut him off forever from the possibility of salvation. The gravity of his condition is made clear by Beatrice when she attempts to convince Virgil to go to the aid of her desperate friend:

> I fear he may have gone so far astray,
>   from what report has come to me in Heaven,
>   that I may have started to his aid too late.
>   (*Inf.* II, 64–66)

The resolution of the pilgrim's crisis will be a moral and religious regeneration expressed in terms of a rebirth that takes the form of a journey through Hell, Purgatory, and Heaven. But we learn from the very first lines of the poem that Dante's drama of redemption is meant to be exemplary as well as confessional. The personal dimension of the protagonist's identity as Dante Alighieri, Florentine poet, unfolds gradually over the course of the poem. The allegorical dimension of the protagonist is introduced, instead, at the beginning. The pilgrim's journey is somehow analogous to the readers' experience; the drama of the poem takes place in the midst of "the journey of *our* life"[2] (emphasis mine).

The exemplary function of Dante's protagonist is logically cast in terms of the poem's cultural context. His pilgrim is a deliberately Christian "Everyman," meaning that he carries with him, according to Dante's theological framework, the dangerous consequences of original sin. Because of the Fall, human nature, which had originally been created in perfect harmony with the will of God, was forever corrupted. As Beatrice will tell the pilgrim in the seventh canto of *Paradiso*, human nature "sinned once and for all / in its first root" (vv. 85–86). The price for that transgression was exile from the original state of perfect harmony, not only for the first parents but for all their descendants. The subsequent stain, which St. Thomas termed the *vulneratio naturae* (the "wound of nature"), left all humans susceptible to the inclination to sin.[3] The dire consequence of original sin, Beatrice explains, was that Adam, "damning himself, damned all his progeny" (*Par.* VII, 27).

In the opening scene of the *Inferno*, the pilgrim embodies the fallen human condition. Like all humans since the Fall, he is removed from that original union with the creator that was known only by Adam and Eve. If he is to regain that oneness, he must make the difficult journey back from the state of exile in which we find him at the beginning of the poem. In the prologue scene of the first canto, marked by its vague allegorical landscape so unlike the realistic landscape of Hell itself, we see a physical manifestation of the pilgrim's contaminated soul. In his effort to climb the hill that seems to promise liberation from the terror of the dark wood, the pilgrim is hindered not only by the three beasts that block his path, but also by the "stronger foot" (v. 30) that causes him to limp awkwardly up the hillside.[4] We need not be concerned here with the many possible interpretations of both the hill and the "stronger foot"; in broad terms, it seems clear that the pilgrim's physical impediment suggests the "wound of nature" that he shares with all humans and which makes everyone on "the journey of our life" susceptible to sin, thus impeding their return to the God from which they were alienated by the sin of the first parents.

The pilgrim will succeed in his attempt to climb a hill, that of Purgatory, but not until he has first completed his journey down through the depths of Hell, where he will come face to face with the darkness of his own soul. His futile attempt to climb the hill in *Inferno* I is an ingenuous act of self-reliance motivated by pride and ignorance.[5] The pride implicit in that act is the antithesis of the humility he must acquire if he is to return to God. His abortive attempt must fail because, according to Dante, it is an attempt to do what the Christian pilgrim cannot do on his own. Liberation from the contamination of sin can come only as a gift of divine grace, represented by the intervention, in Canto II, of the three heavenly ladies and the subsequent guidance of Virgil. The journey to redemption begins only when the pilgrim opens himself to accepting that intervention.

The humility required for the successful ascent to God will be attained through the pilgrim's descent into Hell, and it will be earned through the awareness gained on that descent of his own sinful inclination. At the outset the pilgrim is ignorant not only of the path that leads to truth but also of the terms of his human condition. He must first understand the inherent weakness of that human condition before he can hope to understand the God that created him. The first step toward acquiring the strength that will guide him away from sin and toward redemption must be an acknowledgment of his susceptibility to sin that defines him as a fallen human being.

The impediments that block his initial ascent—the three beasts and the "stronger foot" that figure the pilgrim's flawed condition—will not be overcome until the pilgrim reaches the top of the mountain of Purgatory. It is only then, after he has not only recognized but turned his back on sin, that Virgil will pronounce him free:

> Now is your will upright, wholesome and free,
>   and not to heed its pleasure would be wrong:
>   I crown and miter you lord of yourself.
>   (*Purg.* XXVII, 140–142)

During his ascent of the purgatorial mountain, the pilgrim bears visible signs of his inclination to sin. When he is about to pass through the gate of Purgatory, an angel inscribes on his forehead seven *p*'s, representing the seven capital vices to be purged, and admonishes the pilgrim to purify himself:

> Then with his sword he traced upon my brow
>   the scars of seven P's. "Once entered here,
>   be sure you cleanse away these wounds," he said.
>   (*Purg.* IX, 112–114)

One by one, the seven *p*'s will be erased as the pilgrim leaves each of the seven terraces of Purgatory.

If the pilgrim's initial condition in the prologue scene of *Inferno* I is a manifestation of the universal susceptibility to sin, and if his inclination to sin is visibly portrayed by the inscription and subsequent erasure of the seven *p*'s in Purgatory, it is logical to ask how, or if, his susceptibility to sin is exhibited in his journey in the *Inferno*. Given the pilgrim's explicit participation in the process of purgation, is there a similar manifestation of his sinful nature as he makes his way through Hell? In other words, does the poet sustain the portrayal of his flawed protagonist once the narrative proper begins in Canto III of the *Inferno*?

Within the *Inferno* no visible sign comparable to the seven *p*'s of the *Purgatorio* is borne by the pilgrim. The "stronger foot" that hinders him in the opening scene disappears along with the other allegorical markers of the first canto, such as the dark wood and the three beasts. That symbolic limp may be deemed by the poet to be inappropriate once the protagonist enters the concrete geographical reality of Hell, yet the moral and spiritual limitations indicated by the "stronger foot" cannot be left behind. Those limitations are, after all, the reason the journey is necessary.

The journey through Hell is at once a chronicle of the disorder and chaos loose in the world and an acknowledgment that the same disorder and chaos exist, in potentiality if not actuality, within the protagonist. His journey is, figuratively, a descent into the depths of his own soul, an encounter with the darkest reality of his own fallibility. Were it not so, were the pilgrim not to acknowledge his own weakness, his journey through Hell would be informative but not redemptive. Objective knowledge of sin might lead to a sense of moral righteousness in the pilgrim, but subjective awareness of his own capacity for wrongdoing is the necessary first step toward repentance.

The manner in which the poet depicts the pilgrim's acknowledgment of his fallibility and potential to sin is consistent with his portrayal of the sinners throughout the *Inferno*. One of the obvious marks of Dante's poetic genius is his ability to depict his sinners not as awkward allegorical representations of specific sins, but as compelling human beings. Dante's sinners engage the attention of the pilgrim, and of the reader, by their immediacy and believability; they act out their sins, they do not merely "represent" them. Similarly, the poet depicts the pilgrim's vulnerability to sin dramatically, not didactically, in the form of the pilgrim's mimetic response to the sinners he encounters. Beyond the gates of Hell, the vague sense of confusion and sinfulness suggested by the image of the dark wood in the opening scene becomes articulated in the specific sins encountered in the nine circles. What was, in the prologue scene, depicted as potentiality—the pilgrim's limp as a sign of wounded human nature—is, within Hell proper, portrayed as the fulfillment of that negative potentiality. The condemned are in Hell because they refused to find the way out of their own dark woods, succumbing instead to their vulnerability to sin as children of Adam.

The souls in Hell have chosen to turn away from the option of pursuing the Highest Good and by so doing have isolated themselves from God, shutting themselves off forever, because of their limited vision, from the possibilities of the infinite. While he is in this realm of limited vision, the pilgrim himself is contaminated by its atmosphere. Faced with the immediate drama of the sinful disposition of the shades in Hell, he temporarily shares in their contamination. It is in this way that the poet depicts the pilgrim's recognition of his own potentiality to sin, wherein lies his acquisition of humility.

This mimetic behavior will be evident in the *Purgatorio* as well. There, in addition to having the seven *p*'s inscribed on his forehead, the pilgrim will imitate, in varying ways, the purgative process acted out by the penitent shades. Like the souls in the Antepurgatory, he is inclined to procrastinate; he is lulled by Casella's song (Canto II), captivated by Manfred's story (Canto III), and, like the indolent in Canto V, he is weary and sluggish. Like the proud, he walks with his head lowered; like the wrathful, he is deprived of his eyesight. In the *Inferno*, with its much greater variety of sin and punishment, the pilgrim's symbolic involvement in sin is more varied; it is at times verbal, at times visual, at times obvious, at times subtle. A few brief examples will have to suffice here to illustrate the nature of the pilgrim's mimetic behavior.

In Limbo (Canto IV) the pilgrim is greeted by the great classical poets—Homer, Horace, Ovid, and Lucan—who, together with Virgil, accept him as one of them: "Greater honor still they deigned to grant me: / they welcomed me as one of their own group" (vv. 100–101). The pilgrim, here clearly functioning in his biographical role as the Florentine poet, is logically delighted by this honor, as he and his fellow poets walk and talk of "things that here are best kept silent" (v. 104). The privileged zone of Limbo that these poets and their fellow shades inhabit represents the most perfect human condition they could imagine. But as the pilgrim shares his thoughts with these great minds, for whom reason was the key to knowledge, he is forgetting that they will spend eternity in Limbo "cut off from hope" (v. 42), knowing as they now do that there is a higher truth that their rationality failed to comprehend. The pilgrim, unlike these shades, will move on, but for the moment he shares with them their limited vision of human existence.

At the end of Canto V, overcome by pity in response to Francesca, the pilgrim faints. He is, in effect, seduced by Francesca's speech and, like those in the circle of lust, his reason (which should recognize the justness of her punishment) is overcome by passion. In Canto VIII, after having responded to the sinners' condition with pity in Cantos IV, V, and VI, the pilgrim suddenly becomes wrathful, precisely in the canto of wrath. His anger toward Filippo Argenti seems to be unprovoked by the sinner, and to search for a biographical motivation for Dante's behavior takes us needlessly outside the text. What we witness in the circle of wrath is not the vendetta of the poet toward a personal enemy, but the mimetic behavior of the protagonist who responds throughout the *Inferno* to the particular atmosphere in which he finds himself.

In the circle of heresy (Canto X), the pilgrim engages in a rancorous political dialogue with Farinata, rejoicing in the ultimate victory of *his* party over that of his Ghibelline enemy. Farinata is portrayed as the consummate "party man," yet the pilgrim is no less fanatical in his devotion to the kind of factional political strife that Dante the poet clearly portrays as the seed of the degeneration of Florence. Again, this time near the end of the *Inferno*, the poet will engage in a verbal political duel. Mosca dei Lamberti, condemned among the sowers of discord in the ninth *bolgia* for initiating the Guelph-Ghibelline feud that would divide Florence throughout the thirteenth century, boasts that it was he who "'sowed the seed of discord for the Tuscans'" (*Inf.* XXVIII, 108). The pilgrim immediately fires back: "'And of death for all your clan,'" adding a "fresh wound" to Mosca, who "went off like one gone mad from pain" (vv. 109–111).

In the Ninth Circle of Hell, where fraud is joined with violence, the pilgrim encounters shades who are punished in the frozen lake of Cocytus. In the region of Antenora, which holds those sinners who betrayed their country or party, the pilgrim attempts to trick one of the shades into revealing his identity, thinking that he may be Bocca degli Abati, who betrayed the Florentine Guelphs at the battle of Montaperti. When Bocca scoffs at Dante's offer to speak of him when he returns to the world of the living, the pilgrim resorts to violence, pulling out the sinner's hair until yet another shade betrays Bocca by revealing his identity. In the circle of treachery, the pilgrim's behavior mirrors the very sin being punished.[6]

This particular example of the pilgrim's mimetic involvement underlines the ironic stance that distinguishes the voice of the poet from that of the pilgrim. Clearly the pilgrim's harsh behavior toward Bocca is not contradictory to the poet's judgment of the sin of treachery. At the same time, the pilgrim's behavior in this episode is so harsh, and so curiously like the very sin being punished, that it calls attention to itself. There is no dramatic justification for the pilgrim's violence; he has done nothing like this before, and his actions are not necessary to advance the narrative proper. As is true throughout the *Inferno*, the pilgrim's mimetic behavior is the dramatic manifestation of the contamination that makes him susceptible to sin and makes his journey through Hell necessary.

Through his imitative response, the pilgrim acknowledges that whatever human impulses motivate the sinners in Hell, they exist potentially within himself as well. Each of the sinners he meets is a potential other self. In his exemplary role as a wayfarer on "the journey of our life," the pilgrim has within him the capability of committing any sin he witnesses in the varied gallery of Hell. Through the strategy of mimesis, the poet reveals the protagonist's acknowledgment of his vulnerability to each of the sins he encounters, an acknowledgment that is the essence of humility and the necessary prelude to the purgation of that vulnerability which will take place in the *Purgatorio*. The same inclination to sin that will be erased on the ascent of the mountain of Purgatory is acknowledged by his symbolic involvement with the sinners in Hell. As long as he is in the blind world of Hell, his is susceptible to its effects.[7]

In essence, the pilgrim/protagonist is a "reader" in the *Inferno*. As a reader of the distinct "texts" he encounters in each circle of Hell, he is tested by his reading of those texts. Unlike the poet who has completed the journey, the pilgrim cannot see the text as a whole—an image that the poet will use at the end of the poem (*Par.* XXXIII, 82–87) to suggest the totality of vision achieved at journey's end. To the pilgrim, the text unfolds page by page, and his imitative response to the sins of the *Inferno* is an indication of his limited ability to decipher the text properly.

If the pilgrim is a reader of the texts he encounters and an active participant in the journey, the reader of Dante's text is, in turn, a pilgrim, one who is drawn into the journey of the protagonist both by the dramatic immediacy of the poet's descriptive power and by the poet's direct addresses to the reader, which I shall discuss in a moment. Because he portrays sin dramatically, not didactically, Dante requires his reader to take an active role in the reading of the text; meaning requires a collaborative effort by both poet and reader. The relation between poet and reader, then, is no less significant than that between poet and protagonist. It is a relation that is explicit as well as implicit, since Dante addresses his reader no less than twenty times in the *Comedy*.[8]

In his essay on "Dante's Addresses to the Reader," Erich Auerbach points out the newness of these addresses relative to classical and medieval precedents. The originality of Dante's addresses, argues Auerbach, is a symptom of a new relation between poet and reader, one in which Dante assumes a stance of "brotherly solidarity" with the reader. Yet the reader is never on an equal footing with the poet. In fact, Auerbach concludes that "Dante creates his reader," a reader who is a "disciple" who is "not expected to discuss or to judge, but to follow, using his own forces, but the way Dante orders him to" (p. 46).

As significant as Auerbach's study is in establishing the historical originality of Dante's approach to his reader, it neglects the ironic duality of the distinct voices of the poet and pilgrim. Auerbach's image of the prophet revealing truth to the willing disciple is misleading in that it suggests a passive reader. The poet does guide the reader, as Auerbach suggests, but even in the direct addresses Dante coaxes the reader to see the truth but does not reveal it directly. It is the obligation of the reader to read the signs properly; the poet's obligation is to report what he witnessed on his journey as pilgrim. In one of his direct addresses to the reader, Dante states what may be taken as a guiding principle of the poet's approach throughout the *Comedy*: "I put the food out; now you feed yourself" (*Par.* X, 25). I would argue that throughout the *Inferno*, Dante challenges and tests the reader, who must come to terms with the ironic duality of the poet and the protagonist. At every step of the journey the reader must be careful to listen to both voices in order to read the signs properly.

In an ironic twist of his own, Auerbach, in a later essay, implicitly denies Dante's reader the possibility of understanding the poet. The fault, however, lies with Dante himself, according to Auerbach, who maintains that Dante ultimately undermines the allegorical intent of the *Comedy*. Because Dante creates characters that are so realistic and fascinating, especially in the *Inferno*, the reader is likely to focus on the human element of the poem and forget about the signification behind the image. According to Auerbach, "the image of man eclipses the image of God."[9]

Auerbach's conclusion suggests a naive failure on Dante's part to merge form and function. Having established a complex framework whose goal is to enlighten the reader, Dante subverts that framework by the power of his realism. Essentially, Auerbach is refuting his claim, made in the earlier essay, for the authoritative and even prophetic voice of Dante by arguing that the poet unwittingly sabotages the purpose of the poem by infusing it with compelling images of humanity that distract the reader from the professed redemptive function of the poem.

The danger to which Auerbach calls our attention is indeed real. Individual episodes of the *Inferno*, featuring fascinating sinners, often seem at odds with the thematic thrust of the poem as a whole, so much so that the consistency of form and content is called into question. The details of the text would seem to resist stubbornly the conclusiveness that the structure seeks to impose on them. It is not surprising, then, that modern readers for whom the didactic message of the *Comedy* does not strike a responsive chord may succumb to the temptation to read the *Inferno* as a series of dramatic episodes featuring interesting characters who coax the reader's mind away from the governing structure of the poem.

On the other hand, it may be that Dante was expecting more of his readers than Auerbach is willing to grant them. Implicit in his interpretation is the duality that characterizes much of twentieth-century Dante criticism. It is a critical response that suggests an essentially schizophrenic view of Dante as either poet or prophet, as the maker of powerful but fragmented poetic images, or as the *scriba Dei* who fashions an allegorical work designed to lead his readers to God.

But are there, in fact, two Dantes—the poet and the prophet—and are we as readers forced to choose one or the other? Or is the creation of images that would seem to distract us, and the pilgrim/protagonist, from the poem's purpose in fact part of that purpose? Might it not be the case that the temptation to be diverted from the final goal is part of the poet's strategy, part of the challenge he poses both to his protagonist and to his reader? The challenge to both is to not lose sight of the purpose of the whole, to not be distracted by the images of the finite and limited vision encountered in Hell but to maintain the commitment to the journey to its end, through Purgatory and Paradise, so that the failures of the damned may be seen in their proper perspective? On rare occasions the challenge to the reader is posed explicitly by the poet, and it may be helpful to examine one of those instances.

In the twentieth canto of the *Inferno*, the pilgrim encounters the soothsayers whose punishment for having tried to look into the future is to have their heads twisted 180 degrees so that their faces look to the rear. Forced to walk backward, they move slowly and silently, weeping as they walk. The pilgrim is overcome by the startling sight of these deformed shades; leaning against a rock, he weeps in pity. And the poet interrupts the narrative to ask the reader to understand why he, as the pilgrim, behaved as he did at that moment of his journey:

> So may God grant you, Reader, benefit
>> from reading of my poem, just ask yourself
>> how I could keep my eyes dry when, close by,
>
> I saw the image of our human form
>> so twisted—the tears their eyes were shedding
>> streamed down to wet their buttocks at the cleft.
>
> Indeed I did weep, as I leaned by body
>> against a jut of rugged rock.
>> <div align="right">(<i>Inf.</i> XX, 19–26)</div>

If we hear in these lines only the literal request for a sympathetic understanding of the pilgrim's behavior, the poet's address seems to be an appeal to our humanity, essentially asking us: wouldn't you have done the same thing had you been in my place? But if we read the poet's address in an ironic vein, we see that what appears to be a request for sympathy for the pilgrim is at the same time a challenge to the reader to see the possibility of other behavior in that situation: "May God grant you, Reader, *benefit* from reading of my poem, just ask yourself *how* I could keep my eyes dry."

By keeping in mind the context of the situation, the reader might conclude that the pilgrim could have kept his eyes dry by remembering that what he was witnessing was not the physical distortion of the human body but the punishment of the condemned sinners' souls. The distortion of their shade bodies is, of course, a metaphor of their own willful distortion of their vision; their twisted bodies are a visual representation of their failure to "see" in the proper way. The pity expressed by the pilgrim is indicative of his limited vision. He fails to see the signification behind the sign; unable to grasp the spiritual significance of the sinners' torment, he can only respond to their physical predicament: "I saw the image of our *human form* so twisted." The pilgrim's failure to keep the scene he witnesses in its proper context is rendered even more blatant for the reader by the poet's reminder, in the unusually prosaic opening lines of the canto, that what he is writing, and what we are reading, is a poem about Hell:

> Now I must turn strange torments into verse
>> to form the matter of the twentieth canto
>> of the first chant, the one about the damned.
>> <div align="right">(<i>Inf.</i> XX, 1–3)</div>

Unlike the pilgrim, Virgil is aware of the scene's context, as he quickly reminds his errant pupil:

"So you are still like all the other fools?

In this place piety lives when pity is dead,
for who could be more wicked than that man
who tries to bend divine will to his own!"
(*Inf.* XX, 27–30)

The final two verses of his passage are, I think, purposely ambiguous, referring to both the sinners and to the pilgrim. Both tried to bend divine will to their own, the soothsayers by usurping a power belonging rightly to God alone, the pilgrim by questioning the appropriateness of divine justice, displaying pity where piety is the appropriate response. Caught up in the immediate drama of the scene he witnesses, and forgetting where he is and why, the pilgrim mirrors the behavior of the sinners; like them he weeps and "'bend[s] divine will to his own.'" He fails to read the text properly.

I cite this particular example to underscore the ambiguous relation between the poet, the protagonist, and the reader. Throughout the *Inferno*, the reading process is analogous to the journey of the pilgrim; the signs are there, but they require careful and attentive reading if they are to be properly interpreted.

But this conclusion raises an obvious question: if the poem is didactic, if its purpose is to lead the reader to an awareness of the truth, why does the poet challenge the reader's ability to understand the text? Why, especially in the *Inferno*, are there potential stumbling blocks, not only for the reader but for the pilgrim as well?

Throughout the *Comedy*, comprehension is rendered difficult by the poet's requirement that he, and his readers, recognize all aspects of God and his creation in all their detailed particulars. Vagueness simply will not do for Dante, and his quest for knowledge strains not only his poetic imagination but also the reader's ability to comprehend the products of that imagination. Just as Ulysses exhorts his crew to journey with him into the unknown, Dante urges his readers to follow him on his quest for knowledge. But whereas Ulysses coaxed his men with the promise of discovery, Dante is a more honest rhetorician, warning his followers of the potential danger of getting lost in his wake:

All you who in your wish to hear my words
have followed thus far in your little boat
behind my ship that singing sails these waters

go back now while you still can see your shores;
do not attempt the deep: it well could be
that losing me you would be lost yourselves.
(*Par.* II, 1–6)

Here Dante addresses those about to embark on the final stage of the journey in the *Paradiso*, and the danger to which he alludes presumably has to do with the sheer intellectual weight of philosophy and doctrine that may overwhelm the reader. The *Inferno* poses challenges which are perhaps more subtle, having to do, at least in part, with the poet's mode of depicting sin. The nature of sin, as Dante portrays it, is that it is often seductive and beguiling. (Keep in mind that almost half the cantos in the *Inferno* are devoted to sins of fraud.) Precisely because the sinners are painted with realistic strokes, they appear to the pilgrim, and to the reader, as complex and ambiguous characters, not as blank stereotypes of sin. A few shades may reveal the baseness of their character in their language and behavior, but many evoke sympathy, pity, respect, even admiration. Dante's sinners are drawn with a precision and clarity that makes them come alive in the present moment, so much so that they may seem to be living human beings temporarily misplaced in the eternal environment of Hell. So too do they appear to the pilgrim, who often responds to the shades as if they were living characters encountered on the streets of Florence; he echoes the narrative ambience established by their voices and often neglects to deal with them in terms of the broader context of place that defines their eternal reality as inhabitants of Hell. If that context is neglected by the reader, perspective is distorted and the sinners in Hell may be seen as the lead players in their own brief dramas rather than as signs pointing the way for the pilgrim.

As the passage from *Paradiso* II cited above attests, Dante is aware of the high demands he places on his readers. Though his professed goal in the *Divine Comedy* is nothing less than the salvation of humankind, both in this life and the next, he refuses to patronize his audience. As a poet, he chooses instead to confront his readers with the challenge of properly reading the signs he places before them. The ironic tensions evident throughout the *Inferno*—between the wayfaring pilgrim and the enlightened poet, between image and theme, between the compelling immediacy of single episodes and the structure of the whole that puts them into proper perspective—all of these contribute to an ambiguity which both challenges the reader and enriches the poetry. The precise detail of the poet's depiction of Hell and its inhabitants contains the potentiality, for the pilgrim and the reader, of both enlightenment and distraction from the goal. But that is as it should be in the first canticle of the *Comedy*, where pilgrim and reader alike must confront the danger of wandering away from "the straight path." If the reader of the *Inferno* fails, along with the pilgrim, to see through the veil, all is not lost. The truth will be revealed gradually and the attentive reader who is willing to maintain the commitment will learn step by step, along with the pilgrim, as the journey progresses and the text unfolds itself.

1. Of the many scholars who have discussed the distinction between the poet and the protagonist, among the first were Leo Spitzer, "A Note on the Poetic and the Empirical 'I' in Medieval Authors," *Traditio* 4 (1946): 414–22, and Charles S. Singleton, in *An Essay on the Vita Nuova* (Cambridge: Harvard University Press, 1949), repr. (Baltimore: Johns Hopkins University Press, 1977), 25.

2. The allegorical nature of Dante's protagonist is discussed by Charles S. Singleton in *Dante Studies 1: Commedia, Elements of Structure* (Cambridge: Harvard University Press, 1954), esp. chap. 1.

3. *Summa Theologica*, I–II, q.85, a.3.

4. For a summary of the various interpretations of the meaning of the hill, see Anthony K. Cassell, *Inferno I*, Lectura Dantis Americana (Philadelphia: University of Pennsylvania Press, 1989), 142 n. 1. On the "stronger foot," see Musa's note to *Inf.* I, 30, and John Freccero, "Dante's Firm Foot and the Journey without a Guide," *Harvard Theological Review* LII (1959): 245–81 (repr. in *Dante: The Poetics of Conversion* [Cambridge: Harvard University Press, 1986], 29–54).

5. For a discussion of Dante's failed climb, see Cassell, *Inferno I*, esp. chap. 2.

6. For a more complete discussion of this episode, see my essay, "Dante's Hardened Heart: The Cocytus Cantos," in *Lectura Dantis Newberryana*, vol. 2, ed. Paolo Cherchi and Antonio Mastrobuono (Evanston, IL: Northwestern University Press, 1990), 3–20.

7. In the first canto of *Purgatorio* (vv. 94–99), Cato will instruct Virgil to wash Dante's face so as to remove the filth of Hell that clouds his vision.

8. For discussions of the "reader" in *The Divine Comedy*, see Erich Auerbach, "Dante's Addresses to the Reader," *Romance Philology* 3 (1949): 1–26; Leo Spitzer, "The Addresses to the Reader in the *Commedia*", *Italica* XXXII (1955): 143–65; Howard H. Schless, "Dante, Comedy and Conversion," *Genre* IX, no. 4 (Winter 1976–77): 413–27.

9. "Farinata and Cavalcante," in *Mimesis: The Representation of Reality in Western Literature* (Princeton: Princeton University Press, 1953), 202.

Dante's Beloved Yet Damned Virgil

GUY P. RAFFA

A great Latin poet who "sang of arms and of a man" and who made the founding of the Roman Empire the subject of his *Aeneid*, Virgil articulated the goal of Dante's political philosophy: a universal monarchy headed by a strong and just ruler. He also told of heroic descents to the Underworld—Aeneas in the *Aeneid* (Book VI) and Orpheus in the *Georgics* (Book IV)—which gave Dante models for imagining his own infernal journey. Just as important, however, was Virgil's reputation as a prophet in the Middle Ages. According to this legend, the Latin poet unknowingly predicted the birth of Christ in his *Fourth Eclogue* (Virgil died in 19 B.C.). Together, these three aspects of Virgil's poetry and literary reputation—Empire, Underworld and Prophecy—help to explain Dante's decision to choose him as the pilgrim's guide through the circles of Hell and around the terraces of Purgatory. But Dante's Virgil, particularly in the *Inferno*, is far more than a prophetic author and exemplary guide. He is also a tragic figure whose intellectual, emotional and psychological complexity accounts for much of the dramatic energy in Dante's poem. After all, most of the action of the journey through Hell involves Virgil in some way, usually through his relationship to the pilgrim, himself a creation of the poet. Although Virgil appears most often as a wise guide and a source of knowledge for the pilgrim, there are crucial moments when Dante the poet seems to undermine Virgil's authority and credibility in order to enrich the aesthetic and moral structure of his poetic universe.[1]

Virgil, as the author of the *Eclogues*, the *Georgics*, and the *Aeneid*, provided Dante with an abundance of mythological, historical and political material. While the *Eclogues* (the earliest Latin pastoral poetry) and the *Georgics* (four long poems treating farm life) are significant works of Latin literature in themselves, Virgil's fame as a poet is due far more to the *Aeneid*, his tale of Aeneas's wanderings from the fall of Troy to the foundation of a new civilization in Italy. More than any other poet, Virgil exemplified for Dante the relentless hard work necessary for translating a poetic vision into well-wrought verse. Working within the demanding constraints of dactylic hexameter (six feet according to precise metrical patterns), Virgil's attention to the nuances of style and poetic structure served as both a model and a challenge for Dante. The Italian poet answered that challenge admirably with the 14,233 lines of *terza rima* (Dante's invention) that make up the *Divine Comedy*.

Dante clearly drew on his knowledge of Virgil's poetry in his conception of the *Inferno*. In *Aeneid* VI, the story of Aeneas's visit to the world of shades, Dante found themes, characters, and topographical features that he could transform to meet the demands of his own poem. Of course, Dante does not take all of the Virgilian elements, he adds innumerable touches of his own, and much (if not most) of what he does borrow from Virgil is barely recognizable in its new setting. For example, Dante inserts most of the rivers and marshes of Virgil's Underworld—Acheron, Styx, Phlegethon and Cocytus[2]—into an elaborate, interconnected hydraulic system whose source is the flow of tears from the Old Man of Crete, an immense statue symbolizing the degradation of civilization from a mythological Golden Age to the religious and political corruption of Dante's time (Canto XIV). Virgilian creatures from *Aeneid* VI who inhabit Dante's Hell include Charon the demonic ferryman (Canto III), Minòs the infernal judge (Canto V), Cerberus the three-throated dog (Canto VI), Phlegyas (Canto VIII), the Furies and the Medusa (Canto IX), the Minotaur and the Centaurs (Canto XII), the Harpies (Canto XIII), Geryon (Cantos XVI–XVII) and several Giants (Canto XXXI). The very name of Virgil's Underworld—"House of Dis"—comes to designate Dante's Lower Hell where heresy, violence, and fraud are punished.

Dante's Underworld and the figures contained therein are generally more sharply drawn and tangible than their Virgilian counterparts. For example, whereas Virgil's Minotaur appears as one of Daedalus's sculpted figures on Apollo's temple, Dante brings the hybrid monster to life as the guardian and symbolic representative of the entire circle of violence. And Geryon, whom Virgil only mentions in *Aeneid* VI as a "three-bodied shade," is one of Dante's most complex creatures. With the face of an honest man, a serpent's body with hairy paws, a scorpion's tail, and an intricately patterned hide, Geryon functions as a symbol of, and transporter to, the realm of fraud. Typical of Dante's monstrous creations, Geryon also reveals some psychological complexity, in this case a sullen, resentful attitude toward the travelers. Dante's attention to detail accords with his desire to highlight the reality of the pilgrim's journey through Hell. Virgil, on the other hand, creates a more phantasmagoric atmosphere in his account of Aeneas's journey to the world of shades. By having Aeneas leave the Underworld through the Gate of False Dreams, Virgil perhaps suggests "the uncertainty of his own religious vision."[3]

Although there is no question as to the sincerity of Dante's religious vision, the success of the pilgrim's journey through Hell occasionally appears less certain. Virgil's account of Orpheus's tragic mistake in *Georgics*

IV—he looks back, thereby losing Eurydice forever—provided Dante with the example of a decidedly unsuccessful journey to the Underworld. Moreover, just as Virgil's Aeneas receives prophecies of imminent hardships as well as a glimpse into the future glory of Rome, so Dante's pilgrim learns that his journey to the Other World will not spare him the pain of exile and political failure back on earth. Virgil's two stories thus combine to illuminate the double-edge of the pilgrim's journey through Hell: it is a divinely sanctioned mission, but not without fears and doubts concerning both the journey itself and the future life of the protagonist.

Virgil's literary reputation offered Dante not only a model of poetic excellence but also a vehicle for dramatizing issues of poetic truth and falsehood in the *Inferno*. It is therefore no surprise that Virgil's role as an author figures so prominently throughout the journey. In fact, Virgil's status as an *auctor*—an author and an authority—helps to shape his relationship to the pilgrim right from the start. Consistent with his attempt to underscore the historical veracity of his poem, Dante has the character Virgil introduce himself to the pilgrim with pertinent biographical details:

> "I was born, though somewhat late, *sub Julio*,
>   and lived in Rome when good Augustus reigned,
>   when still the false and lying gods were worshipped.
>
> I was a poet and sang of that just man,
>   son of Anchises, who sailed off from Troy
>   after burning of proud Ilium."
>
> (I, 70–75)[4]

Identifying himself as the poet of the *Aeneid*, Virgil firmly establishes a political theme central to Dante's poem: the celebration of the Roman Empire as the apex of civilization. Descendants of "that just man" Aeneas, the Romans reached the heights of their greatness under "good Augustus." Yet this was still the time of "false and lying gods," an admission on the part of Dante's Virgil that implies at least a partial Christian perspective. Dante will develop and exploit Virgil's limited Christian vision at key junctures in the *Inferno*.

As the pilgrim pleads for help to escape from the she-wolf, he recognizes the immense literary debt he owes Virgil. In characteristic fashion, Dante acknowledges and propagates his own literary reputation at the same time that he praises the Latin poet:

> "O light and honor of the other poets,
>   may my long years of study, and that deep love
>   that made me search your verses, help me now!
>
> You are my teacher, the first of all my authors,
>   and you alone the one from whom I took
>   the beautiful style that was to bring me honor."
>
> (I, 82–87)

We will never know if Dante refers here to a specific period of his own literary production (parts of the *Vita nuova*, certain *canzoni* treating political themes, etc.), but it is clear that Virgil has served as a significant literary model in a general sense. This is the Virgil known for the excellence of his dactylic hexameters, the perfection of his poetic skills from the *Eclogues* to the *Georgics* and culminating in the *Aeneid*. That the pilgrim attributes his own poetic honor to Virgil alone, "light and honor of the other poets," establishes an intimate relationship with both professional and personal overtones. The "deep love" that compelled the pilgrim to study Virgil's poetry now forms the bond of affection developed in the poem between the teacher and his student.

The pilgrim's familiarity with Virgil's literature strongly affects his thoughts and actions. In Canto II his recollection of Aeneas's visit to the Underworld in *Aeneid* VI nearly keeps him from following Virgil into Hell in order to evade the she-wolf and regain the "straight path." The pilgrim, in fact, reminds Virgil that he wrote about Aeneas, who made his journey "'with flesh corruptible, / with all his senses, to the immortal realm'" (14–15). But whereas Aeneas clearly earned such an honor as "'father of glorious Rome and of her empire'" (21),[5] the pilgrim sees no reason why he should embark on such a journey himself. Virgil must finally convince his reluctant companion that this journey too is divinely sanctioned. Celestial intervention in the form of three "gracious ladies" (Mary, Lucy and Beatrice) mercifully lies behind Virgil's selection as the pilgrim's guide through Hell and Purgatory. The pilgrim's reference to Aeneas as a historical figure underscores Dante's concern with poetic truth and the intersections of fiction and reality. By creating a character out of the historical Virgil and by having the pilgrim compare himself to Aeneas, the protagonist of Virgil's poem, Dante sets up a reciprocal relationship between his *Comedy* and Virgil's *Aeneid*.

This poetic reciprocity becomes most apparent when the travelers enter Limbo, the First Circle of Hell and Virgil's permanent abode as a great-hearted man who lived before Christ. Along with the Latin poets Horace, Ovid and Lucan, the Greek poet Homer bestows praise on Virgil with the words, "'Now let us honor our illustrious poet, / his shade that left is now returned to us'" (IV, 80–81). Soon thereafter Dante obliquely yet assertively lays claim to his own literary potential by having these eminent poets from antiquity extend their welcome to him as well as to Virgil:

> Greater honor still they deigned to grant me:
> they welcomed me as one of their own group,
> so that I numbered sixth among such minds.
> (100–102)

Once again the pilgrim, speaking as an author, turns an opportunity for paying homage to Virgil into a daring—yet prescient—act of self-promotion.

Dante's depiction of Virgil's literary reputation in the *Inferno* determines more than the relationship between the pilgrim and his learned guide. It can also shape the pilgrim's encounter with an individual sinner, as in the case of Pier delle Vigne in the wood of the suicides. Virgil's literary influence, moreover, extends beyond his authorship of Aeneas's journey to the Underworld in *Aeneid* VI. In Canto XIII Dante represents the Polydorus episode from *Aeneid* III in order to dramatize the power of literature to convey incredible truths. Having crossed the Phlegethon with the centaur Nessus, Dante and Virgil enter a strange forest. The twisted black trees provide nests for the Harpies, hybrid creatures of human females and birds who, Dante tells us, "drove the Trojans from the Strophades / with filthy forecasts of their close disaster" (11–12). This reminiscence of an event from Aeneas's travels recounted in Book III of the *Aeneid* thus anticipates Dante's reworking of the Polydorus episode from the same book.

Hearing "wails of grief" with no apparent source, the pilgrim is encouraged by Virgil to break off a branch from one of the gnarled trees. When a voice cries out "'Why are you tearing me?'" (33) and from the cut flows a mixture of words and blood (43–44), the pilgrim learns that the trees are in fact the form of the souls punished in this horrid place. Virgil immediately apologizes to the offended spirit with an explicit reference to his own poetry:

> "O wounded soul," my sage replied to him,
>   "if he had only let himself believe
>   what he had read in verses I once wrote,
>
> he never would have raised his hand against you,
>   but the truth itself was so incredible,
>   I urged him on to do the thing that grieves me."
>   (46–51)

In *Aeneid* III Virgil tells of Aeneas's frightening encounter with Polydorus, Priam's youngest son, who was betrayed and murdered by the King of Thrace out of lust for gold. Transfixed by iron lances, Polydorus's pierced body grew into a myrtle bush. When Aeneas plucks the plant's stems, to be used as covering for an altar, he shudders to see drops of black blood and then to hear a piteous voice arise from the plant's severed roots:

> Why are you mangling me, Aeneas? Spare
> my body. I am buried here. Do spare
> the profanation of your pious hands.
> I am no stranger to you; I am Trojan.
>   (52–55)[6]

Virgil thus feels that the pilgrim, who has studied his literary guide's verses with "'deep love'" (I, 83), could not perceive the literal truth of something as incredible as a human plant. By re-creating the episode in the *Inferno*, Dante allows Virgil to reaffirm the truth value of his *Aeneid*: plants *can* become the form of a human being. This strategic reenactment therefore supports the consideration of Virgil's epic as a historically accurate account of Aeneas's wanderings and eventual conquest of Italy, the future center of the Empire and the Church. Here it is the pilgrim whose faith (in literature) is put into question.[7]

However, the fault for such disbelief does not lie with the pilgrim alone, for Virgil ultimately failed to convey the truthfulness of Polydorus's transformation into a talking, bleeding bush in the *Aeneid*. Dante dramatizes this failure by having Virgil force the pilgrim to repeat Aeneas's action of wounding the human plant. The pilgrim is thus able to see with his own eyes (and hear with his own ears) what Virgil's verses could not convince him to believe, namely, that a human being—in this case a suicide—could take the form of a plant. But Dante does one step further in this staged critique of Virgil's limited capacity to represent incredible events truthfully. In his presentation of Geryon's arrival, a strange and wondrous event, Dante actually models the dilemma of a reader confronted with an incredible—yet true—situation. The Italian poet thereby one-ups his Latin predecessor by challenging the reader of the *Comedy* to believe in the reality of even the most fantastic of the sights and sounds of the pilgrim's journey through Hell.

Toward the end of Canto XVI the travelers have reached the innermost edge of the Seventh Circle, where the burning sand of the sodomites and the usurers meets a rocky precipice leading down to the final two circles of Hell. In a highly symbolic act, Virgil takes a cord, previously worn by the pilgrim, and flings it down into the abyss. The pilgrim's revelation that he had once considered using this cord "to catch the leopard with the gaudy skin" (108) and Virgil's order for him to hand over the cord "looped into a coil" (111) unequivocally announce the travelers' proximity to the realm of fraud. As readers we are now thrust into an atmosphere of suspense, thinking, as the pilgrim does, that "something strange is going to happen . . . to answer the strange signal" sent by Virgil to the circles below (115–116). It is at this point that Dante the poet, who obviously knows what is about to happen, interrupts the narrative to speak directly to his reader:

> It is always better to hold one's tongue than speak
> a truth that seems a bold-face lie when uttered,
> since to tell this truth could be embarrassing;
>
> but I shall not keep quiet; and by the verses
> of my *Comedy*—so may they be received
> with lasting favor, Reader—I swear to you. . . .
>   (124–129)

And he goes on to describe what he "saw": a figure swimming up through the murky air to the edge of the cliff where the travelers are waiting. Only in the next canto do we learn that this strange creature is Geryon, a hybrid monster with "the face of any honest man," a serpentine body, clawed paws "hairy to the armpits," and a scorpion-like tail. With physical attributes decidedly more intricate and colorful than other creatures in Dante's Hell, Geryon serves as an appropriate image of the fraudulent realm whence he came, a place where appearances disguise dangers as great as the slyly concealed intentions of the malicious sinners punished therein.

However, just as striking as Geryon's dramatic appearance is Dante's strategy for convincing his reader he really saw this strange creature swimming up like a diver returning to the surface of the sea (XVI, 130–136). The poet now cleverly proclaims the truthfulness of his account of Geryon's exciting arrival by saying, in effect, "I know you won't believe this, but it really happened." Implicitly recalling and thus highlighting Virgil's difficulty in Canto XIII, Dante anticipates his reader's potential objections as he makes the very question of poetic truth a legitimate subject of his verses.[8] To complicate matters, Dante swears on these very same verses that he's telling the truth! Ultimately, Dante has faith in the power of his verses to convince his reader of the reality of Geryon's arrival, whereas Virgil considered his own speech incapable of convincing the pilgrim that the trees in the wood were really suicides. What remains crystal clear, therefore, is Virgil's destiny to come out second best in this staged competition in which Dante pulls all the strings.

The Virgil of the *Aeneid* and the *Georgics* thus plays a major role in Dante's ideas of fiction and poetic truth, most notably through his portrayals of Aeneas's encounter with Polydorus and visit to the Underworld and Orpheus's tragic attempt to bring Eurydice back to the world of the living. The Virgil of the *Eclogues*, however, also informs Dante's conception of the pilgrim's guide for the journey through Hell and up the Mountain of Purgatory. In fact, one of the *Comedy*'s most poignant moments occurs when Statius, a fellow Latin poet, credits Virgil with both his conversion to Christianity and his poetic vocation by paraphrasing verses from the *Fourth Eclogue*:

> for you once wrote: "The world is born again;
> Justice returns, and the first age of man,
> and a new progeny descends from Heaven."

> Through you I was a poet, through you, a Christian.
> (*Purg.* XXII, 70–73)

Through Statius' gracious speech Dante follows the medieval tradition that interpreted Virgil's *Fourth Eclogue* (written c. 42–39 B.C.) as a prophecy announcing the birth of the Christ child. A passage from Virgil's text more complete than the verses cited by Statius reveals the basis of such an interpretation:

> Now the last age of Cumae's prophecy has come;
> The great succession of centuries is born afresh.
> Now too returns the Virgin, Saturn's rule returns;
> A new begetting now descends from heaven's height.
> O chaste Lucina, look with blessing on the boy
> Whose birth will end the iron race at last and raise
> A golden through the world: now your Apollo rules.
>
> $(4-10)^9$

That Virgil most likely based his prophetic hopes on a child born to Antony and Octavia, the leading Roman couple of the time, matters little. The prophecy of messianic renewal, with specific references to a virgin and child, evidently sufficed for medieval Christianity to adopt Virgil as a prophet. And such a legend clearly informed Dante's depiction of the Latin poet as one who could lead others to a truth which he himself could not know.

Along with this view of Virgil as a Christian prophet, the Middle Ages fostered the image of the Latin poet as a magician or sorcerer. This more ominous reputation, which, as Comparetti demonstrates, existed primarily in the popular imagination, actually functions as the flip side to Virgil's prophetic status.[10] Prophecy and sorcery, after all, both offer insights into the future, often with the hopes of changing it. In his *Eighth Eclogue* Virgil presents the contrasting love songs of Damon and Alphesiboeus, in a male and female voice respectively. Alphesiboeus' song describes the magic and witchcraft used by a jealous woman to win back her lover:

> Fetch water and around this altar wind soft wool
> And burn the sappy vervain and male frankincense,
> For by these magical rituals I hope to turn
> My sweetheart's sanity; only spells are lacking now.
>
> (64–67)

The woman then describes the power of such spells as she creates her own magical incantation by chanting the refrain, "Draw Daphnis back from town, my spells, draw Daphnis home." As one of her examples of such witchcraft, the lover tells of Circe, who "by spells transformed the shipmates of Ulysses" (70). Dante's Ulysses, in fact, begins the famous account of his final voyage with the words, "When I / set sail from Circe—" (*Inf.* XXVI, 90–91). But what concerns us here is the way in which Virgil invokes the spirit of Ulysses to tell his tale in *Inferno* XXVI. Addressing the "two-horned flame" concealing Ulysses and Diomed in the eighth *bolgia* of the Eighth Circle of Hell, Virgil pronounces what sounds suspiciously like a magical incantation:

> "O you who are two souls within one fire,
>   if I have deserved from you when I was living,
>   if I have deserved from you much praise or little,

when in the world I wrote my lofty verses,
   do not move on; let one of you tell where
   he lost himself through his own fault, and died."
                          (79–84)

While Virgil undoubtedly refers to the "lofty verses" of his *Aeneid*, the magical spells described in the *Eighth Eclogue* seem more consonant with his act of inducing Ulysses to speak.[11]

Alphesiboeus's magical song also provides a negative example for Dante's theological conception of the Trinity. At the end of his vision in the *Paradiso*, the pilgrim will perceive the Christian Godhead as "three circles / in three clear colors bound in one same place" (XXXIII, 116–117). While Virgil's verses lack the geometric dimension of Dante's vision, they describe a similar blend of number and color:

First with these triple threads in separate colors three
I bind you, then about this altar thrice I bear
Your puppet self; uneven numbers please the god.
. . . .
Tie the three colors, Amaryllis, in three knots;
Just tie them and repeat "the Venus knot I tie."
                          (73–78)

Indeed, it is not difficult to think of this "Venus knot"—three knots of three colors—as an infernal parody of Dante's celestial vision of the Trinity. Virgil's magical eclogue might therefore provide a key to understanding Dante's exploitation of the Latin poet's reputation as a sorcerer.

Perhaps the most striking association of Virgil with the magical arts occurs in *Inferno* IX, when the pilgrim asks for reassurance that his guide indeed knows the way down to Lower Hell. Virgil's response shows that he has in fact been a victim of the sort of witchcraft he described in his *Eighth Eclogue*:

"But it happens as I was down here once before,
   conjured by that heartless witch, Erichtho
   (who could recall the spirit to its body).

Soon after I had left my flesh in death
   she sent me through these walls, and down as far
   as the pit of Judas to bring a spirit out."
                          (22–27)

A probable invention of Dante's, this story of Erichtho conjuring Virgil to fetch a spirit provides a credible explanation for the Latin poet's knowledge of the structure of Hell. But Virgil's association with Erichtho cannot help but bring to mind his reputation as a sorcerer in the medieval popular imagination. In addition, Virgil's Alphesiboeus in the *Eighth Eclogue* mentions a certain Moeris, a necromancer who "has often called up ghosts from deepest graves" (98). In Dante's hands, Virgil's own poetry sometimes produces or exacerbates an unflattering image of the Latin poet. Yet, rather than merely calling attention to Virgil's reputation as a sorcerer and leaving it at that, Dante goes further by having Virgil indirectly defend himself against these charges. The poet thus cleverly incorporates the issue of Virgil's reputation into the thematics of his poem, just as he did with the matter of poetic truth in Cantos XIII and XVI. We shall see, in fact, that these two thorny problems—poetic truth and Virgil's association with magic—are closely related in the *Inferno*.

In Canto XX, as the travelers observe the sinners in the fourth *bolgia*, Virgil strikes an unusually harsh pose by castigating the pilgrim for shedding tears at the sight of the contorted figures of the soothsayers:

"So you are still like all the other fools?

In this place piety lives when pity is dead,
for who could be more wicked than that man
who tries to bend divine will to his own!"
(27–30)

On the one hand, Virgil's rebuke here reminds us that the pilgrim has yet to learn completely—emotionally, that is, as well as intellectually—the true nature of sin. Though he proved perfectly capable of responding in an appropriately indignant manner to such sinners as Filippo Argenti (Canto VIII) and Pope Nicholas III (Canto XIX), the pilgrim's present misplaced pity and his later voyeuristic enjoyment of the vulgar altercation between Master Adam and Simon the Greek (Canto XXX) clearly demonstrate that his spiritual progress is marred by occasional setbacks. On the other hand, Virgil's authoritative outburst puts him in a precariously lofty position from which he may soon tumble.

Such a fall, in fact, begins here in Canto XX and continues uninterrupted through Cantos XXI–XXIII, the longest single episode of the *Inferno*. After pointing out various augurs and seers to the pilgrim, Virgil catches sight of the prophetess Manto down below in the fourth *bolgia*. He immediately announces his intention to tell the pilgrim "'something of her story'" (57). What follows is a forty-two verse digression on the founding of Mantua, Virgil's native city (the pilgrim addressed him as a "'courteous Mantuan'" in Canto II, 58). Most of the speech, however, has little or nothing to do with Manto. After mentioning the death of Manto's father, Tireseus, and the enslavement of Thebes, Virgil vaguely states that "'she wandered through the world for many years'" (60). Then, instead of specifying the nature of Manto's extensive travels, he launches into a lyrical hymn to the beautiful topography of north-central Italy all centered on Lake Benaco (the present-day Lake Garda): streams flow down from the Alps into this lake, which overflows into a river, the Mencio, that joins with the larger Po river at Governol. Virgil finally gets back to his point about Manto and Mantua by backtracking through his geography lesson. Referring to the Mencio river, he recalls:

"but before its course is run it strikes a lowland
   on which it spreads and turns into a marsh
   that can become unbearable in summer."
                                        (79–81)

To this spot came Manto "'to escape all human intercourse'" and "'to
practice magic with her servants'" (85–86).

Virgil clearly has no intention of trying to challenge Manto's reputa-
tion as a diviner. Indeed he drew the pretext for his story from her
appearance in the *bolgia* designed to punish such persons. He does, how-
ever, wish to remove any trace of sorcery from the founding of his native
city, obviously named for the prophetess. In fact, his description of the
founding of Mantua is perfectly ordinary, almost banal:[12]

"Later on, the men who lived around there gathered
   on that very spot, for it was well-protected
   by the bog that girded it on every side.

They built a city over her dead bones,
   and for her, the first to choose that place, they named it
   Mantua, without recourse to sorcery."
                                        (88–93)

The striking detail, of course, is the phrase "without recourse to sorcery,"
meaning that no one interpreted omens or performed other magical rites
to name the city. The builders simply named it after the first inhabitant of
the marshy area. By extension, Virgil probably wishes to counter the
charge that he too was connected with sorcery because he was so closely
identified with his native city.

If Virgil's account ended here we could conclude that Dante has al-
luded to Virgil's damaging reputation as a sorcerer in the action of the
Inferno primarily in order to allow the Latin poet to clear himself of such
a label once and for all. However, this is not the case, for Virgil adds a
coda to his story that calls into question his truthfulness. "'And so, I warn
you,'" he says to the pilgrim, "'should you ever hear / my city's origin told
otherwise, / let no false tales adulterate the truth'" (97–99). It so happens
that the pilgrim would have heard Virgil's "city's origin told otherwise" in
no less authoritative a text than the Latin poet's own *Aeneid*. In Book X
of his epic, Virgil explicitly attributes both the founding and the naming
of Mantua to Manto's son Ocnus, a Tuscan warrior who comes to the aid
of Aeneas in the Italian wars:

There, too, another chieftain comes who from
his native coasts has mustered squadrons: Ocnus,
the son of prophesying Manto and
the Tuscan river; Mantua, he gave you
walls and his mother's name—o Mantua. . . .
                                        (278–282)

While this account by the author of the *Aeneid* does not contradict the claim by the Virgil of Dante's *Inferno* that Mantua was named "without recourse to sorcery," it is nonetheless an example of the "city's origin told otherwise." Was Mantua built and named by "'men who lived around there'" (*Inf.* XX, 88) or by the chieftain Ocnus, "son of prophesying Manto" (*Aen.* X)? To make matters worse, when Virgil later identifies Eurypylus in the fourth *bolgia*, he says that the pilgrim should already know this augur's story from the *Aeneid*, a text which, Virgil claims, the pilgrim knows inside out ("'you know it, every line,'" XX, 114).[13]

What, then, is the pilgrim (and the reader) to think? Not only has Virgil contradicted himself but he has also called considerable attention to his inconsistency. Either the *Aeneid*—the work for which Virgil is "'light and honor of the other poets'" (I, 82)—contains an error or Dante's Virgil is telling a "false tale" in Canto XX. Although it is ultimately impossible to choose between the two stories, the pilgrim's reaction to Virgil's account in Canto XX clearly supports this version over the version told in the *Aeneid*:

> "Master, your explanations
> are truth for me, winning my faith entirely;
> any others would be just like burned-out coals."
> (100–102)

If the pilgrim indeed knows Virgil's *Aeneid* line by line, his unequivocal response implies that the "other" story from the great epic is as dead as a "burned-out coal." Yet, given his immense respect for Virgil's literary reputation, the pilgrim may have decided to concur politely with his guide's account in Canto XX while secretly believing the story of the founding and naming of Mantua from *Aeneid* X. In either case, Virgil pays a high price for exonerating himself from the charge of sorcery inasmuch as he creates a major inconsistency that calls into question his truthfulness. The long shadow of doubt cast by Virgil's contradictory stories sets the stage for the episode in Cantos XXI-XXIII, an episode in which Virgil has the dubious honor of playing the starring role.

Critics generally agree that Cantos XXI-XXIII comprise the most sustained example of comedy, in the modern sense of the word, in the entire poem.[14] The episode displays a style that is unique for the *Comedy*, in terms of tone, language and action. Fowlie, for example, maintains that "the fifth *bolgia* illustrates the theory of a literary genre in which the element of the grotesque will be pushed very far."[15] Equally noteworthy is the narrative structure of this episode in Lower Hell: whereas the action begun in one *bolgia* normally ends when the travelers advance to the next *bolgia*, here the resolution to the action begun in the fifth *bolgia* (Cantos XXI-XXII) coincides with the end to the action of the sixth *bolgia* (Canto XXIII). Virgil learns that he has been duped by Malacoda (XXI, 106–111) only when Friar Catalano, a hypocrite, mockingly informs him that the devil is the "'father of all lies'" (XXIII, 144). Clearly, this overlap of one *bolgia* onto the next serves to link the sins of barratry (political corruption) and hypocrisy as part of the poet's general strategy to connect the sins of Malebolge to one another. Simony, for example, connects back to flattery insofar as the prostitute Thaïs (Canto XVIII) prefigures the simonists who prostitute the Church (Canto XIX). And the punishing flames which "steal" the sinners from view in the eighth *bolgia* arise from the previous *bolgia* housing the thieves. Yet the fifth and sixth *bolge* are unique in their function as a single dramatic unit.

Canto XXI opens with the travelers reaching the top of the bridge over the fifth *bolgia* and observing the strange darkness below. Following a busy simile comparing the swelling mass which fills the *bolgia* to the tenacious, boiling pitch used in the Venetian shipyard for repairing boats, the narrator describes the sudden, frightening arrival of a black devil, one of the Malebranche ("evil-claws"), carrying a barrator from Lucca. After the devil has tossed the sinner into the pitch, there appear other Malebranche. They taunt the hapless barrator and stick him with their hooks, like cooks who keep meat from floating up to the surface in a pot. It is at this point that Virgil instructs the pilgrim to hide behind a rock, thereby dramatizing the travelers' complicity in the aesthetic of concealment, a leitmotif in this episode and an important aspect of Dante's *contrapasso* for the sin of barratry. More important, Virgil tells the pilgrim not to worry because he, the trustworthy guide, "'know[s] how things are run here'"; he has "'been caught in as bad a fix before'" (62–63).

While most commentators think Virgil refers here to his previous journey to the pit of Hell under the spell of the necromancer Erichtho (IX, 22–27), his supposed reassurance also recalls, whatever his intentions, his near disaster at the gates of Dis. In fact, Virgil's dismal performance during this earlier stage in the journey sheds considerable light on his imminent problems with the Malebranche. According to Musa, Virgil failed at the gates of Dis in Cantos VIII–IX because he neglected to capitalize on the journey's divine origin: instead of proclaiming the invincible formula ("It is so willed, there where the power is / for what is willed," III, 95–96), he tried to parley with the fallen angels. Further, when the Furies appeared and called on the Medusa to turn the pilgrim to stone, the Latin poet, who wrote about such mythological creatures in his *Aeneid*, really thought that the pilgrim's life was in danger. It took the arrival of a messenger from Heaven, in an allegorical representation of Christ's Harrowing of Hell, to restore order and allow the travelers to continue into Lower Hell. At this juncture, therefore, Virgil's attitude was one of "disbelief." Dante figuratively transported him back to his own pre-Christian world in order to stage the elaborate reenactment of Christ's Harrowing.[16]

In Cantos XXI–XXIII, on the other hand, Virgil's attitude is completely different. In fact, his performance here is so radically different from what he displayed at the gates of Dis that it may very well resemble

some form of over-compensation. As part of Dante's psychological real-
ism, his characters possess memory. I suggest, therefore, that Virgil's
recollection of what he did wrong at the gates of Dis now causes him to
over-react in the fifth *bolgia*. The two episodes function as flip sides of the
same coin: the Latin poet's unassertiveness, in the first case, and his naive
overconfidence in the second each put the success of the pilgrim's infer-
nal journey at risk. From the pilgrim's point of view, moreover, Virgil's
reminder of an earlier failure, together with the inconsistencies sur-
rounding the founding of Mantua in the previous *bolgia*, cannot help but
weaken his trust in the Latin poet during the ensuing action.

Virgil is not the only actor in the lively episode whose behavior and
trustworthiness affect the success of the pilgrim's journey. With the pil-
grim safely hidden from view, Virgil crosses the rest of the bridge and
boldly commands the aggressive Malebranche to send forth one of their
troop to hear him out. They send Malacoda ("evil-tail"), who, after learn-
ing that Virgil is leading another on a journey with divine sanction, drops
his hook and tells the rest of the black devils not to attack. In complete
control of the situation, Virgil now tells the pilgrim to come out from
behind the rock and cross the bridge. It appears, then, that Virgil's return
to the sort of assertive behavior which served him so well with Charon,
Minòs, Cerberus, and Plutus—and which he failed to display at the gates
of Dis—will enable the travelers to pass the Malebranche unharmed. The
similar reactions of Plutus in Upper Hell and Malacoda here in Lower Hell
would seem to confirm this observation:

> As sails swollen by wind when the ship's mast breaks,
>   collapse, deflated, tangled in a heap,
>   just so the savage beast fell to the ground.
> (Plutus in VII, 13–15)

> With this the devil's arrogance collapsed,
>   his pitchfork, too, dropped right down to his feet,
>   as he announced to all: "Don't touch this man!"
> (Malacoda in XXI, 85–87)

The obvious difference, yet one Virgil may fail to take into account, is that
Malacoda belongs to the Eighth Circle of Hell. This place, as Virgil himself
instructed the pilgrim, houses the sinners who practiced the sort of fraud
that "'seems only to destroy / the bond of love that Nature gives to man'"
(XI, 55–56). Such fraud could occur, for example, when a sentinel or
escort deliberately misinforms travelers passing through his region. Thus
Malacoda and the other Malebranche, as both guardians and representa-
tives of this *bolgia* in the realm of fraud, are hardly to be trusted. While
the pilgrim adopts an appropriately suspicious attitude, Virgil remains
hopelessly ingenuous.

One reason for the pilgrim's justified caution is simple observation.
He quickly ascertains that the faces of the devils have "nothing good

about them" (XXI, 99), and the pilgrim's distrust surely grows when Malacoda must intervene to prevent the fiends from sticking him in the rump with their pitchforks (100–105). Virgil, on the other hand, seems oblivious to the danger posed by the Malebranche. In fact, his misplaced trust in Malacoda probably increases when the devil informs the travelers that the bridge they have been following does not cross the next *bolgia* and then commands ten of the Malebranche to escort the travelers along the ridge to the next intact bridge. This information, we shall discover later, is only partially true: while the present bridge does indeed lie broken in the sixth *bolgia*, so in fact does the next such bridge. Malacoda knows this full well. Moreover, his account of the broken bridge contains the sort of precise factual information that would surely impress and possibly disorient Virgil:

> "Five more hours and it will be one thousand,
>   two hundred sixty-six years and a day
>   since the bridge-way here fell crumbling to the ground."
>   (112–114)

In a later canto we will hear a black cherubim taunt a sinner by claiming to be "'somewhat of a logician'" (XXVII, 123). Malacoda is surely that as he dates Christ's Crucifixion and Harrowing of Hell—the cause of the broken bridge—to the hour! Virgil himself previously attributed cracks in the infernal landscape to Christ's Harrowing, "'the coming of that One / who took from Hell's first circle the great spoil'" (XII, 38–39). Thus Malacoda's logical and detailed explanation of an event Virgil actually witnessed cannot help but bolster the Latin poet's trust in the devil. When the pilgrim objects to Malacoda's offer of an escort and asks his guide to observe how the Malebranche grind their teeth and wink at one another, Virgil tries to reassure him: "'they do it for the boiling souls, not us'" (XXI, 135). Despite Virgil's well-meaning intentions, this too is only a partial truth.

Malacoda's blatant lie sandwiched between a partial truth and an accurate fact sets the stage for a series of tricks and lies in the action of Canto XXII. As Virgil and the pilgrim travel with the Malebranche along the ridge dividing the fifth and sixth *bolge*, they see a sinner in the pitch hooked by Graffiacane and brought before the other devils for further torture. This barrator, usually identified as a certain Ciampolo of Navarre, proves to be at least as cunning as his torturers.[17] Having already suffered several attacks, Ciampolo tries to strike a deal with the eager Malebranche: if they back up a bit he will call seven additional barrators up to the surface by whistling, the signal that the coast is clear. Cagnazzo, for one, thinks the sinner is lying in order to escape, but the other Malebranche, especially Alichino, cannot resist the challenge and they all back away from the edge as Ciampolo asked. Sure enough, the crafty sinner, with a perfectly timed leap, escapes from the Malebranche by diving back into the pitch. Alichino chases him in vain and another devil, Calcabrina, having hoped that Ciampolo would escape, now picks a fight with Alichino. The two Malebranche, equally matched for fighting, fall into the boiling pitch and are unable to lift themselves out of it. Not only has Ciampolo lied to the Malebranche but the devils were less than truthful with one another: while going along with Alichino's proposal to trust Ciampolo, Calcabrina hid his desire to fight with Alichino. As the rest of the devils work to rescue their stranded brothers, Virgil and the pilgrim sneak off.

The web of lies and deceits developed in Cantos XXI–XXII undoubtedly serves as the opening act for the presentation of the hypocrites in Canto XXIII. Encased in gilded cloaks lined with lead, these sinners now bear the full weight of the false pretexts which they used to deceive others on earth. Saying one thing and meaning another, hypocrisy seems closely related to the sort of behavior exhibited by Ciampolo and the Malebranche in the previous canto. In fact, the travelers have not seen the last of these devils. Once again, it is the pilgrim who perceives the imminent danger:

> "O master," I said, "if you do not hide
>
> both of us, and very quick, I am afraid
>   of the Malebranche—right now they're on our trail—
>   I feel they're there, I think I hear them now."
>   (XXIII, 21–24)

This time, however, Virgil acknowledges the pilgrim's valid fear and, as he contemplates an escape route, the fiends appear, "their wings wide-open" (35), clearly intending to harm the travelers. So much for Virgil's earlier reassurance that the Malebranche's intimidations were directed only at the sinners in the pitch! Acting finally out of instinct (which should have alerted him to the danger in the first place), Virgil now grabs the pilgrim, like a mother rescuing her child from a burning house:

> And over the edge, then down the stony bank
>   he slid, on his back, along the sloping rock
>   that walls the higher side of the next *bolgia*.
>   (43–45)

In this unflattering image of the great Latin poet and dignified guide, maternal instinct triumphs over macho overconfidence. His ego bruised and his backside smarting, Virgil has barely averted a disaster largely of his own making.

Dante's conception of the sin of hypocrisy derives in part from Christ's harsh judgment in Matthew 23:27–28:

> Woe to you, scribes and Pharisees, hypocrites! for you are like white-washed tombs, which outwardly appear beautiful, but within they are full of dead men's bones and all uncleanness. So you also outwardly appear righteous to men, but within you are full of hypocrisy and iniquity.

Comparing the cloaks and hoods of the hypocrites in the sixth *bolgia* to the dress of the Benedictine monks at Cluny, Dante evokes a monastic atmosphere for his presentation of the sinners. In fact, the two hypocrites who address the pilgrim identify themselves as Catalano and Loderingo, Jovial Friars from Bologna. The climax to the drama of the sixth *bolgia* occurs when the travelers see a figure crucified to the floor of the ditch with three stakes. In line with the biblical depiction of hypocrisy cited above, Catalano explains that the impaled sinner "'advised the Pharisees it was expedient / to sacrifice one man for all the people'" (XXIII, 116–117). Thus the pilgrim learns that Caiaphas and his father-in-law Annas suffer a special *contrapasso* for their role in Christ's Crucifixion: they are stretched out naked across the narrow floor of the ditch (in a crucified position) so that all the other hypocrites must walk over them in their leadlined cloaks.

While the sight of the crucified Caiaphas forces the pilgrim to interrupt his speech to Catalano, it elicits even greater perplexity in Virgil:

> And I saw Virgil staring down amazed
>   at this body stretching out in crucifixion,
>   so vilely punished in the eternal exile.
>   (124–126)

Virgil's amazement may result from an association between Caiaphas's crucified figure and the "sign of victory"—a cross inscribed within a halo—born by Christ during his descent to Virgil's permanent home in the First Circle of Hell (IV, 54).[18] Virgil then learns from Catalano that the travelers will soon reach the ruins of another bridge, the one Malacoda claimed was intact. On the one hand, the discovery of this second broken bridge is a blessing insofar as the toppled rocks will serve as stairs for the travelers' climb out of the *bolgia*. On the other hand, this revelation confirms what Virgil must by now suspect: he has been had by Malacoda, and the pilgrim was right not to trust the devil.

If Virgil's earlier breakdown at the gates of Dis occasioned Dante's allegorical representation of Christ's Harrowing of Hell, the Latin poet's poor judgment in dealing with the Malebranche results from the most visible sign of this event. Virgil breaks down right before the place where the bridges are literally broken due to Christ's Harrowing of Hell. A structural image of the cross, the broken bridges anticipate the figure of Caiaphas crucified on the floor of the sixth *bolgia*, a figure who elicits uncharacteristic amazement on the part of Virgil. The Latin poet must wonder at the similarities between this crucified figure and the cross—the "sign of victory"—which he saw at the time of the Harrowing. In sum, Virgil breaks down at moments of significant Christian iconography: before the gates of Dis with the fallen angels and before the broken bridges with the Malebranche (black devils). Little wonder that Virgil, a stranger to both Christ and the Anti-Christ, should be defeated by representatives of the latter.

Whereas Virgil is usually presented as the wiser, more enlightened of the two travelers, Dante occasionally emerges as the more astute observer of infernal wickedness and trickery. This points to the pilgrim's generally progressive movement toward greater knowledge and repudiation of sin. The fact that he can react appropriately to an unexpected situation attests in part to Virgil's successful teaching. However, the fact that it is the student-pilgrim and not his learned guide who catches on, say, to the Malebranche's ruse in the fifth *bolgia* (Cantos XXI–XXIII) raises serious questions about Virgil's authority and credibility. In this sense, we might conclude that the pilgrim learns at Virgil's expense.

In Canto XX Virgil authoritatively tells the pilgrim to "'let no false tales adulterate the truth'"(99)—this following a tale of the founding of Mantua that blatantly contradicts his tale in *Aeneid* X. One of these tales, both told by Virgil, is clearly false. Dante the poet thus devises a punishment for Virgil's presumption by having him fall victim to Malacoda's lie in Cantos XXI–XXIII. To add insult to injury, Virgil receives confirmation of Malacoda's deception from a sinner, a hypocrite to boot. Catalano tells Virgil what every schoolboy at Bologna knows: the devil is, among other things, the "father of all lies." Virgil's childish reaction says it all:

> In haste, taking great strides, my guide walked off,
> his face revealing traces of his anger.
> (XXIII, 145–146)

Seeing Virgil in such a vulnerable state, the pilgrim can only feel a more intense bond with his guide and mentor:

> I turned and left the heavy-weighted souls
>
> to make my way behind those cherished footprints.
> (XXIII, 147–148)

Thus Virgil's failure and subsequent humiliation do not make him a less powerful figure in the *Inferno*. On the contrary, it is his involvement in the humanity and occasional humor of the poem that so endears him to readers as well as to the pilgrim. With every reading of the *Divine Comedy*, therefore, we join the pilgrim "behind those cherished footprints" of Dante's beloved yet damned Virgil.

NOTES

1. A recent sampling of criticism on Dante's creative use of Virgilian sources can be found in *The Poetry of Allusion: Virgil and Ovid in Dante's Commedia*, Rachel Jacoff and Jeffrey T. Schnapp, eds. (Stanford: Stanford University Press, 1991).

2. Dante locates Lethe, the river of forgetfulness, in the Terrestrial Paradise on the Mountain of Purgatory (cf. *Purg.* XXVIII, 127–132).

3. R. D. Williams, *The Aeneid of Virgil: Books 1–6* (Basingstoke: Macmillan, 1972), 517.

4. I cite Mark Musa's translation of the *Divine Comedy* throughout this essay.

5. With the pilgrim's description of Aeneas as "father of glorious Rome," the future seat of the papacy, Dante displays the strategy of "christianizing" Virgil's epic that he develops throughout the *Divine Comedy*.

6. I cite Allen Mandelbaum's translation of the *Aeneid* (Berkeley: University of California Press, 1981). Line numbers are Mandelbaum's.

7. For another interpretation of Dante's revisitation of Virgil's Polydorus episode, see Douglas Biow, "From Ignorance to Knowledge: The Marvelous in *Inferno* 13" (in *Poetry of Allusion*, 45–61). Exploring Dante's strategy "to historicize the marvelous" (51), Biow argues that Dante's scene in the wood of the suicides represents the fulfillment of Virgil's episode.

8. Leo Spitzer writes in "The Addresses to the Reader in the *Commedia*" (*Italica* 32 [1955]: 152): "To give the reader 'something to do' about a matter difficult to imagine is a psychological inducement to make him accept this subject matter." Teodolinda Barolini, in her article "Narrative and Style in Lower Hell" (*Annali d'Italianistica* 8 [1990]: 314–44), notes that the Pier delle Vigne episode from Canto XIII and Geryon's arrival in Canto XVI are linked through "the question of the text's credibility" (p. 320).

9. I cite Guy Lee's translation of Virgil's *Eclogues*, with modifications for American spelling (Harmondsworth: Penguin, 1984).

10. See Domenico Comparetti, *Vergil in the Middle Ages*, trans. E. F. M. Benecke (Hamden, CT: Archon, 1966), especially Part II, chapters I–VII. Comparetti, however, refutes the idea that Dante incorporates Virgil's reputation as a magician into the *Divine Comedy*: "The purely popular reputation of a literary man could not be of any account to one who held art so high as Dante did and had so lofty a conception of the ancient poets" (219).

I will argue just the opposite by showing, first, that Virgil's own literature (the *Eighth Eclogue* in particular) could support his association with magic in the popular imagination; and, second, that Dante's "high art" could take some very low turns, as in the scatological humor in Cantos XXI–XXIII.

11. I thus follow Dorothy L. Sayers, who speaks of "the Virgil of mediaeval folk-lore, Virgilius Magus, the great White Magician, who could conjure the spirits, and who once at least in the 26th canto of the *Inferno* does very magnificently and in his own power conjure them" ("Dante's Virgil," in *Further Papers on Dante* [London: Methuen, 1957], 59).

12. Barolini, "True and False See-ers in *Inferno* XX" (*Lectura Dantis* 4 [1989]: 42–54), interprets the "unexciting prosaic manner" of Virgil's digression as an intentional stylistic device (staged by Dante) to counter and "correct" the lofty, tragic style of the *Aeneid* (48–50).

13. Moreover, Virgil's identification of Eurypylus as an augur in Canto XX constitutes yet another distortion, willful or otherwise, of the text of the *Aeneid*. In the words of Robert Hollander, "to make amends for the first lie, Dante has Virgil create a second, adding an augur to the cast of the *Aeneid*" ("Dante's Misreadings of the *Aeneid* in *Inferno* 20" [in *Poetry of Allusion* 88]).

14. For an excellent discussion of this episode, see Christopher Kleinhenz, "Deceivers Deceived: Devilish Doubletalk in *Inferno* 21–23" (*Quaderni d'Italianistica* 10.1–2 [1989]: 133–56).

15. Wallace Fowlie, *A Reading of Dante's* Inferno (Chicago: University of Chicago Press, 1981), 137.

16. Mark Musa, *Advent at the Gates* (Bloomington: Indiana University Press, 1974), 65–84.

17. In the words of Kleinhenz, "just as Malacoda conditioned Dante and Virgil's response by embedding a lie in the middle of truthful statements, so the

Navarrese barrator, with his own special linguistic trick, turns the tables on his captors and does them one better" ("Deceivers Deceived," 145).

18. Charles S. Singleton relates Christ's "sign of victory" to the cruciform nimbus in medieval iconography (*The Divine Comedy*, 6 vols. [Princeton: Princeton University Press, 1970–75], *Inferno*, 2: *Commentary*, 60).

Inferno I: Breaking the Silence

DENISE HEILBRONN-GAINES

The *Divine Comedy* opens at an extraordinary moment of moral awakening, in the midst of a crisis. Dante has found himself again:[1] he is in a dark wood, because the straight path has been lost. Conscious of his own perilous situation, he is filled with fear. This event is described retrospectively as having occurred in the past, "in the middle of the road of our life." The dread Dante felt then is renewed now, in the retelling. Just how he entered that dark place is hard to say, so full of sleep was he when he abandoned the true way.

Dante, an anonymous character until Beatrice pronounces his name at the top of the mountain of Purgatory, is a wayfarer whose fear is powerfully real. Yet the transparent moral symbolism of the opening verses of Canto I raises the question whether the wood in which Dante finds himself is literally a "place," or rather a symbolic wood that serves primarily to represent the wayfarer's spiritual condition. The darkness is so bitter as to resemble death. Such darkness precisely describes a state of sin, the death of the soul. The road the wayfarer has abandoned (abandonment implies a willful act) is the "straight" or "true" way. It readily calls to mind its opposites, the many crooked, false paths he must have taken to arrive at his sinful state. The darkness too evokes its opposites, the light and life, the state of happiness in the divine presence, to be reached at the end of life's journey when the right path is chosen. The first three tercets do not express these positive values but imply them by their absence, while the text focuses on the protagonist's overwhelming sense of fear. Nevertheless, the dark wood does hold some good, and Dante will deal with this by talking about the other things he saw there—things other than the good (vv. 8–9). The story seems to arise from a negative moral landscape, in which a real wayfarer, truly terrified, realizes that he has lost his way.

Besides creating the implied moral contrasts of darkness and light, straight and crooked, true and false, good and something other than good (its absence, or evil), the twelve initial verses contain two additional important dichotomies. Dante has lost his way along the road of *our* life. It is his journey as well as ours. He represents himself, the one, and all humanity, the many who participate in his condition and his experience, including the reader. Furthermore, it *is* hard (now) to talk of that dark place where he *was* lost (then), for the thought of it renews his fear (vv. 4, 6). Dante is the lost wayfarer in the narrative, and he is also the narrator, the poet, who remembers and retells his experience for the sake of revealing the good that he discovered in it. By that fact alone, the reader knows from the outset that, as dark and oppressive as the story's beginning may be, its outcome will be good. And since this is the story of a remembered experience, we are to accept it as something that literally happened.

Yet, in the first half of Canto I, it is difficult to grasp an objective, literal meaning. Its dreamlike or symbolic quality has often been commented upon.[2] The wayfarer looks up from the dark wood to see a sunlit height. The wood has become a valley, a low place, in contrast to the hilltop illuminated by the sun, the planet which, in its symbolic reflection of the divine light, "leads men straight ahead on every road." The "road of life" may now be seen as an ascent, as the sinner struggles to flee from the darkness of sin to the light of salvation, no longer implied but expressed in visible symbolism.[3] Here the shifting metaphors become increasingly perplexing. The hill, the valley, the rays of light that briefly allay the wayfarer's fear, the panting swimmer emerging from a dangerous sea, the deserted slope, the firm foot (the lower one in an attempted uphill climb), all seem to mean something more than themselves while lacking a clearly objective reality of their own. They have been explained allegorically in spiritual and moral terms, in terms of the soul, its strivings, its higher and lower faculties that direct the soul either to God or to the things of this world.[4]

In the unfolding narrative, meanwhile, the initial darkness has given way to an atmosphere suffused with light. As the wayfarer begins to climb, beasts appear on the hillside to block his ascent. Their sudden presence, coming as if from nowhere, suggests their symbolic character.[5] The first one, a leopard with a dappled coat, a colorful pelt, effectively dispels any lingering impression of darkness. Even though this beast impedes the wayfarer's ascent, the sunlit hilltop and morning stars that call to mind divine love inspire hope of some good to come from it. But then a lion advances with a raging hunger that seems to make the air tremble. Fear returns, and with the appearance of a she-wolf, the terrified wayfarer loses all hope of reaching the summit. The she-wolf finally forces the wayfarer down from the slope toward the darkness of the opening verses. That darkness is now equated with silence in the memorable closing image of the first major division of Canto I: "she forced me back to where the sun is mute" (v. 60).

This metaphor, darkness expressed as silence, opens a new poetic dimension as the imagery expands from the visual to the auditory sense. Looking back over the first sixty verses, we realize that the unique feature of the moral landscape in which the wayfarer has found himself is not its darkness but its silence. There are dark places in Hell, even in Purgatory; but the opening section of Canto I is the only passage in the entire *Divine Comedy* where no inanimate sound or animate voice is mentioned. Even the menacing lion paradoxically seems to cause the air to tremble without making a sound. This is all the more remarkable in view of the vast range of sonorities that fill the rest of the poem.

When explained allegorically, the "silence" of the sun has been associated with the darkness at noon on Good Friday, for this is the day of the journey's beginning; or with unbelief and death of the soul, a state in which one cannot or will not express God's word. It may also suggest God's silence.[6] As St. Augustine points out in his sermon on Psalm 49 (Vulgate; 50 in modern numeration), in this world, God speaks in many ways: He has spoken through the Angels, the Prophets, His own mouth, the Apostles; and He speaks through the faithful whenever they utter the truth. But He is silent for those who do not hear.[7] This is precisely the condition of Dante, the sinner, lost in a silent space where he too is mute.

In offering yet another interpretation of this much-discussed canto, I wish to focus on the two transitional tercets (vv. 61–66). Here a radical shift in poetic expression occurs. A symbolic, subjective mode whose literal meaning remains singularly elusive gives way to the objective narrative of a journey through the other world, whose primary sense is literal. The shift depends upon and coincides with a profound spiritual change undergone by Dante in his dual role as sinner-protagonist and as poet-narrator, while his silence turns to speech. I hope to show that David, the psalmist, is Dante's model in both aspects of this transformation.

While the wayfarer is falling down the hillside toward the valley and before he touches the depths, a meeting takes place—not between Dante and Virgil as we tend to think of it, but between two nameless characters whose anonymity confirms the primacy of the meeting itself as a spiritual event. One is a lost traveler on "the road of our life," the other a shadowy presence of unknown provenance, the unidentifiable figure of a human being. This personage is introduced in the verse "dinanzi a li occhi mi si fu offerto" (v. 62). Because of the particle *si*, the verse shares in the ambiguities of the first half of Canto I. It can be translated literally in two ways, meaning either "before my eyes [someone] had offered himself to me" (reflexive), or "before my eyes [someone] had been offered to me" (passive impersonal construction). There is a considerable difference between these two alternatives. The reader learns later, but does not know now, that the one who will soon turn out to be Virgil does not offer himself on his own initiative but comes in response to a complex series of petitions made on behalf of the sinner. The preterit perfect, *fu offerto*, suggests prior events to be narrated in Canto II. Therefore when retrospectively understood, the passive construction is the only correct reading. It is impossible to grasp this initially, but even without the requisite hindsight, the attentive reader may glimpse in the ambiguous *si* the still hidden fact, or at least the possibility, that there is an agent: an external source of intervention having a real existence independent of the wayfarer.

Virgil's coming is very unlike that of the three beasts, who simply appear on the scene as though in a dream: "Ed ecco . . . una lonza . . . la vista . . . m'apparve d'un leone. Ed una lupa" (and behold . . . a leopard, . . . the sight . . . of a lion . . . appeared to me, and a she-wolf). Virgil does not *appear*, but is *offered*. As reported in Canto II, he leaves his honored place in Limbo in response to the urgent and compassionate entreaties of three women, Mary, Lucy, and Beatrice. But the ultimate source of help is divine. With the suggestion of an agent who exists outside of the wayfarer's own psyche, the passive construction moves the narrative, almost imperceptibly, toward the objective account of a journey willed by God.

The help that is offered consists of someone, *chi*, who at first sight partakes of the unreal, visionary quality of the initial part of the canto, expressed in the problematical verse "chi per lungo silenzio parea fioco" (who because of long silence appeared faint, v. 63). Whether or not this potential rescuer acquires a concrete existence in the narrative depends entirely on the wayfarer's response to the offer.

The problems regarding the literal and symbolic sense of verse 63 have called forth a great deal of commentary, which focuses mainly on *lungo silenzio* (long silence) and *fioco* (faint).[8] The latter term is ambiguous because it may refer to either sight or hearing (visually indistinct or weak of voice). The former, equally ambiguous term, however, is the more essential to understanding the verse. If taken literally, whose silence is it? And what does "long" refer to? Without some qualifier other than the descriptive adjective (there is no article, no possessive adjective), the answer is unclear. This obscurity on the literal level allows the verse to convey more than one meaning metaphorically. Robert Hollander connects the "silence" with the *silentes* (i.e., the dead) of the *Aeneid* and proposes the literal interpretation that Virgil, because he has been long dead, appears indistinct to the wayfarer's eyes; metaphorically, the silence points to Virgil's ignorance of Christ and to his failure to proclaim the divine Word.[9]

Throughout the verse's lengthy exegetical tradition, the "long silence" has been attributed almost unanimously to Virgil.[10] However, there are difficulties with this approach on both the literal and the metaphoric level. At the moment Dante and Virgil meet, the wayfarer does not know whether the person offered to his eyes is alive or dead, and he therefore addresses the shadowy figure as "qual che tu sii, od ombra od omo certo!" (whatever you may be, either shade or living man, v. 66). If the long silence (his long abode among the dead, his failure to acknowledge the true God) is indeed Virgil's and is the cause of his indistinct appearance (*fioco* understood visually), this fact could not have been immediately perceived by the protagonist.[11]

Furthermore, if "long silence" is understood auditively to mean that Virgil has not spoken in a long time (i.e., according to a common allegorical explanation the voice of Human Reason has been silent within the wayfarer), this would pertain more to Dante's inability to hear than to silence on the part of Virgil. It also disregards the literal level of the unfolding text. The reader will soon learn, but has not yet been told, that Virgil and the other magnanimous pagan poets condemned to Limbo are not at all silent but converse in harmoniously pleasing voices (*Inf.* IV, 97, 104–105, 114), and that Virgil has just had a long dialogue with Beatrice before coming to Dante's aid (*Inf.* II). Consequently, the literal attribution of the "long silence" to Virgil will only be contradicted in later cantos; and symbolically, the inscrutable figure on the slope cannot be made to stand for Human Reason or otherwise explained until the reader, having proceeded further into the poem, is able to realize the full interpretive potential of Canto I. Finally, while *fioco* (faint) can indeed be taken to mean literally that Virgil is visually indistinct, the text must be forced if the term is understood auditively to mean that even before he speaks, Virgil's voice seems hoarse or weak from disuse. We must assume that verse 63, which has long been a challenge to commentators, is deliberately written in such a way as to resist any attempt at a clear-cut interpretation.[12] Even though the newly introduced person, defined as human solely by the pronoun *chi*, is offered to the wayfarer's *eyes* ("dinanzi a li occhi mi si fu offerto"), verse 63 offers no mental picture to the reader's imagination. As a result, it resonates as an open question throughout the transitional tercets and takes on a decisive role in their interpretation.

Because these tercets coincide with a critical turning point along the wayfarer's spiritual road, it should be useful to examine verse 63 from an alternate point of view. Virgil is unknown and silent when he appears to Dante. Neither the wayfarer nor the reader will know anything further about the new character until he reveals himself through his speech in the second half of Canto I. Only the omniscient narrator might call Virgil's initial silence "long." However, even the reader may attribute a "long" silence to the wayfarer, whose spiritual crisis is the subject of the first half of the canto. In attempting to understand "long silence," then, we can look forward in the narrative, as is customarily done, and interpret Virgil's arrival in verse 63 from the broad perspective of the *Inferno* and the *Purgatorio* as a whole; or we can look backward at Dante's role as wayfarer and sinner at the beginning of the poem. The latter perspective is that of the ideal first-time reader. We shall adopt this viewpoint to re-examine the transitional tercets.

The all-pervading silence characterizing the first sixty verses is never explicitly described, but it is epitomized in the image of the silent sun that concludes them. The protagonist participates in this silence by not uttering a word. Although his silence could have been a long one, we are not informed of its duration for he does not remember how he entered the dark wood: "Io non so ben ridir com' i' v'intrai, / tant'era pien di sonno a quel punto / che la verace via abbandonai" (I cannot well retell how I entered there, / so full of sleep was I at that point / when I abandoned the true way, vv. 10–12). The only possible reference to time is "at that point," and it is indeterminate. Surely "long" need not be taken as an absolute temporal reference: if "silence" metaphorically represents a sinful state in which one neither hears nor speaks of God, then any such period during which the sinner turns away from God is long, too long. Without doubt, Dante has been silent both literally and figuratively.

The negative aspect of Dante's silence may be glossed with some verses from a *lauda* by the poet's older contemporary, the Franciscan friar, Jacopone da Todi. In his poem, the friar is engaged in a battle with the Enemy, whose temptations he overcomes one by one with succinct, logical arguments. Silence is usually considered to be more virtuous than speech; therefore the Devil urges Jacopone to be silent ("If you did not speak, Brother, it would be edifying"). But the friar astutely replies that silence can sometimes be a vice: "to say nothing about God's goodness when one must announce it" (*Lauda* XLVII, 67–74).

To announce the good that he found in the dark wood, Dante will tell about the other things he perceived there. If the wood is understood in its narrower metaphoric sense as the wayfarer's own sinfulness, the "good" found there is Virgil's arrival to rescue the sinner, leading to his salvation, and this is how Singleton, Cassell, and others interpret it.[13] Yet Virgil is not the only good seen while the wayfarer is lost: Dante also sees the stars ("quelle stelle . . . quelle cose belle," *Inf.* I, 38, 40) that will reappear as though in confirmation of a promise when the pilgrim and his guide finally emerge from Hell to climb the mountain of Purgatory ("le cose belle . . . le stelle," *Inf.* XXXIV, 137, 139).[14]

This observation leads us to consider the poet's larger purpose: to celebrate the goodness of God. If Dante is seen as a representative of all human wayfarers, the "dark wood" may be taken in its extended, more general sense as the unrepented sinful life with its inevitable consequences in Hell. This clarifies the meaning of those "other things" the poet will tell about, those things that are not good in themselves and yet will show forth divine goodness. Hell will reveal the good (*il bene*) that it lacks once Dante gives an account of his journey through the underworld. As written over its entrance gate, Hell was made by the three divine Persons: the Power, Wisdom, and Love of the triune God, moved by Justice (*Inf.* III, 4–6). These are the divine attributes whose effects must be recognized even in Hell; this is the Good that is the subject of the first canticle, as it is of the entire *Comedy*.

The Italian scholar, Giovanni Getto, appropriately refers to the transitional tercets in *Inferno* I as a "passage between the zone of silence and the zone of speech."[15] Both the protagonist and the poet make this transition in a single pivotal verse. While the she-wolf forces Dante toward the "low place," he sees the shadowy personage offered to him in the vast emptiness. Instantly he calls out, "Have pity on me!" (v. 65). These words are the first sound, the first human speech recorded in the *Comedy*. These crucial words, the words that break the silence, are Dante's, and they also belong to David the psalmist, whose great penitential psalm begins "Miserere mei" (Ps. 50, Vulgate). Dante cites the first word in Latin and translates the second into the vernacular: "Miserere di me." By thus linking the two languages, he indissolubly binds, through poetic meter, his own spoken Tuscan to the scriptural language of the psalmist. In this poetic design we may infer Dante's intention to reshape and transform his native tongue, making it capable of expressing the highest form of praise. Like the psalms (David's *tëodia: Par*. XXV, 73), the *Comedy* will be a song in honor of God.

Let us now consider David's place in the *Comedy* and his importance to Dante. Dante greatly cherished David's example. The *Divine Comedy* shows his high regard for the biblical king in its many references to him (*Inf*. IV, 58; XXVIII, 138; *Purg*. X, 64–66; *Par*. XX, 37–42; XXV, 70–74; XXXII, 11–12). In *Purgatorio* X, sculpted reliefs on the terrace of the Proud depict David, the humble psalmist, dancing in front of the ark as an example of humility. In *Paradiso* XX, in the heaven of Jupiter, a multitude of souls arrange themselves in the shape of an eagle, the symbol of Justice: David alone shines in the middle of the eagle's eye, forming its pupil. The inspired singer of the Holy Spirit deserves this exalted position because of the judgment (*consiglio*) he used in choosing to praise God in song. Thus the above two passages illustrate David's humility and the merit of his own moral discernment.

Later in the journey, when Dante undergoes an examination on the virtue of Hope (*Par*. XXV, 70–78), he says that David first instilled hope in his heart before becoming the "highest singer of the Highest Lord." Then, Dante continues, his examiner, St. James, also gave him hope in his Epistle. The Epistle of James ends in the assurance that anyone who strays from the truth can be brought back from his misguided ways and saved. James's lesson of hope clearly applies to Dante's situation in *Inferno* I, as does the example of David, who was a sinner before he became the psalmist.[16] Dante concludes his examination with the statement that he himself, now filled with hope, is showering it on others. This means that the *Comedy*, with its story of a penitent who is saved, should be a source of hope to its readers.

Dante's contemporaries saw in David's life the example of a great sinner who openly and humbly acknowledged his sins, repented, and received divine mercy. Before he composed his psalms, he had committed adultery with Bathsheba and caused her husband, Uriah, to be killed. Because he was forgiven such great sins, he shows the power of true repentance and teaches us never to despair. To biblical commentators of

Dante's time, Psalm 50 exemplified David as a penitent man restored to divine grace.[17] Dante himself will be such a man after he confesses his deeply repented sins and is absolved at the summit of the mountain of Purgatory while he hears the psalmist's words, "Asperges me," sweetly sung (Ps. 50:9; *Purg.* XXXI, 98). Soon thereafter Beatrice confers upon him the obligation to write for the sake of the living (*Purg.* XXXIII, 52–78).

Psalm 50, therefore, is both a penitential psalm and a song of hope. Like other scriptural fragments cited in the *Comedy*, its first verse conveys the full import of the entire text, constituting the background against which Dante's *Miserere* in *Inf.* I, 65 should be read. The psalm expresses acknowledgment of sins and hope in spiritual renewal and joy (vv. 5–6, 9–10); the converted sinner will be an example to others (v. 15); his tongue will exult in God's Justice (v. 16); the Lord will open the lips of the sinner, who will proclaim divine praise (v. 17).

We may now see the relevance of the first spoken words in the *Comedy*, the words that, in response to divine assistance freely offered, open the wayfarer's lips: "Miserere di me." The idea that the Lord also opens the *poet's* lips, however, does not occur to us until we read in *Purgatorio* XXIII, 11, the words "Labia mea Domine" (Ps. 50:17) sung by the repentant Gluttons. The entire verse reads, "O Lord, open my lips and my mouth shall proclaim your praise." The Gluttons are asking for the grace to use their mouth in a more worthy way than they did in life: that is, the grace to praise God.[18]

It turns out that an important meeting between poets takes place on the terrace of the Gluttons. While the two Roman poets, Virgil and Statius, stay in the background, Dante speaks with two contemporaries, Forese Donati and Bonagiunta da Lucca, minor poets or perhaps mere versifiers. The former wrote poetry of vituperation in an exchange of sonnets with Dante; the latter did not quite succeed in writing true poetry of praise. In the course of their conversation, in which he summarizes his entire itinerary from the dark wood to the summit of Purgatory, Dante defines his own way of writing poetry: "I' mi son un che, quando / Amor mi spira, noto, e a quel modo / ch'e' ditta dentro vo significando" (I am one who, when love inspires me, takes note, and in that manner in which he dictates within me I give forth meaning, *Purg.* XXIV, 52–54). Two words in this statement may carry more than one sense. In the case of *Amor*, the context calls to mind that the Holy spirit is Love. The other term, *notare*, can mean "to take note" but also "to sing," to follow the notes of a musical text, as it does in *Purg.* XXX, 92. Dante follows the inner promptings of Love and in fact tells us that he sings in the *Comedy* ("I shall sing [canterò] about that second realm," *Purg.* I, 4).[19] Both David and Dante have the same source of inspiration; both are singers. Other poets in the vernacular, Dante's medieval predecessors and contemporaries and he himself in his earlier lyric compositions, speak: the verb *dire*, in such expressions as *dire parole per rima*, means to compose verses.[20] Thus Dante recognizes an immense spiritual and literary gulf between himself as poet of the *Comedy* and the other poets of his time, as well as his earlier self.[21] It could be that he also has in mind those two Romans who are standing quietly in the background. Though Virgil and Statius did sing,[22] both lacked divine inspiration as poets: both failed to celebrate the true God in their song.

In *Inferno* I Dante breaks the silence by crying out "Miserere di me" in his time of despair, but he remembers the psalmist once more near the end of his journey and of his poem shortly before falling again into silence where human language reaches its limits of expression. There he identifies David as "the singer who cried for his sin: *Miserere mei*" (*Par.* XXXII, 11–12). In the end, the Latin text stays intact as if to honor the singer.

To return to the transitional tercets in Canto I: Dante the wayfarer tries to climb the hill as the morning stars rising with the sun remind him of divine love and give him hope even as the fleet and colorful leopard obstructs his way. But when the other beasts re-instill fear and deprive him of that hope, Virgil is there on the deserted slope enveloped in silence. It is essential to respect the ambiguity with which the poet has shrouded the moment when the wayfarer, encumbered by his sinfulness, first perceives Virgil. The important aspect of the meeting between the two poets is that it is Dante who breaks the silence with the psalmist's *Miserere*.

The instant Virgil comes into view Dante cries out David's humble words of repentance, not to God directly but to the dim figure that has been offered. He breaks first of all his own silence which, as a manifestation of his sinfulness, prevented him from seeing Virgil clearly. By crying out, he also breaks Virgil's silence, a component of the general silence that surrounded the wayfarer as long as he was spiritually lost. The silence gives way to speech: first Dante's, then Virgil's. When Virgil speaks, his eloquence becomes an instrument of divine grace. Ultimately, the "silence" of the sun is broken as, in the course of the journey, the divine Word becomes audible to the protagonist and, through the poet, to the reader.

By choosing the opening of Psalm 50, "Miserere mei Deus secundum magnam misericordiam tuam" (Have pity on me O God, according to your great mercy), the poet leaves no doubt that "Miserere di me" is the cry of a repentant sinner who in his misery implores divine mercy. His heart filled with fear and despair (cf. vv. 14–15, 54), Dante cries out in response to a freely given grace, causing his first guide on the journey to salvation to take on a concrete existence.

The wayfarer's outcry is followed immediately by *Rispuosemi* (He answered me). This term, in this context, goes far beyond simply indicating a change of speaker in a dialogue. It marks the first positive event in the literal account of the journey: the enabling, life-giving response to the sinner's plea. *He answered*. With this, the narrative has moved to a different plane, leaving nothing indistinct or ambiguous. Virgil discloses his condition as a shade and without naming himself allows Dante to recognize him. Once a man, he was of Mantuan parentage, born in late antiquity, and lived in Rome. Most importantly, he is the poet of the *Aeneid*. Dante acknowledges Virgil as his "master and author."

Now, an *auctor* was to medieval literary and biblical commentators a writer whose statements possess authority, someone to be read, respected, and believed; someone whose writings contained truth and wisdom and eloquence worthy of imitation. The term was applied to biblical and secular authors of antiquity alike.[23] By calling Virgil his "master and author," expressing a disciple's great love and admiration for him, the protagonist identifies himself as a poet as well and locates himself and his work in a precise literary tradition. This tradition, this connection to Virgil's epic poem about Troy and Rome, gives Dante's poem strong roots in literary and world history, lending authority to its literal sense and to Dante's interpretation of Virgil and of history as well.

While the historical Virgil connects Dante's poem to the past of Italy, the fictitious Virgil links it to Italy's future through his mysterious prophecy of the Greyhound. The hound, or *Veltro*, is someone who will come to save humble Italy by killing the she-wolf—the very one that is threatening the wayfarer—and putting her back into Hell whence she came.

As Virgil urges Dante to follow him down another road, one that descends before it leads to the mountain top, his role as guide on Dante's fictional journey becomes clear and so do his limitations as a pagan excluded from the city of God. Finally, Virgil summarizes the itinerary and goal of the journey and Dante beseeches him to lead on, in the name of that God whom Virgil did not know. With this dialogue Virgil has been transformed into an actual character in the narrative and Dante, once his sacred goal has been defined and freely accepted, becomes truly a pilgrim.

The beast that caused Dante's outcry, bringing the historical Virgil into the fiction, continues to be present while the two poets converse ("You see the beast that forced me to retreat," v. 88). But the she-wolf soon is absorbed into Virgil's prophecy, where she continues to be a powerful symbol, devoid of materiality.

In Canto II Dante is still "on that dark slope" (v. 40) where he first caught sight of Virgil, for he has not yet entered Hell. Unlike the topography of Hell proper, which exists as a continuum with its various sections joined by ferrymen, rivers, bridges, craggy paths, etc., and whose moral structure is laid out in Canto XI, the landscape of the dark wood and sunlit hill is a disconnected space. It is mentioned two more times in the retrospective digression of Canto II ("a desert slope," v. 62, and "that river the sea shall never conquer," v. 108). Like the wolf, that landscape (and the action it holds) then persists as a metaphor to inform the entire poem:

again and again as we read and interpret, we look back to Canto I, which enriches our understanding of the *Comedy* and in turn grows in significance in relation to the poem as a whole. The narrative of the journey, on the other hand, acquires its literalness precisely at the moment of the wayfarer's spiritual turning point, where he breaks the silence with his *Miserere*, humbly admitting his sinfulness. When he finally sets out with his guide "on that deep and rugged road" (*Inf.* II, 142), the description of the road refers first of all to the rough, difficult terrain of Hell. At the same time, the road to be traveled through the three realms of the other world remains colored in its spiritual dimension by the metaphoric ambiance of Canto I. The journey and the poem end in a final reference to the sun and those same stars first glimpsed by the lost wayfarer as a summons and a source of hope.[24] In the end (as in the beginning, we now understand), they are not only symbols but also literally the sun and stars. The goal that has been attained is the divine Love that first set them in motion and ever moves them.

NOTES

1. Anthony K. Cassell, *Inferno I*, Lectura Dantis Americana (Philadelphia: University of Pennsylvania Press, 1989), proposes a different interpretation stressing the sense of repetitiveness in the verb *ritrovarsi*. In this view, the prefix *ri-* expresses habitual sin or backsliding: "at midlife he found himself yet again in a state of sin" (p. 9). For a full discussion of *mi ritrovai*, see pp. 8–14. In my view the opening of the *Inferno* describes a unique event in the spiritual life of the protagonist, who gains consciousness of the sinful state in which he has persisted and still persists. Hence the fear and the struggle to flee. I agree with those critics who see in the prefix an expression of renewed self-awareness, an awakening from sleep (on sleep as a metaphor of habitual sin, see Cassell, *Inferno I*, 4).

2. See, for example, Cassell, ibid., 115; Giovanni Getto remarks on "la prima parte del canto, in cui parlano soltanto i simboli," on p. 9 of "Il canto introduttivo della *Divina Commedia*," in *Aspetti della poesia di Dante* (Florence: Sansoni, 1966 [rpt. of *Il canto I dell' Inferno. Lectura dantis scaligera* (Florence: Le Monnier, 1960)]; Zygmunt G. Barański, "La lezione esegetica di *Inferno* I: allegoria, storia e letteratura nella 'Commedia,'" in *Dante e le forme dell'allegoresi*, ed. Michelangelo Picone (Ravenna: Longo, 1987), 79–97; Tibor Wlassics, "L'onirismo dell'*incipit*: appunti su *Inferno* I, 1–63," in *Letture classensi*, XVIII (1989): 31–39.

3. According to Cassell, who follows Freccero, the wayfarer attempts his ascent in self-deception and pride (*Inferno I*, 6, 123–25). I rather agree with Antonio C. Mastrobuono, *Dante's Journey of Sanctification* (Washington, D.C.: Regnery Gateway, 1990), 229–31, that the upward struggle is motivated by hope. The she-wolf causes the wayfarer to lose hope ("la speranza de l'altezza," v. 54) because, as Cassell rightly shows, he is unable to reach the summit unaided by divine grace. Nevertheless, the wayfarer's instinctive upward movement, initially spurred by fear that pierces the heart (vv. 14–15: "quella valle / che m'avea di paura il cor compunto"—compunction suggests an awareness of guilt), cannot be prideful or in any sense negative. It is an expression of the natural inclination of all human beings toward their ultimate goal, the supreme good, or God: see *Purg.* XVII, 94.

When fear of the wolf turns the wayfarer back from the attempted ascent, the help of God is already assured (Canto II). Dante's spiritual itinerary in Canto I is from fear to hope to despair to free acceptance of divine assistance offered through Virgil.

4. See especially Charles S. Singleton, *Dante Studies I: Commedia, Elements of Structure* (Cambridge: Harvard University Press, 1954), ch. 1; idem, "In Exitu Israel de Aegypto," *Annual Report of the Dante Society* 78 (1960): 1–24; idem, *The Divine Comedy, Translated, with a Commentary*, vol. I, *Inferno*, pt. 2: *Commentary* (Princeton: Princeton University Press, 1970); John Freccero, "Dante's Firm Foot and the Journey without a Guide," *Harvard Theological Review* 52 (1959): 245–81, and "Dante's Prologue Scene," *Dante Studies* 84 (1966): 1–25; Mastrobuono, *Dante's Journey*, and Cassell, *Inferno I*, which also provides a comprehensive bibliography.

5. The beasts are generally considered to represent sinful dispositions, or the three categories of sin punished in the major divisions of Hell. See Mark Musa's note on vv. 32–60.

6. Robert Hollander, *Il Virgilio dantesco: tragedia nella "Commedia"* (Florence: Olschki, 1983) 69–77 on "dove 'l sol tace" and "chi per lungo silenzio parea fioco," which are seen as closely related. Cassell (*Inferno I*, 87–88) builds on Hollander in his own interpretation of the symbolism of silence.

7. St. Augustine of Hippo, *Enarrationes in Psalmos*, in J. -P. Migne, ed., *Patrologiae cursus completus: series latina* [*P.L.*] (Paris, 1844–64), vol. 36, cols. 563–85.

8. The long exegetical history of verse 63 has been carefully reviewed by Hollander in chapter 1 of *Il Virgilio dantesco*.

9. Hollander, ibid., 67–77.

10. Exceptions cited by Hollander either attribute or relate the "long silence" to the sun.

11. According to Cassell (*Inferno I*, 92–93), the poet-narrator describes Virgil's initial appearance from the perspective of the subsequent journey, which allows the "long silence" to be attributed to Virgil's lack of faith.

12. Singleton (*Commentary*) considers verse 63 to be "deliberately ambiguous."

13. For Singleton, the "good" found in the wood is "the wayfarer's rescue by Virgil" (*Commentary*, v. 8). For Cassell (*Inferno I*, 120–25) it is the conversion of the sinner who, after a series of "negative" events (the ascent attempted in pride, the temporary failure of the fall) learns a lesson in humility which prepares him for the reception of grace and makes the journey and the poem possible.

14. Note the linking of the rhyme words in *Inf*. I and *Inf*. XXXIV by means of a remote chiasmus: *stelle—belle* / *belle—stelle*.

15. Getto, "Il canto introduttivo," 9.

16. Robert Hollander points out that David's penitence prefigures that of Dante, "a later singer who feels grief for a fault and who sings *Miserere*." See "Dante's Use of the Fiftieth Psalm (a Note on *Purg*. XXX, 84)," *Dante Studies* XCI (1973): 147. On David as a model for Dante, see also Teodolinda Barolini, *Dante's Poets: Textuality and Truth in the COMEDY* (Princeton: Princeton University Press, 1984), 275–78.

17. Alastair J. Minnis, *Medieval Theory of Authorship: Scholastic Literary Attitudes in the Later Middle Ages* (London: Scolar Press, 1984), 103–112.

18. Isidore of Seville hints at the relationship between gluttony and speech in his explanation of the term "mouth": "Os dictum, quod per ipsum quasi per ostium et cibos intus mittimus et sputum foris proicimus; vel quia inde ingrediuntur cibi, inde egrediuntur sermones" (*Etymologiae sive Originum libri XX*, ed. W. M. Lindsay [Oxford: Clarendon Press, 1911], Lib. XI, 1, 49). Barolini, *Dante's Poets*, 51–52, discusses the connection between *Labia mea* and lyric poetry of praise.

19. See also *Inf*. XVI, 127–128; *Inf*. XXI, 2; *Par*. V, 139.

20. *Dire* recurs throughout the *Vita nuova* with this meaning. See especially ch. 25: "dire per rima, sapere dire, dicitori per rima"; see also ch. 3: "l'arte del dire parole per rima." Cf. Giacomo da Lentini's "Madonna, dir vo voglio"; Guido Cavalcanti's "Donna me prega—perch'eo voglio dire"; Dante's "Donne ch'avete 'ntelletto d'amore / i' vo' con voi de la mia donna dire," cited in *Purg.* XXIV, 51.

21. I basically agree with those critics who see in Dante's words to Bonagiunta a statement on the poetics of the *Comedy*. See Mark Musa, *Advent at the Gates: Dante's COMEDY* (Bloomington: Indiana University Press, 1974), ch. 6; and Teodolinda Barolini, *The Undivine COMEDY: Detheologizing Dante* (Princeton: Princeton University Press, 1992), 52–53. Lino Pertile, on the other hand, argues persuasively that the declaration of *Purg.* XXIV is Dante the character's definition of the *dolce stil novo*, not an explanation of the radically new poetics of the *Comedy*. See "Dante's *Comedy* Beyond the *Stilnovo*," in *Lectura Dantis* 13 (1993), 47–77, especially 55–68. Nevertheless, the poet's extraordinary claim to be divinely inspired is concealed in the double meanings of *Amor* and *noto*.

22. Dante refers to Virgil as a singer in *Inf.* I, 73, *Inf.* XX, 112, and *Purg.* XXII, 57; and to Statius in *Purg.* XXI, 126 and XXII, 55.

23. Minnis, pp. 10–11.

24. Cf. *Inf.* I, 38–40, *Par.* XXXIII, 145.

Dante's *Inferno*, Canto IV

AMILCARE A. IANNUCCI

It is tempting in a *lectura Dantis* to claim for the canto one is explicating a special status: the key to the whole poem. This is understandable from a psychological point of view, but the phenomenon also has a textual basis. The allusive quality of the *Comedy*'s literal narrative is such that it is possible to develop an elaborate intratextual discourse starting from virtually any point. Obviously, this is not the place to discuss the poem's distinctive textual characteristics. That is another story, and a long one at that. Perhaps Contini treats the subject best, albeit obliquely, when he speaks of the *Comedy*'s "altra polisemia," and I refer you to him.[1]

For our purposes, it is sufficient to say that there are essentially two kinds of cantos, which we may label, rather inelegantly, as "local" and "structurally determining." A "local" canto is one whose meaning is largely, if not completely, exhausted within its immediate context. On the other hand, a "structurally determining" canto is one whose meaning extends far beyond its immediate or "local" context. It is a constant point of reference and continues to determine meaning throughout the poem. *Inferno* IV is such a canto.

Inferno IV—Limbo—occupies a privileged position in the poem's structure. It is the First Circle of Hell, yet it stands outside Hell proper (by which I mean the hell of personal sin), suspended as it is between Charon and Minòs. And Dante chooses this liminal setting as the location for one of the most extraordinary cultural operations in literary history. By placing the virtuous pagans in Limbo, he departs radically from the theological tradition on the subject. In so doing, he also banishes pagan civilization from the center and relocates it at the margin of history. The gesture is more than a mere indication of his attitude toward established authority and traditional sources, whatever their origin: historical, philosophical, theological, or literary. His bold "rewriting" of Limbo changes its significance and its role in the structure of Christian history. Moreover, it brings into focus some of the major themes of his great "theological romance": the place of pagan civilization in providential history, the limits of reason in the absence of revelation, the relationship between free will and grace, the myopic limits of human judgment, and the inscrutable nature of divine justice.

Theological themes all of them. However, instead of suffocating the poetry,[2] theology is the very source of it. Sparked by Dante's repositioning of pagan civilization at the margin of history, these themes are treated not abstractly but dramatically. Moreover, Dante's gesture turns "comedy" into "tragedy." This he accomplishes in another daring move. He turns the Harrowing of Hell for the virtuous pagans from an event of release and fulfillment into a disquieting reminder of incompletion: "sanza speme vivemo in disio" (*Inf.* IV, 42.).[3] Virgil, the virtuous pagan *par excellence*, assures that the tragedy of the virtuous pagans (and all that it entails) becomes not a "local" issue but one which invests the structure of the whole poem.[4]

And there is more. The initial encounter with the great poets of antiquity, the first souls Dante meets in the "afterlife," is another significant gesture of repositioning, this time within the more restricted sphere of literary history. With this meeting, Dante effectively redraws the literary map: he issues an implicit poetic challenge to his illustrious classical precursors, against whom he wishes to be measured. By the end of the poem, Dante can and does claim victory. They, Virgil included, are pushed to the margin, into the "noble castle" of Limbo. What Dante wins is more than the laurel crown, for what was at stake was no less than salvation and damnation. In *Inferno* IV Dante focuses on the losers (poetic and otherwise) and it is primarily through their loss that he articulates a complex vision of Christian history which includes "tragedy" as well as "comedy." I will concentrate on this aspect of the canto. In deference to the *lectura Dantis* tradition, I shall try to limit my analysis as much as possible to the canto itself—not an easy task for a canto which is as "structurally determining," as *Inferno* IV.

The theologians of Dante's time distinguished between two Limbos, the *limbus patrum* and the *limbus puerorum*, which occupied more or less the same spot at the edge of Hell's pit.[5] The *limbus patrum* was the theological counterpart to the biblical bosom of Abraham. By Dante's time it was considered to be the place where the righteous patriarchs of the Old Testament and those fortunate gentiles to whom God had extended a special grace awaited in a state of anxious but hopeful expectation Christ's Harrowing of Hell. The *limbus puerorum*, on the other hand, was essentially a child of the Middle Ages and grew out of the need to distinguish between original sin and the sin of person. The *limbus puerorum* was the exclusive domain of those, principally the unbaptized infants, who died in a state of original sin. Since these souls did not commit any personal sin, their punishment is not the pain of sense, that is, actual physical torment, but rather the pain of loss, the *poena damni*. They suffer the loss of grace, the withdrawal of original justice and of the sight of God. Within this shadowy landscape Dante constructs a "noble castle" in which he houses Virgil and other virtuous pagans. By introducing virtuous pagans into Limbo, Dante breaks abruptly with the theological tradition that had evolved in the West from the New Testament through St. Augustine and Gregory the Great to St. Thomas.[6]

This unexpected departure from tradition has led some commentators to make the rather extravagant assertion that Dante created Limbo in order to construct the "noble castle."[7] Although untenable from the point of view of the poem's theological structure—given this structure Dante had to present some sort of Limbo in his Hell—this claim nonetheless captures the spirit of Dante's Limbo and individualizes its poetic focus. But the "noble castle" is not an autonomous image independent of the rest of Limbo, as other commentators have maintained. It is not simply a "temple" that Dante erected in the middle of his Christian poem to celebrate pagan civilization.[8] Nor is it merely a tribute to reason,[9] although the episode is indeed an expression of Dante's prehumanistic spirit. Certainly one of the factors that brought him to rescue Virgil and the virtuous pagans from lower Hell and to disregard the theological tradition on Limbo was his great admiration for pagan poetry and philosophy.[10] However, the principal subject of the canto is neither poetry nor philosophy, but the limits of humanism when it is not illuminated by revelation. In other words, the "noble castle" is an expression both of Dante's humanism and of his painful awareness of its limits.[11]

The duality of the Limbo theme is conveyed primarily through the melancholic and tragic figure of Virgil. Virgil is aware from the outset that he is not one of the elect. Referring to his exclusion from the City of God in *Inferno* I, 125–126, he exclaims with a sense of profound regret, "oh felice colui cu' ivi elegge!" (*Inf.* I, 129). This passage defines the nature of Virgil's tragedy and sets its tone. All further references to Virgil's condition and that of his fellow Limbo-dwellers are references to predestination. In order to make the tragedy of predestination more compelling and more perplexing, Dante takes an extreme case to exemplify it, that of the virtuous pagans whom he presents within the structure of the poem as completely sinless, damned only because they lived in an age of ignorance, "nel tempo de li dèi falsi e bugiardi" (*Inf.* I, 72).[12]

As Virgil explains more than once in the course of the poem, he and his companions in Limbo are completely free of personal sin, and, furthermore, possess great positive merits (vv. 33–42):

Or vo' che sappi, innanzi che più andi,
   ch'ei non peccaro; e s'elli hanno mercedi,
non basta, perché non ebber battesmo,
ch'è porta de la fede che tu credi;
   e s'e' furon dinanzi al cristianesmo,
non adorar debitamente a Dio:
e di questi cotai son io medesmo.

> Per tai difetti, non per altro rio,
> semo perduti, e sol di tanto offesi
> che sanza speme vivemo in disio.

Despite their virtue, they are lost, suspended in Limbo, simply because they were not baptized and lacked faith in Christ, learning of him too late (cf. *Purg.* VII, 25–36). Dante bars the gates of Heaven to the virtuous pagans; he locks them in the "noble castle" instead. Their existence is not one of hopeful expectation like that of the Hebrew fathers of the *limbus patrum*, but one of expectation without hope, like that of the children of the *limbus puerorum*.

How does Dante go about dramatizing the tragedy of the virtuous pagans? I have already stated that Dante deviates from theological tradition on Limbo; he also completely alters the typical poetic representation of Limbo, which focuses exclusively on the *limbus patrum* and the Harrowing of Hell. Indeed, the Harrowing of Hell or the *Descensus Christi ad Inferos* was a favorite theme in the Middle Ages.[13] Its popularity stemmed from the fact that Christ's descent into Hell symbolized the resurrection and the redemption. The redemption, especially in the West, was conceived of as a victory of Christ over death and Satan, who with original sin had acquired control over man. The Harrowing of Hell dramatizes Christ's release of man from the bondage of sin and ignorance that had prevailed since the fall, and His rule over all creatures both living and dead. In particular, it dramatizes His liberation of the Hebrew patriarchs from Hell. An arsenal of stock images, drawn more from the apocryphal fifth-century Gospel of Nicodemus than from the sparse reports of the Harrowing in the New Testament, existed to represent this pivotal event in Christian history. Needless to say, the structure of these accounts is naturally "comic" and the tone celebratory.

Dante changes all of this. He overturns the usual poetic representation of Limbo by shifting the emphasis from the Harrowing of Hell to the "noble castle." In his representation of Limbo, Dante is interested in neither the *limbus puerorum* nor the *limbus patrum* and the Harrowing of Hell. Rather he is concerned with the *limbus paganorum integrorum* or the "noble castle," which he created to emphasize the tragedy of the virtuous pagans. In *Inferno* IV Dante strips Christ's descent into Hell of the bold agonistic imagery which vivifies traditional representations (vv. 52–63):

> Io era nuovo in questo stato,
> quando ci vidi venire un possente,
> con segno di vittoria coronato.
>   Trasseci l'ombra del primo parente,
> d'Abèl suo figlio e quella di Noè,
> di Moïsè legista e ubidente;
>   Abraàm patrïarca e Davìd re,
> Israèl con lo padre e co' suoi nati
> e con Rachele, per cui tanto fé,

e altri molti, e feceli beati.
E vo' che sappi che, dinanzi ad essi,
spiriti umani non eran salvati.

No longer the focal point of Dante's Limbo, the Harrowing's primary function is to set in dramatic relief the tragedy of the virtuous pagans. In its new context, it announces not so much victory as defeat, for Dante transfers the poetic focus from those whom Christ released from the prison of Hell to those who were left behind. For this reason, the tone of Dante's Limbo is the exact opposite of that of his contemporaries' depictions of that realm. Unlike traditional accounts, Dante's does not evoke the Hebrew patriarchs' triumphant entry into paradise nor their hymn of praise to their redeemer.[14] Instead Dante gives us the sighs of those who are left behind (vv. 25–30):

Quivi, secondo che per ascoltare,
non avea pianto mai che di sospiri
che l'aura etterna facevan tremare;
ciò avvenia di duol sanza martìri,
ch'avean le turbe, ch'eran molte e grandi
d'infanti e di femmine e di viri.

By turning comedy into tragedy, Dante succeeds in creating in his Limbo one of the most gripping and poignant episodes in the entire *Comedy*.

Despite this change in focus, poetically Dante's brief evocation of the descent into Hell remains pivotal in his representation of Limbo. When Dante the wayfarer realizes that Limbo is populated by Virgil and other men of great worth, he is seized with pity (vv. 43–45). He asks Virgil a question that may at first seem puzzling, if not downright naive (vv. 46–50):

"Dimmi, maestro mio, dimmi, segnore,"
comincia' io per volere esser certo
di quella fede che vince ogne errore:
"uscicci mai alcuno, o per suo merto
o per altrui, che poi fosse beato?"

Surely Dante was familiar with the theology of the Harrowing of Hell.[15] An article of faith of the Apostle's Creed, it concentrated on the deliverance of the Hebrew fathers from Hell. In his commentary on the *Divine Comedy*, Boccaccio argues that Dante poses the question in order to discover whether there is any way that he can save those meritorious souls left behind in Limbo by Christ.[16] Boccaccio's is a fanciful interpretation, but it nonetheless indicates the nature of the wayfarer's perplexity at this point. He is bewildered at the thought that the virtuous pagans were forsaken despite their great personal merit, while the Hebrew patriarchs were saved, and this disquieting thought puts a momentary strain on his faith (v. 48). If this were the motive behind the pilgrim's question, he must have been disappointed by Virgil's response. Virgil does nothing more than relate a conventional account of the Harrowing. He does not resolve the intellectual dilemma which provoked the question, the problem of why the Hebrew fathers were released from Limbo and the equally meritorious gentiles were not. Nor does he reveal whether any gentiles were saved. This unanswered question will haunt the wayfarer throughout his journey, even after Virgil's pathetic and impassioned *quia* speech in *Purgatorio* III.

Dante's "great thirst" for this knowledge is not satisfied until the Eagle in *Paradiso* XIX explains to him that there is no path to salvation save through Christ: "A questo regno / non salì mai chi non credette 'n Cristo, / né pria né poi ch'el si chiavasse al legno" (*Par.* XIX, 103–105). Even the pagans Ripheus and Trajan, whom Dante sees to his surprise in the Eagle's brow, had to have explicit faith in the passion and resurrection of Christ in order to be saved (*Par.* XX, 103–105). If Dante the wayfarer is necessarily disappointed by Virgil's response, Dante the poet is not (v. 51). The poet needs the Harrowing as a foil to accentuate the tragic plight of Virgil and his virtuous companions, who remain locked forever in the "noble castle."

The poetic power of Dante's Limbo lies precisely in the surprising juxtaposition of two images—the Harrowing of Hell and the "noble castle"—one an image of release and fulfillment, the other of confinement and melancholy; one of comedy and the other of tragedy. In order to emphasize the tragedy of the virtuous pagans and the related paradox of unrewarded merit, Dante deliberately dramatizes it in a context traditionally used by poets and theologians to represent the "comic" turning-point in history. Dante's Limbo is not a place of jubilation; it dwells rather on the sadness and melancholy of the virtuous pagans which result from their awareness that they can never attain spiritual fulfillment: "sanza speme vivemo in disio" (v. 42). Dante downplays the imagery connected with the descent into Hell in *Inferno* IV because he wants to depict not the fullness of time—*plenitudo temporis*—but the emptiness of time.

Christ came, but not for Virgil and his kind. Nothing survives in Dante's Limbo of the evangelizing Christ who preached the Gospel in Hell and thereby despoiled it not only of the Hebrew fathers but also of all those He managed to convert there. According to this notion, prevalent in the Primitive Church and preserved in the Eastern tradition,[17] the choice the souls of B.C. time were denied in this life, because of their invincible ignorance, they were granted in the next. Although Dante suggests that if the virtuous pagans had known Christ, they would certainly have been Christians, for them it is too late, *tardi*. This adverb, which escapes from Virgil's lips on more than one occasion, has a pathetic ring to it. With the release of the just from Limbo at the Harrowing, hellmouth locked its jaws. Those who were left behind are caught forever in its grip.

Ironically, for the majority of Dante's virtuous pagans, it is with Christ's descent into Hell that their terrestrial "comedy" becomes an eschatological "tragedy." Before the coming of Christ, they lived in blissful ignorance. With His coming, their pagan Elysium is suddenly transformed into the "noble castle" of Christian Limbo, natural happiness into sadness, spiritual contentment into hopeless desire. The event tears them out of the context of pagan culture and inserts them abruptly into the flow of Christian history. All continuity is shattered. The state of natural bliss that they had enjoyed in the Elysian Fields is now seen as inadequate in the light of the supernatural bliss that they have lost irrevocably. The inadequacy of natural bliss is reflected in the image of the "noble castle" itself.

Dante's overall representation of the "noble castle" is, as has often been observed, modeled on the ancient poets' depiction of the Elysian Fields and especially Virgil's in Book VI of the *Aeneid*.[18] Stylistically, however, Dante's "noble castle" is a pale image of paradise as conceived by Virgil (vv. 106–111):

> Venimmo al piè d'un nobile castello,
> sette volte cerchiato d'alte mura,
> difeso intorno d'un bel fiumicello.
>   Questo passammo come terra dura;
> per sette porte intrai con questi savi:
> giugnemmo in prato di fresca verdura.

The absence of descriptive detail betrays its diminished status. Within Dante's Christian universe, natural happiness, achieved through reason alone, is no longer man's ultimate goal. It is no more than a way station in the quest for eternal bliss, figured by the Celestial Paradise (*Monarchia* III, xvi), to which Dante ascends via the new, redeemed Earthly Paradise at the top of Mount Purgatory. It is not surprising, therefore, that Dante should save Virgil's Elysian imagery to describe not the former pagan paradise, but Christian paradise, in both its early (*Purg.* XXVIII) and celestial (*Par.* XXXI) manifestations.[19] Dante's despoiled Elysium is an image of the extent to which Eden can be recovered without Christ.

A more detailed consideration of the castle's intricate imagery from this perspective is in order.[20] Although the "noble castle" occupies a special place in Dante's lower world, segregated as it is from the rest of Hell, it is an image not only of segregation but also of containment. The castle's seven walls separate reason from passion and malice, but they also separate reason from revelation and grace; in other words, they divide the pagan world from the Christian. In this light, of all the interpretations of the seven walls and gates (the seven liberal arts, the seven parts of philosophy, etc.) the most cogent is that they stand for the four cardinal and three intellectual virtues. The *Monarchia* (III, xvi) supports this view. Here Dante states that natural happiness can be attained through studying philosophy and practicing the four cardinal and three intellectual virtues. On the other hand, supernatural happiness can only be realized by following spiritual precepts, which transcend human reason, that is, by pursuing the three theological virtues of faith, hope, and charity. The virtuous pagans are armed with the human virtues but lack the theological ones.

The blaze of light which circumscribes the "noble castle" must also be seen from a double perspective. In terms of its symbolic value within the structure of "Hell," the light emanating from the castle is expansive and liberating. It is the light of reason, which overcomes ignorance: "io vidi un foco / ch'emisperio di tenebre vincia" (vv. 68–69). However, without God's grace, what we take to be light is darkness, or at best a shadow (*Par.* XIX, 64–66):

> Lume non è, se non vien dal sereno
> che non si turba mai; anzi è tenèbra
> od ombra de la carne o suo veleno.

Original sin disfranchised man and cast a shadow over him; B.C. man was thus dimly illuminated by God's grace: "del lume suo poco s'imbianca" (*Par.* VII, 81). The glow over the "noble castle," over the Eden of unredeemed time, corresponds to the shadow which descended over mankind after the fall, a shadow that was not dispersed until the redemption (*Par.* VII, 55–120).

If we consider the "noble castle" as a symbol of the extent to which Eden could be recovered before the coming of Christ, the image of the river encircling the castle, which has so engaged the commentators' imagination, also finds a simple and natural explanation. Variously interpreted as the vanities of this world, and, more positively, as eloquence, virtue, or good deeds, it is (within this interpretative framework) yet another symbol of reason, that reason which both segregates the virtuous pagans from the rest of Hell and confines them there. The curious manner in which the poets cross the river as though it were dry land can also be explained simply and naturally from this point of view. It is a sign of failed baptism.

Dante has turned a literary reminiscence—Virgil's "many-watered Eridanus" (*Aen.* VI, 659)—into a symbol charged with Christian signification. Baptism, as Virgil himself indicates to Dante, is the door to the Christian faith, "porta de la fede che tu credi" (v. 36). In its absence, damnation is certain no matter how eloquent or virtuous a man may be.[21] From this perspective, the river at the threshold of the Eden of unredeemed time is in obvious contrast to both the river Lethe at the threshold of the restored Christian Eden (*Purg.* XXXI, 94–96) and the river of lights which opens up into a vision of the Celestial Rose (*Par.* XXX, 61ff.). Unlike these purveyors of eternity, the river of Limbo shackles those inside the castle to the timebound pattern of their own thought. Unfortunately, because of their place in history, the virtuous pagans were cut off from the sanctifying water of grace, "l'acqua onde la femminetta / samaritana domandò la grazia" (*Purg.* XXI, 2–3). Unbaptized, they are locked within the confining and hopeless circularity of

Christian Limbo: "sanza speme vivemo in disio" (v. 42). As a symbol of the extent to which man can recover Eden without divine aid, the "noble castle" expresses both the dignity and the frailty of man, both the conquests of humanism and its shortcomings, both the achievements of pagan civilization and its limits.

Dante uses the Limbo theme in the *Comedy* to articulate, among other things, a vision of history which is Christian and hence ultimately comic in nature, but one that does not exclude tragedy. In order to express this tragic vision, especially as it relates to that unredeemed, graceless section of time between the fall and the redemption, Dante the poet revolutionizes the traditional theological and poetical conception of Limbo. First he introduces the virtuous pagans into the bosom of Abraham, but instead of having them freed along with the righteous Hebrews at the Harrowing of Hell, as others before him had done, he locks them securely within that realm, leaving them to sigh hopelessly forever with the infants of the *limbus puerorum*. By shifting the focus from the Harrowing of Hell and the idea of release to the image of the "noble castle" and containment, he completely overturns the tone and the meaning of the traditional medieval depiction of Limbo. Dante represents defeat not victory, tragedy not comedy. The terrestrial "comedy" of the virtuous pagans becomes an eschatological "tragedy." The implications of the virtuous pagans' exclusion from grace are such that Dante returns to the theme repeatedly in the course of the poem.

From a Christian perspective, the condition of these souls—their state of perpetual longing without hope of spiritual fulfillment—reflects the existential plight of man before the redemption. They lived in the emptiness of time and are now doomed to the empty hope of Limbo. The tragedy of the virtuous pagans resembles, therefore, a Greek tragedy of necessity rather than a Christian tragedy of possibility. Their tragedy is not one of free will like Ulysses', the positive infidels', or indeed that of the neutrals who chose not to choose, but one of predestination. Although they made all the right choices in this life, they were pursued by an unsympathetic fate which would verify itself only in the afterlife. This fate or destiny determined by the God of Christianity Himself, is undoubtedly just (*Par.* XXXII, 55–57); and myopic, timebound man must ultimately accept God's judgment, although as a man he has compassion for the suffering of his kind. From this human perspective, for all the divine justness of the virtuous pagans' destiny, their tragedy evokes pity and compassion. For a Christian like Dante, it cannot create terror, for he can never share their state. But the virtuous pagans' predicament remains a tragedy and a double one at that. They were irrevocably stained by the sin of the First Adam and forsaken by the saving grace of the Second Adam.

Lecture given at the University of Virginia on September 15, 1989. This essay is a revision and an elaboration of a small portion of an earlier, much more extensive treatment of *Inferno* IV in "Limbo: The Emptiness of Time." *Studi danteschi* LII (1979–80), 69–128. For the immense bibliography on the subject, I refer the reader to this essay, as well as to Francesco Mazzoni, "Saggio di un nuovo commento alla *Commedia*: il canto IV dell'*Inferno*." *Studi danteschi* XLII (1965), 29–206, and Fausto Montanari, "Limbo," *Enciclopedia dantesca* III, 651–54.

1. Gianfranco Contini, *Un'idea di Dante* (Torino: Einaudi, 1976), 119ff.

2. As Benedetto Croce argues in *La poesia di Dante* (Bari: Laterza, 1966), 72–73. Others have also held this view. See, for instance, Giovanni Getto, *Aspetti della poesia di Dante* (Sansoni, 1966), 159.

3. All quotations from the *Divine Comedy* are taken from *La Commedia secondo l'antica vulgata*, a cura di Giorgio Petrocchi, 4 vols. (Milan: Mondadori, 1966–67).

4. My understanding of Virgil's "tragedy" in this essay is substantially different from that of Robert Hollander in *Il Virgilio dantesco: Tragedia nella "Commedia"* (Firenze: Olschki, 1983), 117–54. My position on the subject was outlined in my earlier essay on Limbo cited above.

5. For the concept of Limbo in theological thought, see A. Gaudet, "Limbes," *Dictionnaire de Théologie Catholique*, IX, 1 (1926), cols. 760–72.

6. For a full discussion of the theological implications of such a move, see Iannucci, "Limbo: The Emptiness of Time."

7. See, for example, Carlo Grabher, "Il Limbo e il Nobile Castello," *Studi danteschi* XXIX (1950): 49.

8. The common view that the "noble castle" is a temple erected in honor of pagan culture is perhaps stated most elegantly by Francesco De Sanctis, *Storia della letteratura italiana* (Milano: Feltrinelli, 1970), 181. Cf. Fiorenzo Forti, *Magnanimitade: studi su un tema dantesco* (Bologna: Pàtron Editore, 1977), 9–48.

9. Getto, *Aspetti*, 156–61.

10. Augustin Renaudet, *Dante Ilumaniste* (Paris: Les Belles Lettres, 1952), 123.

11. For another, substantially different perspective on the duality which animates the episode, see Kenelm Foster, *The Two Dantes* (London: Darton, Longman and Todd, 1977), 156–253.

12. That Dante's virtuous pagans are not, as Tito P. Bottagisio, in *Il limbo dantesco* (Padova: Tipografia e Libreria Editrice Antoniana, 1898), 12, remarks flippantly, all "fior di galantuomini," matters little.

13. On the Harrowing of Hell, see, for example, Jean Monnier, *La Descente aux Enfers* (Paris: Librairie Fischbacher, 1904); and, H. Quillet, "Descente de Jésus aux Enfers," *Dictionnaire de Théologie Catholique*, IV (1911), cols. 565–619, still the most comprehensive and useful treatment of the subject.

14. For a comparison of traditional accounts of the Harrowing and Dante's novel use of the theme in the *Divine Comedy*, see Amilcare A. Iannucci, *Forma ed evento nella* Divina Commedia (Roma: Bulzoni, 1984), 51–81.

15. The theology of the Harrowing which evolved over a long period of time does allow for the possibility of pagans being saved. And Dante is aware of this, as the later appearance of Cato, Ripheus, and Trajan makes clear. But in Limbo this possibility is raised only to be set aside. On the complex problem of the salvation of infidels, see S. Harent, S.J., "Infidèles (Salut des)," *Dictionnaire de Théologie Catholique*, VII, 2 (1923), cols. 1726–1930. On Dante's unorthodox treatment of the issue, I refer you again to "Limbo: The Emptiness of Time." See also Michel-

angelo Picone, "La 'viva speranza' di Dante e il problema della salvezza dei pagani virtuosi. Una lettura di *Paradiso* 20," *Dante Today*, ed. Amilcare A. Iannucci, special volume of *Quaderni d'italianistica* X, 1–2 (1989): 251–68.

16. Giovanni Boccaccio, *Esposizioni sopra la Comedia di Dante*, a cura di Giorgio Padoan (Milan: Mondadori, 1965), 178–79.

17. On the "evangelizing" theory of the redemption and the related interpretation of Christ's descent into Hell, see Quillet, "Descente," cols. 597–98.

18. See, for example, Benvenuti de Rambaldis de Imola, *Comentum super Dantis Aldigherij Comoediam*, curante Jacopo Philippo Lacaita, vol. I (Florentiae: Barbèra, 1887), 159, for an early and clear statement on the subject: "pratum virens figurat viredinem famae illustrium virorum, quia similiter Virgilius VI Eneydos, et Homerus XI Odysseae fingunt viros illustres stare in prato virenti."

19. See Bartlett A. Giamatti, *The Earthly Paradise and the Renaissance Epic* (Princeton: Princeton University Press, 1969), 15. See also L. Pertile, "Il nobile castello, il paradiso terrestre e l'umanesimo di Dante," *Filologia e critica* V (1980): 1–29.

20. For a survey of the various interpretations of the "noble castle," its walls, its gates, the river surrounding it, etc., see Mazzoni, "Saggio," 156–68.

21. See John 3:5: "Nisi quis renatus fuerit ex aqua et Spiritu Sanctu, non potest introire in regnum Dei." Cf. Heb. 11:6: "Sine fide autem impossibile est placere Deo."

Behold Francesca Who
Speaks So Well (*Inferno* V)

MARK MUSA

The majority of scholars who have treated the figure of Francesca have presented her in a highly favorable light. To such an extent is this true, in some cases, that they seem to suggest that the attractiveness of her personality is great enough to atone for her sin.[1] Since they treat her only on the surface, this favorable picture is surely understandable, as is their tone of affection, respect and compassion. For on the surface she is truly one of the most charming creatures to appear (though hers was such a brief appearance) in world literature.

What her words most clearly reveal is the good breeding of the speaker: hers is an aristocratic nature, now fired by ardent memories, now tempered by sweetness and feminine grace. Toward the Pilgrim she shows the quintessence of courtesy and graciousness—as is already revealed in her opening words, "O animal grazioso . . ." (88), themselves an echo of the Pilgrim's address to the pair of lovers "O anime affiannate . . ." (80); indeed, it was surely her gratitude for the Pilgrim's tender greeting that inspired her gracious response. And in the wish suggested by her offer "noi pregheremmo . . . della tua pace," her graciousness seems to be inspired by true magnanimity: it is precisely that "peace" which she craves so ardently (and which is surely reflected in her description of the waters of the river Po: "dove 'l Po discende / per aver pace"), a peace which she will never know, that she would like to have assured for the Pilgrim. And how ready she is to comply with his requests; to his summons (81), "Venite a noi parlar," she answers,

> "Di quel che udire e che parlar vi piace
> noi udiremo e parleremo a voi . . ." (94–95)

> ("Whatever pleases you to hear or speak
> we will hear and we will speak about with you . . .").

And when he asks her to tell him how Paolo and she had allowed themselves to confess their love to each other (118–120), she acquiesces, even though the telling will cause her pain:

310

E quella a me: "Nessun maggior dolore
    che ricordarsi del tempo felice
    ne la miseria; e ciò sa 'l tuo dottore.
Ma s'a conoscer la prima radice
    del nostro amor tu hai cotanto affetto,
    dirò come colui che piange e dice . . ." (121–126)

(And she to me: "There is no greater pain
    than to remember, in our present grief,
    past happiness—as well your teacher knows!
But if your great desire is to learn
    the very root of such a love as ours,
    I shall tell you, but in words of flowing tears . . .").

Nor is she sparing with her words—which seem to flow naturally from her heart.

Her courtesy extends also to Virgil, though he has not addressed her; on two occasions she shows her awareness of his presence. In lines 94–95, when she promises to answer the Pilgrim's first request, she shifts from the *tu* with which she had been addressing him to the *vi* and *voi* that would include Virgil (remembering, no doubt, the form of the Pilgrim's request: "Venite a *noi* parlar"); and before she begins her second confession, she ends her aphorism "Nessun maggior dolore," with a reference to the Pilgrim's "dottore" that she sees before her.[2]

Francesca's aristocratic background is suggested not only by her delicate manners but also by her delicate and often noble language (revealing her familiarity with contemporary literature)—a feature which has impressed most critics, though in describing her style they do little more than point out the "dolce stil nuovo" flavor of her two characterizations of "Love" (100 and 103): "Amor, ch'al cor gentil ratto s'apprende" and "Amor, ch'a nullo amato amar perdona." But her style is not limited to the preciosity of the two lines just mentioned; it reveals a considerable variety of nuances. There is the powerful impact of the entire passage (100–106) beginning with "Amor" and ending "ad una morte," which contains the threefold description of the (sinister) part played by Love in the development of the feelings between her young kinsman and herself, and in the tragic outcome of their feelings. There is the lofty, yet graceful and tender tone of the description of her birthplace (97–99): "Siede la terra dove nata fui. . . ." And there is the delicacy, one might even say the femininity, of her words indirectly alluding to the hideous fact of their murder: "noi che *tignemmo* il mondo di *sanguigno*." Not the basic word *sangue* but its derivative *sanguigno*—and the blood which she mentions is a "tint." Finally the poet has even endowed Francesca with a superb mastery of narrative exposition: the story of her fall, opening so casually, so unpretentiously, with the words, "Noi leggiavamo un giorno per diletto" (127), leads up to the passionately dramatic climax (whose inevitability we are made to feel): ". . . la bocca mi basciò tutto tremante."

The tension is maintained in the following line with its epigrammatic interpretation of causality: "Galeotto fu 'l libro e chi lo scrisse," then the tension subsides with the calm, haunting, accents of the concluding line (that seems to suggest, delicately, the cessation of all activity): "quel giorno più non vi leggemmo avante."

But the more carefully we study the words of the courteous and cultivated Francesca, the more clearly we become aware of the flaws in her character which she is inadvertently revealing. Her basic weakness is her self-centeredness, and this can be seen even in her gracious attitude toward the Pilgrim. That the caressing words which open her address are inspired by gratitude for his expression of compassion, and for the invitation he extended to the lovers, already suggests, if only slightly, her hunger for appreciation, her pleasure at having been singled out for consideration from among the many others flying there: since the Pilgrim treats Francesca this way, he must be "grazioso e benigno."

The implied wish that follows, "Se fosse amico il re de l'universo, / noi pregheremmo lui de la tua pace" (91–92), was earlier characterized as (perhaps) revealing true magnanimity; but while one cannot deny that her wish springs from a generous impulse, one must also sense a frustrated desire on the part of the aristocratic Francesca to use her influence with the powers that be: with the one of highest rank, "il re de l'universo." Surely, the nobly-born Francesca would delight in the opportunity to intercede with a king for a humble pilgrim.[3] Again, as evidence of her graciousness, I have already mentioned her readiness to comply with the Pilgrim's invitation ("Venite a noi parlar"), her words flowing forth so freely. But surely this flow, this effusiveness is slightly ridiculous: in lines 94–95 the Pilgrim's simple *parlare* has been extended to *parlare* and *udire*, and this pair of verbs is (chiastically) repeated:[4] "Di quel che udire e che parlar vi piace / noi udiremo e parleremo a voi" (94–95). Moreover, while here she gives the Pilgrim *carte blanche* to speak on any theme he may desire—instead of pausing at this point (she has already been speaking for three tercets) to allow him to explain what he had wished to talk about when he called the lovers to him, Francesca flows on with a description of her birthplace. And, as she continues, we are reminded that the Pilgrim had expressed his desire to talk to both of the lovers, and she has just acceded to his request in the same terms,[5] yet neither here nor at any other point in the canto will Paolo be given a chance to speak.[6] In fact, except for her reference to *costui* (101 and 104) and *questi* (135), she appears to completely ignore his presence. She is clearly the dominating member of the pair.

As for the theme with which she chooses to continue her speech, we may note the assured way in which she takes for granted the Pilgrim's interest in such a detail as the location of her birthplace. Could it be that, counting on the widespread circulation of her story, she hopes that this allusion to her birthplace will aid the Pilgrim to identify her (as, indeed, it will)? If so, does this not mean that she would be willing to exploit her own scandal in order to let the Pilgrim realize that he is talking to a well-known person?[7]

The poetic style of the description of her birthplace has already been pointed out, but in spite of the undeniable beauty of the passage, it must make the reader smile. Given the speaker, the lofty tone of the opening lines is incongruous: "Siede la terra dove nata fui / su la marina dove 'l Po discende" (97–98). It could recall the words of Adrian in *Purgatorio* XIX, after he has revealed his Papal identity ("scias quod ego fui successor Petri"):

> "Intra Sïestri e Chiaveri s'adima
>   una fiumana bella, e del suo nome
>   lo titol del mio sangue fa sua crima." (100–102)

> ("Between Sestri and Chiaveri descends
>   a lovely stream, and from its name derives
>   the noble title of my family.")

or Cunizza's elaborate self-identification (*Paradiso* IX, 25–32) in topographical terms, which begins:

> "In quella parte de la terra prava
>   italica che siede tra Rialto
>   e le fontane di Brenta e di Piava,
> si leva un colle, e non surge molt'alto,
>   là onde scese già una facella,
>   che fece a la contrada un grande assalto.
> D'una radice nacqui e io ed ella:
>   Cunizza fui chiamata, e qui refulgo . . ."

> ("There in that part of sinful Italy
>   which lies between Rialto's shores and where
>   the Piave and the Brenta rivers spring,
> rises a hill of no great height from which,
>   some years ago, there plunged a flaming torch
>   who laid waste all the countryside around.
> Both he and I were born from the same root:
>   Cunizza was my name, and I shine here
>   for I was overcome by this star's light.")

That Francesca loves to talk, that she knows she talks beautifully and is quite conscious of putting on a performance for the Pilgrim, should be evident by now (incidentally, Francesca is the only woman allowed to speak in the whole of the *Inferno*). Her histrionic self-consciousness is also borne out by certain expressions in her "second confession"; in her first, she needed three tercets to get started (88–96); now, having warmed up, she still needs two (121–126) before she can really begin. In the two tercets opening with "Nessun maggior dolore," we see a figure plunged into grief by the Pilgrim's question but heroically forcing herself to comply with his desire, attempting to adopt a philosophical attitude (the senten-tiousness of "ciò sa 'l tuo dottore"!), only at the end to remind us of the tears she is restraining ("come colui che piange e dice").

Up to the present, Francesca has occasionally been grandiloquent or pompous; she has never been pedantic. But her description of Paolo's kiss, "Questi, che mai da me non fia diviso, / la bocca mi basciò tutto tremante," is preceded by a dependent clause, describing Lancelot's kiss, which con-tains a rare latinate version of the construction *accusativus cum infinitivo*:

> "Quando leggemmo *il disïato riso*
>   *esser basciato* da cotanto amante. . . ." (133–134)

> ("It was when we read about those longed-for lips
>   now being kissed by such a famous lover. . . .")

—literally, "when we read the longed-for lips / to be kissed." Was her choice of construction due to her desire to display her culture, the degree to which she had profited by her extensive reading? Or was it the gentle-woman in her (rather than the blue-stocking) that chose to describe Lancelot's kiss in such antiseptic terms? In either case, with this frigid pre-lude to the account of Paolo's kiss, itself vibrating with passion, we are offered a most incongruous juxtaposition.[8]

Now in Francesca's painful words, "Nessun maggior dolore," used to introduce the story of Paolo's kiss, there is obviously contained an appeal to the Pilgrim for his sympathy. This may remind us of the reason she offers for desiring the Pilgrim's peace: "poi c'hai pietà del nostro mal per-verso"—words that both show her gratitude for his pity and make a further bid for it by referring to her punishment as "mal perverso." And this should make us wonder what other indications she gives of her atti-tude toward the sentence passed upon her; to what extent does she seem to recognize her guilt, her responsibility for her sin?

Francesca's autobiographical account is unique, for twice she tells the story of her love, her sin. The first confession she herself volunteers, re-minding us, in this regard, of Guido da Montefeltro, the only other sinner who takes it upon himself to explain why he is in Hell; her second con-fession is an answer to a question from the Pilgrim who wishes to probe more deeply into the occasion of her fall. (This is the first and only time the Pilgrim will invite a sinner to give his own version of how he yielded to temptation.)

In her twofold account of her love-affair with Paolo, three move-ments are indicated: when she and Paolo fell in love; when they revealed their feelings to each other (while reading the story of Lancelot); Paolo's kiss. (The fourth stage is only hinted at.) At each step she presents herself as the victim of an irresistible force: it was the tyranny of Love that made her reciprocate Paolo's passion, it was the hypnotic spell of the Old French romance that drew their eyes together in a mute avowal, it was the quivering lips of Paolo which brought her to complete surrender.

It is in her description of the first movement—the first movement toward her death—that the irresistibility of the force to which she yields is stressed the most; whereas the power of the Old French romance and that of Paolo's kiss happened to find her vulnerable (as they might not have found another), the power of Love on the person loved is declared to be such that no one could possibly resist it: "Amor, ch'a *nullo amato amar perdona*." (In presenting herself as the victim of an irresistible force she is again like Guido da Montefeltro, and him alone.) And Paolo, too, who began the movement, is presented as obeying a similarly imperious law: "Amor, ch'al cor gentil *ratto s'apprende*," a line evoking the idealistic love sung by Guinizelli and other so-called "dolce stilnovisti."[9]

Thus, according to the two famous lines just quoted, it was not only inevitable that Paolo fall in love with her and she, therefore, with him, but the nature of the love that inspired them was beyond reproach. What, then, are we to think of the words that follow the Guinizellian reminiscence:

> ["Amor, ch'al cor gentil ratto s'apprende,]
> *prese costui de la bella persona*
> *che mi fu tolta . . ."* (100–102)

> (["Love quick to kindle in the gentle heart,]
> *seized this one for the beauty of my body,*
> *torn from me . . .").*

Has Francesca read her poets so carelessly that she can believe that the love they praise will admit of desire for the lady's "beautiful body"? The two ideas, the two kinds of love, here juxtaposed, are mutually exclusive according to the literature she had obviously read. And it must, of course, be the second of these that represents Paolo's love as it really was: sensual love (the simple declarative statement annuls the pretentious relative clause that precedes)—as her love, too, had to be, since she did respond to his feelings. Perhaps Francesca knew full well the nature of the love "ch'al cor gentil ratto s'apprende," which should mean that she saw clearly the difference between that love and the one that brought her to her death. But perhaps she did not see clearly. On the one hand she surely knew that it was the carnal elements of love between her and Paolo that led them to adultery and to Hell; on the other, being a woman, she may have wanted to stress the sweeter, more tender, more exalted aspects of that love and, being well-bred, accustomed to observe the ambiguous code (whereby gentility leads insensibly to hypocrisy) of always showing herself at her best and presenting situations in their most favorable light, she could not face steadily the nature of her sin.[10] And, perhaps, there is also a touch of snobbish poetic aspiration: she must lay claim, somehow, in spite of the evidence, to a love as refined as that treated by the most refined poets.

In the description of the second movement of her love, involving the lovers' revelation to each other of their feelings, even more obvious is the influential role played in their love-affair by literature (in this case a single text), and this is recognized explicitly in Francesca's allusion (137) to the go-between, Galehot, in the Old French romance: "Galeotto fu il libro e chi lo scrisse." But again we must wonder if Francesca was a careless reader, for the event which she is supposedly retelling from the text the lovers read, and which, according to her, inspired Paolo's passionate kiss, never took place in the text in question. As is now well known (and the problem involved has engaged the attention of a number of critics), it was not the timid Lancelot who kissed the "disïato riso" of the queen; it was the sophisticated and coquettish Guinevere who, at the urging of Galehot, decided to kiss the lovesick knight: "et la roine voit que li chevaliers nen ose plus faire, si le prent par le menton e le baise devant Galehot asses longement, si que la Dame de Malohaut seit qu'ele le baise."

It is difficult to believe that Francesca read carelessly the text which made the loves flush and pale, and drew their eyes together. (And, incidentally, careless reading on her part would imply careless reading on the part of Dante, who is letting her retell the story.) It is also difficult to believe—and with this we now approach the third movement of their love—that a kiss given by Guinevere to Lancelot would have inspired Paolo to give a kiss to Francesca (unless, of course, he too were reading carelessly the passage which inspired him to adultery). Indeed, it would be more likely that the Old French text, which they had before their eyes, would have inspired Francesca to follow the queen's example and to kiss Paolo.

And, indeed, I have proposed that the incident of the kiss between Francesca and Paolo was the reverse of what she describes: that it was Francesca who took the initiative in the lovemaking.[11] If this is true, it is now understandable why she also inverted the roles played by Lancelot and Guinevere: since she had made the Old French romance responsible for their kiss, and since she wished to present Paolo as taking the first step in the expression of their guilty love, she had to present the Lancelot of the romance as taking the first step. Two false versions, the first one that she gives (that Lancelot kissed the queen) made necessary by the ensuing one that she plans to give (that Paolo kissed her). Must we then think of Francesca as a calculating person who knowingly tells a double lie in order to put the blame on her lover for what she herself has done—two lies in order to betray?

I think one cannot use the word "calculating" and "knowingly" of Francesca and her misrepresentation (though, in my earlier article, I was somewhat more harsh toward her). If we remember the confusion that she showed in her first confession, how her hypocritical suggestion of the purity of their love is immediately contradicted in the next line by her own reference to her beautiful body—it is difficult to attribute to her, in her second confession, such a degree of mental clarity as could enable her to foresee the necessity of planting one lie in order to make a second one credible. Perhaps, here, too, we have to do with mental confusion, which must also imply moral confusion. Perhaps Francesca, like so many persons concerned with their own prestige, has developed the ability to remember past events in a way that redounds to her credit. It would have been only "normal" if Paolo had been the one to give the first kiss, and so her memory conveniently allows her to believe that this is what happened. She has "forgotten" that it was she who kissed first, inspired by the text they were reading—consequently she must "forget" that in that text it was Guinevere who kissed Lancelot. The image of the self-assured queen who took the timid Lancelot by the chin and kissed him "longuement" had faded in her memory, replaced by a gentle figure of sweet compliancy such as she now "remembers" herself to have been.[12]

So far we have presented Francesca's story of her love with its three movements as if it were a continuous flow from the first to the second to the third. Actually, of course, there is a sharp break after her first confession, ending line 106, which contains a description of the initial stage of her love and a sudden reference to the death of the two lovers. In this confession the second and third stages are not mentioned; we are told only about the birth of Love and, suddenly, about death. And Francesca surely believed that with her depiction of the efficacy of love:

"Amor, ch'al cor gentil ratto s'apprende
. . . .
Amor, ch'a nullo amato amar perdona
. . . .
Amor condusse noi ad una morte,"

her story is told. But the Pilgrim (moved to tender compassion by her words, and perhaps puzzled by her implication that such a sweet love could lead to sin and death) asks her a question (118–120): how did it come about that love allowed them to recognize their dubious desires and reveal them to each other? (He asks her to tell him about the second stage.) Francesca will answer this question by telling about the day when she and Paolo read the love story of Lancelot, which moved them so deeply—ending with a delicate allusion to the third stage (sensuous indulgence) about which the Pilgrim had not inquired.

But the words that introduce her second account are curious indeed, and they seem to reveal another example of confusion or disingenuousness on her part. Francesca agrees to tell the Pilgrim, since he so desires, about "the first root" of their love:

"Ma s'a conoscer la prima radice
    del nostro amor tu hai cotanto affetto,
    dirò . . ." (124–126)

("But if your great desire is to learn
   the very root of such a love as ours,
   I shall tell you . . .").

But this is not what the Pilgrim had inquired about (in fact, Francesca had already described "the first root" in her description of love); he is urging her to tell him how the first tender stirrings then *took shape*, how the un-avowed longings were allowed to reveal themselves—which is, in fact, what Francesca proceeds to do in her reference to the Old French prose romance. Why then does she preface her account of the reading of the book with a reference to "la prima radice"? Is she trying to pretend that their reading together represented the very beginning, "the root" of their love; that, if it had not been for the text of *Lancelot du Lac*, they would never have fallen in love? This, of course, would be in flagrant contra-diction to her first analysis of causality: the love "ch'al cor gentil ratto s'apprende" needs no book.[13] The total confusion manifest in Francesca's attempts to remember, and to explain—a confusion mainly caused by her determination to see herself, and to present herself, in as favorable a light as possible—this has been sensed by none of the critics I have read.[14] In fact, Foscolo was able to speak of the "truthfulness [which] beautifies her confession of desire" and Renato Poggioli (see n. 5 above) says that she "has given proof of intellectual and moral courage by facing truth in all its nakedness" (p. 339).

We have already seen that Francesca in her two confessions uses every means possible to excuse her sin by presenting it as caused by forces beyond her control, and of course we could not possibly have expected to find in her words any indication of repentance: it is the law of Hell that the sinner, once damned for his failure to repent on earth, is not given a second chance to repent. But, in addition to a total lack of repentance, do we also find any indications of defiance against Divine Justice (if so, we must expect them to be implicit rather than explicit)? Many scholars believe to have found them, insofar as they read into Francesca's words a fierce loyalty to her lover, to her love, to her sin. They speak in terms of an undying love which has triumphed over death and over Hell, a love in which she glories. Perhaps Grandgent may be quoted briefly as one of the more sober exponents of that theory: "Amid the tortures of Hell, where all is hatred, her love does not forsake her, and she glories in the thought that she and Paolo shall never be parted."[15]

The two passages that have inspired these words of Grandgent, and on which others, too, have based their opinion, are the following:

"Amor . . .
   mi prese del costui piacer sì forte
   che, come vedi, *ancor non m'abbandona.*" (103–105)

("Love . . .
   seized me so strongly with delight in him

that, as you see, he never leaves my side.")

and

"Quando leggemmo . . . ,
. . . .
questi, *che mai de me non fia diviso*
la bocca mi basciò. . . ." (133–136)
. . . .

(" . . . when we read . . . ,
. . . this one, who shall never leave my side,
then kissed my mouth. . . .")

On the surface the words italicized in each passage may seem to justify the interpretation suggested above: happy, triumphant insistence on the inseparability of the two lovers. But such a "triumph over Hell" would contradict the principles of divine punitive justice as these are reflected throughout the *Inferno*. How can we believe that the poet would make an exception of Paolo and Francesca, whom he presents (as a lesson to the Pilgrim) as the first sinners he encounters in Hell?

But there are other reasons that speak against this romantic amoral interpretation. In the first place eternal togetherness in itself is not necessarily a cause for exultation, it may also be the cause of deepest anguish (one may think of Sartre's *Huis clos*). We must see Francesca's words as ambiguous, and I prefer to take them in the second, more tragic sense. We cannot, of course, imagine that their constant companionship represents a choice on the part of the two lovers, the indulgence of a mutual desire. No, if they go always together it must be because they are forced to do so (together in Hell because they were slain together in their sin). And how could it make Francesca happy—or rather, how could it alleviate her suffering—to know herself never to be free of the naked body of her dead lover, this constant reminder of passion spent, of the sin that condemned them, of shameful exposure and death? Rather, their inseparability could well be the bitterest aspect of their punishment. And the silent, weeping figure of Paolo certainly does not suggest one who is glorying in his love.[16]

Nor, during the scene where Francesca holds the center of the stage, does she give the slightest indication of enjoying the presence of her lover. We have already seen how Paolo is immediately eclipsed as soon as she begins to speak. She never turns to him, even for a brief moment, to address him. As has already been said, if it were not for the *costui* and the *questi* with which she reminds us of his presence, we could easily forget that he is on stage (until she finishes speaking, and we learn that Paolo has been weeping all the while). She does not call him by his name or by any endearing term (and, of course, there is no *tu*); she merely points to a nearby figure: *costui, questi*. These two deictic, distantiating pronouns evoke a minimum of humanity, of individuality.

As we listen to Francesca's words, with their adverbial reminders of eternity, "che . . . *ancor* non mi abbandona," and "che *mai* da me non fia diviso," referring to the figure who will always be by her side, we must hear in her words bitterness, hopelessness, dull anguish, terrible resignation.

In fact, I am so convinced that Francesca loathes Paolo's presence that I should like to offer a new interpretation of the much-debated line 102: "e 'l modo ancor m'offende." I agree with those who see in *modo* a reference to the manner of the lovers' death and, more specifically, with those who see, in the "offense" mentioned, the exposure of the lovers in their intimacy.[17] But there may well be an additional element in this "offense": not only were they exposed together, they were killed together. For this reason, they must remain together forever in Hell, and I believe it is this that "offends" Francesca more than the temporary exposure of the lovers in their intimacy. Note that the *ancor* of line 102 is paralleled by the *ancor* that follows three lines later which, in turn, points toward the *mai* of line 135:

> " . . . la bella persona
> che mi fu tolta; e 'l modo *ancor* m'offende." (101–102)

> " . . . come vedi, *ancor* non m'abbandona." (105)

> "questi, che *mai* da me non fia diviso,
>   la bocca mi basciò. . . ." (135–136)

Thus, her two references to their fated inseparability are stylistically linked with the reference to the manner of their death ("e 'l modo . . ."). The "manner" of their death "still" torments her, for she is "still" linked with Paolo who will "never" leave her.

Thus Francesca's words themselves spell out her doom. For a brief moment, with the Pilgrim, she could perform, she could pretend, she could be the gracious lady she had been in the beautiful life on earth. But when the Pilgrim, with his "doctor" will have taken his leave, she will be left alone with her silent lover Paolo, in Hell, forever.

We have seen the Pilgrim prostrate and unconscious on the floor of Hell, symbolizing the subjection of his reason to sentiment. This is Francesca, the figure of a woman so appealing on the surface and, within, so vain, so confused, and ultimately so treacherous to her lover, who stirred the Pilgrim to such overwhelming compassion. This is the figure, condemned to Hell for having indulged in adulterous, incestuous lust (of which she is totally unrepentant), who has caused the Pilgrim to fail so ignominiously his test. For surely his encounter with Francesca was intended as a test—a test of his ability to see Francesca's sin for what it was.

Now, granted that I am right about the falsity that I see revealed in Francesca's words, one might object that the Pilgrim in his brief encounter with her, dazed and shaken as he had to be by his recent experiences, could hardly be expected to take in the various levels of Francesca's *vanitas*. But it was not for vanity, or emptiness, or phoniness, or any other flaw in her personality that Francesca was condemned to Hell; she was condemned to the Second Circle for her lust. And that she was lustful the Pilgrim did know. It is not because he failed to analyze her personality with more acumen that he is tacitly condemned by the author of the *Divine Comedy*; it is because he reacted to her personality, he reacted to Francesca as to an individual lady, with a name of her own, such as might be encountered in society (or in romantic literature)—and not to the incarnation of lust unrepented. Instead of allowing her charm to mitigate her sinfulness, the Pilgrim should have seen her sinfulness against the background of her arrant lack of penitence—as revealed so clearly in her words.

I have said that Francesca is the only woman in the *Inferno* allowed to speak; and she is the first speaker in Hell, the first sinner. In the role she plays with Paolo, this "first sinner" must remind us of the first human being to sin in Christian history. Is not Francesca Eve? And not content with having seduced Paolo in the flesh, this *figura Evae* has attempted successfully to seduce the Pilgrim, who is Everyman, into committing not the sin of lust itself but what has been defined as the essence of Lust: the subjection of reason to emotion. And this is precisely what the original Eve did to Adam, the father of Everyman. And this is why we see the Pilgrim prostrate and unconscious on the floor of Hell at the close of the canto. In fact, the abstract formula offered by Virgil defines not only the essence of lust but also the essence of sin itself—which first came into the world through Eve.

Canto V of the *Inferno* that introduces us to the realm of the damned in Hell is the only one in which Dante the Poet allows the Pilgrim to be tempted by a sinner. His *descensus ad infernum* had to begin with his total surrender to temptation.

NOTES

1. Two striking exceptions to the tendency to glorify Francesca are represented by the studies of Busnelli ("La ruina del secondo cerchio e Francesca da Rimini," in *Miscellanea dantesca* [Padova, 1922], 51–60) and Trombadori ("Saggio critico sull'episodio di Francesca da Rimini," in *Annuario . . . 1927–28 del R. Liceo-Ginnasio M. Foscarini, Venezia*). Trombadori sees Francesca·as "la donna demoniaca che la bella persona, gli allettamenti sensuali, adopera ad assopire la virtù del cor gentile e transcinarlo alla perdizione." Busnelli finds in her words "note dolenti, nelle quali fremeranno gli impeti della colpa c della disperazione, l'ostinazione nel pervertimento sensuale, e lo scianto dell'immenso rancore" (p. 54). But the two treatments are determined by quite disparate points of view: Busnelli makes no attempt to analyze Francesca's words in any detail nor does he treat her as an individual; she is a paradigmatic figure, representing the unrepent sinner condemned to Hell. And if her words reveal desperation and perseverance in evil, it

is because, according to Catholic dogma (Busnelli quotes Thomas Aquinas at greater length than he does Francesca) such are the characteristics of the state of mind of the damned. To Trombadori, however, she is a figure in her own right and should be seen as the guilty one of the pair of lovers, having seduced the more spiritual Paolo into sin. But the evidence that he offers for his interpretation (an interpretation which Barbi rightly rejects) is highly questionable: for the greater purity of Paolo he can appeal only to the line "Amor, che *al cor gentil* ratto s'apprende" (100) which attributes to Paolo a "cor gentil." and in order to justify his interpretation of the dominant role played by Francesca he was forced to interpret line 103, "Amor, che *a nullo amato* amar perdona" as referring not to herself, as all other critics have assumed, but to Paolo; in other words, she would be saying that the kind of love that seized her demanded that she be loved in turn. But such an interpretation of line 103 would completely destroy the logical consistency of the two tercets (100–105) in which it is embedded.

Between the two extreme interpretations of Francesca there can, of course, be found, especially in recent years, judgments of a more sober, unbiased nature.

2. I believe that Francesca's words "il tuo dottore" refer to Virgil: not to the historical Virgil (whose epic poem she may or may not have read) but simply to the figure she sees accompanying the Pilgrim; Francesca easily could have sensed the monitory role of the Pilgrim's companion ("il tuo dottore") and, knowing that he is a spirit condemned to Hell, who must regret his happier days on earth, she could attribute to him the sad knowledge he must share with her.

3. Once in the *Purgatorio* and again in the *Paradiso* God is called a King: "rege eterno," but in both cases his majesty is indicated within the vast framework of celestial mechanics; he is a Being unapproachable, from whom no individual would solicit a favor for another individual—as Francesca, to judge by her words, would seem to think possible:

> se fosse amico il re de l'universo,
> noi pregheremmo lui de la tua pace. . . .

4. According to Michele Barbi (*Dante* [Firenze, 1952], 197) the tercet 94–96, containing the words *parlare* and *udire* twice expressed, has been described by G. Vitali as "lungo e inutile preambulo a un discorso che sarà così breve." And the terzina describing Francesca's birthplace as well as the three preceding tercets he considers pleonastic. He, however, is evidently here voicing criticism of Dante's style, not of Francesca's tendency to loquacity.

5. Poggioli ("Paolo and Francesca: Tragedy or Romance?" *PMLA* LXXII: 328–29), however, suggests that Francesca's *noi* in line 95, "Noi udiremo e parleremo a voi," does not include a reference to Paolo, but is a *pluralis majestatis* (he also interprets the *voi* of the same line as an honorific).

6. It is true that in the last half of the scene with Francesca the Pilgrim himself excludes Paolo from the conversation by addressing himself to Francesca alone.

Incidentally, according to Poggioli "many scholars" have argued that Paolo is indeed given the chance to speak—if only one line: from Francesca's first confession of twenty lines (88–107) they would remove the last one ("Caina attende chi a vita ci spense"), referring to the punishment awaiting the lovers' murderer, to put it into the mouth of the murdered brother. In this way the following line ("Queste parole *da lor* ci fur porte") can be interpreted literally as referring to two speakers and not, as most critics assume, to Francesca who has been speaking for the two of them.

But even though the use of the plural pronoun must be "explained away" if Francesca has been the only speaker (compare also line 109: "Quand'io intesi *quell'anime offense* . . ."), still, what has been proposed to justify the literal interpretation of *da lor* is surely unacceptable: it would imply incredible carelessness on the part of the narrator (who would have failed to announce the change from one speaker to another); moreover, if the hitherto mute Paolo were suddenly to chime in, this would offer a comically melodramatic conclusion to the deeply moving words of Francesca.

7. The possibility that Francesca might be willing to exploit her own scandal in order to let the Pilgrim realize that he is talking to a well-known person—this apparently does not shock Barbi, who has this to say of the Pilgrim's recognition of Francesca and of his calling her by name (*Dante*, p. 196):

> Quanta tenerezza in quel semplice vocativo premesso ad ogni altra parola! Giunge come il conforto di persona familiare. Il poeta mostra d'essere già stato toccato nel mondo dal caso pietoso di quella gentile, e riesce a farle subito intendere che partecipa al suo dolore *con l'interesse che si ha per persona ben nota.*

Ercole Di Marco (*Letture dell'Inferno,* ed. V. Vettori [Milano, 1963], 70–71) believes that the *noi* of line 90 ("noi che tignemmo il mondo di sanguigno") refers not to all those of "Dido's flock" but only to Francesca and her lover. But not only would this reveal a degree of self-infatuation (of which Di Marco does not seem to be aware) hardly conceivable even in the self-infatuated Francesca: it would imply her belief that the Pilgrim was able to recognize her, which, in turn, would make unnecessary her self-identification by reference to her birthplace.

8. Is it not possible that Francesca's latinate construction ("il disiato riso / esser baciato") would have been ridiculous even in Latin? Was *legere* one of the verbs that took the *accusativus cum infinitivo?*

9. Barbi (*Dante*, p. 202), contesting such critics as Romani and Parodi, believes that Francesca's pronouncements about love are "pur dottrina di Dante"—instead of representing her own transformation of a personal experience into a universal law for the purpose of self-justification.

10. Could the same failure to recognize the extent of her sinfulness also be reflected in Francesca's words: "noi che tignemmo il mondo di sanguigno"? (This line has already been discussed from a stylistic point of view: the "delicacy" of her choice of words.) Perhaps this self-characterization is meant to imply that the only sin committed by those in "Dido's flock" was that of staining the earth with blood.

11. I have argued that Dido's name, not given in Virgil's list of lustful women, was reserved to be applied to the whole group of lustful spirits seen by the Pilgrim ("la schiera ov'è Dido"). Actually, it would be more accurate to say that Dido's name is reserved to be applied to Francesca and Paolo: it is only after the Pilgrim's attention has been called to the figures of the two lovers and he has invited them to stop and speak with him that the phrase in question appears:

> Quali colombe dal disio chiamate . . .
> vegnon per l'aere dal voler portate
> cotali uscir *de la schiere ov'è Dido,*
> a noi venendo . . . (82–86).

Why should Dante the Poet wish to remind his reader of Dido just when Francesca makes her appearance? If we turn to the scene in Book IV of the *Aeneid* describing the first intimacy of Dido and Aeneas, we learn that it was Dido who took the initiative in the lovemaking.

12. Caretti (*Il Canto V dell' "Inferno"* [Firenze, 1967], 35), though he admits that in her first confession Francesca is confused and seeks only to justify herself, believes that in the second one she abandons herself to true confession with absolute frankness.

13. Plinio Carli (*Saggi danteschi ricordi e scritti vari* [Firenze, 1954], 3–17), who believes that the love of Paolo and Francesca was pure at the beginning and would have remained so if they had not revealed their feelings to each other, is able to see in the reading of the *Lancelot du Lac* "la prima radice del nostro amor" since it marked the beginning of their love as a shared feeling, and he distinguishes the "nostro amor" of this line describing their passion from the "amor" mentioned three times at the beginning of Francesca's confession. The possibility of the innocent beginnings of the adulterous love of Paolo and Francesca has also been suggested by Professor Simonelli in Volume 30 of *Studi danteschi* [Florence, 1951], 235.

14. Certain scholars (Brandeis and Montano) have seen that Francesca was confused as to the relationship between her sin and her punishment, and this is necessarily true of all of those condemned to hell; since they have not repented, they cannot see their sin for what it truly is. But the "total confusion" to which I refer involves a·network of inconsistencies that runs through her confessions from beginning to end.

15. Compare with Grandgent's picture of sin triumphant, as exemplified in Francesca, that of Torraca (*Studi danteschi* [Naples, 1912], 427):

> Ah sì, lealmente le ha tenuto fede [Paolo a Francesca]; con lei, tra le braccia di lei, morì; fu e sarà con lei, come aveva promesso; onde il grido trionfale, che sfida la bufera e l'eternità della pena, e sembrerebbe sfidar il cielo stesso, se non vi si potesse distinguere una nota di profonda gratitudine: *Mai da me non fia diviso!*

According to Barbi (*Dante*, pp. 180–181) certain scholars (Fedeli Romani and Enrico Corradini) have seen in the treatment of Francesca "persino la glorificazione del talento sulla ragione e la rivendicazione dei diritti dell'umanità contro i divieti della religione."

16. Barbi, for one, in his polemic with Foscolo, ventures the same pessimistic interpretation of the inseparability of the lovers, and mentions the detail of Paolo's tears (*Dante*, p. 172).

17. Some scholars, Pagliaro for one (*Saggi di critica semantica* [Messina, 1953], 335–55), believe that the *modo* of line 102 ("e 'l modo ancor m'offende") refers to the "manner" of Paolo's love for Francesca: she is still "offended" at the thought of his violent passion. The favorite interpretation of those who see Francesca as complaining about the manner of her death is that she regrets having been prevented thereby from repentance. (Cf. Pagliaro for his summary of the different interpretations of this line.)

Iconographic Parody in *Inferno* XXI

CHRISTOPHER KLEINHENZ

Although critical opinion is generally divided regarding the definition of comic elements and *comicità* in the *Divina Commedia*, the grotesque and farcical activities of the Malebranche in *Inferno* XXI–XXII should certainly give us some indication of Dante's sense of the parodic and ludicrous.[1] More general consensus has been reached on the similarity of the scene in the fifth *bolgia* with those presented on the stage in contemporary religious dramas, particularly in the transalpine regions, and the interaction here between "performers" (devils, sinners) and "observers" (Dante, Virgil) most probably derives from those interludes in medieval plays when the "devils" would run about among the audience, inspiring both laughter and fear.[2] In the *Inferno*, of course, there is no such "interlude", no "intermission" in the performance, nor are the *dramatis personae* wearing masks and costumes. Indeed, the everpresent, diabolical undercurrent attacks the superficially "festive" atmosphere and gradually subverts it.

Our perception of the events in Cantos XXI–XXII is determined in large part by two contradictory thematic currents: devilish playfulness and diabolical cunning. On the one hand, the devilish antics, or *diableries*, seem to provide the mainstay of the action, affecting all the participants and reducing them to a common denominator;[3] even Dante the Pilgrim expresses his camaraderie with the proverbial "Ahi fiera compagnia! ma ne la chiesa / coi santi, e in taverna coi ghiottoni" (*Inf.* XXII, 14–15).[4] On the other hand, since every coin has two sides, the *rovescio* of this "innocent" activity may be glimpsed from time to time in the machinations contrived both by the devils (Malacoda's lie, which aims to entrap Dante and Virgil) and by the sinners (Ciampolo's ruse calculated to free himself from the Malebranche). There are, then, in simultaneous operation, two levels on which the events of these cantos should be understood: 1) grotesque humor and 2) profound seriousness, the latter underlying and consistently undermining the former.

Several factors contribute to the successful representation of this duality. One is the basic and ironic dichotomy between appearance and reality. Dante extends the opening simile by describing the intense activity in the Venetian shipyard:

> Quale ne l'arzanà de' Viniziani
> bolle l'inverno la tenace pece
> a rimpalmare i legni lor non sani,
>   ché navicar non ponno—in quella vece
> chi fa suo legno novo e chi ristoppa
> le coste a quel che più vïaggi fece;
>   chi ribatte da proda e chi da poppa;
> altri fa remi e altri volge sarte;
> chi terzeruolo e artimon rintoppa.
>   (*Inf.* XXI, 7–15)

The impression created by this image is one of openness, energy and productivity, and consequently this well-populated scene in the Arsenal contrasts sharply both with the seemingly deserted *bolgia* and, further, with the unproductive and secretive undertakings of the grafters. Just as these secular counterparts to the simonists, ignoring the greater and more important needs of the state,[5] thought in life only of personal gain, so here in Hell they continue their nefarious operations in darkness (under the pitch) and with deceit (the tricks played on their guardians, the Malebranche). The nature of the *contrapasso* has, therefore, a direct relationship to the overall structure of the episode. By concealing the sinners, the pitch itself—bubbling, hot and black—presents a false appearance, which initially "deceives" the Pilgrim as to its true content:

> I' vedea lei, ma non vedëa in essa
> mai che le bolle che 'l bollor levava,
> e gonfiar tutta, e riseder compressa.
>   (*Inf.* XXI, 19–21)

The dichotomy between appearance and reality may be seen even more clearly in the two lies, the first spoken by Malacoda, who intends to entrap the wayfarers by telling them a half-truth:

> "Più oltre andar per questo
> iscoglio non si può, però che giace
> tutto spezzato al fondo l'arco sesto.
>   E se l'andare avante pur vi piace,
> andatevene su per questa grotta;
> presso è un altro scoglio che via face.
>   Ier, più oltre cinqu' ore che quest'otta,
> mille dugento con sessanta sei
> anni compié che qui la via fu rotta."
>   (*Inf.* XXI, 106–114)

The reference here to the Harrowing of Hell (which comprises the true portion of the speech) is not without significance, as we will see later in this essay.

The second lie is told by the barrator from Navarre, known as Ciampolo, who as it were pays the Malebranche back in kind with a deceitful intrigue of his own; in exchange for his freedom he "promises" to make other sinners come out of the pitch:[6]

> " . . . io, seggendo in questo loco stesso,
>   per un ch'io son, ne farò venir sette
> quand'io suffolerò, com' è nostro uso
> di fare allor che fori alcun si mette."
>   Cagnazzo a cotal motto levò 'l muso,
> crollando 'l capo, e disse: "Odi malizia
> ch'elli ha pensata per gittarsi giuso!".
>   Ond' ei, ch'avea lacciuoli a gran divizia,
> rispuose: "Malizioso son io troppo,
> quand' io procuro a' mis maggior trestizia."
>   (*Inf.* XXII, 102–111)

Another manner of enhancing the duality of vision in these cantos involves the use of certain parodic elements. The "trumpet" blast, on whose note Canto XXI ends ("ed elli avea del cul fatto trombetta," v. 139), gives rise to the marvelous mock-heroic introduction to Canto XXII, where Dante, by "elevating" this *diversa cennamella*, effectively lowers it to its proper level and underscores its base nature:

> Io vidi già cavalier muover campo,
> e cominciare stormo e far lor mostra,
> e talvolta partir per loro scampo;
>   corridor vidi per la terra vostra,
> o Aretini, e vidi gir gualdane,
> fedir torneamenti e correr giostra;
>   quando con trombe, e quando con campane,
> con tamburi e con cenni di castella,
> e con cose nostrali e con istrane;
>   né già con sì diversa cennamella
> cavalier vidi muover né pedoni,
> né nave a segno di terra o di stella.
>   (*Inf.* XXII, 1–12)

Litotes is incorporated for ironic effect, as, for example, when the devil declares that everyone in Lucca is a "barattier, *fuor che Bonturo*" (*Inf.* XXI, 41 emphasis mine). Bonturo Dati is, of course, the most notorious criminal of all.

Irony is also present in the allusion to religious art, which is obviously not immune from ridicule, not "sacred" as it were. In Canto XXI the Santo Volto of Lucca furnishes an appropriate referent for the irreverent remarks of the devils. Having just been hurled into the pitch by the devil, the unidentified Lucchese barrator

> . . . tornò sù convolto;
> ma i demon che del ponte avean coperchio,

gridar: "Qui non ha loco il Santo Volto!
qui si nuota altrimenti che nel Serchio!"
(*Inf.* XXI, 46–49)

Here, as in other places, in the *Commedia*, Dante expects his readers to have a certain familiarity with the object in question (the Santo Volto, a crucifix reputedly carved by Nicodemus), so that they will be able to understand the full import of the reference.[7] Because of its dark wood and particular veneration in Lucca, the "Holy Face" is especially pertinent to the events at hand, as Singleton's gloss of the verse makes abundantly clear:[8]

> *Convolto*, 'hunched up.' His shape suggests to the humorous demons the attitude of prayer. But the meaning of *convolto*, in this context, may well be 'rump up'—and in this case it would be a rump covered with blackest pitch. Now the most striking feature of the *Holy Face* is that it is ebony black. The thrust, then, and the devilish taunting humor are therefore the more pungent.

The generally parodic atmosphere of these cantos reaches a high (or, perhaps better, low?) point with this allusion; indeed, it would be fair to say that the Santo Volto is actually present on the scene, but in the parodic guise of its infernal opposite or perversion.

It is not surprising that Dante should have recourse here to the figurative or plastic arts as a means of glossing his poem. In fact, this occurs two cantos earlier, where, as Singleton has rightly noted,[9] the upended position of the simonists in the "baptismal fonts" recalls the usual representation of Simon Magus in medieval art. Several parallels and connections between *Inferno* XIX and XXI–XXIII will help clarify the points in question. As suggested above, the two sins punished in the third and fifth *bolge* are complementary, corruption in the Church (simony) having as its secular counterpart graft in public office. Moreover, both episodes are partially based on specific autobiographical details: in Canto XIX Dante refers overtly (but enigmatically) to his breaking of a baptismal font in San Giovanni;[10] in Cantos XXI–XXIII the fact that Dante himself was accused (albeit falsely) of barratry lies behind and informs the events. Although the accusation is not mentioned in Cantos XXI–XXIII, knowledge of it enables us to understand the Pilgrim's extreme anxiety in this *bolgia*, and it also helps to explain why this should be the only time in the *Commedia* when Dante is constantly threatened with real physical harm.[11] Furthermore, with one notable exception, it is only in these two *bolge* that Virgil carries his protégé.[12] In Canto XIX this action, as a token of his affection, demonstrates primarily his approval of Dante's rebuke of Nicholas III (and of simonists in general);[13] in Cantos XXI–XXIII it is motivated by his concern for his charge's safety and by the necessity of escaping the real menace posed by the Malebranche. Finally, in addition to the above points, the incorporation of parodic inversion, as seen in the upside-down position of the simonists and in the ironic use made of the Santo Volto, would point to a common principle behind and inspiration for the creation of these two episodes.

I would argue, therefore, that just as medieval art establishes a frame of reference for the interpretation of Canto XIX, here in Canto XXI, through the allusion to one work of art (the Santo Volto), Dante gives us an indication, a clue, as to how we should read and interpret the entire episode. Indeed, by asking that we conceive and visualize an important part of the scene in artistic terms, he encourages us to consider the possibility of other artistic parallels which, perhaps less obvious than the Santo Volto, are no less important. Along these lines, I would like to suggest a further iconographic (and ultimately literary) interpretation of one element of this episode that should enrich our appreciation and understanding of Dante's art.

The formal action of the fifth *bolgia* begins when Dante sees a

> . . . diavol nero
> correndo su per lo scoglio venire.
> > (*Inf.* XXI, 29–30)

He continues by describing the devil and by reporting his words and actions:

> Ahi quant' elli era ne l'aspetto fero!
> e quanto mi parea ne l'atto acerbo,
> con l'ali aperte e sovra i piè leggero!
> L'omero suo, ch'era aguto e superbo,
> carcava un peccator con ambo l'anche,
> e quei tenea de' piè ghermito 'l nerbo.
> Del nostro ponte disse: "O Malebranche,
> ecco un de li anzïan di Santa Zita!
> Mettetel sotto, ch'i' torno per anche
> a quella terra, che n'è ben fornita:
> ogn'uom v'è barattier, fuor che Bonturo;
> del no, per li denar, vi si fa *ita*."
> Là giù 'l buttò, e per lo scoglio duro
> si volse; e mai non fu mastino sciolto
> con tanta fretta a seguitar lo furo.
> > (*Inf.* XXI, 31–45)

The sinner subsequently returns to the surface of the pitch, *convolto*, and this sight elicits the sacrilegious jeers of the Malebranche relating to the Santo Volto.

The grotesque image which the devil projects in his first appearance was likened by Benvenuto da Imola to that of a butcher carrying the carcass of an animal:[14]

> Quod iste daemon portabat unum peccatorem in spatula, et
> corpus pendebat per renes cum capite deorsum, et diabolus cum

unguibus suis tenebat eum ante per pedes, sicut recte macellar-
ius portat animal jungulatum nigrum ad macellum ad
excoriandum et vendendum ipsum.

And this has become the standard interpretation of the image.

Of the numerous critics and commentators on this canto, no one has,
to my knowledge, noted that the figure of the devil who carries the
sinner would appear to be a direct imitation and parody of the artistic
representation of Christ the Good Shepherd, who bears the lost sheep on
his shoulders.[15] Several passages in both the Old and the New Testaments
provide the literary basis for this manner of depiction:[16] for example, the
parable of the lost sheep in Luke (15:4–6):

> Quis ex vobis homo, qui habet centum oves: et si perdiderit unam ex
> illis, nonne dimittit nonaginta novem in deserto, e vadit ad illam quae
> perierat, donec inveniat eam? Et cum invenerit eam, imponit in hume-
> ros suos gaudens: et veniens domum convocat amicos et vicinos, dicens
> illis: Congratulamini mihi, quia inveni ovem meam, quae perierat?

and the following more explicit passage in John (10:11, 14, 27–28):

> Ego sum pastor bonus. Bonus pastor animam suam dat pro ovibus
> suis. . . . Ego sum pastor bonus: et cognosco meas, et cognoscunt me
> meae. . . . Oves meae vocem meam audiunt, et ego cognosco eas, et
> sequuntur me: et ego vitam aeternam do eis, et non peribunt in aeter-
> num, et non rapiet eas quisquam de manu mea.

Besides specific references to this tradition in patristic literature,[17] the
Good Shepherd was a very popular figure and theme in early Christian
art.[18] Early on, as demonstrated by his appearance on numerous sar-
cophagi, the *Pastor Bonus* was associated typologically with the concepts
of baptism and resurrection. In addition to these associations, the notion
of Christ as Good Shepherd is complemented and enriched by his descrip-
tion in the Apocalypse (7:15–17) as the Agnus[19] who functions in the role
of psychopomp:

> Ideo sunt ante thronum Dei, et serviunt ei die ac nocte in templo eius:
> et qui sedet in throno, habitabit super illos: non esurient, neque sitient
> amplius; nec cadet super illos sol, neque ullus aestus: quoniam Agnus,
> qui in medio throni est, reget illos et deducet eos ad vitae fontes aq-
> uarum, et absterget Deus omnem lacrymam ab oculis eorum.

These two related aspects of Christ—*Pator Bonus* and *Agnus Psychopompos*—
were conflated early in the Christian era, as may be observed in the
following passage taken from a prayer for the dead in the Gelasian Sacra-
mentary:[20]

> Debitum humani corporis sepeliendi officium fidelium more com-
> plentes. Deum, cui omnia vivunt, fideliter deprecemur: ut hoc corpus a
> nobis in infirmitate sepultum, in virtute et ordine sanctorum resuscitet:
> et ejus animam sanctis fidelibus jubeat adgregari; cuique in judicio mis-

ericordiam tribuat: quemque morte redemptum, debitis solutum, Patri reconciliatum, boni Pastoris humeris reportatum, in comitatu aeterni Regis perenni gaudio et sanctorum consortio perfrui concedat. Per Dominum nostrum.

Although the popularity of the Good Shepherd as an artistic and literary motif waned in the later Middle Ages, we do find some evidence of its continued vitality.[21] It is very appropriate for the present study that several such artistic examples are found in Lucca. The baptismal font in San Frediano is adorned with a series of relief sculptures, executed by a certain magister Robertus, perhaps in 1177.[22] In one of these, Christ is depicted carrying the lamb on his shoulders and standing in the middle of a group of six figures, who have been identified variously as allegorical representations of the days of the week[23] or as prophets.[24] During a sojourn in Lucca, Dante may have viewed this very baptismal font, or another of these representations, and may thus have come into direct contact with the traditional image of the Good Shepherd; and more than likely he viewed the Santo Volto under similar circumstances.[25] Although purely hypothetical, such an encounter in Lucca would be fortuitous for the unity of thought, the coordination of images and the presentation of events in this canto. It is also possible, of course, that, if not in Lucca, Dante could have received his iconographic inspiration from viewing representations of the *Pastor Bonus* in the numerous churches in Rome during his stay there.[26]

In the anti-clerical literature of the later Middle Ages, the image of the Good Shepherd is employed ironically and parodically, as, for example, in the following verses from the *Apocalypsis Goliae Episcopi*:[27]

Vae genti mutilae cornutis ducibus!
qui mulctant mutilos armatis frontibus,
dum habet quilibet foenum in cornibus,
non pastor ovium sed pastus ovibus.
Non tantum cogitat ille de miseris,
de claudis ovibus, aegris vel teneris,
quantum de compoto lactis et velleris;
sic ovem perditam refert in humeris.
Si vulgi noverit excessus pauculos,
causatur fidei laesos articulos,
trahit jus ovium in causae tribulos,
vellens exuvias et mungens loculos.
Errantem sequitur grex errans praevium,
quem pastor devius ducens per devium,
post lac et vellera, dat carnes ovium
luporum dentibus et rostris avium.
(vv. 129–44)

Although he does not refer overtly to Christ as the Good Shepherd in his works, Dante, by inveighing against "Bad Shepherds" on more than one occasion, demonstrates his familiarity both with the general concept and with this specific kind of adaptation.[28] Moreover, he endows certain characters (especially Virgil) with pastoral attributes, as will be made clear below.

Against this artistic and literary background, the scene in Canto XXI assumes greater significance: the devil who hauls the sinner so crudely on his shoulders would be the antithesis of Christ who gently bears the lost sheep (= repentant soul) back to the fold. Furthermore, in this Dantean context the devil acts as the psychopomp, bringing the barrator to eternal perdition.[29] Conversely, Christ as Good Shepherd and psychopomp carries the lamb to eternal salvation.[30] The devil's shoulder, described both physically and metaphorically as *aguto e superbo* (*Inf.* XXI, 34), contrasts with the gentle pose and humble manner of Christ in this office. Other attributes which accompany the Good Shepherd, such as the pastoral crook, find their infernal counterparts here in the instruments of torment—variously termed *raffi, graffi, runcigli,* and *uncini*—which the devils wield to keep the sinners under the boiling pitch. Even the devil's words ("del no, per li denar, vi si fa *ita*," *Inf.* XXI, 42), through their use of clerical Latin *ita* (= "yes"), assist in establishing the ecclesiastical frame of reference and express perfectly the ironic, topsy-turvy nature of the events at hand.

A further consideration: given that the Good Shepherd is sometimes shown seated among or standing watch over a flock of sheep,[31] I would suggest that Dante may have intended the parallel to operate on a more inclusive scale, namely that the unidentified *diavol nero* and his twelve named colleagues (Malacoda, Calcabrina et al.) should be perceived and understood as the infernal counterparts of the *Pastor Bonus* (Christ) and his flock (the twelve Apostles). If this is true, then each time this un-named devil returns from Lucca (or, for that matter, from any earthly city) with a sinner, he would be "reenacting," in parody of course, the Harrowing of Hell: not to save souls, but rather to damn them; not to remove meritorious individuals from Hell to Paradise, but rather to bring sinners to the infernal regions; not to demonstrate his power over death and Hell, but rather to indicate his submission to these forces. Such an interpretation would help to establish the context in which Malacoda's reference to Christ's Harrowing of Hell (which shattered the bridges over the sixth *bolgia*) may be better understood and have greater relevancy.[32] Moreover, it would add yet another dimension to this divinely willed, divinely limited and divinely judged farce.[33]

Parodic inversion is a staple of Dante's art in the *Inferno*, which, being a "perfectly established *regio dissimilitudinis*,"[34] is replete with ironic emblems: three-headed Lucifer represents the infernal perversion of the Trinity;[35] the figure of Farinata, emerging waist up from the sepulchre, parodies the image both of the resurrected Christ and of Christ the Man of Sorrows;[36] and so on. Indeed, as noted above, Dante employed the principle of inversion in a very literal sense in the two preceding cantos

(XIX–XX), perhaps so that the reader would be amply conditioned and properly prepared to think along these lines here. In Canto XIX the simonists are upside-down in the "baptismal fonts," and their feet are as it were baptized with fire; and in Canto XX the twisted torso and backward vision torments the diviners, who engaged in fraudulent magical rites in the attempt to foretell the future. Infernal perversions, however, often have their divine and perfect counterparts elsewhere in the poem. Thus, just as the devil parodies the action of the Good Shepherd in Canto XXI, so Virgil in the same context "imitates" that action. At the end of this episode, which occupies the first third of Canto XXIII, Virgil carries Dante down into the next *bolgia* in order to rescue him from the enraged Malebranche:

> Lo duca mio di sùbito mi prese,
> come la madre ch'al romore è desta
> e vede presso a sé le fiamme accese,
>   che prende il figlio e fugge e non s'arresta,
> avendo più di lui che di sé cura,
> tanto che solo una camiscia vesta;
>   e giù dal collo de la ripa dura
> supin si diede a la pendente roccia,
> che l'un de' lati a l'altra bolgia tura.
>   Non corse mai sì tosto acqua per doccia
> a volger ruota di molin terragno,
> quand' ella più verso le pale approccia,
>   come 'l maestro mio per quel vivagno,
> portandosene me sovra 'l suo petto,
> come suo figlio, non come compagno.
>   (*Inf.* XXIII, 37–51)

The tenderness of the embrace betokens that of the *Pastor Bonus* and contrasts with the devil's brusque hauling of the barrator whom he hurls into the pitch;[37] moreover, this is not the first time Virgil has carried his protégé, nor will it be the last.

Significantly, the only other times this action occurs in the *Inferno* are in Canto XIX, where Virgil bears Dante both down into and up out of the third *bolgia*, and in Canto XXXIV, where he climbs up Lucifer's legs and, ultimately, out of Hell. The connections between Cantos XIX and XXI are, I repeat, several, and not least among them is the fact that both deal with corruption, in Church and State respectively, and with the selling or prostitution of ecclesiastical and secular offices. The sins punished in the third and fifth *bolge* strike at the heart of the two institutions directly responsible for man's temporal and spiritual happiness (the *beatitudo huius vite* and the *beatitudo vite eterne*), and thus in both the idea of the shepherd, the one who leads and governs, should be foremost. It is appropriate that in both instances Virgil, the poet and champion of Empire, should be the Pastor, the one charged with guiding the Pilgrim and the one who contrasts with the image of the Bad Shepherd. In Canto XIX, Virgil's solicitude toward the Pilgrim helps to establish him as the perfect *Pastor*, thus providing an ironic gloss on the evil shepherds punished therein.[38] In Cantos XXI–XXIII, after Dante is exposed to real danger, Virgil "saves" his charge by carrying him, sliding, down into the next *bolgia*, an action which "imitates" in its general outlines Christ's Harrowing of Hell to save the virtuous and contrasts with the parodic image of the Good Shepherd which the devil presents. In the long introductory simile to Canto XXIV, Virgil is depicted as the shepherd who "prende suo vincastro / e fuor le pecorelle a pascer caccia" (*Inf.* XXIV, 14–15), Dante being his "sheep." In *Inferno* XXXIV, the climb up Lucifer's legs and out of Hell, out of the *tomba* (v. 128), would be emblematic of Christ's resurrection from the tomb on the third day and of his Harrowing of Hell. Indeed, Dante and Virgil spend "three days" in the "tomb" of Hell and emerge on the shore of Purgatory just before dawn on Easter Sunday.

The culmination of these shepherd-related actions on Virgil's part comes in *Purgatorio* XXVII, where Dante, at the end of his third day on the mountain and after the long and arduous ascent, sleeps as a *capra* watched over by Virgil and Statius:

> Quali si stanno ruminando manse
> le capre, state rapide e proterve
> sovra le cime avante che sien pranse,
>   tacite a l'ombra, mentre che 'l sol ferve,
> guardate dal pastor, che 'n su la verga
> poggiato s'è e lor di posa serve;
>   e quale il mandrïan che fori alberga,
> lungo il peculio suo queto pernotta,
> guardando perché fiera non lo sperga;
>   tali eravamo tutti e tre allotta,
> io come capra, ed ei come pastori,
> fasciati quinci e quindi d'alta grotta.
>   (*Purg.* XXVII, 76–87)

By carrying Dante or by standing watch over him, Virgil imitates the *Pastor Bonus*, and the several instances of this activity (*Inf.* XIX, 21–24, 34, and *Purg.* XXVII) are intended first of all to counterbalance the parodic scene of the devil carrying the sinner. More generally, in Dante's political ideology or "theology," the emperor is necessarily a *typus Christi*, who assumes the identity of both Good Shepherd and sacrificial *agnus Dei*.[39] Thus, in the pertinent instances from the *Commedia* mentioned above, and especially here in *Inferno* XXI–XXIV, Virgil, the poet of Empire, would embody the notion of the temporal shepherd, the one charged with leading humankind (and in the context of the poem, Dante the Pilgrim) to earthly felicity.[40]

In conclusion, I would suggest that Dante, particularly sensitive to the figurative arts and consciously imitative of them in certain places in the *Commedia*,[41] chose to incorporate here precise attributes from the long iconographic tradition of the Good Shepherd in the rendering of the composite image of devil and sinner. At the same time, this negative version of the *Pastor Bonus* is balanced by the positive one which Virgil exemplifies. The presence of these contradictory images then conforms to and enhances the basic duality, noted earlier, in the presentation of events in this episode. In this scene and in others, Dante expected his readers to create for themselves that "other" artistic context, to visualize the events accordingly, and to increase thereby their comprehension of the episode. If we follow the Poet's expectation, we cannot fail to note that art, and especially iconographic parody play a significant (and heretofore unacknowledged) role in the typological and poetic structure both of this canto and of the entire episode in this section of *Malebolge*.

NOTES

This essay appeared in a slightly different form in *Res Publica Litterarum*, V, pt. 2 (1982), 125–37. I gratefully acknowledge the permission granted by Dott. Cecilia Prete to reprint the essay in this volume.

1. Among the many general and specific treatments of this *bolgia* (and, in particular, Canto XXI) I have consulted the following: Riccardo Bacchelli, "Da Dite a Malebolge: La tragedia delle porte chiuse e la farsa dei ponti rotti," *Giornale storico della letteratura italiana* 131 (1954): 1–32; G. A. Cesareo, "Dante e i diavoli," *Nuova Antologia* (16 marzo 1918): 126–37; Alberto Chiari, "Il Primo canto dei barattieri," *Letture dantesche* (Florence: Le Monnier, 1946), 1–44; Joseph D. Falvo, "*Inferno* XXII," *Dante's "Divine Comedy": Introductory Readings. I: "Inferno"*, ed. Tibor Wlassics (Charlottesville: University of Virginia Press, 1990), 281–96; Guido Favati, "Il 'Jeu di Dante' (Interpretazione del canto XXI dell'*Inferno*," *Cultura neolatina* 25 (1965): 34–52; Egidio Lunardi, "*Inferno* XXI," *Dante's "Divine Comedy": Introductory Readings. I: "Inferno"*, ed. Wlassics, 275–80; Rocco Montano, "L'Episodio dei barattieri e lo stile comico," *Storia della poesia di Dante* (Naples: Quaderni di Delta, 1962), I:487–501; Howard I. Needler, "Linguis Hominum et Angelorum," *Italica* 47 (1970): 265–84; Leonardo Olschki, "Dante, i barattieri e i diavoli," *Giornale dantesco* 38 (1937): 61–81; Antonino Pagliaro, "La Rapsodia dei diavoli," *Ulisse: Ricerche semantiche sulla Divina Commedia* (Messina: D'Anna, 1967), I:311–24; Luigi Pirandello, "Il Canto XXI dell'*Inferno*," *Letture dantesche*, a cura di Giovanni Getto (Florence: Sansoni, 1955), 393–414; Mario Principato, *Il Canto XXI dell'Inferno* (Rome: Signorelli, 1952); Aurelio Roncaglia, "Lectura Dantis: *Inferno* XXI," *Yearbook of Italian Studies* 1 (1971): 3–28; Giambattista Salinari, "Il Comico nella *Divina Commedia*," *Belfagor* 10 (1955): 623–41; Gian Roberto Sarolli, "Musical Symbolism: *Inferno* XXI, 136–39; Exemplum of Musica Diaboli *Versus* Musica Dei," *Prolegomena alla "Divina Commedia"* (Florence: Olschki, 1971), 363–80; Antonio Scolari, "Canto XXI," *Lectura Dantis Scaligera: Inferno* (Florence: Le Monnier, 1971), 725–55; Leo Spitzer, "The Farcical Elements in *Inferno*, Cantos XXI–XXIII," *Modern Language Notes* 59 (1944): 83–88; Vittorio Turri, *Il Canto XXI dell'Inferno* (Florence: Sansoni, 1902); Hope Nash Wolf, "A Study of Dante's Distance from the Creatures of Cantos Twenty–One and Two of the *Inferno* and Its Relation to the Use of Animals in Preceding Cantos," *Italian Quarterly* 12 (1969): 239–51.

2. See Favati, "Il 'Jeu di Dante,'" 41–50, Nash, "Study of Dante's Distance," 247, and Olschki, "Dante," 80, and D. D. R. Owen, "Hell on the Stage," in *The Vision of Hell* (New York: Barnes and Noble, 1970), 224–52.

3. The large number of images involving domestic or non-ferocious animals introduces a "playful" note into this episode, just as the so-called "kitchen humor" does. For this last point, see E. R. Curtius, *European Literature and the Latin Middle Ages*, tr. Willard Trask (New York: Harper and Row, 1963), 431–35.

4. All passages from the *Comedy* follow the Edizione Nazionale of the Società Dantesca Italiana, *La Commedia secondo l'antica vulgata*, 4 vols., ed. Giorgio Petrocchi (Milan: Mondadori, 1966–67).

5. One is tempted in this regard to think of the grafters as saboteurs of the "ship of state," a metaphor countered and corrected by the positive introductory image of the shipyard in Venice.

6. It is interesting to note that this second lie occurs at almost precisely the same place in this canto as the first lie (Malacoda's) in Canto XXI. For a more complete discussion of the duplicitous language found in this episode, see my article, "Deceivers Deceived: Devilish Doubletalk in *Inferno* 21–23," *Quaderni d'italianistica* 10, 1–2 (1989): 133–56.

7. See Giovanni Fallani, "Il Volto Santo di Lucca," *Poesia e teologia nella Divina Commedia* 2 (Milan: Marzorati, 1961): 117–23.

8. Charles S. Singleton, rev. ed., C. H. Grandgent, ed., *La Divina Commedia* (Cambridge, MA: Harvard University Press, 1972), 189.

9. "Inferno 19: O Simon Mago!" *Modern Language Notes* 80 (1965): 92–99.

10. Among the several attempts to resolve this crux, see Mark Musa, "E questo sia suggel ch'ogn'uomo sganni," *Italica* 41 (1964): 134–38; Susan Noakes, "Dino Compagni and the Vow in San Giovanni: *Inferno* 19, 16–21," *Dante Studies* 86 (1968): 41–63; and Leo Spitzer, "Two Dante Notes. I. An Autobiographical Incident in Inferno XIX," *Romanic Review* 34 (1943): 247–56.

11. The range of dangers extends from the playful variety, when the devil remarks: "Vuo' che 'l tocchi / . . . in sul groppone?" (XXI, 100–101) to the very vicious sort, when the Malebranche are in pursuit (XXIII, 34–57).

12. The other instance is his ascent of Lucifer's legs, for which see below.

13. Cf. Virgil's embrace of the Pilgrim in Canto VIII (vv. 43–45).

14. *Comentum super Dantis Aldigherij Comoediam*, a cura di W. W. Vernon and J. P. Lacaita (Florence: Barbèra, 1887), 2:102.

15. In addition to the studies cited in n. 1, I have consulted most of the commentators, ancient (Benvenuto, Ottimo, et al.) and modern (Scartazzini, Momigliano, Grandgent, Gmelin, Singleton, Grabher, Sapegno, et al.). Critics have noted that there are sources, both literary (*Visio Sancti Pauli*) and artistic (the mosaics in the Florentine Baptistery), for the image of the devil carrying a sinner into Hell. On the latter point, see Ernest Hatch Wilkins, "Dante and the Mosaics in His Bel San Giovanni," *The Invention of the Sonnet and Other Studies in Italian Literature* (Rome: Edizioni di Storià e Letteratura, 1959), 51–60. These critics have not, however, perceived the association which I am developing here.

16. Num. 27:17; Ps. 22 (Vulg.); Isa. 40:11; Jer. 3:15; Heb. 13:20; 1 Pet. 2:25 and 5:4.

17. Tertullian, *De pudicitiae*, 7–10, 13 (PL 2:991–1001, 1003–1004); Jerome, *Epistola* 69 "Ad Oceanum" (PL 22:653–654); Augustine, *Sermo* 138 (PL 38:763–769); Gregory the Great, *Homilia* 14 (PL 76:1127–1130); Bede, *In S. Joannis Evangelium expositio* (PL 92:766–768); Petrus Chrysologus, *Sermo* 168 (PL 52:639–641); and Haimo, *Homilia de Tempore* LXXXIII (PL 118:499–506).

18. For the Good Shepherd motif, see the following studies: Anton Legner, *Der gute Hirte* (Düsseldorf: Verlag L. Schwann, 1959), and "Hirt, Guter Hirt," *Lexikon der christlichen Ikonographie* 2 (Freiburg: Herder, 1970), 289–99; Gertrud Schiller,

Iconography of Christian Art, 1, tr. Janet Seligman (London: Lund Humphries, 1971), 130–32; "Pasteur (Bon)," *DACL* 13.2: 2272–2390; L. Charbonneau-Lassay, "Le Christ Pasteur," *Le Mystérieuse emblématique de Jésus-Christ: Le Bestiaire du Christ* (Milan: Toth, 1974 [1940]), 202–206. As was often the case in early Christian art, the figure of the Good Shepherd was based almost wholly on that of a pagan deity, especially on representations of Orpheus and Mercury.

19. Implicit here, too, is the concept of the Lamb of God, slain to take away the sins of the world (cf. John 1:29 and Apoc. 5:6).

20. On this point, see John Block Friedman, *Orpheus in the Middle Ages* (Cambridge, MA: Harvard University Press, 1970), 43. The text follows that in DACL 13.2: 2276.

21. For the survival in art, see Legner, *Der gute Hirte*, 19–23.

22. For an illustration, see Legner, *Der gute Hirte*, pl. 15. This representation is probably modeled on an earlier funereal relief. Also in Lucca are three early Christian sarcophagi which bear the image of the Good Shepherd: two are found in St. Maria Forisportam (one serving as the baptismal font); the other, bearing the date 1198, contains the body of St. Paolino in the homonymous church. Dante may also have seen other artistic examples in Tuscany: a sarcophagus in St. Trinita (Florence) and numerous early Christian sarcophagi in the Camposanto (Pisa). For commentary and illustrations of these, see J. Wilpert, *I sarcofagi cristiani antichi*, 3 vols. (Rome: Pontificio Istituto di Archeologia Cristiana, 1929, 1932, 1936).

23. Placido Campetti, "Il Battistero di San Frediano di Lucca e la sua ricostruzione," *Dedalo* 7 (1926–27): 333–52.

24. Mario Salmi, *Romanesque Sculpture in Tuscany* (Florence: Rinascimento del Libro, 1928), 94–95.

25. For Dante's probable historical association with Lucca, see F. P. Luiso, "Dante e Lucca," *Dante: La vita, le opere, le grandi città dantesche: Dante e l'Europa* (Milan: Treves, 1921), 172–190, and Michele Messina, "Lucca," *Enciclopedia Dantesca* 3 (1971): 702–704.

26. There are numerous depictions in the catacombs in addition to the sarcophagi, relief sculptures, and statues in such places as the Lateran and St. Clement's.

27. *The Latin Poems Commonly Attributed to Walter Mapes*, ed. Thomas Wright (London, 1841; repr. Hildesheim: Georg Olms, 1968). A similar parodic use of the Good Shepherd motif is found in the Old French *fabliau, Le Boucher d'Abeville*, for which see Howard Helsinger, "Pearls in the Swill: Comic Allegory in the French Fabliaux," in *The Humor of the Fabliaux*, ed. Thomas D. Cooke and Benjamin L. Honeycutt (Columbia: University of Missouri Press, 1974), 93–105.

28. See *Inf.* XIX, 104–108; *Purg.* XVI, 92–112; *Par.* XXVII, 55–56; etc. For the several occurrences of *pastore* in Dante's works, see the homonymous article by Antonio Lanci in the *Enciclopedia Dantesca* 4 (1975): 347. References to "bad shepherds" also occur in the Bible (Ezek. 34:1–8; Jer. 23:1–4 and 50:6) and in the writings of the Church Fathers (cf. the passages in Gregory, Bede, and Haimo cited in n. 17 above).

29. There has been some discussion concerning the "direct" route, or "short cut" as it were, from Lucca to the fifth *bolgia*, for this bypassing of Minòs would seem to contradict the general plan of Hell as described earlier in the *Inferno* (V, 4–15; XIII, 94–96; XX, 35–36). In this connection Favati ("Il 'Jeu di Dante,'" 40) refers to him as the *diavolo-psicopompo*.

30. Cf. the verses from the Apocalypse cited above and Psalm 22 (Vulgate).

31. Often such a representation would have twelve sheep to signify the Apostles, and so it is in the mosaic decoration of the apse and triumphal arch in the basilica of St. Apollinare in Classe (Ravenna). Another example with which

Dante was no doubt familiar is in the mausoleum of Galla Placidia (Ravenna), which has only six sheep, however. In the mosaics of the church of San Vitale in Ravenna, Moses is depicted as the Shepherd.

32. It is interesting and perhaps useful to note here that Nicodemus, the supposed author of the apocryphal gospel which tells of the Harrowing of Hell, is also reputed to be the carver of the Santo Volto. Is this merely a fortuitous coincidence, or does it represent conscious planning on Dante's part? The mystery remains.

33. This paraphrases the view of Spitzer, "Two Dante Notes," 88.

34. Gian Roberto Sarolli, *Prolegomena*, 368. For the general notion of the *regio dissimilitudinis*, see Pierre Courcelle, *Les Confessions de Saint Augustine dans la tradition littéraire* (Paris: Etudes Augustiniennes, 1963), 278–88.

35. See, among others, C. S. Singleton, *Dante Studies 1. Commedia: Elements of Structure* (Cambridge, MA: Harvard University Press, 1954), 33–42.

36. Anthony K. Cassell, "Dante's Farinata and the Image of the *Arca*," *Yale Italian Studies* 1 (1977): 335–70, and his chapter on "Farinata" in *Dante's Fearful Art of Justice* (Toronto: University of Toronto Press, 1984), 15–31. See also Robert M. Durling, "Farinata and the Body of Christ," *Stanford Italian Review* 2 (Spring 1981), 5–35.

37. In contrast to the haughtiness of the devil, whose *omero* is *aguto e superbo*, Virgil maintains a humble pose throughout the episode: he is described as a *poverello* (XXI, 68) (which recalls St. Francis); he and Dante move silently in single file as *frati minori* (XXIII, 3).

38. Dante's reference to the Florentine Baptistery ("nel mio bel San Giovanni," *Inf.* XIX, 17) has its correlative in *Par.* XXV, where he speaks of the "bello ovile ov' io dormi' agnello," where he hopes to return eventually in triumph ("Se mai continga che 'l poema sacro," vv. 1–9).

39. Cf. the following two passages from Dante's letters both in reference to Henry VII (the text follows that in *Dantis Alagherii, Epistolae. The Letters of Dante*, ed. Paget Toynbee, 2nd ed. by C. G. Hardie [Oxford: Clarendon Press, 1966]):

> Parcite, parcite, iam ex nunc, o carissimi, qui mecum iniuriam passi estis, ut Hectoreus pastor vos oves de ovili suo cognoscat. (5:85–87)

> Tunc exultavit in me spiritus meus, quum tacitus dixi mecum: "Ecce Agnus Dei, ecce qui tollit peccata mundi!" (7:44–47).

It is doubly appropriate that the penitents on the third terrace of Purgatory recite the *Agnus Dei*, for Marco Lombardo's speech deals precisely with both secular and ecclesiastical shepherds.

40. Some further considerations: in Cantos XXI–XXIII (*bolge* 5 and 6) we are presented with those sinners—grafters and hypocrites—who undermine and eventually destroy the political fabric of the state. Indeed, by describing Virgil as a shepherd in the opening simile of Canto XXIV, Dante sets the end limits for his appearance in the guise of the temporal Good Shepherd, a role begun in Canto XIX which embraces appropriately enough the episode of the hypocrites in Canto XXIII. Because of their ineffectual governance of the Florentine commune, Loderingo and Catalano, although *frati godenti*, also emerge as prime examples of "evil shepherds," as secular counterparts to the simoniac popes, whom they counterbalance in this section of Hell. The irony of this similarity is enhanced by their being clothed in the manner of the monks of Cluny (XXIII, 61–63). Given the nature of the entire scene in these cantos, both in its general design and in its particulars, the two instances of "carrying" (Virgil-Dante, devil-barrator), besides functioning as deliberate contrastive parallels, are laden with political connotations.

41. For example, see the following studies: Enrico de' Negri, "Tema e icono-grafia del *Purgatorio*," *Romanic Review* 49 (1958): 81–104; Giovanni Fallani, *Dante e la cultura figurativa medievale* (Bergamo: Minerva Italica, 1971); Christopher Kleinhenz, "A Nose for Art (*Purgatorio*, 7): Notes of Dante's Iconographical Sense," *Italica* 52 (1975): 372–79; idem, "Dante and the Tradition of Visual Arts in the Middle Ages," *Thought* 65, no. 256 (March 1990): 17–26; and Christie K. Fengler and William A. Stephany, "The Visual Arts: A Basis for Dante's Imagery in *Purgatory* and *Paradise*," *The Michigan Academician* 10 (1977): 127–41.

Virgil and Dante as Mind-Readers
(*Inferno* XXI and XXIII)

ROBERT HOLLANDER

Dante's experience of the sin of barratry, punished in the fifth of the *Malebolge*, at first seems to be limited to a single incident (*Inf.* XXI, 4–57) and to a single exemplary sinner (the unnamed elder of Lucca, first identified as Martino Bottario by Guido da Pisa 1327: 409). This episode comes to an apparent point of closure in the memorable pseudo-simile which compares the tormented sinner to meat being pushed down into a boiling pot the better to be cooked (55–57). Yet immediately thereafter begins the most lengthy episode of all *Inferno*. The ensuing violent yet comic scene (XXI, 58–XXIII, 57, some 290 verses) includes the following narrative details:

XXI, 58–87: Virgil, protecting the hidden Dante, confronts Malacoda, the leader of this army of demons, and comes to terms with him.

XXI, 88–105: Dante, called from his hiding place by Virgil, is eyed by two demons who would like to hook him; they must be restrained by Malacoda.

XXI, 106–117: Malacoda lies successfully to Virgil, insisting that the travelers cannot cross over the sixth *bolgia* at this point because of the broken bridge, but may, under truce, accompany a band of his troops to the next crossing.

XXI, 118–126: Malacoda appoints a squad of ten demons, with Barbariccia to serve as decurion; they are to allow Dante and Virgil to enjoy safe conduct only until they reach this (nonexistent) unbroken *scoglio* ("costor sian salvi infino . . .").

XXI, 127–135: Dante wishes to proceed without such escort; Virgil attempts to soothe his fear.

XXI, 136–139: The squad of demons makes its oral response to Barbariccia's anal signal.

XXII, 1–12: The first of Dante's lengthy canto-opening similes[1] binds the two canti: Barbariccia's anal command is compared to the *cennamella* that signals the start of battle.

XXII, 13–75: The squad treats cruelly the unnamed Navarrese (one

Gian Paolo, or "Ciampolo", according to Lana 1324 and other early commentators).

XXII, 76–96: At Virgil's behest Ciampolo speaks of two others hidden in the pitch.

XXII, 97–108: Ciampolo's stratagem, by which he hopes to escape the clutches of the *Malebranche*, is seen through by Cagnazzo.

XXII, 109–117: Alichino is taken in, nonetheless, and consents to Ciampolo's conditions.

XXII, 118–151: Ciampolo escapes; Alichino fails to catch him; Calcabrina uses Alichino's custodial failure as an excuse to attack *him*; they both fall into the pitch, whence the remaining eight make haste to hook them out.

XXIII, 1–33: Dante and Virgil, now without escort (as Dante had originally hoped they would be), proceed along the ridge; Dante fears that the *Malebranche*, enraged because they were tricked on the traveler's account, must now be in pursuit; Virgil believes his concern justified.

XXIII, 34–57: The *Malebranche* indeed are upon them; Virgil, compared to a mother escaping from a burning house with her babe, slides down into the sixth *bolgia* carrying Dante in his arms, thus effecting their escape.

The immediate relevance of all this activity to one who has been exiled from his *patria* on a trumped-up charge of barratry has occasioned a debate in the discussion of *Inf.* XXI and XXIII.[2] Whatever autobiographical resonance Dante incorporated in the lengthy farcical interlude,[3] and even should it be without such resonance, what has received considerably less attention than it might have occasioned is the deft manipulation of the two major characters' differing responses to what transpires.[4] If we have previously had to acknowledge that Virgil is a less capable guide than we might like to imagine or than he is pleased to admit (see, for example, *Inf.* VIII, 112–IX, 33; XIV, 43–45), we are in this instance for the first time forced to perceive that he is simply and utterly wrong.[5]

1. Teeth as Text and Virgil's Insufficient Gloss (XXI, 127–139).

"Omè, maestro, che è quel ch'i' veggio?"
diss'io, "deh, sanza scorta andianci soli,
se tu sa' ir; ch'i' per me non la cheggio.
　Se tu se' sì accorto come suoli,
non vedi tu ch'e' digrignan li denti
e con le ciglia ne minaccian duoli?".
　Ed elli a me: "Non vo' che tu paventi;
lasciali digrignar pur a loro senno,
ch'e' fanno ciò per li lessi dolenti".
　Per l'argine sinistro volta dienno;
ma prima avea ciascun la lingua stretta
coi denti, verso lor duca, per cenno;
　ed elli avea del cul fatto trombetta.

The first six verses, spoken by the protagonist, doubly impugn Virgil's competence as guide. If he knows how they should proceed, as he has indicated he does at verses 62–63, then why does he want another guide to lead them? As we will discover at XXIII, 133–138, not only does he *not* know that all the bridges over the sixth *bolgia* have been destroyed by the earthquake which occurred at the Crucifixion (another indication that Virgil does not know all that he thinks he does, despite the fact that he has been in the depths of Hell before—see *Inf.* IX, 22–30), but he must swallow a bitter pill when he must subsequently admit that he has been tricked by Malacoda (XXIII, 139–148). He is so chagrined by this recognition that he walks away from Dante, momentarily abandoning his necessary role as guide.[6] The later scene should be in our minds as we examine this text, which is extraordinary. For the first and only time in the *Commedia* Virgil is explicitly (rather than tacitly) shown to have made a mistake in judgment.[7] Virgil, then, does not "sa ire" as well as he thinks he does.[8] Further, and more disturbingly, the "altissimo poeta" turns out to be a rather poor reader of another sort of text, the gnashing of teeth. Our poet's insistence on the very *digrignare* is a clear signal to us, his readers. Dante (correctly) perceives that the *Malebranche*'s grinding is directly menacing to the two travelers (131); yet Virgil opines that the gesture only reveals that they threaten the boiling barrators (134).[9] In the following canto Ciampolo shows that he knows how to read such texts: "Omè, vedete l'altro che digrigna" (XXII, 91), he shouts, correctly inferring from Farfarello's oral gesture that the demon intends to attack him (De Robertis 1981: 3 has noted the parallels between Dante and Ciampolo in this regard), as is confirmed by Barbariccia's restraining command (96). The verb *digrignare* occurs only three times in all of Dante's work. Its purpose here, in these three *loci*, is plainly to show that Virgil has totally failed in his interpretation of the demons' dental behavior. And that fact is underlined in the ensuing action, in which Barbariccia gives the covert signal for their eventual surprise attack to his cohort, all of whom show by their teeth that they understand his order (136–139). This piece of poetic business is deft and sure; we should not be fooled by its scabrous nature—rehearsing a demonic fart—into overlooking the importance of the communicating done among the demons and Virgil's total failure to understand what is occurring before his eyes and ears. Benvenuto's (1373) reading of the demons' gestures remains the most convincing one: "tenebant linguam dispositam et paratam ad trulizandum," that is, the nine of them prepared to acknowledge their leader's signal by so positioning their tongues against their teeth that, once they gave vent to their thoughts, the result would be an oral imitation of the sound of his fart. (See Landino's 1481 similar gloss: "'Stringere la lingua tra denti' significa fare tale strepito con bocca quale fa el vento quando esce per le parti posteriori: el che fanno gl'imprudenti buffoni quando scherniscono alcuno." It is probably best to see that the signal and the response are both a token of understanding among the malefactors and a sign of their derision for Virgil's self-confident misreading of their intentions). Everything here is backwards; Barbariccia turns his anus into a mouth-like orifice; his squad turn their mouths into producers of anus-like noise.[10] The unrecorded sound which they make (we see their preparation—as Benvenuto noted—but do not hear their performance) in answer to their leader's trumpet solo not only is the sign of their agreement to do evil deeds, but is a brutally unkind cut at Virgil as interpreter, since he has just declared that their hostility is aimed elsewhere. With the possible exception of the moving, even excruciating, exploration of Virgil's failure as man, poet, and thinker, presented *seriatim* in *Purg*. III–VI, this must be the high (or the low?) point in Dante's excursions into anti-Virgilian polemic in a poem which seems at first to be centrally dedicated to the pagan poet's restoration in a Christian *poiesis*.

2. *The Missing Link: Dante's Aesopic Second Thought* (XXIII, 1–33). Let us examine the text in two stages:

> Taciti, soli, sanza compagnia
> n'andavam l'un dinanzi e l'altro dopo,
> come frati minor vanno per via.
>   Vòlt'era in su la favola d'Isopo
> lo mio pensier per la presente rissa,
> dov'el parlò de la rana e del topo;
>   ché più non si pareggia "mo" e "issa"
> che l'un con l'altro fa, se ben s'accoppia
> principio e fine con la mente fissa.
>   E come l'un pensier de l'altro scoppia,
> così nacque di quello un altro poi,
> che la prima paura mi fé doppia.
>   (XXIII, 1–12)

The Anonimo Fiorentino (1400) reminds us that, in such Franciscan mendicant pairs as the first *terzina* recalls, the one of greater authority precedes the other (". . . andare l'uno innanzi, quello di più autorità"), a detail that has its ironic overtone when we consider the fact that the conclusion of this canto will reveal Virgil's distress at the way in which his authority has been undermined by Malacoda's lies—lies which he has accepted as truths (139–148); we may also choose to consider the fact that it is Dante, the follower, who in the matter of the reliability of Malacoda and his rout is in fact correct, while his guide and master has been taken in (see Ryan 1982[2]: 21–22 for a similar appreciation). And it is Dante, not Virgil, who first comes to grips with the threat still offered by the momentarily detained *Malebranche*. He does so by recalling 'Aesop's' fable of the mouse and the frog.[11] In its various versions, the story is essentially the same: Needing to cross a stream, a mouse seeks the aid of a frog; the latter attaches a string to one of his own legs and one of the mouse's. His intent is malicious; mid-way across the water he dives in order to drown the mouse. The struggles of the rodent to stay afloat draw the attention of an overflying kite, who seizes the mouse and, with him, the frog, caught in his own trap. To be sure, Dante's first sense of the relevance of the fable is retrospective. The "presente rissa" of verse 5 is the nasty encounter between Alichino and Calcabrina, in which the relations among the three participants are as follows: Ciampolo = mouse, Alichino = frog, Calcabrina = kite.[12] Yet there are at least apparent problems with this formulation. For Ciampolo, unlike the mouse in the fable, is not 'innocent'—not in either sense of the word; further, he does not wish to cross a body of water but to hide in a lake of pitch. And as for Calcabrina, unlike the kite, he is not eventually victorious, but himself a victim. The *rissa* and the fable, Dante says, are alike as "mo" and "issa".[13] But he qualifies the resemblance: "se ben s'accoppia / principio e fine con la mente fissa." In other words the fable and the *rissa* have identical beginnings and endings only if we consider these carefully, that is, they may not seem to do so. But when we do examine them with care, we note that Ciampolo has indeed been compared to a mouse ("sorco" at XXII, 58; Guyler 1972: 32 also notes the reference) fallen among mischievous cats; and if his desire is not so much to cross a stream by agency of a 'frog' as it is to get another creature to help him to return to a relatively greater degree of comfort in the pitch, the beginning of the fable may be understood to fit his plight. And the end, in which the suddenly frog-like Ciampolo, who had "lacciuoli [reminiscent of the *filum* of the fable?] a gran divizia" (XXII, 109),[14] escapes from the clutches of a 'kite', Alichino, who is in fact compared to still other birds of prey, "falcon" (XXII, 131) and "sparvier grifagno" (139), concludes with Calcabrina as the eventual 'kite', clawing Alichino-frog and falling with him into the pitch (137–138). Thus all three of the characters in the fable find their counterparts in *Inf*. XXII, 97–151, if their roles shift as the scene develops. At least the beginning, Ciampolo's mouse-like request for assistance, and the end, which brings unhappiness to the scheming middle-man, are similar.[15]

It has for some time been a puzzle to this reader that Dante should have chosen words that mean 'now' as the instruments of his comparison.[16] Any other pair of like-signifying yet differing terms would have served as well. It now seems to me that his choice was not a casual one. Having considered the relevance of the fable to preterite action, Dante turns his attention to the present: "E come l'un pensier de l'altro scoppia, / così nacque di quello un altro poi, / che la prima paura mi fé doppia." It is as though, while rehearsing the fable and the *rissa*, he unconsciously insisted on the relevance of both matters to what is to happen in the immediate future. And what is indeed transpiring, just out of sight, is the frantic effort of the squad of ten demons to turn Dante into their mouse:

Già mi sentia tutti arricciar li peli
de la paura e stava in dietro intento,

quand'io dissi: "Maestro, se no celi
      te e me tostamente, i' ho pavento
   d'i Malebranche. Noi li avem già dietro;
   io li 'magino sì, che già li sento."
                                    (XXIII, 19–24)

The protagonist, whatever his shortcomings, seems to be more expert than his guide in understanding the devious behavior of such as Malacoda and his demons (a Florentine political background makes even a poet 'streetwise', we may infer). "Noi li avem già dietro; / io li 'magino sì, che già li sento." The double utterance of "già" parallels the two previous uses of words for 'now'. And indeed, at verse 35 we learn that the demons are upon them.

Thus it seems to me that 'Aesop's' fable has not only a preterite reference, but a present (or immediately future) one as well, and in that particular a far more pressing point, both for Dante and for the reader. "If we do not get away from here at once, I am lost" is what Dante (correctly) intuits. It is interesting that while Virgil accepts this intuition (25–33), it is Dante who causes him to act in a helpful matter, thus reversing his usual role as protector and guide. For here he functions rather as aide then guide. And if such is the case, then the reference of the fable is doubly focused and makes some curious suggestions about the interrelationships among the participants in the action.[17] As Larkin (1962: 99; 1966: 87–88) argues, the "principio" of verse 9 refers precisely to the beginning of the episode, where Dante and Virgil, the 'mice' according to him, are trying to enlist Malacoda's aid to make their way across a 'river', i.e., over the sixth *bolgia*. What Dante, with his Aesopic second thought, perceives, is that the 'kite' of the fable is about to reappear in the most threatening way. For if two of the *Malebranche* have temporarily become disabled playing out their roles in their own version of 'frog' and 'kite', once they are hauled from the pitch they will become part of a still more highly motivated tenfold 'kite'.

Mus, rana, milvus. Is it possible that the equivalences are more disturbingly appropriate than has heretofore been appreciated? In XXI Virgil intercedes on behalf of his 'mouse' in order to get him across what seems an unfordable 'stream'. But this 'mouse' objects to his choice of 'frog', Barbariccia's band, because, unlike the mouse in the fable, he perceives that the promised aid is proffered fraudulently. Virgil would reassure him that such is not the case, that the demons are in fact trustworthy 'frogs'.[18] Now that two of the demons have played out their parts in the Aesopic drama precisely in the roles of frog and kite, it is only Dante's receptiveness to a better reading, as he reads their minds, as it were, that allows him to perceive that the *Malebranche* have their own ending for the narrative in mind and are, at the very moment, hastening hence to enforce it on Dante and Virgil. And in this renewed awareness of the aptness of the fable, Dante understands that for the demons he himself is the mouse, while Virgil plays the unwitting frog to their kite (we see their outspread wings from—just barely—a safe distance at XXIII, 35). In Dante's afterthought Virgil has become a frog, no matter how good his intentions. Having tied himself to his guide, he has put himself absolutely at risk beneath the vicious birds of prey.[19] Dante would not be 'crossing' (or actually *not* crossing) in this manner had it not been for Virgil's bad advice.

As though to make amends for his previous lack of intelligence or common sense, Virgil is (finally) galvanized to take the action which Dante might have hoped he would take two *canti* earlier—he leaves the terrain of the *Malebranche* as quickly as he can, holding Dante in his arms as a mother, fleeing a burning house, takes up her babe. And, perhaps to remind us of the earlier 'Aesopics', Virgil's slide into the next *bolgia* is described in aquatic terms by the simile which compares the descent to the rush of a sluice at a mill (46–51). Virgil has finally realized how to perform the frog's role benevolently and efficaciously. The *Commedia* may continue, even if Virgil's anger at having been deceived will temporarily interrupt its forward progress at the end of this canto and the beginning of the next.[20]

This elaborately developed chain of incidents, which would put Virgil in a difficult light even had Dante not intended to do so, is probably better understood as the culminating moment in a series of devaluations of Virgil. Guyler (1972: 40) concludes his study as follows: "As a poet, Dante, with a snicker, has subtly pointed out the superiority of his own Christian poem to that of its pagan model." Those of us who would see such poetic behavior behind the apparent unstinting praise of Virgil must be careful lest we, beguiled by our new vision of Dante's strange behavior toward Virgil, fail to represent adequately the undoubtedly genuine and unquestionably enormous debt of gratitude and affection which Dante does in fact feel toward his *maestro e autore*. Why Dante should have nonetheless wanted to treat him as cruelly as he does is not a question that is readily answered. Before we can attempt it, we need to appreciate how frequently and how intensely he in fact holds Virgil and his work up to probing and antagonistic analysis, while at other moments lavishing the most enthusiastic *encomia* upon them.[21] Praised and damned, Dante's Virgil is perhaps the only truly liminal figure in a poem that loves its own highly defined and strikingly definite symmetries and judgments. In all the *Commedia* it is the figure of Virgil who probably offers us our fullest perception of whatever was unresolved in its author. In that poem which more than any other has come to represent total synthesis for our civilization, Dante's Virgil, liminal and torn, one foot in Eden, the other in Limbo, places a fruitful strain upon our ability to accept the synthesis without a pained awareness of its difficulty and fragility.

Both in text and in footnotes author-date references are to the chronologically ordered bibliographic note. Dates for the earlier commentators are approximate and are based on those found in the apposite entries of the *Enciclopedia Dantesca*. The text of *Inferno* is cited from Petrocchi (1966); of the *Aeneid* from P. Vergili Maronis, *Opera*, ed. F. A. Hirtzel (Oxford, 1900).

1. See also *Inf.* XXIV, 1–18; XXX, 1–27; XXXI, 1–6; *Purg.* VI, 1–12; XVII, 1–12; *Par.* IV, 1–9; XVII, 1–6; XXIII, 1–12; XXIX, 1–9; XXXI, 1–15. That more than one-tenth of Dante's cantos begin in simile underlines the importance that he attached to the figure. For discussion, with bibliography, see Antonino Pagliaro, "similitudine," *Enciclopedia Dantesca* V, 253–59; see also Richard H. Lansing, *From Image to Idea: A Study of the Simile in Dante's "Commedia"* (Ravenna, 1977).

2. For discussion, with bibliography, of the debate over the political allegory discovered in the episode by Rossetti (1826: II, 158–163) and to some degree accepted by such as Torraca (1905), see Mazzoni (1972: 423–24, 425–26); see also Bosco & Reggio (1979: 312–13).

3. See, again, Mazzoni (1972: 423–26), and Bosco & Reggio (1979: 311–14), for discussions of the debate over the precise nature of the comedic element in the two cantos, with bibliography; the most recent discussants of the canto, Conrieri (1981: 35–43), De Robertis (1981), and Ryan (1982²) naturally enough advert to this question, as well as to that concerning the autobiographical nature of the episode (see previous note). For a discussion which goes beyond the limits of this rather arbitrary attempt at a definition in order to explore the wider significance of the "ludic" proclivities displayed by Dante in XXI and XXII, see Sarolli (1971).

4. Upon finishing the first draft of this article I discovered that many of its observations had already been made—and made very well—by Guyler (1972). Thus, much of what I maintain, while not dependent upon his work, is in fact only a latter-day formulation of some of his precise and bold thoughts about this material. Several indications of the closeness of our judgments will be found below. (With only an exception or two, I have not bothered to indicate some less important points upon which we do not agree.)

5. Umberto Bosco, after rejecting two more usual opinions (i.e., Virgil does not suspect Malacoda's treachery because of his high-mindedness—see, for examples, Cesari 1824 and Andreoli 1856; if he is taken in, the reader is also and thus Virgil is not to be blamed in any way for his failure to understand the devil's plot—see Parodi 1909: 169), analyzes the drama of the scene as follows: "Comunque, il fatto che la beffa sia avvertita da Dante e dal lettore fa che la luce del racconto sia proiettata sull'ingenuità di Virgilio, e sottolineata anche dalla sicurezza impervia di lui sino all'ultimo" (citing XXI, 61–62). See Bosco & Reggio (1979: 309); see also Bosco (1975: 33). Bosco is one of the very few to perceive how thoroughly Dante discredits his guide in this scene. (Now see also Conrieri 1981: 33–35.) A similar view, especially as it concerns the relation of this scene to the previous challenge to Virgil's authority found in *Inf.* VIII, is offered by Bacchelli (1954) and by Conrieri (1981: 22–23). Ryan (1982: 1–6) begins his interesting essay on Virgil's shortcomings as Dante's guide with a similar discussion of the two *loci*, apparently without being aware of Bacchelli's study. I have seen no notice of Trucchi's (1936) interesting attempt to grasp the meaning of this surprising reproof of Virgil in his gloss of vv. 127–132: "Dante nella sua paura, illuminata dalla sua conoscenza della natura diabolica, vede giusto; ma Virgilio che si lascia guidar dalla ragione, non potendo di per sé comprendere l'inganno di Malacoda, perché l'altra volta che era stato quaggiù il terremoto non era ancor avvenuto la dà vinta all'astuzia del diavolo."

6. See Margherita Frankel, "Dante's Anti-Virgilian *villanello*" (*Dante Studies* C11 [1984]: 81–89), for a convincing reading of the relation of this scene to the following simile, *Inf.* XXIV, 1–18, a particular also touched on by Guyler (1972: 38).

7. If it accomplished nothing more, the passage might have finally removed the desire, present since the first commentators, to treat the figure of Virgil in Dante's poem as though he were the personification of 'Reason'. If that is what he represents, how could he make a mistake that even the protagonist, errant though he be, does not make? Vellutello's (1544) intervention is of a certain interest. After offering what I believe is the first sure recognition that Virgil is fooled by the demons (" . . . ingannandosi egli ancora non solamente in questo ['digrignar'], ma nel creder a Malacoda dhaver a trovar lo scoglio intero sopra de la sesta bolgia . . . ," he then goes on to argue that " . . . la ragione non sia possente a poterlo difendere, ma perche essa ragione sa . . . chel divino aiuto suplisce sempre in quello che lhuomo per se stesso non puo fare . . . cerca di confortarlo, e di rimoverli il timore." He thus blunts his keen literal reading with a poorly matched allegorical one.

8. We may speculate that he is put off his guard by his previous success in commanding Malacoda's obeisance (XXI, 79–84). Virgil's injunction, ordering the infernal centurion to allow them to pass, recapitulating, as it does, such earlier injunctions of defending demons as are found at *Inf.* III, 94–96; V, 22–24; VII, 8–12; XII, 88–93 (as is noted by Casini & Barbi 1921), is (apparently) met with amazed consternation and consent: Malacoda drops his *uncino* and orders the others not to attack (85–87). Guyler (1972: 34) appreciates the ironic control that lies behind the gesture, a control that is made manifest by subsequent events. His apparent total success evidently blinds Virgil to the possibility that, since he and Dante have now entered the realm of fraud, demons here may conceal their evil intentions behind the façade of defeat before the power of the Lord.

9. The comment of Scartazzini (1874) is instructive: "Dante si è accorto della malizia de' demoni. Senza dubbio Virgilio se ne è pure accorto, ma teme meno e vuol render sicuro il suo allievo." This charitable view, which is shared by Poletto (1894), perhaps indicates a generosity of spirit in the observer, but avoids the clear and pointed purpose of Virgil's misinterpretation. See Bacchelli (1954: 26) for a better reading: "Riluttanza cristiana, e perciò *toto coelo* superiore e più prudente e meglio ispirata di tutta la filosofica sapienza e sicurezza della mente virgiliana."

10. For a keen appreciation of the musical inversions of this scene in relation to a continuing theme of the *Commedia* see Sarolli (1971).

11. For a brief discussion of Dante's probable actual source(s), see Kraus (1970). The fable is not in fact Aesop's, but is likely derived from one of two medieval collections circulating under his name. Guyler (1972: 29–31) offers the fullest discussion (but see also Mandruzzato 1955) and gives convincing arguments for Dante's reliance on the poetic version of the *Liber Esopi* by Walter of England, reviewing the previous discussions of Pietro di Dante (1340), McKenzie (1900), Larkin (1962 and 1966), and Padoan (1965).

12. Singleton (1970), however, in his lengthy discussion of this passage (which is indebted to Paget Toynbee, "Esopo", in his *A Dictionary of Proper Names and Notable Matters in the Works of Dante*, revised by Singleton (Oxford, 1968 [1st ed. 1898], 250–251), argues that the version of the fable found in Marie de France (III, 79–82, in *Die Fabeln der Marie de France*, ed. K. Warnke [Halle, 1898], in which the mouse is eventually set at liberty, is closer to the incident in *Inf.* XXII, in which Ciampolo escapes. While there are attractive aspects to this hypothesis, the fact that Dante would expect his reader to be familiar with one of the more available "tragic" versions argues strongly against it, as does, in my opinion, the context, for Ciampolo's "escape" is hardly a return to life.

13. Pietro di Dante (1340) identifies the words as being, respectively, Lombard and Lucchese dialect for "now"; Guido da Pisa (1327) and Castelvetro (1570) resort to a more "humanistic" set of equivalences: Latin *modo* and *nunc*.

14. I note in passing Castelvetro's (1570) observation that Boccaccio borrowed the phrase at *Decameron* VIII, 7, 146.

15. What probably should be a matter of common consent is that Dante would be unlikely to develop his parallel incident(s) without being certain that we would be able to identify three participants, each of whom takes on the role of one of the creatures in the fable. Yet, from the early days of the commentary tradition, discussions of the passage have given rise to impressively divergent views. I shall attempt to summarize briefly.

That Benvenuto (1373) was correct to call the passage a "fortis . . . passus" is evidenced by the following table, which does not claim to have achieved completeness, but does hope to have included the major variations on our theme.

(1) Ciampolo = mouse; Alichino = frog; Calcabrina = kite: Guido da Pisa (1327); Castelvetro (1570—but see no. 19, below); Wolff (1969).

(2) Alichino = mouse; Calcabrina = frog: Ottimo (1333); Vellutello (1544); Scartazzini (1874); Oelsner (1900); Gmelin (1954).

(3) Alichino = mouse; Calcabrina = frog; the pitch = kite: Benvenuto (1373); Guiniforto (1440); Venturi (1732); Lombardi (1791); McKenzie (1900); Scartazzini (1900); Casini & Barbi (1921); Momigliano (1946); Mattalia (1960); Chimenz (1962); Giacalone (1968). (This is by far the most popular set of equivalences and is found in at least 15 other 19th and 20th–century commentators.)

(4) Alichino = frog; Calcabrina = kite: Buti (1385).

(5) Ciampolo = frog; demons = mouse: Anonimo Fiorentino (1400).

(6) Alichino = mouse; Calcabrina = frog; Barbariccia = kite: Serravalle (1416); Grandgent (1909).

(7) Ciampolo = mouse; [demons = frog?]: Mandruzzato (1955); Fallani (1965).

(8) Dante & Virgil = mouse; demons = frog: Larkin (1962 & 1966). (Andreoli [1856] was the first to suggest this equation, adding the implausible third term, Ciampolo = kite.)

(9) Ciampolo = frog (at beginning); Calcabrina = frog (at end): Padoan (1965); Bosco & Reggio (1979).

(10) Alichino & Dante = mouse; Calcabrina & Virgil = frog; *Malebranche* (twice) = kite: Guyler (1972).

My own formulation, as will become clear, combines (1) and (10):

(11) Ciampolo & Dante = mouse; Alichino & Virgil = frog, Calcaterra & the entire squad = kite.

This debate in the commentaries has come to resemble not only the action which it seeks to analyze, but also the pseudo-Homeric *Batrachomyomachia* which, if unknown to Dante, was the first in a long procession of similar games (see McKenzie 1900: 11).

16. Both will be used again, "mo" in this canto at verse 28, "issa" at *Purg.* XXIV, 55; and see Guido da Montefeltro's speech at *Inf.* XXVII, 20–21, where "mo" and "istra" also signify 'now'.

17. And one such curiosity, as Pietro di Dante (1340) was the first and perhaps only previous commentator to suggest, regards the *Aeneid; Inferno* XXIII, 19 ("Già mi sentia tutti arricciar li peli / de la paura . . .") may ask us to remember *Aeneid* II, 774, describing Aenas, during the fall of Troy, before the ghost of his dead Creusa: "obstipui, steteruntque comae . . . ." And the second part of Dante's speech may recall another moment in that terror-filled narrative: "'Maestro, se non celi / te e me tostamente, i' ho pavento / d'i Malebranche. Noi li avem già dietro . . .'" (21–23) may reflect the words of Anchises to his son, ". . . nate . . .

fuge, nate; propinquant" (II, 733). If these are in fact echoes of the scene describing the fall of Troy—and I offer the citations tentatively—then the terrified, claustrophobic atmosphere of Virgil's Second Book informs the terror felt by the protagonist in *Inf.* XXIII. And in that case we surely expect the sage recorder of the fall of Troy to offer better advice to his pupil than he does here.

18. This *principio* of the extended scene is probably mirrored in XXII, 97–117: in XXI Dante sees through Malacoda's feigned offer of aid while Virgil convinces himself that all is well; in XXII, Cagnazzo sees through Ciampolo's stratagem (97–108) while Alichino convinces himself that the Navarrese may be trusted. The effect of the resulting parallelism between these brief episodes also works against Virgil's authority.

19. Castelvetro (1570), who offers a typically annoyed rejection of what he takes to be Dante's purpose in the Aesopic analogy (" . . . non vedere cose che abbiano meno da fare insieme"), goes on to suggest that Dante's *arrière pensée* ". . . dipendeva dall'esser essi [Dante e Virgilio] tratti come fu il topo e la rana dal nibbio." Whatever his intention, he at least implicitly compares Dante to the mouse and Virgil to the frog. Guyler (1972: 37–39) is more outspoken in his firmly stated interpretation that Virgil is forced to take on the role of the frog. One of my few disagreements with him involves his sense that Virgil has been hypocritical in his dealings with Dante during this extended scene. To be sure, he himself hedges this position, both in the title of his essay ("Virgil the Hypocrite—Almost"), and in the following observation: "Of course Virgil proves through the act of saving Dante that he was not guilty of hypocrisy, but only of overconfidence in his authority" (ibid.), a formulation with which I concur—as does Ryan (1982²: 19–20).

20. See my treatment in "Dante's 'Georgic' *(Inferno* XXIV, 1–18)," *Dante Studies* CII (1984): 111–21.

21. For my own attempt to put this problem into a wider perspective see *Il Virgilio dantesco: tragedia nella "Commedia"* (Florence, 1983). Ryan (1982: 10–25) offers an extended and like-minded treatment of Dante's recondite assault upon Virgilian values in *Purg.* XXX, which parallels my own series of observations on that scene (pp. 131–134, 141–145). See also Albert Rossi, "'A l'ultimo suo': *Paradiso* XXX and its Virgilian Context," *Studies in Medieval and Renaissance History* IV (1981): 64–66. And see Ball (1981: 75–76).

BIBLIOGRAPHY

1324–28 ca. Lana: *Comedia di Dante degli Allaghieri col Commento di Jacopo della Lana bolognese,* a cura de Luciano Scarabelli. Bologna, 1866–67.

1327 Guido da Pisa: *Guido da Pisa's Expositiones et Glose super Comediam Dantis, or Commentary on Dante's Inferno,* edited with Notes and an Introduction by Vincenzo Cioffari. Albany, NY, 1974.

1333 Ottimo: *L'Ottimo Commento della Divina Commedia* [Andrea Lancia]. Testo inedito d'un contemporaneo di Dante . . . [ed. Alessandro Torri]. Pisa, 1827–29.

1340 Pietro di Dante: *Petri Allegherii super Dantis ipsius genitoris Comoediam Commentarium, nunc primum in lucem editum* . . . [ed. Vincenzo Nannucci]. Florentiae, 1845. [See also *Il "Commentarium" di Pietro Alighieri nelle redazioni ashburnhamiana e ottoboniana,* ed. R. della Vedova & M. T. Silvotti. Firenze, 1978 (*Inferno* only)].

1373 Benvenuto: *Benvenuti de Rambaldis de Imola Comentum super Dantis Aldigherij Comoediam, nunc primum integre in lucem editum sumptibus Guilielmi Warren Vernon, curante Jacopo Philippo Lacaita. Florentiae, 1887.*

1385 Buti: *Commento di Francesco da Buti sopra la Divina Commedia di Dante Allighieri* . . . per cura di Crescentino Giannini. Pisa, 1858–62.

1400 ca. Anonimo Fiorentino: *Commento alla Divina Commedia d'Anonimo Fiorentino del secolo XIV, ora per la prima volta stampato,* a cura di Pietro Fanfani. Bologna, 1866–74.

1416 Serravalle: *Fratris Johannis de Serravalle Ord. Min. Episcopi et Principis Firmani Translatio et Comentum totius libri Dantis Aldigherii, cum textu italico Fratris Bartholomaei a Colle eiusdem Ordinis, nunc primum edita,* [a cura di Fr. Marcellino da Civezza & Fr. Teofilo Domenichelli]. Prati, 1891.

1440 ca. Guiniforto: *Lo Inferno della Commedia de Dante Alighieri col comento di Guiniforto delli Bargigi, tratto da due manoscritti inediti del secolo decimo quinto,* con introduzione e note dell'avvo. G. Zac[c]heroni. Marsilia, 1838.

1481 Landino: *Comento di Christophoro Landino fiorentino sopra la Comedia di Danthe Alighieri Poeta fiorentino.* Firenze, 1481.

1544 Vellutello: *La Comedia di Dante Alighieri con la nova espositione di Alessandro Vellutello.* Vinegia, 1544.

1570 ca. Castelvetro: *Sposizione di Lodovico Castelvetro a XXIX Canti dell'Inferno dantesco, ora per la prima volta data in luce* da Giovanni Franciosi. Modena, 1886.

1732 Venturi: *La Divina Commedia di Dante Alighieri* . . . col commento del P. Pompeo Venturi. Firenze, 1821.

1791 Lombardi: *La Divina Commedia, novamente corretta, spiegata e difesa* da F. B. L. M. C. [i.e., Fra Baldassare Lombardi, minore conventuale]. Roma, 1791 [–92].

1824 Cesari: *Bellezze della Divina Commedia di Dante Alighieri. Dialoghi* d'Antonio Cesari P. d. o. Verona, 1824–26.

1826 Rossetti: *La Divina Commedia di Dante Alighieri con comento analitico* di Gabriele Rossetti, Londra, 1826–27. [Only *Inferno;* for *Purgatorio* see the edition of P. Giannantonio. Firenze, 1967 (Biblioteca dell'*AR*, 87)].

1856 Andreoli: *La Divina Commedia di Dante Alighieri,* col Commento di Raffaello Andreoli. Firenze, 1887.

1874 Scartazzini: *La Divina Commedia di Dante Alighieri,* riveduta nel testo e commentata da G. A. Scartazzini. Leipzig, 1874–90. [And see the greatly revised 2nd ed., *ibid.,* 1900; repr. Bologna 1965.]

1894 Poletto: *La Divina Commedia di Dante Alighieri,* con commento del Prof. Giacomo Poletto. Roma, 1894.

1900 McKenzie: Kenneth McKenzie, "Dante's References to Aesop," *Seventeenth Annual Report of the Dante Society.* Boston, 1900, 1–14.

1900 Oelsner: *The Temple Classics Translation of Dante.* London, 1899–1901. [Notes by H. Oelsner & P. H. Wicksteed to *Paradiso* (1899); by Oelsner to *Inferno* (1900) and *Purgatorio* (1901).]

1905 Torraca: *La Divina Commedia di Dante Alighieri* nuovamente commentata da Francesco Torraca, 4th ed. Milano, 1920.

1909 Grandgent: *La Divina Commedia di Dante Alighieri,* edited and annotated by C. H. Grandgent. Boston, 1909–13. [See also the revised ed. of 1933, *ibid.*]

1909 Parodi: E. G. Parodi, "Il comico nella *Divina Commedia,* in his *Poesia e storia nella "Divina Commedia."* Napoli, 1920, 105–209.

1921 Casini & Barbi: *La Divina Commedia di Dante Alighieri* con il commento di Tommaso Casini, 6ª ediz. rinnovata e accresciuta per cura di S. A. Barbi. Firenze, 1944 [repr. *ibid.,* 1973–76. See also Mazzoni 1972–73.]

1936 Trucchi: *Esposizione della Divina Commedia* [di Ernesto Trucchi]. Milano, 1936.

1944 Spitzer: Leo Spitzer, "The Farcical Elements in 'Inferno', Cantos XXI–XXIII," *MLN* 59 (1944): 83–88.

1946 Momigliano: *La Divina Commedia commentata da Attilio Momigliano*. Firenze, 1946–51. [See also Mazzoni 1972.]

1954 Bacchelli: Riccardo Bacchelli, "Da Dite a Malebolge: La tragedia delle porte chiuse e la farsa dei ponti rotti", *GSLI* 131 (1954): 1–32.

1954 Gmelin: *Die göttliche Komödie*. Trans. Hermann Gmelin. *Kommentar*. Stuttgart, 1954–57.

1955 Mandruzzato: Enzo Mandruzzato, "L'apologo 'della rana e del topo' e Dante," *SD* 33 (1955–56): 147–65.

1955 Sapegno: *La Divina Commedia*, a cura di Natalino Sapegno. Milano, 1957. [See also 2nd ed., Firenze, 1968.]

1960 Mattalia: *La Divina Commedia*, a cura di Daniele Mattalia. Milano, 1975.

1962 Chimenz: *La Divina Commedia di Dante Alighieri*, a cura di Siro A. Chimenz. Torino, 1962.

1962 Larkin: Neil M. Larkin, "Another Look at Dante's Frog and Mouse," *MLN* 77 (1962): 94–99.

1965 Fallani: *La Divina Commedia*, a cura di Giovanni Fallani. Messina, 1965.

1965 Padoan: Giorgio Padoan, "Il *Liber Esopi* e due episodi dell'*Inferno*," *SD* 41 (1965): 75–102.

1966 Larkin: Neil M. Larkin, "*Inferno* XXIII, 4–9 Again," *MLN* (1966): 85–88.

1966 Petrocchi: *La Commedia secondo l'antica vulgata*, a cura di Giorgio Petrocchi. Milano, 1966–67.

1968 Giacalone: *La Divina Commedia*, a cura di Giuseppe Giacalone. Roma, 1968.

1969 Wolff: Hope Nash Wolff, "A Study of Dante's Distance from the Creatures of Cantos Twenty-One and Two of the *Inferno* . . . ," *Italian Quarterly* 12 (1969): 239–51.

1970 Kraus: Clara Kraus, "Esopo," in *Enciclopedia dantesca* II, 729–30.

1970 Singleton: *The Divine Comedy*. Translated, with a Commentary, by Charles S. Singleton. Princeton, 1970–75.

1971 Sarolli: Gian Roberto Sarolli, "Musical Symbolism: *Inferno* XXI, 136–139, *exemplum* of Musica Diaboli versus Musica Dei," in his *Prolegomena alla "Divina Commedia*." Firenze, 1971, 363–80.

1972 Guyler: Sam Guyler, "Virgil the Hypocrite—Almost: A Re-interpretation of *Inferno* XXIII," *DS* 90 (1972): 25–42.

1972 Mazzoni: *La Divina Commedia [Inferno* and *Purgatorio]*, con i commenti di T. Casini/S. A. Barbi e di A. Momigliano. Introduzione e aggiornamento bibliografico-critico di Francesco Mazzoni. Firenze, 1972–73.

1975 Bosco: Umberto Bosco, "Il ludo dantesco dei barattieri," in *Essays in Honour of John Humpreys Whitfield*, ed. H. C. Davis et al. London, 1975, 39–40.

1979 Bosco & Reggio: *La Divina Commedia*, a cura di Umberto Bosco e Giovanni Reggio. Firenze, 1979.

1981 Conrieri: Davide Conrieri, "Lettura del canto XXI dell'*Inferno*," *GSLI* 158 (1981): 1–43.

1981 De Robertis: Domenico De Robertis, "In viaggio coi demòni (canto XXII dell'*Inferno*)," *SD* 53 (1981): 1–29.

1982 Ryan: Christopher J. Ryan, "Virgil's Wisdom in the *Divina Commedia*," *Medievalia et Humanistica* 11 (1982): 1–38.

1982² Ryan: C. J. Ryan, "*Inferno* XXI: Virgil and Dante: A Study in Contrasts," *Italica* 59 (1982): 16–31.

The Plot-Line of Myth in Dante's *Inferno*

RICARDO J. QUINONES

We are gradually learning to focus critical attention not only on the story of the *Commedia*—that single line of spiritual development—but also, and now more valuably, on the stories within the *Commedia*. One of the more remarkable unfolding stories within the poem occurs exclusively in the *Inferno*. This drama—and it may accurately be so called—is made up of the series of encounters between the two travelers, Dante and Virgil, and a host of demonic challengers: Charon, Minòs, Cerberus, Pluto, Phlegyas, the demons at the gate of Dis and the Furies who emerge on the ramparts, the Minotaurs, and later the Malebranche.

These encounters are distinctive because through them—and only through them—are revealed in Hell the great patterns of Christian eschatology in which the individual soul knowingly or unknowingly participates—the contest in Heaven, the fall of the rebellious angels (with their resultant roles as devils in Hell), the death of Christ and the Harrowing of Hell. Furthermore, confined to the guards of Hell, all of these encounters exist outside and apart from the exchanges between Dante and the sinners. These encounters set up a separate line of development, and a crucial one it is. Only here in these "extra-curricular" meetings are the larger patterns of Dante's journey established. Only here is his journey taken outside of history and placed in universal myth. It is as if to be in Hell is to be unaware of the larger justifying patterns in which one participates, and as if Dante's own spiritual growth must lie in coming to recognize and understand these patterns. When Dante is brought later to confess that "present things" occupied his attention—and that this was the basis of his straying—we can begin to understand what he meant by that phrase, and why the journey to Hell—in its larger mythic patterning—is the beginning of his restoration.

While it is part of Dante's spiritual growth to learn of these larger patterns, he does so in the canticle that is most atomistic—most concerned with present things—aesthetically and morally. In this canticle we are presented with none of the joined suites of cantos where moral debates, or philosophical questioning, or ongoing drama overflows and extends beyond the limits of individual cantos (think only of *Paradiso* XIV–XVIII). As Dante's aesthetic principles reflect moral ones, such abundance would be misplaced in the *Inferno*, where there is little connection between individual souls, consumed as they are with their own stories, their own obsessive tellings and retellings. It is for this reason that within the *Inferno* the only inter-canto commentary comes from ironic juxtapositions that jostle the reader from too fixed an involvement in the present story (as Ciacco's municipal account in Canto VI separates us physically and spiritually from the tragic story of the *cor gentil* in Canto V). It is for this reason that the larger patterns, unbeknownst to the inhabitants of Hell, are derived from encounters with the guards. That the prisoners are unaware of these larger goings-on is an indication of their benightedness and why they are in Hell itself and why Dante must, as part of his own regeneration, recapture these enlargements, this sense provided of the larger unfoldings of the human drama in which he is involved.

While Christ cannot be mentioned by name in the *Inferno*, it is only here in these episodes that the Harrowing (Canto IV) and the death of Christ (Cantos IX, XII and XXI) are indicated. This last in fact provides the only precise means for dating Christ's death, and consequently the sole means for computing Dante's journey as taking place in the Easter season of the year 1300. These events of Christ's life form the chronological baselines of the poem. Yet, while Christocentric, the pattern is not a full one: it stops short at the Harrowing of Hell, that fabulous piece of Christian legend which tells how Christ used the interval between his death and resurrection to go down to Hell and bring back the great figures of the Old Testament (an adventure that is narrated in *Inferno* IV). This is a pivotal event for the *Inferno* and also highly significant, because it tells us that here in the *Inferno* the issues are not those of the higher possibility of paradisal triumph, but rather of sponsorship and justification. That is, the issues are entirely confined to the meaning of the Journey to the Underworld: who or what provides the support for such a journey, and are those powers sufficient to justify it? Immediately, this requires a debate over entrance, or access: by what right does one attempt such an undertaking? But more importantly it involves a debate over return. To go to Hell might be considered easy, but far more difficult is to go and come back. Hence the higher motif of the Harrowing, which requires return as well (as Dante so pointedly if discreetly inquires of Virgil in Canto IX). True to his creative manner, Dante dramatizes these issues and personalizes them. He himself is most doubtful as to his credentials—and this itself is revealing—but this doubt is cast back onto his more immediate sponsor, Virgil himself.

Another startling fact is that only here, in this line of development, is Virgil ever at a loss in the *Inferno*. And while dramatic episodes—Cantos VIII–IX and XXIII—make this clear, the subtext from Canto II onward suggests Virgil's own limitations. But on the other level, that of history, he is quite adept. And this fact is itself defining of Virgil and his qualities. For instance, the other developing plot-line in the *Inferno* concerns Dante's imminent exile. This story develops in Cantos VI, X, XV, and XXIV—and it will continue in *Purgatorio* VIII before reaching its largest resolution in *Paradiso* XVII, at which point the journey itself will have fulfilled its function and Dante will already have acquired the means for coping with this terrible blow. But in the *Inferno* Virgil is the dominant interpreter of this story, and to further accentuate differences with the other plot-line, all of the pertinent exchanges take place with sinners. It is Virgil who in Canto VII provides the larger discourse on Fortune, and finally in Canto XV, when Dante is able to respond to Brunetto Latini by means of the lessons learned, it is Virgil who applauds his response the way a teacher would an apt pupil. Moreover, at this point, in more ways than one, Dante shows how he has moved from one teacher, Brunetto, to another, Virgil, with all that this implies.

Confined to the sinners, these exchanges show Virgil to be adept at performing on the plane of his proficiency, history. But on the other level, that of myth, Dante's journey to Hell, in its debate over sponsorship and justification, soon becomes a debate over Virgil himself. In the one sphere, that of history, he is uncontested; in the other, that of spiritual justification, he is the contested personage. This is dramatic, revealing and poignant, because of all the mythic journeys of which Dante is aware, those of Theseus, of Hercules, of Aeneas, of Paul, the most significant, the one in which he is deeply immersed in many of its aspects, and the one to which he is most indebted, even when he transforms its essence, is that of Book VI of the *Aeneid*.

History and myth seem to exist for the moment on separate planes in Dante's *Inferno*. Yet there is a point at which they seem to converge, and that is in Canto XXVI, with Ulysses, himself a legendary voyager, who also made a visit to the underworld. It is here that Virgil's world and Virgil's values show a superior value, even if they do not offer the fulfillment that Dante requires.

We have yet to gauge in an imaginatively adequate way the extent of Dante's immersion in Virgil's poem and the magical Book VI. Our lists of citations and echoes, while helpful, do not bring us any closer to the matter. Like that of his predecessor, Dante's journey to the afterlife (and here we mean specifically Hell itself) is not only in quest of, it is defining of essential values. While the *Inferno* is only a partial—in fact a truncated—portion of this vision, only Act One of a three-act drama, it nevertheless participates in the process and is essential to the drama. Dante's visit to Hell is, as it were, the first phase and not the full message. It communicates what must be unlearned; it encourages the ways of disaffection; it exposes false gods. Truly it is a no-man's land (and even more clearly, a no-woman's land) where one's main purpose is to escape. While this must be emphasized, and clearly its limitation to only the Harrowing part of Christian eschatology helps define its nature, it does aspire to essential value, and consequently to representativeness. Its encounters are exemplary, even if they are with anti-heroes.

To arrive at such representativeness requires an extraordinary journey with remarkable engagements. It is not a normal journey and yet it produces patterns in which normal people can participate. On this point the *Commedia* and the *Aeneid* are concurrent. We come here to one of the intriguing paradoxes of great literature—a paradox upon which the leveling radical egalitarianism of our time seems to founder: true representativeness is only achieved rarely and that by an extraordinary person called to a special adventure. The lesson is for everybody but the agonist is not Everyman. Where the mission is one of retrieving essential value, of establishing representativeness, the journey is singular. Moses, Aeneas, Dante are chosen because of their exemplariness. Where the character is most elect his message is most representative. In our own time, when we discount the virtues of special designation, we run the risk of dismantling the importance of representativeness.

In the *Commedia* and the *Aeneid*, the journey undertaken is singular and consequently rare. To be sure, Aeneas has the Sibyl for a guide—and she, unlike Virgil, seems fool-proof and infallible—but not all attempts to secure the golden bough are successful. One cannot fake it, wrest it by willful or conscious violence. A special designation is required, the "right person," and yet that person is representative of the values to be established. The golden bough contains the values of renewal, those values that endure in a culture. If the person is the right person—one called by fate—the golden bough will yield itself to his hands easily, and another will spring up in its place. The charm itself, the talisman, is responsive only to the charmed (*Aeneid*, VI, 208–217).

Similarly with Dante, despite his sponsorship, in fact his dual sponsorship, he is overwhelmingly aware of the singularity of his journey. While all the creatural world is granted respite in the normal rounds of existence, Dante is called to endure an arduous disruption, to experience a definite breach: "Io sol uno. . . ." The emphasis on the singular is in triplicate:

> The day was fading and the darkening air
> was releasing all the creatures on our earth
> from their daily tasks, and I, one man alone,

> was making ready to endure the battle
> of the journey, and of the pity it involved,
> which my memory, unerring, shall now retrace.
> (*Inferno*, II, 1–6)

Such an undertaking is as rare as it is singular. When Virgil intervenes to rescue Dante from his own careening regression, his voice is weak from long silence. In fact, the fullness of the classical voice had not been heard in nearly a millennium. When Dante joins with his classical tradition in *Inferno* IV, he becomes sixth in their group, thus showing his own consciousness that his efforts of restoration are bridging a long period of stunted artistic aspiration and neglect. While we refer to a classical tradition—and such a reference is, I believe, real—it is still noteworthy how sporadic that tradition is, as Virgil himself is similarly aware. The puffed-up and easily angered Charon is deflated instantly by the revelation of the golden bough (which, interestingly enough, the Sibyl held concealed *under* her dress). It is the destined gift, and because of that "one so long unseen." The intermittence of the calling underlines its importance, and reminds us that the outcast, the buffeted one, might also be the son of destiny.

The journey to the Underworld is not an easy one. As the Sibyl makes clear at the outset, and as Dante discovers more than once in the course of his journey, this has a special meaning. If the road to Hell is a slippery slope, then of course it is easy—unconsciously easy, as Dante himself and many of his characters attest. But if the trick is not only to go to Hell but also return then of course that is a different matter.

> The way downward is easy from Avernus.
> Black Dis's door stands open night and day.
> But to retrace your steps to heaven's air,
> That is the trouble, there is the toil. . . .
> (*Aeneid*, VI, 187–190)[1]

The journey to the Underworld is thus difficult in both the aesthetic and moral-spiritual senses. Aesthetically, of course, the easier portion is to describe the journey to the end of the night, show mean streets, and invoke an apocalypse now, even, as Shakespeare did, to dramatize a hell-hound like Richard III. Here one engages the strange propensity we have to identify with evil and power, to be thrilled vicariously. It is much harder to establish aesthetically and with equal or greater power the legitimate bases of a culture and its enduring values. Even Charon—one should say especially Charon, because he reveals the mind over which he presides—was not influenced by the "goodness" of Aeneas's journey, his desire to see his father, but only acceded to the magical pass, the credentials offered by the golden bough. And so it is that Charon's clones throughout the early cantos of the *Inferno* need to be subdued by superior credentials (that is, superior to them but also to Virgil himself). Their recalcitrance only shows their own dim-wittedness, and establishes why they are locked in as guardians of Hell.

But in the moral-spiritual sense, there is another reason why the return from Hell is rare and difficult. It takes a special and resolute intelligence to experience the depths of a culture without being rocked by that revelation. Robert Frost, who certainly understood his own and his culture's depths, called it a mind "too lofty and original to rage." Yet, one can understand the rage of those who go to the depths and do not return, who have had their minds turned and are lost forever. Do they see too much, or not enough? The epic poem, the classical journey is based upon the judgment that they do not see enough, that they lack the requisite courage, resoluteness, higher intelligence to survive the vision into the depth. This is one other reason why the journey is not for Everyman; weaker intelligences are devastated by the revelations. But not so an Oedipus, a Theseus, a Hercules, an Aeneas, a Dante, or a Hamlet—that is, specially designated characters who are charged to carry a terrible burden, a burden under which the normal beneficiaries of their journey would crack.

This is as much as to say that the journey to the underworld, the searching out of essential value through the mediation of another life, participates in larger patterns of consciousness of which Dante and Virgil are well aware. It is at this point that we begin to see the differences between Aeneas's journey in Virgil's poem, and that of the character Dante in the *Commedia*. Unlike Dante, Aeneas understands why he needs to undertake the journey to the underworld. That is, he himself is clear about his purpose and his mission. Confident of his credentials, which he himself supplies, he is able to respond to the Sibyl's dire dissuasions. Orpheus could descend in order to call back his wife's spirit, and Pollux could do so in order to restore his twin—each of these representing large expressions of familial attachment. From Greek culture there were others who succeeded in completing the full journey—they were heroes, Theseus and Hercules. The first two examples are those whom a "benign Jupiter" has loved, and the latter two are those whom a "fiery heroism" has elevated. Aeneas is quite conscious of these precedents, and uses them to assert his own legitimacy: "By birth I too descend from Jove on high. . . ." He, too, is the son of a god, and thus qualified for this undertaking; but more importantly, the fuller meaning is that his own values and those of his culture are sufficient to withstand the scrutiny and to endure the enterprise (*Aeneid*, VI, 175–181).

Aeneas is an active pursuer of his own identity, his own theme and that of his people. He knows why he must undertake the journey to the underworld and is thus able to assert that of which Dante is unaware. He is clear as to his sponsorship, and clear as to his values. There is no need for a shock treatment in regard to Aeneas. What he seeks is confirmation. Thus when the Sibyl conjures up the terrible vision of historical repetition, the same wars in the new land, another Achilles—what he fled from on the plane of history is what he will meet again—this neither surprises Aeneas nor daunts him. He fully comprehends the limitations of the plane on which he exists.

> No novel kinds of hardships, no surprises
> Loom ahead, Sister. I foresaw them all,
> Went through them in my mind.
> (156–158)

And so it is that when Dante responds to Brunetto in Canto XV, he directly echoes these lines: "This prophecy is not new to my ears" ("Non è nuova ali orecchi miei tal arra" [v. 94]).

On all of these matters, Dante's poem differs. Dante is not an active pursuer of his own mission; in fact, at the time of Virgil's intervention, he is backsliding terribly. He requires radical restructuring and redirection. Nor is this an easy adjustment. So heedless has his own attitude been that his recovery demands drastic surgery, an extreme measure, extraordinary disruption, and here within the orbit of the exfoliating meanings, primary must be the fact of exile itself, that terrible fall which finally for Dante came to be so fortunate. While this occupies the historical dimension of the work and is thus only communicated by the inhabitants of Hell, it is clearly something for which he is unprepared and of which he is unaware. That is, unlike the basic method of Virgil's poem, the dramatic shock of the unexpected is critical.

Nor can Dante be so sure about his mission. Within this penumbra of mystery and grace that Virgil's own arrival betokens and that his journey itself will exemplify, Dante cannot know what lays in store for him. His own faith is being tested by his journeying into the unknown, not the known. The vision of which he is in need is only open to a journey of discovery. Yet it was preexisting, one that he had known but lost. Hence Virgil's startling intervention is an act of grace that leads to recovery, to a reassertion of what should never have been lost. This should tell us that Dante's journey transcends the cyclical nature of the historical dimension, that he is proceeding into the philosophical, the poetic, the religious.

Where sponsorship in Virgil's poem is otherwise confident and uncontested, in Dante's poem it is divided, debated, and essential to the dramatic unfolding of the *Inferno* and beyond. Put rather simply, the ongoing debate over Virgil does not only take place in the *Purgatorio*, where his final and necessary demotion takes place, it is essential to the meaning of the poem from the very beginning. From the beginning Virgil needs to be supplemented; while coordinate, his qualities, virtues and guidance are clearly subordinate. But this should come as no surprise, as if Dante had arbitrarily chosen a scapegoat only to eject him at a convenient moment. The entire drama of Virgil is integrally bound up with the essential values of *Aeneid*, Book VI (if not the entire poem). These values show the valid strengths of Roman culture, but also their limitations, the ways in which they needed to be transcended.

The essential value of the *Aeneid* and what it contains is integrally related to the long-standing wish to hold conversation yet again with one's father. This is not an ordinary matter, and like the entire topos itself, it is not normal because it is so universal. Who would not like to talk yet again with his dead father, to show where one has been and what one has done? This larger motive is summary of the essential values of Roman culture, the values of historical and cultural continuity. That is where they will peg their golden bough, on the genealogical tree of communal *pietas*. This is shown in three episodes that both introduce and frame Aeneas's journey.

Immediately after the instructions from the Sibyl, Aeneas discovers that his unburied comrade is Misenus. Before any further advance can be made, Misenus must be properly cremated and inurned. This intervention carries on for more than one hundred lines, but the individual burial has larger cultural import. His name will be forever honored in the promontory named for him, Misenum.

The same transference from individual *pietas* to large cultural import occurs in the next episode, when Aeneas encounters those who cannot be transported across Cocytus for lack of proper burial (normally they have to wait one hundred years). Here Aeneas encounters his helmsman, Palinurus, who disappeared from the boat at the end of Book V and was presumed drowned. As one who cannot move onward with his company, Palinurus harbors thoughts of personal injury, but is assuaged—nay pleased—by the prospect that in compensation for his premature death a tomb will be erected for him, and the cape forever named Palinurus. The compensation of historical continuity assuages the reality of individual loss.

As the revelation of the essential meaning of Roman culture is introduced by these two episodes, so Book VI closes with it. Book VII opens with the burial of Aeneas's nurse, Caieta, who will also have a place named after her. This event assumes added importance in light of Dante's retrospective vision. It is the prospect of such abiding cultural continuity that holds no interest for the adventurous Ulysses in *Inferno* XXVI. Beginning with his long stay with Circe, his own narration is not part of the ongoing cultural processes of civilization.

> When I
> set sail from Circe, who, more than a year,
> had kept me occupied close to Gaeta
> (before Aeneas called it by that name)
> nor sweetness for a son, nor reverence
> for an aging father, nor the debt of love
> I owed Penelope to make her happy,
> could quench deep in myself the burning wish
> to know the world and have experience
> of all men's vices, of all human worth.
> (90–100)

It is this very validity of Roman culture that makes all the more dramatic and intriguing its contested and subordinate place in Dante's poem. Dante in his life was thrown out of the world of known certainties and communal pieties. His purpose was to respond to a higher calling, to undertake a voyage into the unknown, to transcend the valid but diminished compensations of the historical continuity, to discover the larger dispensations of his own theme.

The poem's debate over the validity of Virgil, while clearly presented in *Inferno* IX, begins long before that—in fact, in the two proemial cantos. The poem requires two proemial cantos because sponsorship is divided and debated—there is no single Sibyl, no simple uncontested precedents. When in *Inferno* II Dante reminds Virgil that he is neither Aeneas nor Paul, he is in effect questioning Virgil's own credentials. He is asking what is the transcendent purpose behind his own undertaking. Even if Aeneas were "chosen" to make this visit to the underworld, that was because Rome would later provide the site for Peter. Dante is not Aeneas nor Paul—his own credentials as a chosen being, as a son of god, have been obscured; nor is there an apparent transcendent mission which would justify his being "chosen." Virgil rightly understands the question, and if he disparages the expression of *viltà*, he also fills Dante in on the higher dispensation that inspired his own coming. In short, Dante enjoys better connections than those provided by Virgil himself. The three ladies connect Dante's own experience, his contemporary world, represented by Beatrice herself, the ingredients of his own experience and of his day, with the transcendent possibilities offered by the supreme model of human spirituality, Mary herself. This represents a new order to the epic experience, one which Dante's own questioning leads to, and one which Virgil's response provides.

In episode after episode of demonic challenge, it is Virgil who speaks for the larger sponsorship that Dante enjoys, just as it was Virgil who in Canto II reminded his doubting protégé of the extraordinary dimensions of his own experience. In Canto III, when Dante is told by Charon that he cannot proceed, it is Virgil who responds, "It is so willed, there where the power is / for what is willed; that's all you need to know" (95–96). In Canto IV, he answers Dante's own uneasy question as to whether anyone was ever liberated from Limbo, thus providing a larger pattern of the Harrowing of Hell for Dante's own journey. In Canto V, the issues are more explicit when Minòs warns Dante, "be careful how you enter and whom you trust." But again Virgil pushes the obstacle aside with almost the exact words that he used to subdue Charon. Dante's is a "fatale andare": it is so willed, and that's all you need to know.

Virgil does not believe in wasting too much breath on the demented opposition. In Canto VI he silences Cerberus by throwing a stone. But in Canto VII, he provides additional amplification to Dante's journey. Plutus is called the "lupo" who consumes himself (unlike the *lupa* who consumes others). But he cannot constrain Dante, whose journey is "willed on high, where Michael wrought / a just revenge for the bold assault on God" (11 12). The battle in heaven, which took place even before the fall of humankind, in that great schema of Christian salvation history, was the first phase of the ongoing warfare between good and evil. The pattern is a persistent one, as the same mythic drama is played out again and again. In fact, after Phlegyas is deflated in Canto VIII (18–24) the struggle becomes more explicitly dramatic, partaking of the scenic qualities of a *sacra rappresentazione*. But it is here, where the fullest action of grace is required, that Virgil's own limitations are revealed.

The earlier reference to Michael becomes all the more pertinent because the devils who by the thousands guard the ramparts of the city of Dis are those fallen angels defeated in the first skirmish in heaven. Their challenge is even more ominous because they invoke fears that Dante himself had harbored, fears that his journey was a foolhardy one, a mad act of overreaching hubris. They further challenge Dante to complete if he can, alone, the return journey: "Let him retrace his foolish way alone, / just let him try. . . ." The verbal echoes of "folle strada" return us to Dante's first fears and anticipate the ongoing competition between the journey he undertakes and the challenging one of Ulysses.

At this point Dante is horrified at the prospect of proceeding without Virgil and reminds him of his dependency and of Virgil's prior successes. Virgil's words of encouragement are similar to those that were previously effective: "'Do not fear, the journey we are making / none can prevent: such power did decree it'" (104–105). But the recalcitrant guardians, immune to his persuasions, slam the door in his face. Virgil, himself seeking justification, reaches back for that earlier action that he himself had witnessed.

> This insolence of theirs is nothing new;
>   they used it once at a less secret gate
>   which is, and will forever be, unlocked.
>   (124–126)

Virgil himself is aware that in this ongoing conflict the same powers that opened the gates of Hell ("portae Inferni non praevalebunt"—and the Gates of Hell shall not prevail against them), will be represented by a messenger, who is already descending to their assistance: there "comes one by whom the city will be opened." The tercet with which Canto VIII closes is poised in the simplicity of its language at the outskirts of hope itself, as Virgil reaches back into some dim past, some collective memory, to recall the force that will dissipate the obstacles of despair and distrust.

Here at the start of the second phase of Hell, where violent crimes are punished, Dante returns and recapitulates the tension and the drama that existed at the very outset of the poem.[2] There Virgil was able to chastise him for his faintheartedness, for his *viltà*, but here the question of the *folle strada* does not issue in simple *viltà*, but rather in a larger loss of faith, one for which Virgil himself is dramatically at a loss. He can encourage Dante when heart is lacking, but here against a larger irrationality a greater faith is required. He too can now wonder what would happen if the destined help does not arrive, "Se non. . . ." He can only hold on to the promised aid, ". . . but no, such help was promised," and lament the delay, "O how much time it's taking him to come!"

The fear raised is the essential one, first raised by the Sibyl herself, that one might not be able to effect a return, but may rather be locked forever in the furious antagonisms, the anger of loss and exile. This is the question raised implicitly by Dante in Canto II, indirectly in Canto IV, uttered by the Furies in Canto VIII, and now expressed with full dramatic clarity in Canto IX (16–18):

> "Has anyone before ever descended
> to this sad hollow's depths from that first circle
> whose pain is all in having hope cut off?"

Virgil responds dutifully that he himself made the full journey once before, consigned by the witch Erichtho to fetch a spirit from the lowest circle. But this story is misplaced and its irrelevancy underlined when Dante suddenly drops Virgil's account ("he said other things, but I forget them") because at this point three Furies suddenly appear on the rampart, and Virgil is upstaged if not outmoded.

They themselves recall their defeat by Theseus (with Hercules' aid, in this story), and vow revenge, perhaps providing themselves the image of the defeat they inflict. Virgil identifies the Furies and cautions Dante not to look on these representatives of the horrors of existence, tinged in blood, their own bearing calling up the image of madness itself. This is not the rage that threatens Dante from the outside, but rather from the inside, the fury that unbalances the mind, rendering it hysterical, obsessive, tainted. Not trusting to this disciple, Virgil himself places his hands over Dante's eyes. Should he look on the Gorgon Medusa, "there would be no returning to the world," and his entire project would have indeed succumbed to *follia*.

Similar to what happens in *Purgatorio* XXVII, when it is not Virgil's admonitions but only the name of Beatrice that inspires Dante to pass through the wall of fire, Virgil's actions, while here effective, are still only prohibitive; they do not reveal any positive surge of force, such as is revealed in the arrival of the divine messenger. In fact, his action is violent, indicating a more radical transformation of being at work, as well as a more powerful and positive force. The messenger of grace conveying a more powerful infusion of faith actually puts the gathered enemies to rout. His force is like the wind breaking through a dry forest, and the devils are like frogs fleeing before their enemy, the snake. In this action the very weaknesses of these "destroyed" souls are also revealed, as they scatter before the more powerful force of an active faith, that walks over Styx, with his feet still dry on the water. One can think back to Christ's summons to Peter, and the latter's lack of faith, to suggest that here is represented the great drama of faith, with extraordinary implications for Dante's poem (Matt., 15:25–32; but also Mark, 6:45–52). The need is to maintain the kind of mind and sanity that permits one to address the issues of the day, the causes of one's plight, with conviction, with justice and with right, and not to let the personal demons, the horrors themselves take control.

This plot-line of dramatic challenge and ultimate conquest does not end here. In Canto XII, Virgil again invokes his great model, Theseus, and there are other embarrassing moments in Canto XXIII, where Virgil realizes he has been tricked by Malacoda. But the fullest drama, the one played out in the mythic enlargements provided by the exchanges with the guards of Hell and not with the sinners themselves, has its most intense moments in Cantos VIII and IX. Yet, it is possible that the entire drama does not stay confined to the level of the extra-curricular guardians but finally enters into dramatic contest with one of the sinners themselves. Obviously I here refer to Ulysses, part of whose continuing dramatic attraction derives from the fusion of the interests of history and myth. Ulysses, while the reigning personage in the lower Inferno, is not a guard. Moreover, he, too, made a successful trip to the underworld, a fact Virgil could not include and Dante did not know. Rather, for Virgil Ulysses was the "mastermind of atrocity" and included in Hell only by Deiphobus' account of his treachery (VI, 710). Nevertheless, there are three areas in which the plot-line we have been following and Ulysses' own journey intersect, bringing the latter into the grounds of the contest we have been tracing. The voyages of Dante and of Ulysses are the competing ones. While each runs the risk of *follia*, the charge to which Dante is so keenly sensitive, finally Beatrice, from the higher vision of Paradise, bestows that description on Ulysses' journey, his "varco folle." Of all the souls in the *Inferno*, Ulysses is the only one to have some sense of Purgatory, and hence the continuous nature of his challenge, and is defeated in the very sight of the mountain, "com'altrui piiacque." While clipped and even brutal, this is the same language that supported Dante—a kind of silent will and obscure purpose that seems to operate so mysteriously in its selections.

In order to climb where they might look down on the eighth pocket, Dante and Virgil have to climb over rocks:

> We went along our solitary way
>   among the rocks, among the ridge's crags,
>   where the foot could not advance without the hand.
>   (XXVI, 16–18)

And when Dante rises up to get a better look, "if [he] had not grabbed some jut of rock / [he] could easily have fallen to the bottom." While it is not absolutely clear that these are the same kind of rocks that tumbled at the moment of Christ's death, nevertheless it is the same kind of experience that is part and parcel of the mythic undertaking and revelations from the plot-line we have been following. Not only did Christ break through the locks of Hellgate, but at his death, when the earth shook, many of the bridges and passageways of Hell also crumbled (Cantos XII, XXI-XXIII) and, as a consequence, when Virgil and Dante have to make their way it is frequently over these cascaded rocks. This Virgil relates in Canto XII, 31–45, even if his explanation of its meaning is inadequate. These rocks are then associated with humiliation and defeat, Christ's crucifixion and death. Yet it is to these that Dante clings, and by these that he makes his way, as an act of security and safe passage, particularly here when he compares himself to the lost voyager Ulysses and his destructive fires.

"We only live, only suspire / Consumed by either fire or fire": T. S. Eliot's lines from *Little Gidding* remind us of the alternatives of fire in Dante's poem and in the Ulysses episode. When Dante and Virgil do look at the consuming fire down below in Canto XXVI, Dante resumes the rustic image with which he opened Canto XXIV, and directly associated with Virgil. This is the image of the farmer who represents a kind of *stabilitas* within change, one whose own individual fires are subdued to the larger processes of change and continuity. And of course it is this image— that represented by Roman *pietas*—that is so markedly different in its own observance of continuity within change from what is represented by the footloose, adventurous Ulysses. The death of the nurse—so pointedly mentioned in counterpoint to Ulysses' own experiences—was commemorated by having a city named in her honor. The Romans are the guardians of the perishable goods; theirs is the cult of remembrance, where death and identity, death and naming, go hand in hand. This is one culture, and as far as Dante is concerned it is superior to the other culture, Greek (and perhaps to that of his own time, for which Ulysses is a figure—brilliant, to be sure, but agile intellectually, footloose morally, a cleverness without a center, which becomes mere cunning). While Virgil's culture is superior, and was in fact the basis for the reception and spread of Christianity, it is also insufficient. The drama of Hell, the story within the story, tells us why this is so, representing with remarkable conviction the critical importance of Virgil and hence of Roman culture—understood from within the deepest principle of their achievements—but also showing why this culture, and Virgil in particular, while dimly apprehending that toward which they point, nevertheless failed to provide the fullest assurance and resources that Dante in the trauma of his own personal journey so intensely required.

NOTES

1. All translations from Virgil's poem are from *The Aeneid*, trans. Robert Fitzgerald (New York: Random House, Vintage Classics, 1990).

2. In a valuable *lettura* of Canto IX, Joseph A. Barber reminds us that it also anticipates the actions of Cantos VIII and IX of the *Purgatorio*, where another divine messenger intervenes as an act of special grace in a continuing drama and Dante is mysteriously elevated to the gates of Purgatory. See *Dante's "Divine Comedy," Introductory Readings*, I: *Inferno*, ed. by Tibor Wlassics, *Lectura Dantis*, VI Supplement (1990).

Hell as the Mirror Image of Paradise

JOAN M. FERRANTE

The *Divine Comedy* is a circular poem. Hell only yields its intended message(s) when it is seen as a mirror image of Paradise, when it is understood in terms of what it is not. For Dante, Hell is the least important part of the poem—he would probably have been distressed to know how many people read only Hell. At the very least, Hell must be read within the context of the whole. I will attempt one such reading here in terms of the political or socio-political message of the poem.[1] The political propaganda of the *Comedy* is an aspect which is often ignored by modern critics and readers, though it was obvious to Dante's earliest commentators. The three large socio-political issues which were important in contemporary political theory—and which are not irrelevant now—are the relation of the individual to society, the relative advantages of smaller and larger political structures (city, kingdom, empire), and the conflict between the church and the secular state.

Contemporary political writers from the mid-thirteenth century, following Aristotle, acknowledged the importance of society and social institutions for life on earth, the interdependence of men in supplying their needs. Giles of Rome says there are three possibilities for existence: the life of desire, which is to live as a beast; the life of contemplation, which is to live as an angel; and the civil/political life, which is to live as a man (*De regimine principum*, 1:3). Remigio dei Girolami, a fellow Florentine, puts the common good so far above the individual good that he says one should love the city *more* than oneself, indeed next to God, because of the resemblance it bears to God (*De bono pacis*). Like Remigio, Dante seems to value the good of the whole over the good of the parts, or at least to believe that one is essential to the other; in the *Monarchia*, his essay in political theory, Dante says that only the human race acting as *one* can achieve a restoration of the earthly paradise in which each individual can fulfill his highest potential.

What Dante offers in the *Comedy* is a model in broad outlines for the ideal society on earth, the restoration of that earthly paradise. He begins by revealing in Hell all the traits which must be excluded from the ideal society; in Purgatory, he gives the remedies to counter those traits, and in Paradise he presents the essential qualities and functions of such a society in action. The political message is integral to the poem; all the sins and virtues have social or political implications. Dante is concerned with public issues and the public effects of private actions rather than with private morality. His preferred political structure is the empire which, following the model of heaven, encompasses all smaller units, so that it alone can be the ideal society on earth, a large superstructure mounted over smaller local and national units of government. The major obstacles to the success of empire in Dante's view and in the *Comedy* are Florence, the model of the powerful, rich, corrupt city, the French monarchy, which embodies the worst evils of national states, and the papacy, which usurps temporal power and wealth in defiance of God's will. The audience Dante is writing for includes intellectuals and the powerful—the "big boats" and "highest peaks" he alludes to in Paradise[2]—not only leaders of church and state, but also merchants and financiers, key powerbrokers in Dante's world as in ours. Contemporary merchants' letters cite the *Comedy* and request copies of it, and Dante's use of financial language and his treatment of commercial sins suggest that he had this audience very much in mind.

That the church also knew the poem and understood its critical message is clear from various attacks: a Dominican, Guido Vernani, called Dante's poetry "a poisonous vessel of the father of lies, covered with false and fallacious beauty, by which the author, with poetic phantasms and figments and the eloquence of his words, his siren songs, fraudulently leads not only the sick and ignorant but even the learned to destroy the truth which might save them" (*De reprobatione Monarchiae*). The reading of Dante's poetry was prohibited at a Dominican chapter in Florence in 1335, although it apparently continued to be popular among the brothers; and various passages from the poem—on ecclesiastical corruption—were condemned by church inquisitions. The whole of the *Monarchia* was on the papal index from 1554 to 1881.

Dante chose the poetic mode of the *Comedy* for his political message because it gave not only more freedom of expression, but far more power in the use of imagery than discursive prose would have. In the poem, Dante presents Hell as the greedy, self-centered city-state which serves its own needs at the expense of its neighbors, ignoring the common good, and therefore ultimately self-destructive, like Florence. Paradise, the city of justice, wisdom, love, and harmony, in which the citizens work together for the benefit of all, is the empire which encompasses the world, its peoples, and their needs—Rome. Both are described as cities, but Paradise is city, kingdom, and empire, the total society. Purgatory, a loosely connected "kingdom" with no center like Italy, is never called a city; it is a transitional stage between the corrupt society of Hell and the ideal society of Paradise, its inhabitants waiting to be accepted as "citizens of one true city" (*Purg.* XIII, 94–95). Dante's models for heaven and hell are Rome and Florence rather than the traditional Jerusalem and Babylon, because he is concerned with the immediate problems of his world and he wants his audience to apply his message directly to them.

Dante's personal reasons for casting Florence as Hell are fairly obvious: the city that exiled and rejected him is presented as one no rational being would want to enter; Dante is introduced into it by divine intervention only to show it up for what it is. His political reasons are equally clear: he sees Florence as the major obstacle, along with the church, to the authority of the empire in Italy—Florence is the "viper" that turns against the viscera of her own mother when she "sharpens the horns of rebellion against Rome"³—and worse still, she is the self-styled successor to Rome. In Dante's time, Florence was one of the four largest cities in Europe, expanding its territory in the countryside around it and its power into the world, through its banking and commercial interests; its banks financed kings and popes and wars throughout Europe. It built bridges over the Arno and several new sets of walls (a third set, begun in Dante's time, was designed to be eight times the size of the old walls). What was inexcusable to Dante was that Florence saw herself as the new Rome. Villani, the fourteenth-century chronicler, explains that he began to collect his history of Florence when he saw the impressive ancient buildings of Rome, which reminded him that Florence, "daughter and creation of Rome, was rising and achieving great things, while Rome was declining" (*Istorie Fiorentine*). Indeed, an engraving on the Palazzo del Popolo read: "Florence is full of all wealth; she defeats her enemies in war and civil strife . . . she possesses the sea and the land and the whole earth . . . like Rome she is always triumphant,"⁴ words which Dante echoes sarcastically in his attack on Florence in Purgatory (VI, 127–135): "Fiorenza mia . . . molti han giustizia in cuore . . . ma il popol tuo l'ha in sommo de la bocca. / Molti rifiutan lo comune incarco, / ma il popol tuo solicito risponde / sanza chiamare, e grida: 'Io mi sobbarco'" (My Florence . . . some men have justice in their hearts . . . your people merely shoot off words about it. / Some men think twice when offered public post; / your citizens accept before they're asked, / shouting, "I'll gladly sacrifice myself!").

There are clear physical echoes of Florence in Hell: a series of walls (one outside Hell, another around Limbo, another around the inner city of Dis, and the ten moats of the Malebolge that surround the last circle), as if only Hell could be bigger than Florence and Hell were what Florence was really trying to be. Dante offers several hints of this identification: at the top of Paradise (XXXI, 37ff.), he says he has come from the human to the divine, from time to the eternal, from Florence to the just and sane people; he calls Florence the "devil's plant," which scatters its seed everywhere, that is the florin, Florence's powerful currency, corrupting all it touches. Florentines seem to be the dominant population in Hell, as

Dante notes: "Godi, Fiorenza, poi che sei sì grande / che per mare e per terra batti l'ali / e per lo inferno tuo nome si spande" (*Inf.* XXVI, 1–3: "Be joyful, Florence, since you are so great / that your outstretched wings beat over land and sea, / and your name is spread throughout the realm of Hell!"). The souls in Hell frequently seem to implicate their city in their sins: Florence becomes a glutton in Canto VI, so full of envy that its sack runs over (49–50); Filippo Argenti is "il fiorentino spirito bizzarro" (VIII, 62), both the irascible Florentine spirit and the irascible spirit of Florence; Farinata lures Dante into a miniature Florentine feud (Canto X); the anonymous suicide who made a gallows of his own home (XIII, 151) is identified only by his city, so that Florence seems to be the figure bent on self-destruction; sodomites, most of them Florentines, call their land "nostra terra prava," "our perverted city" (XVI, 9); and the thieves, most of them from major commercial families in Florence, go through metamorphoses just as their city does (Florence also "renews" its people and customs: *Inf.* XXIV, 144, *Purg.* VI, 145–147). Dante goes out of his way to identify his city with particular sins, to suggest that it is gluttonous or greedy, vengeful, self-destructive, deceitful and depraved. Though he moves outward in lower Hell to include many other Italian cities in his condemnation, he comes back throughout the *Comedy* to the attack on Florence, even in Paradise.

Paradise on the contrary, is Rome, the "Roma onde Cristo è Romano" (*Purg.* XXXII, 102), not the contemporary city which was only a shadow of its former self, but the Rome of Roman law, history, poetry, the only city that was both *urbs* and *orbis*, both city and world. To be at once the smallest and the largest political unit is a paradox which can exist only in heaven and in the Roman empire. The empire dominates Paradise from Canto VI, when Justinian gives its history, to Canto XXX, where Dante sees the seat with a crown above it that awaits the emperor Henry VII. Justinian is the only soul in the *Comedy* to speak for an entire canto, that is, the history of Rome is uninterrupted in Dante's poem as in God's plan. Pagan Rome has served God's purpose by preparing the world for the incarnation of Christ, by giving the crucifixion legal validity, and by avenging Christ's death (*Monarchia*, II, 11–12, *Par.* VI, 92), whereas Christian Rome does the devil's work (*Par.* XXVII, 25–27). The rulers of the earth who embody divine justice, pagans and Christians, appear and speak in the eagle, the sign of the Roman empire, "which had brought Rome the reverence of the world" (*Par.* XIX, 101–102); they may not always understand God's will, but they serve it, whereas the church claims to know it, but imposes its will rather than God's—the church withholds the bread that the "pious father denies no one"; the pious father is God, not the pope. The eagle is the only symbolic figure which never speaks to us in individual voices, but only in the unified voice of all its members, a powerful illustration of the harmony that is possible through the empire.

The emperor is the divinely appointed guide to lead mankind to one of its two goals, the restoration of the earthly paradise; the pope is to lead to the other, the heavenly paradise (*Monarchia* III, 16). They are represented in the *Comedy* by Virgil, the poet of empire, who brings Dante to the earthly paradise, and Beatrice, Dante's personal Christ–figure, who brings him to heaven, surrogates not only because of the role they play in Dante's personal conversion, but because neither of the appointed guides is functioning. In the *Comedy*, the dominant pope, the one most frequently alluded to, is Boniface VIII; Boniface was not only involved in Dante's personal troubles, he was also at the center of a struggle for jurisdiction with the major secular powers, the empire and the French monarchy. Boniface's struggle with the French king, Philip IV, is well-documented and fascinating reading. It culminated in a posthumous trial in which the pope was accused of virtually every sin—heresy, blasphemy, fornication, simony, idolatry, demon-worship, war-mongering, sodomy, assassination, violation of the confessional, political intrigue, embezzlement of crusade funds, and saying he would rather be a dog or an ass than a Frenchman.[5] Whatever the truth of these charges, they indicate the scope and persistence of Boniface's reputation as an archvillain, which is echoed in the early commentaries on Dante's poem. I find it intriguing that Boniface was the central figure at this trial, though he could not be present because he was dead, whereas in Dante's Hell, he is a central figure though he cannot be present because he is alive when the story is supposed to be taking place. But even in *Paradiso* XXX, virtually at the end of the poem, we are reminded that Boniface is destined for a hole in Hell.

Boniface is not the only cleric to be condemned. Hell is full of them: Celestine is among the neutrals, despite his holiness—most of the early commentators agree on this identification—not only because he rejected God's will, but also presumably because in resigning from the papacy, denying his responsibility, he left the way open to Boniface and his corruption. The circle of greed is filled with popes and cardinals, whose guard shouts "Papè Satan," a phrase that suggests to an early commentator a bishop calling on his pope Satan; it may also suggest Boniface, since his coins were the only ones in the period in which pope was spelled Papè. A pope as well as a cardinal appear in the circle of heresy; simony is dominated by popes, hypocrisy by monks or friars. There is probably an allegorical reference to the church in the suicide Pier della Vigna (Canto XIII), whose name "Peter of the Vineyard," suggests a perverted image of St. Peter, the first pope, a martyr for the vineyard contemporary popes are laying waste. Pier was at the court of the emperor Frederick, Federico, whose name can mean "rich in faith," though Dante places him among the heretics; members of that court called it the "ecclesia imperialis," the imperial church, with Pier della Vigna as its Peter, the rock on which it was founded, in contrast to the "false vicar of Christ," the pope. Allegorically, this Peter is a pope who abuses the gifts of his office to serve a false faith, a church which uses its powers to interfere with the proper functioning of empire, and commits spiritual suicide. The devils in Hell, fallen angels, can also be identified with the corrupt church, partly by analogy with the angels in Purgatory, who represent the spiritual church,[6] but also by various hints: Satan's legs, last seen upside-down, recall the upside-down legs of the simoniacs, all clerics, in Canto XIX; the body of the friar, Alberigo, is inhabited by a devil on earth while his soul is already with the traitors in Hell (XXXIII, 118ff.). If Dante intended this identification of devils with corrupt churchmen, then it is the church, represented by the devils at the gates of Dis (Canto VIII), which tries to keep God's messengers, Dante and an angel, out of the city, as it kept Dante and the Emperor out of Florence, and it is the church which manipulates corrupt politicians in the circle of barratry. The barratry episode reminds one of the fourteenth-century commentators, Benvenuto da Imola, of *his* experiences at the papal court, so he apparently read the devils this way.

Purgatory may represent the church, to the extent that it is a "rock" on which sit those who carry Peter's keys and the sword of divine justice, and who perform sacraments, but it is significant that the only agents, "officiali" (*Purg.* II, 30) of this church are angels, pure spirit, as far removed from temporal wealth and power as possible. However, we are reminded several times of the historic papacy's interference in political affairs, preventing the emperor from enforcing laws in Italy (Canto VI), and soiling itself and its burden by taking on temporal authority against God's will (Canto XVI). At the end of Purgatory, we are presented with the drama of church history, in which the chariot of the church becomes a monster when it takes on temporal wealth and power. Attacks on the church continue through Paradise, even more forceful because they are put in the mouths of various saints, Bonaventure, Thomas Aquinas, Peter Damian, Benedict, and Peter, the first pope and the one on whom so many claims for papal power were based.

Thomas makes a particularly telling point when he identifies the church with poverty: shortly after Dante has alluded to the church as Christ's bride (X, 140), Thomas calls Poverty Christ's widow (XI, 64). This has to mean that for Dante, at least, Christ did not intend the church to possess worldly riches. But it is Peter who makes the most violent attack on the papacy, in a speech which can be read as a detailed answer to papal claims of extraordinary power for the papacy. In fact, Dante answers a number of the major papalist arguments in the course of the poem: they claimed that priests preceded and even established kings in the Old Testament, therefore kings were subject to priests, so Dante features Jewish kings rather than priests in his heaven. They used the analogy of the sun and moon for the church and empire, as if earthly power derived entirely from spiritual, so Dante posits two suns in the political discourse in Purgatory (Canto XVI) and accuses one, the church, of putting out the light of the other, the empire. Basic to papal claims of universal jurisdiction is the notion of Christendom as one mystical body of which Christ or his vicar, the pope, is the head; Boniface warned that if a body has two heads, it becomes a monster. Dante presents the church as a chariot, not even an animate body, at the end of Purgatory, a chariot which sprouts seven heads when it receives earthly wealth and power, becoming the monster of the Apocalypse. The church called itself the bride of Christ, but Dante emphasizes marital abuses, the popes leading the church into adultery for gold and silver, winning it by deception, raping it, pimping for it, turning it into a whore for kings (*Inf.* XIX); when he speaks of the bride of Christ, Dante means the whole assembly of the faithful (*Par.* XXXI, 1–3). Popes speak of themselves as shepherds, claiming universal jurisdiction on the basis of John 2:16–17, "Feed my sheep"; Dante's shepherd is a wolf, transformed by greed, who leads all the sheep astray (*Par.* IX, 131–132), and the church is filled with wolves in sheep's clothing (*Par.* XXVII, 55–56). The only churchmen Dante praises are those who renounced earthly power to do God's will, though they continued to work in the world, the great teachers and monastic leaders. The major religious figures Dante meets in Paradise were political moderates on the separation of church and state; the only popes he sees there are John XXI, whom he recognizes as a scholar, not as a pope, and Peter, who presided over a church with no wealth or power. Dante's guides on the journey to God are not churchmen, but a pagan poet and a woman.

This is not to say that Dante whitewashes secular rulers; he condemns emperor Frederick II for heresy and criticizes several kings for their corruption. But mainly he features kings and emperors as models of virtue: David and Trajan are examples of humility in Purgatory and incarnations of divine justice in Paradise, and good rulers are seen throughout Paradise as models of love, of wisdom, of self-sacrifice, as well as of justice. The betrayers of empire (of Julius Caesar) are at the center of Hell, in the mouths of Satan, flanking the betrayer of Christ. Heaven awaits the coming of an emperor, while Hell awaits the coming of two popes.

Dante's two major prophecies in the poem, the greyhound in Hell (I) and the "five hundred, ten, and five," the DXV, in Purgatory (XXXIII), both suggest that the only hope for humanity lies in an imperial figure. Early commentators had no doubt that he meant an emperor who would rule over the whole world, bringing peace and despoiling prelates of their wealth, a figure who would free the church of greed by separating it from its possessions. Whatever the particular identity of the prophesied figures, it is clear that Dante intended the empire to set the world straight and the church to have a purely spiritual role, as guide to salvation, without any temporal power or wealth; indeed, only by relinquishing the latter could it accomplish the former.

The model for the ideal society which the empire is to be on earth is Dante's Paradise, while Hell is the model of the corrupt society as it is and Purgatory is the transition stage, where souls move away from a selfish, destructive society, and prepare themselves to take part in a society ordered by justice, wisdom, and love. In Hell, people act for themselves and against the common good, blaming others for their deeds. Dante makes the point that we must be responsible not only for our actions, but for their effects on others, by emphasizing the social aspects of all the sins. In his very arrangement, he makes it clear that sins against society are the worst of all, although all sins have social overtones. Flattery and hypocrisy are further down in Hell than robbery and murder (except murder by treachery), not because Dante considers them more serious, but because their effects on society are more insidious and ultimately more damaging. Dante reverses Aquinas's consideration of theft and robbery; whereas robbery is worse for Aquinas, because it does physical harm to its victim (ST 2.2ae, q.66), the secrecy of theft is worse for Dante, since it opens the way to injustice, incrimination for the innocent, and is a much graver threat to social stability (his theft seems to include commercial crimes). The worst sins for Dante are those that deny the trust on which social and political relations are based—fraud and treachery, and they alone take up half of Hell. But from the beginning of Hell, Dante emphasizes the social effects of our actions: the neutral's failure to act helps others, albeit passively, to commit evil; the circle of lust is filled with queens and princes who indulged their personal desires at the cost of their lands; the glutton is so self-absorbed he can scarcely seek out words to talk to Dante; greed is directly opposed to God's providence (the disposing of wealth and power through the divine minister, Fortune).

In lower Hell, the sins are overtly social. Even heresy is presented as a social sin: not only are the heretics buried with their followers, "i lor seguaci," those they misled, but the main heretic Dante meets, Farinata (Canto X), is an example of political factionalism. Heresy was associated with politics for Dante's audience: political enemies, like Farinata, were posthumously condemned by Florence as heretics so their property could be confiscated; Pope John XXII instigated trials for heresy against many of his political enemies. Farinata applies an essentially heretical position—taking a limited or false view as the truth—to politics, by his devotion to party rather than to city or empire. The destructiveness of such an attitude is revealed when he drags Dante into a kind of feud: by identifying the Guelph Dante as an enemy, the Ghibelline Farinata cuts himself off from an ally, for Dante is not only a fellow Florentine, but a White Guelph, one who like Farinata's Ghibellines supported the imperial cause; by not looking beyond party, Farinata turns an ally into an enemy.

In the circle of violence, Dante classifies the sins by their objects—other people, the self, God—but in each case, the object includes the person and his possessions; since the possessions are an extension of the self, harm to them is on the same level as harm to the body, an attitude that only makes sense within a socio-political morality. From a purely religious standpoint, squandering cannot be as serious as suicide. Even suicide, however, which seems so personal a sin, has public connotations in Dante's Hell: Pier della Vigna is the victim of his own abuse of a public position, and the anonymous Florentine focuses attention on the self-destructiveness of his city. The sodomites include representatives from all major professions, politics, law, the church, letters, and commerce, implying rampant professional perversion; sodomites are homosexuals, whom Dante condemns only for their excesses, since at the top of Purgatory he places the lustful homosexual on the same ledge as the heterosexuals. The usurers are members of major banking and merchant families, or companies. North Italy in this period was dominated by commerce, banking and trade. Dante was involved in commerce directly and through his family and like many contemporary thinkers, including Thomas Aquinas, he accepts the need for trade, even to some extent for usury in a large society. What he condemns are the serious abuses, counterfeiting, bribery, fraud.

By putting usury in the circle of violence rather than fraud, Dante seems to be drawing a distinction between different kinds of lending, not condemning all interest as fraudulent profit, as the church officially did. At the same time, every section of fraud involves illicit profits to some extent, and Dante's language frequently emphasizes the commercial aspect, but it is in the *bolgia* of theft that the connections are most suggestive. Indeed, I think the three metamorphoses can represent three kinds of fraudulent transactions or contracts, white-collar crimes.[7] The words for commercial transactions, *commutationes*, and exchange, *cambium*, echo through the metamorphoses, the exchanging of bodies between souls and serpents; and the souls in this section come from major merchant-banking families—Cavalcanti, Brunelleschi, Donati, names associated with commerce by Dante's audience. Throughout the circle of fraud, Dante emphasizes the victims of the sins, individuals, castles, cities, even nations. Much is made of the abuse of public function: a "mayor" who pimps for his sister, advisors who should correct but instead flatter, churchmen who buy and sell church office, prophets who prostitute their gifts in the service of tyrants, barrators who subvert government for gain, hypocrites who make a pretense of piety to hide their intrigues, thieves, that is businessmen who defraud their clients, counselors of fraud, disseminators of scandal and schism, who rend the fabric of church and state, and falsifiers of various kinds.

The last circle of Hell contains treachery, the worst sin because it is practiced against those to whom one is bound by special ties of family, nation, guest, benefactor. Again there are political overtones in all: many of the souls in the first section murdered relatives to take over their lands and powers; the second section has nothing but political traitors; the third is inhabited by those who betrayed their guests for political reasons; and according to the early commentators, the benefactor, the victim of treachery in the fourth section, is a political lord (*dominus*). The last two sections are shocking for a number of reasons: Ugolino is shown gnawing on the skull of his enemy, a bestial act which denies his humanity, and even more shocking, the souls of Fra Alberigo and Branca Doria are in Hell while their bodies are still on earth. The soul goes to Hell the minute someone commits such an act of betrayal (of a guest), and the body is inhabited by a devil until it dies. That is, this sin removes us altogether from the fellowship of mankind, damns us to Hell without hope, a highly unorthodox position from the religious point of view, but politically and socially sound.

Dante is reminding us at the end of Hell that we create Hell, that we are living in it and, by obstinately committing such sins, we damn ourselves here and there. In the last section of traitors, three souls hang from the mouths of Satan; they are what evil feeds on, and two of them are there because they assassinated the first Roman emperor. So at the center of Hell, its lord consumes his subjects but is imprisoned in the corruption he helped create, the lake of ice. At the same time, his fall from heaven provides the means by which mankind can return to heaven, pushing up the mountain of Purgatory on the other side of earth, just as his body, the total evil they must confront, provides Dante and Virgil the means of beginning their climb out of Hell.

In Purgatory, Dante encounters all the negative lessons of Hell. Here, men and women help each other in the effort to purge themselves of evil tendencies: they guide and comfort each other, they pray for each other, they speak for each other, to praise or to help, not to hurt; they sing together, they show a sense of community, even of family; they are all fellow-citizens of the one true city. Love, we learn here, is the source of all action but must be properly directed, with sufficient force, to the right goals; the love of others can aid in the moral struggle, with prayers which help pay the "debt" of sin, and guidance. Dante seems to be making the psychological point that the love of others gives one strength in the struggle against evil, so even personal morality becomes a social effort. From the first, the souls Dante meets in Purgatory are counters to Hell: the victims of violent deaths are careful to avoid any words that might lead to revenge or continue feuds; they show restraint, forgiveness, a sense of responsibility, all qualities noticeably lacking in Hell. The love of city, which in Hell led Farinata first to speak to Dante and then to fight with him, leads Sordello in Purgatory to speak to Virgil and then to lament the fate of all Europe.

The sins in Purgatory differ from those in Hell, even where they overlap, because they are all the result of love, misdirected, insufficient, or excessive, whereas the sins in Hell result from the failure to follow reason. The lowest sins in Hell are a willful abuse of reason to the harm of others. Similarly, the first three sins in Purgatory are defined as harming or loving the harm of others. On the ledge of pride, Dante shows the failures of religious and secular leaders to use their gifts or positions for the good of others; on envy, their failure to put the good of others before their own, and on wrath, the failure to forgive personal injury in order to avoid public harm. It is on the ledge of wrath, at the center of Purgatory and of the poem, that Dante receives the key lessons of private and public morality: he is taught how love and reason operate through the exercise of free will to guide individual actions, and how the church and state are intended to guide men to the proper choice. On the last three ledges, Dante meets two of the ordained guides, a pope and a king and a series of surrogate guides, poets. The pope's greed was boundless until he achieved the richest office on earth, the papacy; having no further ambitions to fulfil on earth, he turned to heaven. Ironically, it is the material wealth of the papacy that converts the pope, while the king's greed gave rise to over three hundred years of sordid deeds among his descendants. But the poet on the same ledge, Statius, is an example of prodigality, not of greed; he was converted and saved by poetry, Virgil's, and helps now to guide Virgil and Dante toward the earthly paradise, as Dante guides his audience. Poets do what both church and empire fail to do. Before Virgil leaves Dante at the top of Purgatory, the poet crowns him pope and emperor over himself, "io te sovra te corono e mitrio," not only because the individual Dante is now capable of guiding himself but also because the poet Dante must guide mankind where the pope and emperor have failed. The scenes in the earthly paradise are again both personal and public: on the one hand, Dante's confession to Beatrice and symbolic baptism, on the other, his participation in the procession of the books of the Bible (as if he were writing one of them), and his witnessing of the drama of church and state. Dante joins the procession of human and divine history because he is to play a part in it; his poem, as Beatrice and later Cacciaguida intimate, is God's message to mankind, meant to lead toward reform in the church and renewal in the empire.

If Purgatory prepares Dante and mankind to assume a useful role in the ideal society, Paradise shows what that society can be. The souls appear in harmonious groups as they acted in life, first as individuals, acting for themselves but serving the public good, then in groups, in symbolic figures: all those who seek the truth, however diversely and incompatibly, form the circles of the Sun which reflect the Trinity; all those who serve divine justice are part of the eagle of Jupiter. In the Stars, Dante sees all human society as flowers of one garden and finally in the Empyrean as one rose, of which each petal retains its distinct features, the individual achieving his or her highest potential as part of the perfect society. The rose is city, kingdom, and empire, the culmination of all political institutions. Men need society, Dante demonstrates throughout Paradise, because they are different; they have different talents and different wants, and only together can they achieve a full life. In Mercury, harmony is created by souls in different ranks; in Venus, they have different functions, or professions. Man would be worse off if he were not a citizen, Charles Martel and Dante agree, because he needs the talents and functions of others; some men are meant to be lawgivers, others soldiers, priests, artisans. In this sphere, Dante meets a king who appreciated his poetry, a bishop who had been a love-poet, a benefactress of the poor who had been the lover of a poet (and of many others—Dante does not necessarily condemn extra-marital sex), and a prostitute from the Old Testament who helped God's people take the holy land. Rahab represents the good church, in contrast to the corrupt church, now prostituting itself on earth. In the Sun, diversity is seen in approaches to truth and learning; many of the wise reach the truth by the dialectic method, by the opposition of contrary ideas, commenting on, even attacking each others' works; in such processes, the more minds at work, the more can be learned. But despite the intellectual opposition, they now move in harmony to form the circles which reflect God.

At the center of Paradise, Dante meets his ancestor Cacciaguida, whose name suggests the hunt for a leader, and who praises the future deeds of the imperial vicar and Dante's patron, Can Grande. So, at the center of Paradise, we are given praise of the leader who supported the empire, a discussion of the corruption of Florence and of the church's opposition to the empire, Dante's main political themes, as well as the role of Dante's poem, which Cacciaguida tells him is to strike at the highest peaks. Similarly, at the top of Purgatory, in the earthly paradise where he witnessed the drama of church and state, Dante's poetic mission was first announced to him. So there can be little doubt that his poem is meant to serve the cause of empire. In the sphere of Jupiter, the eagle, symbol of empire, is formed by souls of earthly rulers out of the last letter of a biblical phrase written by God in the sky. God uses those souls to make words for Dante to read as he uses people to make history, and Dante reads them as he reads God's message in the Bible and in the movements of men and transmits it to us in his poem. The eagle speaks not only for divine justice, but also to deliver the strongest message of divine mercy and religious conversion in the poem, by the examples of the conversion of two pagans: the emperor Trajan, brought back to life by the prayers of a pope (an unusual instance in the *Comedy* of a pope helping an emperor, though the emperor was already dead); this story is a medieval legend retold even by Thomas Aquinas and therefore not too surprising, but the other conversion is of Ripheus, a figure barely alluded to in the *Aeneid*, for which there is no authorization. Even more startling, Dante has the eagle say that Ripheus was "baptized" by the cardinal virtues before there was baptism, not just saved but baptized before the church existed.

Churchmen predominate in the highest regions of heaven, monastics in Saturn, apostles in the Stars, but they are all religious figures who rejected worldly goods and power, who worked in the world only to do God's will; they represent for Dante the ideal church, not a secular hierarchy which places itself above and in opposition to the empire, but a spiritual army serving God's purpose by serving, not ruling, men. Should we have any lingering doubts of the role of the papacy in Dante's ideal society, Beatrice reminds us that just as there is an empty seat in the rose for the emperor Henry VII, so the pope who opposed him (Clement V) will be thrust into Hell, pushing down even further "the one from Alagna," that is Boniface VIII.

When Dante first sees the rose at the end of Paradise, he feels like a pilgrim who has reached the temple of his vow, a reference to the sacrifice he offered in Mars, where he accepted his mission. The completed poem is the discharge of that mission, a model in broad outlines for the ideal society on earth. A political society should be unified under one rule, with every individual contributing to the common good according to his or her abilities (and the rose does include women in good numbers), motivated by love and justice so that all can realize most fully the potential in each. The community must have certain officers: secular rulers and officials, fighters to defend it, teachers and intellectuals to order and enhance all aspects of earthly life, religious guides to ensure by prayer and example that it remain in harmony with the divine will. But the religious guides must be solely concerned with the spiritual life, completely renounce worldly power and wealth, never interfere in any way with the secular workings of the government; in a word, they are to be the monastic leaders of Saturn, closer to God than any of the other separate groups of souls, but leaving the operation of society in the hands of the rulers in Jupiter, the warriors in Mars, and the teachers in the Sun.

Such is the political society Dante envisages. For the individual within that society, there is a lesson at each level of Paradise: first the need to make a commitment (he learns from those who failed to keep their vows in the Moon), just as the first group in Hell was made up of those who failed to commit themselves; the need to act firmly on that commitment (those active for worldly glory in Mercury), fortified by love for one's fellows (the lovers in Venus), and by all that human learning can offer (the teachers in the Sun); to sacrifice oneself, if necessary, for the common good (the crusaders in Mars); to serve justice rather than self-interest (the rulers in Jupiter); and to dedicate one's actions to God's will (the monastics in Saturn). A society made up of such individuals will be the restored earthly paradise which Dante sees in the garden of the Stars, a reflection of the celestial hierarchy (Primo Mobile), and of God and the eternal city of the Empyrean, the final setting of the *Comedy* which contains all the rest and is the ideal model Dante offers for life on earth, where the individual achieves his or her highest potential as a member of the community, as a distinct petal of the universal rose.

It is this vision of the society mankind might achieve if all worked for it together that makes Dante's condemnation of the souls in Hell understandable and justifiable. Their selfishness, greed, violence, and treachery create a Hell not only for themselves but for their fellows. But mankind is not forced to accept that Hell as its destiny on earth—Paradise presents the alternative, a society that works well for all its citizens because all its citizens contribute to it. Dante wants his audience to reject his vision of Hell, the corrupt society, and adopt his vision of the ideal society, Paradise. That is why one cannot understand his Hell without knowing his Paradise.

NOTES

1. I have developed the arguments of this paper at much greater length and with detailed references in *The Political Vision of the Divine Comedy* (Princeton: Princeton University Press, 1984). Supporting evidence for most of the statements made in this piece can be found there, along with acknowledgments of the sources on which I drew.

2. Dante discourages those in small boats, "in piccioletta barca," that is with insufficient intellect or learning, from following him, II, 1–6, and Cacciaguida tells him his words will be like the wind "striking the hardest at the highest peaks," (le più alte cime, XVII, 133–134), the powerful and famous. I am using Petrocchi for the Italian text and Musa for the English translations.

3. For text and translation, see Paget Toynbee, *Dantis Alagherii Epistolae, The Letters of Dante* (Oxford: Clarendon, 1966), 7.7.

4. Cited by Nicolai Rubinstein, "The Beginnings of Political Thought in Florence," *Journal of the Warburg and Courtauld Institutes* 5 (1942): 213.

5. For a full text of the trial, see Pierre Dupuy, *Histoire du Differend d'entre le pape Boniface VIII et Philippes le bel Roy de France* (Paris: Carmoisy, 1655; reprint, Tucson: Audax, 1963).

6. See Peter Armour, *The Door of Purgatory, A Study of Multiple Symbolism in Dante's Purgatorio* (Oxford: Clarendon, 1983), 36ff. George Holmes, *Dante* (New York: Hill and Wang, 1980), 73, describes Purgatory as a "controlled ecclesiastical environment."

7. See Ferrante, *Political Vision*, 348ff.

Dante in the Cinematic Mode:
An Historical Survey of Dante Movies

JOHN P. WELLE

It may come as a bit of a surprise to discover that Dante Alighieri's Medieval masterpiece known in English as the *Divine Comedy* has had a long and interesting relationship with Italian and world cinema.[1] In addition to Dante's reception in literary high culture, his presence, for example, in T. S. Eliot's *The Wasteland*, the *Cantos* of Ezra Pound, and James Joyce's *Ulysses*, to mention only the most renowned cases of Dantean influence in modern English literature, there are also numerous Dante movies that indicate the enduring attractiveness of his vision at the level of popular culture. Indeed, Dante's reception through the various stages of film history forms part of a larger story involving literature, cinema, and television within changing social, economic, and cultural contexts.

In describing the massive influence of film on the culture of modernity, Raymond Williams has observed that "the remarkable innovations of the cinema . . . might reasonably be described as the invention of a new mode, the *cinematic*, interacting with older kinds, types and forms but also undoubtedly creating some important new forms."[2] Dante movies, i.e., films based on the *Divine Comedy*, on the *Vita nuova*, and on Dante's life, constitute unique and largely unexplored manifestations of what Williams calls "the cinematic mode."[3] Furthermore, Dante movies reveal the *Divine Comedy*'s remarkable adaptability. In reflecting on the qualities inherent in Dante's text that have contributed to its adaptability, Amilcare Iannucci frames the issue as follows:

> How does one explain Dante's enduring popularity, and that of his harsh eschatological poem in particular? The answer, I believe, lies in the poem's distinctive textual characteristics. The *Comedy* is neither an open nor a closed text (Eco, *The Role of the Reader*); it is neither writerly nor readerly (Barthes, *S/Z*). Rather it is more like what Fiske, in *Television Culture*, calls a "producerly" text. A producerly text is polysemous and combines the easy accessibility of the readerly with the complex discursive strategies of the writerly. These peculiar textual qualities allow the poem to produce meaning and pleasure in audiences which run the gamut from the uneducated to the most sophisticated and discerning.[4]

While all Dante movies reflect what Iannucci terms the *Divine Comedy*'s "producerly" qualities, Italian Dante movies in particular point to the centrality of film and literary interactions in the development of twentieth-century Italian culture.[5] As Gian Piero Brunetta asserts: "Among all the histories of national cinemas that of the Italian cinema, along the entire arc of its development, is the most bound to the structures, models, and history of universal literature of all times."[6]

As we shall see in what follows, Dante Alighieri and the cinema intersect and interact in important and interesting ways. While providing a brief but historical survey of Dante movies, we shall give particular attention to Dante's position in the Italian cinema. Because Dante is known as the "founding father" of the Italian language, and has been constructed as the Italian national poet since the late eighteenth century, Dante movies are particularly well-suited for charting the historical continuities and innovations that the cinema has brought about in Italy. For this reason, in order to understand the significance of Dante's relationship with Italian film history, we first need to sketch the broad contours of Italian linguistic history, and to trace the process through which the Medieval Florentine emerged as the Italian national poet in the nineteenth century. Having gained an understanding of Dante's special status in Italian culture, we shall then be better equipped to trace the trajectory of his reception in film history, while giving special attention to the Italian silent cinema.

A rich but problematic linguistic diversity has been one of the salient characteristics of Italian civilization throughout its long history. Centuries of political disunity, strong regional cultural centers, and a geographical situation unfavorable to rapid communication have all contributed to the depth and continuity of Italian linguistic diversity. In *De vulgari eloquentia*, for example, written around 1303, Dante divides the peninsula into some fourteen sections according to the various tongues of Italy. During the Italian Renaissance, in the debates concerning the search for a national literary standard—the famous *questione della lingua*—the written Tuscan variety as encodified by Dante, Petrarch, and Boccaccio during the Trecento emerged victorious in the Cinquecento as the preferred national literary language. From the sixteenth century onward, the other regional idioms of the Italian peninsula were relegated to dialect status.

In describing the subsequent linguistic situation, Hermann W. Haller observes that "Italian evolved over many centuries as a minority language, while the Italy of the masses resembled a 'selva di dialetti,' a thick dialect forest."[7] For example, during the Risorgimento, the movement for Italian independence and national unification in the second half of the nineteenth century, it is estimated that perhaps as few as 2.5 percent of Italians were able to use the so-called national language for everyday purposes.[8] The other 90 to 97.5 percent of the Italian people communicated in the various regional and local dialects. These statistics provide the most graphic illustration of the linguistic and cultural realities underlying (and undermining) Italian national unity on the eve of the twentieth century. In the well-known phrase of Massimo D'Azeglio, concerning the lack of national consciousness in Italy at the conclusion of the wars of unification in 1870, "We have made Italy, now we have to make Italians."[9]

In the process of "making Italy" during the nineteenth century, i.e., in the process of gaining independence from foreign and papal rule, and in creating political unification, Dante, although long since dead, contributed significantly. In fact, beginning in 1780 and throughout the nineteenth century, Dante was resurrected, rehabilitated, and reconstructed.[10] He was resurrected from three centuries of relative neglect stemming from Renaissance critical ideals, from the widespread vogue of European Petrarchism, and from neo-classical norms which favored Petrarch, Ariosto, and Tasso as canonical poets. Dante was rehabilitated first of all outside Italy by being transformed from a "gothic" primitive to an individual genius along the lines favored by German and European Romanticism. Subsequently, he was reconstructed within Italy in order to serve as the prophet and proponent of Italian liberation and national unification. A series of historical events and a variety of cultural and literary currents created the cult of Dante as national bard. This process parallels and is indebted to the development of the cult of Shakespeare as the national poet of England.

Carlo Dionisotti points out that from 1791 on, publications of *La Divina commedia*, as well as praise for Dante the poet and the man, become ever more numerous (259–60). "The first, decisive impetus of the revolutionary wave that shook Italy in 1796 and 1797 stems from the new attribution of a national and civil mission to literature and also from a public celebration of literature configured as a kind of national, civil religion" (Dionisotti 267). The tomb of Dante in Ravenna was restored in 1780 and the event was consecrated in contemporary poetry. After the French invasion, amid the trees of liberty constructed in the public squares, the Italian people were called forth to celebrate their ancient poets: Virgil in Mantova, Ariosto in Ferrara, and on January 3, 1798, Dante in Ravenna.

In characterizing the relationship of poetry to politics during this period, Adrian Lyttelton writes:

> In the age of nationalism, poets enjoyed a peculiarly privileged role as the guardians and even creators of national identity. Nowhere was this more true than in Italy. After all, Dante was the founding father of the Italian language. The diffusion of the Italian language had been the work of a literary and humanistic elite, unassisted by a powerful central state, as in France, or by a vernacular reformation, as in Germany. Dante and the other great poets of the past were elevated to the status of patron saints in the national revolutionary cult.[11]

In 1865, the sixth centenary of Dante's birth was celebrated for the first time in Florence, the new capital of the new Kingdom of Italy. In

1900, with the celebration of the new century, the sixth centenary of Dante's vision was also celebrated. However, this celebration, "was the sign, not of the vitality, but of the survival of a formal cult that in that moment could not serve any useful purpose" (Dionisotti 288). In fact, Dante scholars themselves, including Benedetto Croce, complained that the cult of Dante was distracting them from more useful scholarly endeavors. One Italian Dante scholar dubbed this phenomenon "Dantephilia, Dantology, Dante-mania" (Dionisotti 289).

In turn-of-the-century England and in the United States, a similar Dante craze had taken hold. Henry Beers, author of a book entitled *A History of English Romanticism in the Nineteenth Century*, published in 1901 writes:

> Since the middle of the century Dante study and Dante literature in English-speaking lands have waxed enormously. Dante societies have been founded in England and America. Almost every year sees another edition, a new commentary or a fresh translation in prose, in blank verse in *terza rima*, or in some form of stanza. . . . Not that he will ever be popular, in Shakespeare's way; and yet it is far gone when the aesthete in a comic opera is described as a "Francesca da Rimini young man."[12]

While the cult of Dante in Italy had outlived its political usefulness, having already served its purpose in helping to "make Italy" in the nineteenth century, the myth of Dante would still prove central to the ongoing cultural project of "making Italians" in the twentieth century. Dante movies flourish during the silent period, particularly during the golden age of Italian cinema prior to World War I.[13] Dante's strong presence in the early Italian cinema reflects the widespread popularity of filmic adaptations during this period. Moreover, the particular role of the Florentine poet within this process also points to the continuation of the cult of Dante established in the nineteenth century.

In 1896, the first films were exhibited in Italy at fair grounds, carnivals, and in the public spaces of the growing urban centers. In 1905, a decade after the Lumière brothers began making films in France, the first Italian film with a complex plot was produced: *La presa di Roma* (The capture of Rome, produced by Filo Albertini), an historical film celebrating the liberation of the eternal city from papal control. At this time, permanent film theatres began to be constructed in the large cities. In 1906, for example, Naples boasted twenty-five cinemas, Rome had twenty-three, Turin nine, and Milan seven.[14]

Three genres dominate this early period in Italian film history. First of all, historical subjects, such as *La presa di Roma*, provided grist for the cinematic mill, particularly films dealing with the Risorgimento, but also short films about the Renaissance and Roman antiquity. Secondly, the Italians developed successful comedies around such comic actors as Fregoli, the quick-change artist; Polidor, Fricot, and Tontolini, who achieved international followings. Thirdly, and most importantly for our puposes, the Italians created numerous short films based on literary and theatrical works.[15] Canonical authors such as Dante, Tasso, and Manzoni were reduced to the ten-to-twenty minute format of these early films as were texts by such popular writers as Carolina Invernizio, Eugene Sue, and Alexander Dumas. The Italian film industry's widespread borrowing from literature has been described by Gian Piero Brunetta as "a migration of genres from literature to film."[16] Among the many works adapted to the screen we note the following: five versions of Alessandro Manzoni's nineteenth-century novel *I promessi sposi* (The betrothed), between 1908 and 1923, as well as other films based on the nineteenth-century historical novel; films derived from the epic tradition, including the *Illiad*, the *Odyssey*, *La Gerusalemme liberata* (Jerusalem delivered), and the *Pilgrim's Progress* of John Bunyan, and even a film entitled *La cavallina storna* (The dappled mare), a film based on Giovanni Pascoli's poem of the same title.[17] Films derived from lyric opera were popular: *Rigoletto*, for example, and *Il trovatore*, to name but two. The works of Shakespeare were also reduced to this ten minute format and Italians produced short films based on Romeo and Juliet, Macbeth, Othello, and Hamlet.

Reflecting the importance of the "literary-film" genre, and mirroring Dante's status as the national bard, the Italian film industry, between 1908 and 1912, produced no fewer than eleven films based on the *Divine Comedy*, on Dante's life, and on figures and scenes of Dantean inspiration.[18] Of these eleven films, Dante's *Inferno*, launched by Milano Films in 1911, is by far the most important and most influential. This film set a new standard for production quality and signifies the first serious artistic encounter between the nascent film industry and the Italian literary tradition. In this way, Dante's *Inferno* represents the culmination of the early Italian cinema's use of literary texts, and it established a number of records.

It was the longest film yet made at 1200 meters and it was the most costly, at more than 100,000 lire.[19] Its length, its cost, its innovative special effects, and its publicity campaign, distinguish *L'Inferno* by Milano Films as the first true, Italian colossal. It revolutionized the cinema by extending the viewing format beyond the then canonical ten to twenty minutes. The passage from the short to the longer feature film, inaugurated by Dante's *Inferno*, represents the boom movement of the Italian cinema and allows film to compete favorably with the theatre for the first time as a spectacle worthy of serious attention.

L'Inferno became the prototype of such historical films as *Quo vadis?* (1913), *Gli ultimi giorni di Pompei* (The last days of Pompeii, 1913), *Marcantonio e Cleopatra* (1913), *Giulio Cesare* (1914), and of course, *Cabiria* (1914), the historical epic by Giovanni Pastrone with the collaboration of Gabriele D'Annunzio, a film which would exert a profound influence on D. W. Griffith and other filmmakers around the world. *L'Inferno* by Milano Films helped to establish the genre of the costume epic in which the Italian film industry would excel between 1912 and 1915. The Italian cinema at this moment competes with France for the dominance of world markets. Gian Piero Brunetta describes the expansion of the Italian film industry in these terms:

> The years between 1912 and 1914 mark therefore the great expansion and the consolidation of the structures: the Italian industry enjoys its maximum splendor and success in the United States, but it also enters triumphantly into Great Britain, Argentina, Russia, Switzerland, France.[20]

Dante's *Inferno*, along with the other film colossals of which it was the prototype, also had a profound effect on the way films were exhibited. Longer films meant that there would be fewer films screened during the day's programming. More people would need to be accommodated at a single showing. Consequently, film theatres were built that could seat as many as a thousand people. These cinemas had names like "Splendor," "Eden," and "Fulgor." In Venice the cinema "Rossini" resembled architecturally the famous Venetian theatre "La fenice." At Turin, "il Ghersi" was constructed, at Florence "il Gambrinus," at Genoa "l'Olimpia," and at Naples "l'Excelsior,"[21]

L'Inferno was accompanied by an advertising campaign aimed at achieving high visibility for the new film product.[22] Gustavo Lombardo, the future owner of the Titanus film production company and the producer of *L'Inferno*, also founded *Lux*, a weekly magazine devoted to films, entertainment, and culture. *Lux*, both before the debut of Dante's *Inferno* and after it began its run, published a number of articles about the film. On October 16, 1911, four months before the film's debut, *Lux* published a parody of the opening stanzas of the *Divine Comedy*. Entitled "La Divina Visione," this poem brings Dante back to life to view the film that his poem had inspired. Here, the medieval poet's "dark wood," is transformed into a film theatre. The parody includes the following tercet of hendecasyllables, the traditional Italian line, in which Dante the poet testifies to the fidelity of the filmmaker's vision:

> la Commedia interamente
> io vidi riprodotta al naturale
> come sgorgata m'era dalla mente.

> [the Comedy in its entirety
> I witnessed reproduced naturally
> as it flowed from my mind.]

"La Divina Visione" even includes a parody of the notes at the bottom of the page which are prevalent in Italian scholastic editions. In the text of the parody, Dante affirms "Li parenti miei furon Lombardi" (My parents were Lombards). Although this line is spoken by Virgil in the original, in the parody the line is spoken by Dante. As noted above, the film was produced by a certain Gustavo Lombardo. A note at the bottom of the page points out that Dante, in claiming that his relatives were Lombards, seeks to establish his family relationship to Gustavo Lombardo so that, in good Italian fashion, he can enter the movie theatre without having to buy a ticket.

Prepared by a long and colorful advertising campaign, the film had its Neapolitan debut at the Regio Teatro Mercadante in the spring of 1911. Those attending included the dramatist Roberto Bracco, the novelist Matilde Serao, and the philosopher Benedetto Croce. Matilde Serao admits to having been impressed by the film and comments on its iconographic typology:

> For us, the film by the Milano Company of Dante's *Inferno* has rehabilitated the cinematograph. . . . And if Gustave Doré has written with the pencil of the draftsman the best graphic comment to the Divine Poem, this film has brought back to life Doré's work.[23]

We have already noted the impact that this film had on the early Italian cinema as a culture industry. We should also point out that the film includes a shot of the monument to Dante at Trento. This image ties the film to the nineteenth-century historical currents that promoted Dante to the status of Italian national poet. In this way, the series of monuments in marble and concrete constructed at Florence, Ravenna, Verona, and Trento during the course of the nineteenth century prepare the way for this monument of the silent cinema constructed in celluloid.[24]

Dante's *Inferno* was also the subject of a lecture at the École des hautes études by Ricciotto Canudo, a poet and writer from Bari residing in Paris who authored the first treatise on film aesthetics (Brunetta, *Storia del cinema* 144). The increased cultural status that this film gained for the cinema can be documented by the sympathetic response it prompted from Italian intellectuals, who also recognized the potential of the new medium to contribute to Italian cultural unification. As a reviewer wrote in an article from 1911: "We judge the Dantean film to be a work that will contribute mightily to the development of national culture and civil consciousness" (Brunetta, *Storia del cinema* 144).

The continuity that we have been tracing between the cult of Dante in the nineteenth century and his reception in the early Italian cinema was disrupted, in part, by Benito Mussolini, who came to power one year after the celebration in 1921 of the centenary of Dante's death. According to Dionisotti (295), Fascism

> had rendered useless the cult of Dante as national poet. Other cults, that of Imperial Rome or of Machiavellian politics, lent themselves much better to the new order of things. . . . the nationalistic myth of Dante, first revolutionary and then of the Risorgimento, declined precipitously and died out during the first half of this century, between one and the other European and world wars. Dante, of course, remained and he reappeared isolated, different, and in part new in the difficult times.[25]

If the rhetorical cult of Dante as national poet died out during the Fascist *ventennio*, he was rediscovered as a model for living writers, and indeed had been enjoying one of his periods of greatest influence outside of Italy, as demonstrated by his importance for Anglo-American modernist poets and writers such as T. S. Eliot, Ezra Pound, James Joyce, Hart Crane, and others.

While Dante's *Inferno* by Milano Films in 1911 constitutes one of the high points of the golden age of Italian film and represents one of Dante's most significant encounters to date with the cinema, there are also other Dante movies worthy of brief attention. These films include two American productions, both entitled *Dante's Inferno*, one released in 1924 and the other eleven years later starring Spencer Tracy. In both cases Dante serves as a pretext for commercial ventures that exploit the visual possibilities inherent in Dante's vision of the underworld. *Variety Film Reviews* of October 1, 1924, provides the following report:

> It's the naked stuff only that is going to make the picture. . . . The modern story is by far the weakest portion. However, it is as good an excuse as any for the ringing in of a visualization of Dante's Inferno on the screen. It is a dream idea. That modern portion bespeaks a modern money-grabber, grown hard in the pursuit of wealth. He has practically brought about the ruin of his neighbor and the latter, in the last minute before he decides to end it all, sends a copy of the Inferno to his financial enemy and on the fly-leaf inscribes a curse. As the recipient reads the opening passages, the screen shows a visualization of the Inferno. Evidently the illustrations of Gustave Doré have been faithfully followed. . . . In the end of the modern story is a happy ending. When the money-grabber has the dream that the reading of the book has brought, he realizes the error of his ways and has an according change of heart.[26]

The reviewer concludes on a moralizing note: "This in reality is a subject that tends to put the fear of God into the hearts of the transgressors, providing they take time enough to think while trying to get a flash of the undressed mob."

The 1935 film entitled *Dante's Inferno,* starring Spencer Tracy, elicited this response from a reviewer for the *New York Times* on August 2, 1935:

> This parenthetical study of the fate which awaits us all is the vision of Henry B. Walthall, who operates a concession known as "Dante's Inferno." Here he provides brief but significant glimpses of the satanic torture chambers, together with pointed advice to his customers on how to keep out of them. The old man is a prophet crying in the wilderness until Spencer Tracy, who marries the professor's ward, introduces high-pressure ballyhoo and puts hell on a paying basis.[27]

This film circulated in Italy in 1935 under the title, "La nave di Satana" (Satan's ship).

Americans are not the only non-Italians to have produced Dante movies or films that at least refer to Dante in some fashion. A Swedish film from 1931 bears the title *Dante's Mysterier* (Dante's mysteries). In

1967, Ken Russell, a British director, produced for television a film about Dante Gabriel Rossetti entitled *Dante's Inferno*, which the director himself described as "a peep into the nightmare world of the Pre-Raphaelite brotherhood."[28] In the same year, Spain gave the world a film entitled *Dante no es unicamente severo* (Dante is not only severe). In 1982, the Canadian director Philip Marshak produced yet another *Dante's Inferno*. In 1984, Tom Phillips and Peter Greenaway began their series of video adaptations of the *Inferno* for British Channel Four Television. Entitled *A TV Dante*, this project currently includes adaptations of the first fourteen cantos of the *Inferno*.[29] Finally, an animated film made in 1958 bears the title *Dante Dreamer*.

Returning to Italy, we should mention the 1949 version of *Conte Ugolino* directed by Riccardo Freda with the collaboration of Mario Monicelli. In this film, according to Cristina Bragaglia, "Dante is only a distant memory. Freda won fame for himself (and an audience) by fattening up the genre of the historical film . . . with Hollywood-type stylemes, situations and rhythms and a dash of Gothic atmosphere" (135). In a similar fashion, Raffaele Matarazzo's 1950 film *Paolo e Francesca*, based on Dante's star-crossed lovers, constitutes an important step in this director's move toward melodrama.[30] Matarazzo was one of the most successful Italian directors of the 1950s. His melodramatic films, particularly *Catene* (Chains, 1950), while box office sensations in Italy, were not exported. His version of Paolo and Francesca points to the enduring popularity of the short passage in *Inferno* V which has been elaborated and retold by numerous painters, dramatists, and filmmakers.[31]

Our itinerary thus far has concentrated on Dante movies in the strict sense. However, Dante also serves as a frame of reference in numerous Italian films in the 1960s, 1970s, and 1980s. For example, not a few critics have analyzed the Dantean elements in the films of Federico Fellini.[32] Pier Paolo Pasolini expresses his engagement with Dante in poetry, novels, and films. Pasolini's *La Divina Mimesis* (The divine mimesis), for example, which rewrites the first four cantos of the *Inferno*, opens with Pasolini poet-protagonist lost in the "'Dark Wood' of the reality of 1963."[33] In this literary text contaminated with cinematic elements, Pasolini finds himself "in front of the cinema Splendid . . . or Splendor or Emerald?" and glimpses "a happy and evil light: between the two doors of the film theater" (*La divina mimesis* 5–6).

Pasolini championed Dante's mixture of linguistic levels, resuscitated interest in Italian dialect poetry, and wrote in Dantean inspired tercets. He also saw himself as Dante's heir as a civil poet, i.e., as a critic of Italian society. Moreover, Pasolini's film and literary appropriation of Dante reflect not only the poet's specific interest in the medieval poet but is also indicative of wider trends: by the late 1960s, Dante had become a pervasive presence in Italian popular culture. Zygmunt Baranski, following Gianfranco Contini, describes the issue at hand:

Since his rehabilitation at the end of the Settecento, Dante, via his successive canonizations, has become an integral part of Italian life. Elements ranging from his writings and biography have become, thanks to their dissemination through the schools, public life, and everyday linguistic usage, ever increasingly part of the cultural memory of generations of Italians. Contini termed such knowledge (and use) of Dante part of the "memoria nazionale" [national memory] ("Power of Influence" 346).

For the purpose of drawing a contrast between Dante's presence in the contemporary "national memory" and his presence in popular culture prior to WWI, it is of interest to note a conversation overheard and reported by Michele Mastropaolo, a Neapolitan educator, following the screening of Dante's *Inferno* in 1911:

> I was present at the very dramatic action inspired by the miserable end of Count Ugolino . . . but the crowd remained unmoved, they did not comprehend nor did they hear "He spoke these words; then, glaring down in rage, / attacked again the live skull with his teeth. . . . " "What, do they take turns eating each other?" a woman exclaimed with a voice hoarse from laughter. "It's clear that they haven't eaten for awhile."[34]

This woman's reaction suggests a lack of familiarity with the details of Dante's text. To be sure, this lack of knowledge is not surprising given the high rate of illiteracy at the time, the restricted access to education, and the still weak diffusion of the Italian language.[35]

In 1865, during the first celebration of the Dantean centenary, only a small percentage of Italians were familiar with the literary standard. In 1965, Italians celebrated for the second time in their history the centenary of Dante's birth. In the previous year, Pier Paolo Pasolini had dramatically declared the birth of Italian as a national spoken language. While linguists, scholars, and professors took issue with the finer points of his argument, history has proved him correct with regard to the language. By the 1980s, a majority of Italians spoke Standard Italian at home, many of them along with their regional dialects.[36] Thus, more or less during the span of time measured by the Dantean celebrations, Italian, which had been for centuries a "minority language" based on the medieval literary Florentine of Dante, Petrarch, and Boccaccio, the language of Italian high culture useful for writing lyric poetry and spoken only by an educated elite, became, over the course of the twentieth century but particularly in the postwar period, the basis for the spoken idiom of a modern nation.

In the process of "making Italians," the Italian cinema, together with the press, radio, television, and the other cultural industries, has played a fundamental role. The mass media have been a powerful instrument of modernization throughout the West, but particularly in Italy, where, due to its longstanding linguistic divisions, lack of national consciousness, and late political unification, the cinema has occupied a central place in twentieth-century culture. Together with the press, radio, and television, the cinema promoted the diffusion of Italian as a national language, contributed to the growth of a national identity (however problematic), and mediated the rapid social changes that Italy has undergone in the transformation from a rural, chiefly agricultural and traditional society to becoming one of the most highly industrialized and technologically advanced countries in the world.

Our survey of Dante movies, while admittedly glossing over the heterogeneous character of the films mentioned, also reveals some dominant tendencies and recurring patterns. Between 1908 and 1912, the nineteenth-century cult of Dante is carried over in a new artistic medium, the cinema, which seeks the status of art by adapting literary classics for a broad, still largely illiterate public. In the process, the film colossal is born, exhibition practices are transformed, and a wider spectrum of Italian society becomes familiar with the iconology of Dante's *Inferno*. This iconology, as formulated by Gustave Doré, finds expression in the 1911 *Inferno* by Milano Films, and will also inform an American Dante movie produced in 1935 starring Spencer Tracy. In this way, Dante's Hell emerges at an early date and remains through the present (via Tom Phillips and Peter Greenaway's *A TV Dante*) a textual site that lends itself to visualization in a popular vein. Furthermore, Paolo and Francesca, together with Count Ugolino, are the Dantean characters most frequently revisited by the cinema.

Finally, and most importantly, in the process of "making Italians," Dante and the cinema, particularly in the silent period, but also in the more recent past, have contributed to the formation of a more widely-diffused national culture, a "national memory," and a truly national spoken language. Dante, the "father" of the Italian language, the Italian national poet, and the subject of numerous films demonstrating the innovations and continuities of the cinematic mode, remains and will no doubt always remain a fundamental symbol of Italian national identity.

NOTES

1. An earlier version of this material was presented at the conference "Dante Now: Current Trends in Dante Studies" at the University of Notre Dame, October 29–30, 1993.

2. Raymond Williams, *The Sociology of Culture* (New York: Schocken, 1981), 202.

3. For scholarship dealing with various aspects of Dante and the cinema, see Aldo Bernardini, "L'Inferno della Milano-Films," *Bianco e nero* 2 (April–June 1985): 91–111; Antonio Costa, "Dante, D'Annunzio, Pirandello," in *Sperduto nel buio: Il cinema italiano muto e il suo tempo (1905–1930)*, ed. Renzo Renzi (Bologna: Cappelli editore, 1991), 59–69; Cristina Bragaglia, *Il piacere del racconto: narrativa*

italiana e cinema (1895–1990) (Florence: La nuova Italia, 1993); William Uricchio and Roberta E. Pearson, *Reframing Culture: The Case of the Vitagraph Quality Films* (Princeton: Princeton University Press, 1993); and the entry by Alfredo Barbina on cinema in the *Enciclopedia Dantesca*, Istituto della Enciclopedia italiana, Fondata da Giovanni Treccani (Rome: 1970), 4–5. All translations in this article, unless noted otherwise, are my own.

4. Amilcare A. Iannucci, "Foreword," *Dante Today*, a special issue of *Quaderni d'italianistica* X, nos. 1–2 (1989): iv.

5. For an historical overview of film and literary interactions in Italian culture, see John P. Welle, "Introduction. From Pastrone to Calvino: New Perspectives on Italian Film and Literature," *Annali d'Italianistica* 6 (1988): 4–17. See also Gian Piero Brunetta, *Forma e parola nei cinema* (Padua: Liviana, 1970); idem, ed., *Letteratura e cinema* (Bologna: Zanichelli, 1976); and idem, "Letteratura e cinema: Da un rapporto di subalternità ad uno di prevalenza," in *Cinema e letteratura in Italia: Attualità di un dialogo* (Lugano: Cenobio, 1983).

6. G. P. Brunetta, as cited and translated by Millicent Marcus, *Filmmaking by the Book: Italian Cinema and Literary Adaptation* (Baltimore: Johns Hopkins University Press, 1993), 2. Marcus's *Filmmaking by the Book* discusses the theoretical aspects of film adaptation, provides a brief chronology of adaptation in Italy, and analyzes ten post-World War II Italian films based on literary texts.

7. Hermann W. Haller, "Introduction," *The Hidden Italy: A Bilingual Anthology of Italian Dialect Poetry* (Detroit: Wayne State University Press, 1986), 35.

8. Describing the situation with greater precision, Giulio Lepschy writes: "De Mauro after a careful and systematic study of the available documents reached the conclusion that 2.5 percent of Italians knew Italian in 1860. The figure has a special poignancy because it is close to that given in official statistics for the *minoranze alloglotte*, that is Italian citizens who had a foreign language (French, German, Slovenian, Greek, Catalan etc) as their mother tongue: these were about 1 percent in 1860, and about 2 percent in 1918. Another linguist, Arrigo Castellani . . . one of the foremost specialists of Old Tuscan . . . decided to look afresh at all the material, to see if he could reach a different conclusion. The figure he arrived at, despite all his efforts, is lower than 10 percent. It appears that this is the range we have to accept. When the Italian state was proclaimed, in 1860, the number of Italians, who could use the national language was at most 10 percent, perhaps as little as 2.5 percent. The social, political and cultural implications of this state of affairs are clearly far-reaching and ought to receive due consideration in any account of modern Italian history" (65–66). Giulio Lepschy, "How Popular Is Italian?" in *Culture and Conflict in Postwar Italy: Essays on Mass and Popular Culture*, eds. Zygmunt G. Baran'ski and Robert Lumley (New York: St. Martin's Press, 1990), 63–75.

9. Cited by E. J. Hobsbawm, *Nations and Nationalism Since 1780: Programme, Myth, Reality* (Cambridge: Cambridge University Press, 1990), 44.

10. The historical description that follows is largely indebted to Carlo Dionisotti's essay, "Varia fortuna di Dante," in his *Geografia e storia della letteratura italiana* (Turin: Einaudi, 1967), 255–303. Subsequent references will be given in the text.

11. Adrian Lyttelton, "The National Question in Italy," in *The National Question in Europe in Historical Context*, eds. Mikulás Teich and Roy Porter (Cambridge: Cambridge University Press, 1993), 72.

12. Cited in William Uricchio and Roberta E. Pearson, *Reframing Culture: The Case of the Vitagraph Quality Films* (Princeton: Princeton University Press, 1993), 95–97. These authors also provide the following interesting information regarding Dante's reception in American universities and in popular culture: "In the United States, upper and middle-class women seemed particularly enamoured of the Italian poet. The *Ladies' Home Journal* published William Dean Howells's ar-

ticle on the poet, and 'enterprising publishers tried to exploit this Dante furore by issuing elegant Dante calendars.' In general, though, Dante ephemera seem to have been less widely available than Shakespearean and were never, as far as we know, distributed gratis. A set of Dante postcards, 'A visit to Hell with Dante—The Italian Poet,' dating from around 1900, cost fifty cents for twenty-five 'views,' at least half-a-day's pay for wage earners such as elevator men, tailors, and grocery clerks. But at the universities Dante societies and courses proliferated. . . . Nor was Dante's penetration into popular culture limited to the cinema. For example, George B. Bunnel, a nineteenth-century entrepreneur touted as the 'legitimate successor to P. T. Barnum,' featured a 'Dante's Inferno' of 'waxworks, mechanical contrivances and pictorial views' as the principle [sic] attraction in his Bowery Dime museum. This carnivalesque encounter with the Italian poet apparently extended beyond dime museums to amusement parks. Even today the decaying Coney Island has a ride called 'Dante's Inferno,' while the 1935 film of the same name told the story of a park built around an elaborate reproduction of the circles of hell" (97–98). We shall return briefly to the Dante film from 1935 at a later point in this essay.

13. On the Italian silent period in general see Maria A. Prolo, *Storia del cinema muto italiano (1896–1915)* (Milan: Poligono, 1951); Aldo Bernardini, *Cinema muto italiano. I. Ambiente, spettacoli e spettatori (1896–1904)* (Bari: Laterza, 1980); *Cinema muto italiano. II. Industria e organizzazione dello spettacolo (1905–1909)* (Bari: Laterza, 1981); *III. Cinema muto italiano. Arte, divismo e mercato (1910–1914)* (Bari: Laterza, 1982); A. Bernardini and Jean Gili, eds., *Le cinéma italien de "La prise de Rome" (1905) à "Rome ville ouverte" (1945)* (Paris: Centre Georges Pompidou, 1986); Massimo Cardillo, *Tra le quinte del cinematografo: Cinema, cultura e società in Italia 1900–1937* (Bari: Edizioni dedalo, 1987). *Sperduto nel buio: Il cinema italiano muto e il suo tempo (1905–1930)*, ed. Renzo Renzi (Bologna: Cappelli editore, 1991); Gian Piero Brunetta, *Storia del cinema italiano, 1895–1945* (Rome: Editori riuniti, 1979); Vittorio Martinelli, *Il cinema muto italiano. I film del dopoguerra*, 4 vols. (Rome: Edizioni di Bianco e nero, 1980–81); and Peter Bondanella, *Italian Cinema. From Neorealism to the Present* (New York: Continuum, 1990), 1–12.

14. See Aldo Bernardini, "Le sale cinematografiche nel 1906," in his *Cinema muto italiano*, II, 227–29.

15. See Bragaglia, *Il piacere del racconto*, for an exhaustive chronicle of the Italian cinema's use of literary texts from its origins through 1990.

16. Gian Piero Brunetta, "La migrazione dei generi dalla biblioteca alla filmoteca dell'italiano," *Italian Quarterly* 21 (Summer 1980): 83–90.

17. For a list of films produced in Italy between 1904 and 1915, see Prolo, *Storia del cinema*.

18. These films, according to Prolo, ibid., 117–84, include "Pia dei Tolomei" (Cines, Rome, Mario Caserini, 1908), "Francesca da Rimini" (Comerio, Milan, 1908), "Il conte Ugolino" (Itala Film, Turin, 1909), "L'Inferno da La Divina Commedia di Dante Alighieri," Francesco Bertolini and Adolfo Padovan, with Giuseppe De Liguoro as chief actor (1909, Milano Films, Milan, 1000 meters), "L'Inferno dalla Divina Commedia di D. Alighieri" (1910, Helios Film, Velletri, 400 meters), "Il Conte Ugolino," (Itala Film, Turin, 1910 [a re-issue of the 1909 film by the same name]), "Il Purgatorio," (Ambrosio Films, Turin, 1911), "Guido Cavalcanti" (Cines, Rome, 1911), "Il Purgatorio dalla Divina commedia di D. Alighieri" (Helios Films, Velletri, 1911). "Il Paradiso" dalla Divina Commedia di D. Alighieri" (Psiche Film, Albano Laziale, 1911, 660 meters), "Dante e Beatrice" (Ambrosio, Turin, 1912). Cristina Bragaglia (*Il piacere del racconto*, 15) provides the following information regarding the production dates of *Dante's Inferno* by Milano Films: "Dante returns on the screen in . . . 1909, when in October, at the I Concorso Cinematografico di Milano (First Milanese Film Competition) the

Saffi-Comerio Company presents *Saggi dell'Inferno dantesco* (Scenes from Dante's Inferno). They are parts of a longer film that the Milanese company started working on and that will be finished only in 1911 (at that time the Saffi-Comerio Company will be transformed into Milano Films). " In 1920, Floreal-Film of Rome produced *Francesca da Rimini* (Barbina, *Enciclopedia Dantesca*, 5). In 1921, Domenico Gaido directed a costume epic entitled *Dante* (Brunetta, *Storia del cinema italiano*, 270). The *International Film Index 1895–1990* (Goble: vol. on film titles, London: Bowker-Sauer, 1991) lists Luigi Caramba as the director of a 1921 Dante film entitled simply *Dante*. Known in Italian as *La mirabile visione* (The heavenly vision), this film was produced explicitly to coincide with and benefit from the sixth centenary of Dante's death in 1321. See Arnoldo Frateili, "Grandezza e decadenza del cinema romano (1919–1921)," *Scenario* 5 (1933), now in *Almanacco del cinema muto italiano*, ed. Roberto Chiti et al. (Forlì: Centro Studi Cinetelevisivi, 1988), 225–26.

19. This information is adapted from Costa, "Dante, D'Annunzio, Pirandello," 59–60.

20. Gian Piero Brunetta, "La nascita dell'industria cinematografica in Italia," in *C'era il Cinema. L'Italia al cinema tra Otto e Novecento* (Reggio Emilia, 1896–1915), ed. Flavia De Lucis (Comune di Reggio Emilia: Edizioni Panini, 1983), 22–23.

21. On the Italian cinema's transition from being primarily a spectacle for the lower classes toward its establishment as a form of bourgeois entertainment, see Aldo Bernardini, "Industrializzazione e classi sociali," in *Sperduto nel buio* 22–23. On the early film theatres, see also Gian Piero Brunetta, *Buio in sala. Cent'anni di passioni dello spettatore cinematografico* (Venice: Marsilio, 1989).

22. The information that follows is found in Costa, "Dante, D'Annunzio, Pirandello," 59–60.

23. Matilde Serao as cited in Bragaglia, *Il piacere del racconto*, 16.

24. In the original Italian version of 1911, the shot depicting the monument to Dante at Trento occurs at the end of the film. According to Bernardini (see L'Inferno della Milano-Films," 108), this scene, which stirred Italian irredentist emotions, was later suppressed by the Italian censors in 1914 for political reasons. In the English-language version currently in distribution in the United States through the Rohauer Collection, the Dante monument at Trento occurs at the beginning of the film.

25. The early 1920s saw the production of three Italian Dante films. In 1920, Floreal-Film of Rome produced *Francesca da Rimini* and in 1922, Domenico Gaida directed *Dante nella vita dei suoi tempi* and Luigi Caramba directed *La mirabile visione*. The later film, although it appeared one year later than scheduled, was produced explicitly to coincide with and benefit from the celebrations in 1921 marking the centenary of Dante's death. See Arnoldo Frateili, "Grandezza e decadenza del cinema romano (1919–1921)," *Scenario* 5 (1933), now in *Almanacco del cinema muto italiano*, ed. Roberto Chiti et al. (Forlì: Centro Studi Cinetelevisivi, 1988), 225–26.

26. *Variety Film Reviews 1907–1980*, vol. 2, 1921–1925 (New York: Garland, 1983).

27. *New York Times Film Reviews 1913–1968*, vol. 2: 1932–1938 (New York: New York Times and Arno Press, 1970), 1195.

28. Ken Russell, *Altered States: the Autobiography of Ken Russell* (New York: Bantam Books, 1991), 87.

29. See Amilcare Iannucci, "Dante, Television, and Education," in "Dante Today," 1–33. Iannucci also discusses various video and television projects involving Dante sponsored by the RAI and the Media Centre of the University of Toronto, respectively. See also idem, "Dante Produces Television," *Lectura Dantis* 13 (Fall 1993): 32–46.

30. According to Angela Prudenzi, this film "marks . . . the exact moment in which the melodramatic convention makes its entrance into Matarazzo's work. It is the ideal bridge towards his following production" (cited in Bragaglia, *Il piacere del racconto*, 136).

31. William Uricchio and Roberta E. Pearson discuss adaptations of the tale of Francesca of Rimini in their *Reframing Culture*, 95–110.

32. Barbara K. Lewalski, for example, analyzes the analogies between Fellini's *8 1/2* and Dante's *Purgatorio* in her "Federico Fellini's *Purgatorio*," in *Federico Fellini: Essays in Criticism*, ed. Peter Bondanella (New York: Oxford University Press, 1978), 113–15. See also Zygmunt Baran'ski, "The Power of Influence: Aspects of Dante's Presence in Twentieth-Century Italian Culture," *Strumenti critici* n.s. 1 (September 1986): 343–76; and John P. Welle, "Fellini's Use of Dante in *La dolce vita*," *Studies in Medievalism* II, 3 (1983): 53–65, now in *Perspectives on Federico Fellini*, eds. Peter Bondanella and Cristina Degli-Esposti (New York: G. K. Hall, 1993), 110–18.

33. Pier Paolo Pasolini, *La divina mimesis* (Turin: Einaudi, 1975), 5.

34. Cited in Massimo Cardillo, *Tra le quinte*, 27. The translation of *Inferno* XXXIII, 76–77 is Mark Musa's.

35. See David Forgacs, *Italian Culture in the Industrial Era 1880–1980: Cultural Industries, Politics and the Public* (Manchester: Manchester University Press, 1990).

36. See G. C. Cecioni, "La lingua italiana oggi: la crisi della tradizione aulica," in *Lingua letteraria e lingua dei media nell'italiano contemporaneo*, Atti di un convegno svoltosi a Siena, 11–13 ottobre 1985, ed. G. Cecioni and G. Del Lungo Camiciotti (Florence: Le Monnier, 1987), 1–6. See also A. L. Lepschy and G. Lepschy, *The Italian Language Today*, 2nd ed. (London: Hutchinson, 1988).

SELECTED BIBLIOGRAPHY:
INFERNO

The newest and most authoritative Italian edition of Dante's *Comedy* is by Giorgio Petrocchi (*La Commedia secondo l'antica vulgata* in 4 vols., Milan: Mondadori, 1966–67). The Petrocchi edition is the one used by Charles S. Singleton in his commentary (Bollingen Series 80, Princeton, 1970–75).

Among the most useful general introductory studies on Dante are those by Thomas Bergin (*Dante* [Westport, CT, 1976]), Francis Fergusson (*Dante* [London, 1966]), Michele Barbi (*Life of Dante* [Berkeley, 1954]).

Of the many prose translations of the *Commedia*, the two outstanding ones are the Modern Library edition by Carlyle-Wickstead and the John Sinclair version (New York, 1961) which is straightforward and faithful to the original.

Important reference and bibliographical sources include Umberto Bosco (*Handbook to Dante Studies* [Oxford, 1950]); the journal *Dante Studies* with a thorough, descriptive bibliography of Dante scholarship in the United States (edited by Anthony L. Pellegrini for many years and now by Christopher Kleinhenz, published by the State University of New York at Binghamton); Charles Dinsmore (*Aids to the Study of Dante* [New York: Houghton Mifflin, 1903]; the *Enciclopedia Dantesca* edited by Umberto Bosco (6 volumes [Rome, 1970]); the most useful bibliographical reference book in Italian is by Enzo Esposito (*Bibliografia analitica degli scritti su Dante, 1950–1970* [Florence: Olschki, 1990]); Edmund Gardner (*Dante* [London, 1985]); Paget Toynbee (*A Dictionary of Proper Names and Notable Matters in the Works of Dante*, revised by Charles S. Singleton [Oxford, 1968]); and E. H. Wilkins, T. G. Bergin, et al. (*A Concordance to the Divine Comedy of Dante Alighieri* [London, 1965]).

CRITICAL STUDIES

Auerbach, Erich. *Dante: Poet of the Secular World.* Trans. Ralph Manheim. Chicago, 1961.
———. *Mimesis.* Princeton, NJ, 1953.
Barolini, Teodolinda. *Dante's Poets, Textuality and Truth in the "Comedy."* Princeton, NJ, 1984.
——— . *The Undivine "Comedy," Detheologizing Dante.* Princeton, NJ, 1992.
Boyde, Patrick. *Dante Philomythes and Philosopher: Man in the Cosmos.* Cambridge, 1981.
Brandeis, Irma. *The Ladder of Vision: A Study of Dante's Comedy.* New York, 1961.
Comparetti, Domenico. *Virgil in the Middle Ages.* Trans. E. F. M. Benecke. New York, 1895.

Davis, Charles Till. *Dante and the Idea of Rome.* Oxford, 1957.

Demaray, John I. *The Invention of Dante's "Commedia."* New Haven, CT, 1974.

d'Entrèves, Passerini. *Dante as a Political Thinker.* Oxford, 1952.

Dunbar, H. Flanders. *Symbolism in Medieval Thought and Its Culmination in the Divine Comedy.* New York, 1961.

Ferrante, Joan M. *The Political Vision of the "Divine Comedy."* Princeton, NJ, 1986.

Fletcher, Jefferson Butler. "The 'True Meaning' of Dante's *Vita nuova.*" *Romanic Review* XI (1920): 95–148.

———. *Dante.* Notre Dame, IN, 1965.

Foster, Kenelm. *The Two Dantes and Other Studies.* Berkeley, 1977.

Freccero, John. *Dante: The Poetics of Conversion.* Ed. R. Jacoff. Cambridge, MA, 1986.

Gardner, Edmund G. *Dante and the Mystics.* London, 1913.

Gilson, Etienne. *Dante the Philosopher.* New York, 1949.

Grandgent, Charles H. *Companion to the "Divine Comedy."* Ed. Charles Singleton. Cambridge, MA, 1975.

Hollander, Robert. "*Vita Nuova*: Dante's Perceptions of Beatrice." *Dante Studies* 92 (1974): 1–18.

———. *Allegory in Dante's "Commedia."* Princeton, NJ, 1969.

Lansing, Richard H. *From Image to Idea: A Study of the Simile in Dante's* Commedia. Ravenna: Longo Editore, 1977.

Masciandaro, Franco. *Dante as Dramatist.* Philadelphia: University of Pennsylvania Press, 1991.

Mazzeo, Joseph Anthony. *Medieval Cultural Tradition in Dante's "Divine Comedy."* Ithaca, NY, 1960.

Mazzotta, Giuseppe. *Dante, Poet of the Desert.* Princeton, NJ, 1979.

Montanari, Fausto. *L'Esperienza poetica di Dante.* Florence, 1959.

Montano, Rocco. *Storia della poesia di Dante.* Naples, 1962.

Musa, Mark. *Advent at the Gates: Dante's Comedy.* Bloomington, IN, 1974.

———. *Essays on Dante.* Bloomington, IN, 1964.

Nardi, Bruno. *Nel mondo di Dante.* Rome, 1944.

Nolan, David, ed. *Dante Commentaries.* New Jersey, 1977.

Orr, M. A. *Dante and the Early Astronomers.* Rev. ed. London, 1956.

Ruggiers, Paul R. *Florence in the Age of Dante.* Norman, OK, 1964.

Sayers, Dorothy. *Introductory Papers on Dante.* New York, 1959.

———. *Further Papers on Dante.* New York, 1957.

Seznec, Jean. *The Survival of the Pagan Gods: The Mythological Tradition and Its Place in Renaissance Humanism and Art.* Trans. B. Sessions. Princeton, NJ, 1953.

Singleton, Charles S. *An Essay on the "Vita Nuova."* 1949. Cambridge, MA: Harvard University Press, 1958.

———. *Dante Studies I.* Cambridge, 1954.

Sowell, Madison, ed. *Dante and Ovid, Essays in Intertextuality.* Binghamton, NY, 1991.

CONTRIBUTORS

Mark Musa is Distinguished Professor of Italian at Indiana University. He has translated and edited critical editions of many Italian literary classics, including *The Poetry of Panuccio del Bagno*, Dante's *Divine Comedy* and *Vita nuova*, *The Decameron*, *The Portable Machiavelli*, and *Petrarch's Lyrics*. He is also author of *Advent at the Gates: Dante's Comedy*.

Lawrence Baldassaro is Professor of French and Italian at the University of Wisconsin-Milwaukee and the author of numerous articles on medieval and Renaissance Italian literature. He has coordinated an oral history of the Italians in Milwaukee and is coeditor of the intermediate text *In terza pagina*. He has also written extensively on the subject of baseball and is editor of *The Ted Williams Reader*.

Joan M. Ferrante is Professor of Comparative Literature at Columbia University. She is the author of *The Political Vision of the "Divine Comedy,"* as well as articles on Dante's language and poetics.

Denise Heilbronn-Gaines is retired from the faculty of North Illinois University. Her work has appeared in *Dante Studies, Italian Culture, Lectura Dantis, Studies in Philology, Rivista di Studi Italiani*, and other journals.

Robert Hollander is Chair of the Department of Comparative Literature at Princeton University. His publications include *Boccaccio's Two Venuses, Studies in Dante, Boccaccio's Last Fiction*, and *Dante's Epistle to Cangrande*.

Amilcare A. Iannucci is Professor of Italian at the University of Toronto. He is the author of *Forma ed evento nella 'Divina Commedia'* and articles on medieval and Renaissance Italian literature.

Christopher Kleinhenz is Professor of Italian and Chair of the Medieval Studies Program at the University of Wisconsin-Madison. He is the editor of *Dante Studies* and has published widely on medieval Italian literature, including *The Early Italian Sonnet*.

Ricardo J. Quinones is Director, Gould Center, Claremont-McKenna College. He is the author of, most recently, *The Changes of Cain*.

Guy P. Raffa is Assistant Professor of Italian at the University of Texas at Austin. His articles on Dante have appeared in *Lectura Dantis, Italian Culture*, and *Dante Studies*.

John P. Welle is Associate Professor of Italian at the University of Notre Dame. He is the author of *The Poetry of Andrea Zanzotto* and editor of "Film and Literature," *Annuli d'Italianistica* 1988. His essays on modern Italian literature, film, and translation have appeared in *World Literature Today, Cinema & Cinema*, and *Rivista di studi italiani*, among other journals.

INDEX

barratry, sin of, 159, 173, 278, 280–81, 340
Bartolomeo dei Folcacchieri, 215
Batrachomyomachia, 349
Beatrice, role of in *Inferno*, 32, 361, 363, 364, 371, 379
Beers, Henry, 384
Benvenuto da Imola, 208, 329, 342, 349, 372
Bernard, St., 80, 172
Bernardini, Aldo, 391, 394
Bertran de Born, 209
bestiality, sins of, 99, 100
betrayal, sins of, 375–76
Biow, Douglas, 284
blasphemy, sin of, 113–14, 186
Bocca degli Abati, 235, 259
Boccaccio, Giovanni, 65–66, 86, 126, 127, 180, 303, 382
Boethius, 67
Bonagiunta da Lucca, 293, 298
Boniface VIII (pope), 60, 145, 200, 201, 202, 371
Bonturo Dati, 327
Bosco, Umberto, 347
Bottagisio, Tito P., 308
Bragaglia, Cristina, 389, 391, 393
Branca Doria, 242, 376
Briareus (son of Uranus), 229
Brunetta, Gian Piero, 382, 385, 386, 392, 394
Brunetto Latini, 120, 121, 355, 359
Brutus (Marcus), 248
Bunnel, George B., 393
Buoso da Duera, 235

Caccia d'Asciano, 215
Cacciaguida, 378, 380
Cacus (centaur), 186
Caiaphas (High Priest of Jews), 172, 282
Caïna (division of Cocytus), 55
Camicion de' Pazzi, 234
Camilla (daughter of King Metabus), 25, 46
Can Grande della Scala (ruler of Verona), 25, 378
canto, "local" and "structurally determining" types of, 299
Canudo, Ricciotto, 387
Capaneus, 113–14
Carli, Plinio, 324
Carlino de' Pazzi, 234
Casalodi, Alberto da, 153

Cassell, Anthony K., 265, 291, 296, 297
Cassius (Caius Cassius Longinus), 248
Castelvetro, 349, 350
castle, allegorical construction of, 45–46, 301, 304, 305–307, 308
Catalano de' Malavolti, 172, 338
Cato, 113, 265, 308
Cavalcanti, Guido, 86–87, 298
Cavalcanti de' Cavalcanti, 86–87
Celestine V (pope), 38, 201, 371
Centaurs, 99, 186
Cerberus, 59–60, 81, 361
Cesari, Antonio, 347
La Chanson de Roland (medieval French epic), 227
Charbonneau-Lassay, L., 337
Charlemagne, 227
Charles of Anjou, 207, 235
Charon, 38–39, 357, 361
Chiron, 100
Christianity: demonic challengers and patterns of eschatology, 353; medieval belief in three Advents of Christ, 80–81; representations of Good Shepherd in art and literature, 330–32, 334–35; Virgil as prophet, 272–73. *See also* Church; theology
Church: anti–clerical literature of later Middle Ages, 331; criticism of clergy in *Inferno*, 66–67, 282, 371, 372, 373; Crusades and Boniface VIII, 201; doctrine on Limbo, 44; doctrine in the *Purgatory*, 92; sin of simony and, 144–47; socio-political reading of *Divine Comedy*, 367–80. *See also* Christianity; theology
Ciacco, political prophecy of, 60
Cicero, 46, 47, 139, 248
Circe, 194, 273, 360
Clement IV (pope), 172
Clement V (pope), 145, 208, 379
Cleopatra, 53
clergy. *See* Church
comedy: Cantos XXI–XXIII as example of, 277; iconographic parody in Canto XXI, 325–35; and theological themes in *Inferno*, 300
Comparetti, Domenico, 273, 284
Conrieri, Davide, 347
Constantine the Great (emperor of Rome), 146
Conte Ugolino (film, 1949), 389
Contini, Gianfranco, 299

Florence: as Dante's model for Hell, 368–70; Dante's rhetorical condemnation of, 127, 193; exile of Dante from, 87, 145; patrons of, 108; pilgrim and debates on politics in, 259; political prophecies concerning, 60, 120–21; theme of decadence and materialism of, 132
Forese Donati, 293
Fortune, as theme of medieval and renaissance writers, 67
Foster, Kenelm, 308
Fowlie, Wallace, 277
Francesca da Rimini, figure of in Canto V, 52, 54–55, 258, 310–21
Francesco Cavalcanti, 187, 188
Francesco d'Accorso, 121
Frankel, Margherita, 348
fraud, sin of, 127, 132, 166, 172–73, 195, 202, 222, 279. *See also* Falsifiers, sins of the
Freccero, John, 265
Frederick II (emperor), 88, 107, 172, 373
Friedman, John Block, 337
Frost, Robert, 357–58
Furies, 79, 80, 278, 363

Galasso da Montefeltro, 200
Galen, 47
Ganelon (betrayer of Roland), 235
Gaudet, A., 308
Georgics (Virgil), 266, 267–68, 272
Geri del Bello, 214
Geryon, 127, 132, 133, 267, 271–72
Getto, Giovanni, 291–92, 296
Giacomo da Lentini, 298
Giacomo da Sant'Andrea, 107, 108
Gianni Schicchi, 220
Gianni de' Soldanier, 235
giants, in pagan mythology, 227–29
Giles of Rome, 367
Giovanni Buiamonte, 132–33
Giovanni Villani, 101, 146
gluttony, sin of, 59–60, 293, 297, 374
graft, sin of, 326, 336, 338
Grandgent, Charles H., 318–19, 324
Griffolino da Arezzo, 215
Gualdrada, 126
Guglielmo Borsiere, 126
Guido Bonatti, 153
Guido da Montefeltro, 195, 200, 201, 202, 314, 349

Guido da Pisa, 340, 349
Guido del Cassero, 208
Guido Guerra, 126
Guido Vecchio, 200
Guiscard, Robert, 207
Guy de Montfort, 101
Guyler, Sam, 346, 347, 348, 350

Haller, Hermann W., 382
Harent, S., 308
Harpies, 106, 107
Harrowing of Hell: as literary theme in Middle Ages, 302; parodic inversion of in Canto XXI, 332; as pivotal event for *Inferno*, 354. *See also* Limbo
Hecate, 87
Hector, 46
Hecuba (wife of Priam), 220
Helen of Troy, 53
Hell: beasts as representations of major divisions of, 23–24, 127; corporeal forms of shades in, 60; landscape of in Canto I, 23, 26, 255, 295–96; implications of return from, 357–58; as mirror image of Paradise, 367–80; time in depths of, 153; Vestibule of, 38; worldly fame and the damned in, 60. *See also* Harrowing of Hell; Limbo
Helsinger, Howard, 337
Henry II, 209
Henry VII, 338, 370, 379
Heraclitus, 47
Hercules, 194–95, 358
heresy, sin of, 81, 228, 374
Hippocrates, 47
history: Dante's repositioning of literary, 300; framework of three Advents in Christian, 80–81; interpretations of by Dante and Virgil, 295–96, 355; Limbo and structure of Christian, 299–300, 307; and myth in *Inferno*, 353–65. *See also* film history
Hollander, Robert, 284, 289, 297, 308, 350
Holmes, George, 380
Homer, 45, 193, 269. *See also* Ulysses
Horace, 45
humanism, as subject of Canto IV, 301
human nature: exemplary function of protagonist, 255–56, 257

humility: exemplary function of protagonist, 255–56, 258
hypocrisy, sin of, 172, 173–74, 281–82, 338, 374
Hypsipyle, 138

Iannucci, Amilcare A., 308, 381–82, 394
Icarus, 133
iconography: and parody in Canto XXI, 325–35; Virgil and Christian, 282, 285
identity, Dante and Italian national, 381–91
image, theme and textual irony in *Inferno*, 264
incontinence, sins of, 94, 228
Inferno: figure of Francesca in Canto V, 310–21; figure of Virgil in, 266–83, 340–46; iconographic parody in Canto XXI, 325–35; moral symbolism in Canto I, 286–96; plotline of myth in, 353–65; reconstruction of Limbo in Canto IV, 299–307; textual irony and narrative voice of, 253–64. *See also* Dante Alighieri; *Divine Comedy*
L'Inferno (Milano Films, 1911), 385–88, 391, 394
insanity, of sinners in *Divine Comedy*, 220
Isidore of Seville, 297
Islam. *See* Mahomet; Mohammedanism
Italy, Dante films and development of twentieth-century culture, 382–84, 387, 389–90, 390–91

Jacopone da Todi, 291
Jacopo Rusticucci, 60, 126
James, St., 292
Jason, 138, 145
Jehosaphat, valley of, 86
John XXII (pope), 374
John the Baptist, 108
John the Evangelist, St., 146
journey: as central motif of *Divine Comedy*, 23, 268, 287; encounters with demonic challengers and patterns of, 353, 356; narrative voice and motif of, 253–55, 257
Joyce, James, 381
Judas, 247–48
Julius Caesar, 46, 208, 248

Justinian, 370

Kleinhenz, Christopher, 284–85
Kraus, Clara, 348

Lancelot du Lac (medieval French romance), 54, 234, 315, 316, 317–18
Lanci, Antonio, 337
language, development of Italian, 292, 382–83, 390–91, 392
Larkin, Neil M., 345
Latinus, 46
Lee, Guy, 284
Legner, Anton, 336, 337
Leo the Great (pope), 101
Lepschy, Giulio, 392
Lethe, river of, 115, 283, 306
Lewalski, Barbara K., 395
Liber Esopi (Walter of England), 348
Limbo: narrative voice and concept of, 258; reconstruction of in Canto IV, 299–307, 308; Virgil and structure of, 32, 44. *See also* Harrowing of Hell; Hell; paganism
literature: anti–clerical in later Middle Ages, 331; Dante's repositioning of literary history, 300; influence of Dante on modern English, 381; medieval French romances, 54, 227, 234, 315, 316, 317–18. *See also* author; poet
Lithgow, William, 120
Livres dou Tresor (Brunetto), 120, 121
Livy, 207
Loderingo degli Andalò, 172, 338
Lucan, 45, 101, 180, 187
Lucius Annaeus Seneca. *See* Seneca
Lucia, heavenly ladies and Divine Grace, 32
Lucifer, 247, 248–49, 332
Lucius Junius Brutus, 46
Lucretia, 46
Luiso, F. P., 337
lust, sin of, 52, 320–21, 323
Lyttelton, Adrian, 383

Maghinardo Pagani da Susinana, 200
magic, association of Virgil with, 273–77, 284
Mahomet (Mohammed, founder of Islam), 207–208
Malacoda (leader of devils), 159–60, 166, 173, 277–78, 279–80, 283, 284, 343, 348, 350, 364

Malatesta (lord of Rimini), 200
Malatestino (lord of Rimini), 200, 208
Malebranche (devils), 159, 166, 173,
    278, 279, 280–81, 283, 325–35,
    345–46
malice, sins of, 94
Mandelbaum, Allen, 284
Mandruzzato, Enzo, 348
Manfred (king of Sicily), 207, 235
Manno Branca (mayor of Florence),
    160
Mantua, founding of, 152, 275–77
Marcia (wife of Cato of Utica), 46
Marco Lombardo, 338
Marcus, Millicent, 392
Marcus Tullius Cicero. See Cicero
Margaret of Trent, 208
Marie de France, 348
Mars (god of war), 108, 228
Martel, Charles, 378
Martino Bottario, 340
Mary, Virgin, 32, 361
Mastrobuono, Antonio C., 296
Mastropaolo, Michele, 390
Matarazzo, Raffaele, 389
materialism, sins of, 66–67
Mazzoni, Francesco, 309, 347
Medusa, 79, 80, 278, 363
Messina, Michele, 337
metamorphosis: in opening image of
    Canto XXIV, 179–80; types of in
    Cantos XXIV–XXV, 187
Michael (archangel), 66, 362
Michael Scot (Scottish philosopher),
    153
Michele Zanche (governor of
    Logodoro), 166, 242
military: imagery in Canto XXI and
    Canto XXII, 159; and sin of fraud,
    202
mimesis: narrative voice and strategy
    of, 258, 259
Minòs, 52, 53, 99, 337, 361
Minotaur, 267
La mirabile visione (film, 1921), 394
Misenus, 360
Miserly, sins of the, 66–67
Mohammedanism, medieval view of
    schism between Christian Church
    and, 207–208
De monarchia (Dante), 24, 305
monarchy, goals of Dante's political
    philosophy, 266, 368

Montaperti, battle of, 87
morality, symbolism of Canto I of
    Inferno, 26, 286–96. See also sin
Mordred (nephew of King Arthur),
    234
Moroello Malaspina, 181
Mosca dei Lamberti, 259
Moses, 356
Musa, Mark, 278, 297, 298, 336
Muses, invocations to, 31, 234
Myrrha, 221
myth, plotline of in Inferno, 353–65

Narcissus, 221
narrative voice: of Dante the Poet as
    author and Dante the Pilgrim as
    protagonist, 55, 138, 253–64; use of
    first person singular, 23
Nessus (centaur), 100, 101
neutrality, sins of, 38
Niccolò da Prato (cardinal), 193
Niccolò de' Salimbeni, 215
Nicholas III (pope), 145, 146, 275, 328
Nicodemus, Gospel of, 302
Nimrod, 227, 228
Nino Visconti (governor of Pisa), 166,
    240
Nisus (Trojan warrior), 25
Noakes, Susan, 336

Obizzo d'Esti (Marquis of Ferrara),
    100
Ocnus (son of Manto), 276–77
Orpheus, 267–68, 358
Ottaviano degli Ubaldini, Cardinal, 88
Ovid, 45, 54, 114, 133, 152, 187

paganism: Dante's reconstruction of
    Limbo, 299–307; Virgil's
    terminology and, 25, 44, 67, 99
Pagliaro, Antonino, 347
Palinurus (helmsman of Aeneid), 360
Paolo (lover of Francesca), 310–21,
    322–23, 324
Paolo e Francesca (film, 1950), 389
Paradise, as mirror image of Hell,
    367–80
Paris (son of Priam), 53, 54
Parodi, E. G., 323, 347
parody, iconographic in Canto XXI,
    325–35
Pasiphaë (wife of Minos), 99
Pasolini, Pier Paolo, 389, 390

Paul (apostle), 32
Paulus Orosius, 53
Pearson, Roberta E., 392, 395
Penthesilea (queen of the Amazons),
46
Pertile, Lino, 298
Peter, St., 371, 372, 373
Petrarch, 382
Phaëton (son of Apollo), 133
Phalaris (ruler of Argentum), 200
Philip the Fair (king of France), 145
Philip IV (king of France), 371
Phlegethon (river of fire), 99–100,
115, 127
Phlegyas (son of Mars), 73, 133, 361
phoenix, 180
Pholus (centaur), 100
Physics (Aristotle), 94
Picone, Michelangelo, 309
Pier da Medicina, 208
Pier della Vigna, 107, 270, 371–72,
375
Pietro di Dante, 349
Pimps, sins of the, 138
pity: Limbo and Virgil's expression of,
44; theme of pilgrim's, 31, 152, 258,
262; and theology of Harrowing of
Hell, 303
Plato, 46
Pliny the Elder, 132
Plutus, 66, 279, 361
poet: relationship to reader, 260–61,
263–64; role of Dante as, 45
Poggioli, Renato, 318, 322
Poletto, Giacomo, 348
politics: fascism in twentieth-century
Italian, 387–88; grafters and
hypocrites in, 338; pilgrim and
debates on Florentine, 258–59;
prophecies on Florentine, 60,
120–21; socio-political reading of
Divine Comedy, 367–80; Virgil and
goal of Dante's philosophy on, 266.
See also Church; Florence; monarchy
Pollux, 358
Polydorus, 270–71, 284
Polynices (son of Oedipus), 193, 194
Pontius Pilate, 38
Potiphar's wife, 221
Pound, Ezra, 381
predestination, and Dante's concept of
Limbo, 307
pride: exemplary function of

protagonist, 255–56; sin of, 228
Prodigal, the, 66–67
Profligates, sins of the, 107, 108
Prolo, Maria A., 393–94
prophets and prophecy: Dante as poet
and, 261; Virgil's reputation as
Christian, 266, 272–73
Proserpina, 87
Prudenzi, Angela, 395
Psalms, influence on Dante, 288,
292–94, 297
psychology, pilgrim's condition as
mid-life crisis, 254
Ptolemy, 47, 241
Puccio Sciancato, 187–88
Pyrrhus (king of Epirus), 101

Quillet, H., 308, 309

reader: address to in Canto VIII,
79–80; Dante's approach to, 260–61,
263–64; pilgrim/protagonist as,
259–60
realism/reality: historical Virgil as
character, 269; Dante's approach to
reader, 261, 264, 272; dichotomy
between appearance and, in Canto
XXI, 325–26; psychological, of
characters, 279
reason, Virgil as representation of, 24,
25, 87
Reggio, Giovanni, 347
Remigio dei Girolami, 367
Ripheus, 304, 308, 378
Roland, 227, 235
romances, medieval French, 54, 227,
234, 315, 316, 317–18
Rome: *Aeneid* and values of culture,
359–60, 363; as Dante's model for
Paradise, 368–69, 370
Rossetti, Gabriele, 347
Ruggieri degli Ubaldini (archbishop),
240, 241
Ryan, Christopher J., 347, 350

Saladin (sultan of Egypt and Syria), 46
Sarolli, Gian Roberto, 348
Sassol Mascheroni, 234
Sayers, Dorothy L., 187, 284
Scartazzini, G. A., 348
Schiller, Gertrud, 336
Schless, Howard H., 265
Seducers, sins of the, 138

history, 295–96; Dante's selection of as guide, 24; description of as shepherd, 338; figure of in *Inferno,* 266–83, 284, 340–46; influence of on Dante, 266–83, 305; paganism of and theological terminology, 44, 67, 99; as representation of reason, 24, 25, 87; role of as teacher, 88, 355; silence of as metaphor in Canto I of *Inferno,* 289–90, 294; and structure of Limbo, 32. See also *Aeneid*

Visio Sancti Pauli, 32

Vita nuova (Dante), 86, 269

Vitali, G., 322

voyage, as central metaphor of *Divine Comedy,* 201

Walter of England, 348

Welle, John P., 392, 395

Wenzel, Siegfried, 67–68

Wilkins, Ernest Hatch, 336

Williams, Raymond, 381

Wlassics, Tibor, 296

wrath, sin of, 67, 68

Zeno, 47

Zita, Santa, 159